ANATOLIAN INTERFACES

HITTITES, GREEKS AND THEIR NEIGHBOURS

Proceedings of an International Conference on Cross-Cultural Interaction, September 17–19, 2004, Emory University, Atlanta, GA

edited by

Billie Jean Collins, Mary R. Bachvarova and Ian C. Rutherford

Oxbow Books

First published in the United Kingdom in 2008. Printed in paperback in 2010 and reprinted in 2017 by
OXBOW BOOKS
The Old Music Hall, 106–108 Cowley Road, Oxford OX4 1JE

and in the United States by
OXBOW BOOKS
1950 Lawrence Road, Havertown, PA 19083

Paperback Edition: ISBN 978-1-84217-963-5
Digital Edition: ISBN 978-1-78297-475-8 (epub)

A CIP record for this book is available from the British Library

For a complete list of Oxbow titles, please contact:

UNITED KINGDOM
Oxbow Books
Telephone (01865) 241249, Fax (01865) 794449
Email: oxbow@oxbowbooks.com
www.oxbowbooks.com

UNITED STATES OF AMERICA
Oxbow Books
Telephone (800) 791-9354, Fax (610) 853-9146
Email: queries@casemateacademic.com
www.casemateacademic.com/oxbow

Oxbow Books is part of the Casemate Group

Cover illustrations
Drawing of Mycenaean warrior on a clay fragment from Boghazköy (courtesy of the Bogazköy-Archive, Deutsches Archäologisches Institut).
Photo of the relief of Tarkasnawa, king of Mira, at Karabel (courtesy of Billie Jean Collins).

CONTENTS

PART 4
IDENTITY AND LANGUAGE CHANGE

PART 5
ANATOLIA AS INTERMEDIARY: THE FIRST MILLENNIUM

PREFACE

When Ian Rutherford and Mary Bachvarova first conceived the idea for a conference on cross-cultural interaction in Anatolia, they found a willing collaborator in Billie Jean Collins, who volunteered Emory University in Atlanta, Georgia as the location for the conference. Its purpose would be to bring together scholars who might not normally travel in the same academic circles to engage in a discussion about Anatolia's many cultural "interfaces." Cross-cultural interaction in ancient Anatolia between indigenous groups, such as the Hattians, Indo-Europeans, including Hittites and Greeks, and Near Eastern cultures, particularly the Hurrians, resulted in a unique environment in which Anatolian peoples interacted with, and reacted to, one another in different ways. These cultural interfaces occurred on many levels, including political, economic, religious, literary, architectural and iconographic. The rich and varied archives, inscriptions and archaeological remains of ancient Anatolia and the Aegean promised much material for study and discussion. After a year of planning, on September 17–19, 2004, an international body of scholars, more or less equally divided between Classicists and Anatolianists, met at Emory University. These Proceedings present the rich fruits of the discussion that took place over those three days in Atlanta.

Hosted and co-sponsored by the Department of Middle Eastern and South Asian Studies of Emory University, the conference, "Hittites, Greeks and Their Neighbors in Ancient Anatolia: An International Conference on Cross-Cultural Interaction" was made possible by the generous support of many sponsors. From within Emory, the sponsors include the Center for Humanistic Inquiry, the Department of Anthropology, the Department of Art History, the Department of Classics, the Department of Religion, the Graduate Division of Religion, the Graduate Program in Culture, History and Theory, the Graduate School of Arts and Sciences, the Institute for Comparative and International Studies, the Michael C. Carlos Museum, the Office of International Affairs, the Program in Classical Studies, the Program in Mediterranean Archaeology and the Program in Linguistics. Support from outside the University came from the American Schools of Oriental Research, the Georgia Middle East Studies Consortium, the Georgia Humanities Council, the Foundation for Biblical Archaeology and the Hightower Fund. The publication of these proceedings was made possible by a subvention from Emory College and the Emory Graduate School of Arts & Sciences. Thanks also go to Susanne Wilhelm of Archaeoplan for preparing the maps for the volume.

The conference "Hittites, Greeks and Their Neighbors" underscored how all our fields of study can benefit from a cross-cultural, cross-disciplinary approach. If, in publishing these proceedings, we draw attention to the importance of Anatolia in recovering the cultural heritage of the western world, then our efforts have been worthwhile. Many at the conference expressed the hope that it might be the beginning of a regular series of formal conversations on the topic, and one participant predicted that the conference would usher in a new era of cross-disciplinary cooperation. We certainly hope so.

ABBREVIATIONS

ABAW	Abhandlungen der Bayrischen Akademie der Wissenschaften
AHw	W. von Soden, *Akkadisches Handwörterbuch*. Wiesbaden, Harrassowitz, 1958–1981.
Alc.	Alcaeus
Anac.	Anacreon
AOAT	Alter Orient und Altes Testament
AP	*Anthologia Palatina*
Euphorion, *ap Ath.*	Euphorion, *ap Athenaeus "Deipnosophistae"*
Ar., *Thesm.*	Aristophanes, *Thesmophoriazusae*
Archil.	Archilochus
Arnobius, *Adv. nat.*	Arnobius, *Adversus nationes*
Ath.	Athenaeus
ca.	circa
CAD	*The Assyrian Dictionary of the Oriental Institute of the University of Chicago*. Chicago, The Oriental Institute of the University of Chicago, 1956–
CAH	*Cambridge Ancient History*
CANE	*Civilizations of the Ancient Near East*. New York, Scribner's Sons, 1995
CDA	J. Black, A. George, and N. Postgate, *A Concise Dictionary of Akkadian*. 2nd correctted printing. Wiesbaden, Harrtassowitz, 2000.
CHD	*The Hittite Dictionary of the Oriental Institute of the University of Chicago*. Chicago, The Oriental Institute of the University of Chicago, 1980–
Clement of Alexandria, *Protrep.*	Clement of Alexandria, *Protrepticus*
CLL	H. C. Melchert, *Cuneiform Luvian Lexicon*. Chapel Hill, N.C., self-published, 1993.
CLuw.	Cuneiform Luwian
CNR	Consiglio Nazionale delle Ricerche
CTH	E. Laroche, *Catalogue des textes hittites*. Paris, Klincksieck, 1971.
CTH suppl.	E. Laroche, Premier supplement, *RHA* 30 (1972), 94–133.
Diog. Laert.	Diogenes Laertius
DLL	E. Laroche, *Dictionnaire de la language louvite*. Paris, Maisonneuve, 1959.
DLU	G. del Olmo Lete and J. Sanmartín, *Diccionario de la lengua ugarítica*. Aula Orientalis Suppl. 7–8. Barcelona, AUSA, 1996.
FGrH	F. Jacoby, ed. *Die Fragmente der griechischen Historiker*, Berlin, Weidmann, and Leiden, Brill, 1923–.
Firmicus Maternus, *De. err. prof. rel.*	Firmicus Maternus, *De errore profanarum religionum*
fl.	floruit
fr.	fragment
Gr.	Greek
HED	J. Puhvel, *Hittite Etymological Dictionary*. Berlin, Mouton, 1984–
HEG	J. Tischler, *Hethitisches etymologisches Glossar*. Innsbruck, Institut für Sprachwissenschaft der Universität Innsbruck, 1977–
Hitt.	Hittite
HLuw.	Hieroglyphic Luwian
Homer, *Il.*	Homer, *Iliad*
Homer, *Od.*	Homer, *Odyssey*
[Hom.], *Marg. P.Oxy.*	Pseudo-Homer, *Margites*, Oxyrhynchus Papyrus

HW	J. Friedrich, *Hethitisches Wörterbuch*. Heidelberg, Carl Winter, 1952.
HW^{2}	J. Friedrich and A. Kammenhuber, Hethitisches Wörterbuch. 2. Auflage. Heidelberg, Carl Winter Universitätsverlag, 1975–
Iamblichus, *De Myst.*	Iamblichus, *De mysteriis*
IBoT	*Istanbul Arkeoloji Müzelerinde bulunan Bogazköy Tabletleri.* Istanbul 1944, 1947, 1954, Ankara 1988.
IBS	Innsbrucker Beiträge zur Sprachwissenschaft
IEG	M. L. West, *Iambi et elegi graeci*. 2 vols. Oxford, Oxford University Press, 1991–1992.
Il. Comm. ad. Π	R. Janko, *The Iliad: A Commentary*, vol. IV: *Books 13-16*. Cambridge, Cambridge University Press.
KBo	*Keilschrifttexte aus Boghazköi*. Berlin, Gebr. Mann, 1916–.
KUB	*Keilschrifturkunden aus Boghazköi*. 60 volumes. Berlin, Akademie Verlag, 1921–1990
KN	Knossos tablet
Lith.	Lithuanian
Luw.	Luwian
Lyc.	Lycian
Lyd.	Lydian
MesZL	R. Borger, *Mesopotamisches Zeichenlexikon*. Münster, Ugarit-Verlag, 2003.
MHG	Middle High German
MSL XIII	B. Landsberger et al., *Materialien zum sumerischen Lexikon*, vol. 13. Rome, Pontifico Istituto Biblico, 1971.
MY	Mycenae tablet
Myc.	Mycenaean
Myl.	Mylesian
Nic. Dam.	Nicolaus Damascenus
OBO	Orbis Biblicus et Orientalis
OLA	Orientalia Lovaniensia Analecta
Or.	*Oratio*
Pal.	Palaic
PIHANS	Publication de l'Institut Historique et Archéologique Néerlandais de Stamboul
[Plutarch], *De mus.*	Pseudo-Plutarch, *De musica*
Plutarch, *Mor.*	Plutarch, *Moralia*
PMG	D. Page, *Poetae Melici Graeci*, Oxford, Clarendon, 1962.
PN	personal name
PRU 4	C. F.-A. Schaeffer, *Le palais royal d'Ugarit IV*. Paris, Imprimerie Nationale & Klincksieck, 1956.
PY	Pylos tablet
r.	ruled
RHA	*Revue hittite et asianique*
StBoT	Studien zu den Boğazköy-Texten
Strabo, *Geog.*	Strabo, *Geography*
s.v.	sub voce
Theoc.	Theocritus
trans.	translated by
TrGF	*Tragicorum Graecorum Fragmenta*. Göttingen, Vandenhoeck & Ruprecht, 1971–.
Ugar.	Ugaritic
Ugaritica V	J. Nougayrol et al., *Ugaritica V*. Paris, Geuthner, 1968.
UT-PASP	University of Texas at Austin Program in Aegean Scripts and Prehistory
vel sim.	*vel similia* "similar word"
Verg.	Virgil
WAW	Writings from the Ancient World

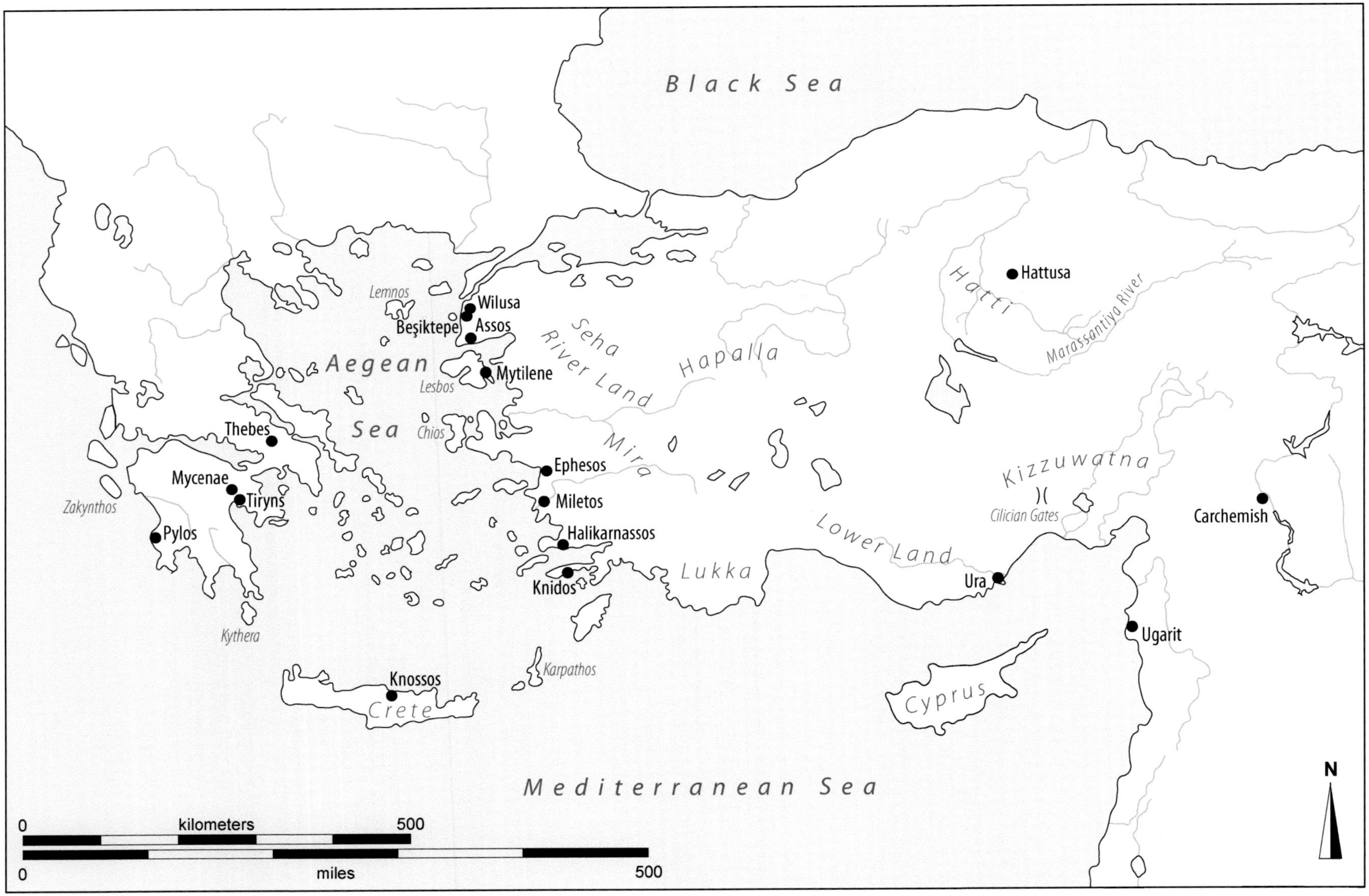

Anatolia and the Aegean in the Late Bronze Age.

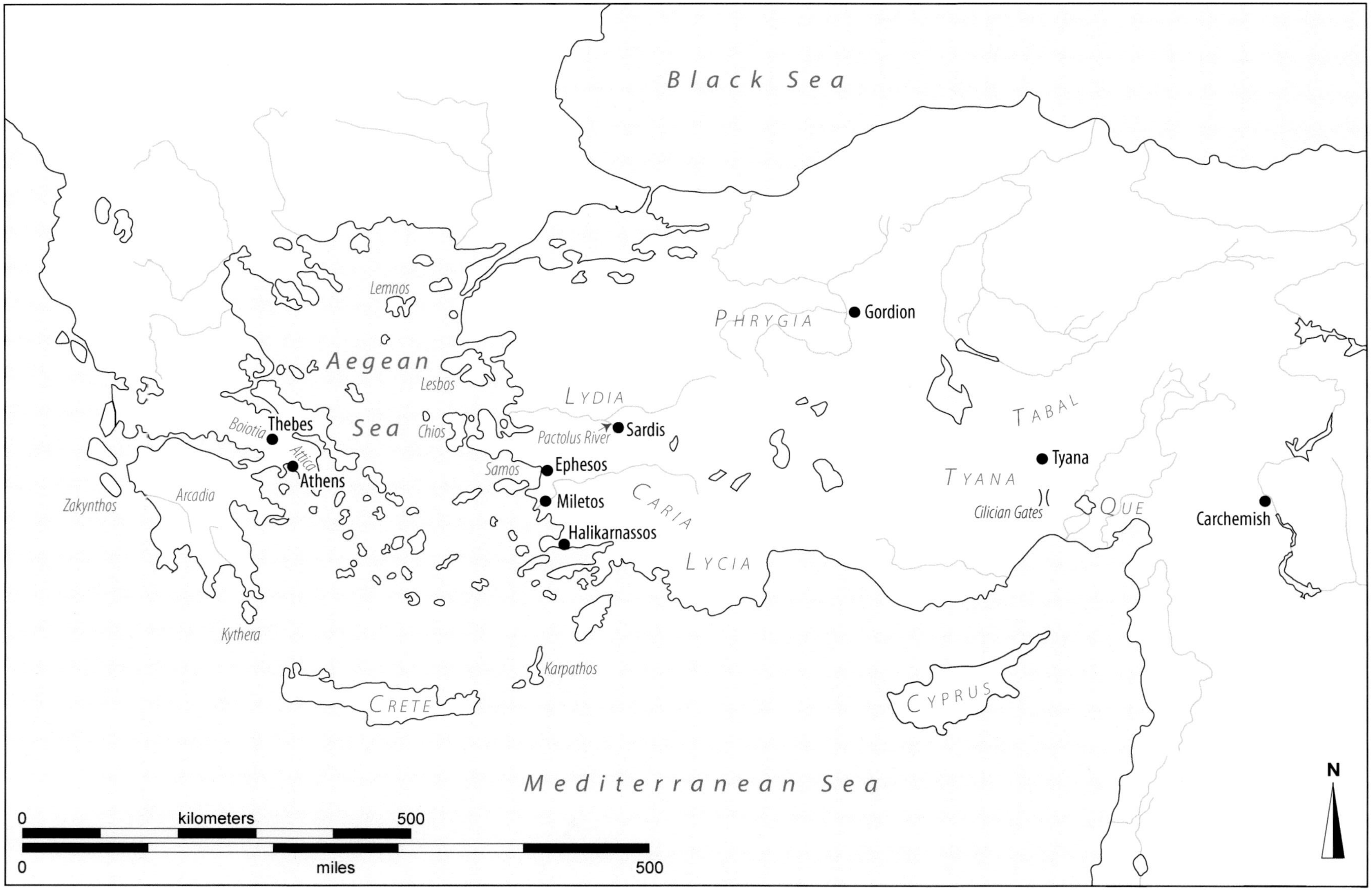

Anatolia and the Aegean in the Iron Age

INTRODUCTION

Billie Jean Collins, Mary R. Bachvarova
and Ian C. Rutherford

By the Late Bronze Age, the territories in the eastern Mediterranean and Near East seem to have come to constitute a distinctive cultural zone comprising similar palace-states linked in a political and religious network. The term "koiné" (a metaphor from the idea of a "common language") has sometimes been applied to the region (see, e.g., Bergquist 1993 on animal sacrifice), and that usage is justifiable as long as it is taken to imply not that the different cultures are the same, but rather that they have a number of key features in common that facilitate interaction and exchange. This situation is likely to have come about through a long and complex process of cultural diffusion and population movement in the region. Important aspects of this process include the following:

1. The great migrations. It is an almost universally held and probably correct view that the speakers of the Indo-European languages Luwian and Hittite entered Anatolia, whether from the northeast or northwest, probably some time in the third millennium BC (see Crossland and Birchall 1974; Jasink 1983; Melchert 2003, 24–26). There they will have encountered other cultures that were indigenous or had been established in the region for a long time, such as that of the speakers of the Hattic language. Similarly, Indo-European speaking Greeks must have entered Greece at about the same time, where they encountered various other cultures, including that of Minoan Crete.
2. Center-periphery cultural transmission from Mesopotamia. We know that cuneiform writing spreads from Mesopotamia to several other cultures, among them the Hittites and Hurrians. We also know that certain religious practices spread in a similar direction. This has been analyzed as a "center-periphery" or "world systems" relationship (Algaze 1993; Wallenstein 1974). On this model, Anatolia could be thought of either as part of the periphery, or as part of a semi-peripheral area, itself in a hegemonic situation with respect to even more peripheral areas (such as the Aegean). One institutional mechanism by which such transmission could have happened is the Assyrian trade colonies in Cappadocia, which can be said to constitute a "trade diaspora" (Stein 1999, 2002).
3. Cultural interaction within Anatolia. The state archives of Hattusa show that the Hittite kingdom kept ritual texts belonging to several other cultures of Anatolia and composed in their languages. One of these is Hattic, which seems to have been the language of the people whose territory the "Hittites" ultimately came to control, appropriating from them the label "Hatti" as the designation for their new state after they moved on from the earlier seat at Kanes (see Gilan, this volume; the modern name "Hittite" seems to be a misunderstanding based on references in the Hebrew Bible). Other cultures elements of whose religion the Hittites appropriated were those of the Hurrian state of Mitanni in North Syria, and the Indo-European Luwian cultures of Arzawa in the West and Kizzuwatna

in the South; in Kizzuwatna, Luwian religion had already undergone a process of fusion with Hurrian ritual by the time the Hittites came into intensive contact with the region.

4. Cultural interaction between the Aegean and Anatolia. It has long been clear that there was considerable interaction in this dimension (Ramsay 1928). Linear B tablets seem to refer to cities of Asia Minor and even a goddess whose name may be "Mistress of Asia" (Morris 2000). We know that there were Mycenaean Greeks in southwestern Asia Minor in the thirteenth century BC (the area called the "Interface" by Mountjoy 1998), and that the geographical term Ahhiyawa used in Hittite texts has now been shown after all to refer to Mycenaean Greece (Hawkins 1998). A deity associated with Ahhiyawa is attested at the Hittite court, which suggests that cultural transmission could go both ways. In some cases, it is possible that Anatolia functions as an intermediary for the passage of cultural or ritual practices from Mesopotamia to Greece (see, e.g., Bremmer 2001 on the "scapegoat ritual," which is best known in different forms in Iron Age Greece and Israel, but is first attested in Early Bronze Age Ebla; Zatelli 1998).
5. Cultural interaction within the Aegean Sea. Early Minoan civilization may have been influenced from Anatolia (see Lévêque 1975) and the iconography of seals point to a degree of influence from Egypt (Weingarten 1991). To judge from iconography and archaeology, Crete exerted a heavy cultural influence on mainland Greece in the middle of the second millennium BC (Hägg 1984). From about 1400 BC, however, when the presence of Mycenaeans is first attested on Crete, probably as the consequence of invasion, their hybrid Mycenaean-Minoan culture is dominant in the region. So here we seem to see the direction of influence shifting from Crete —> Greece to Greece —> Crete.

The volume of scholarly work that has been done on these issues is considerable, drawing particularly on texts (chiefly comparing Late Bronze Age Hittite texts with Iron Age Greek ones), but also on archaeology. The most popular area has probably been aspects of religion, ritual and mythology. The best collection of essays on cross-cultural interaction in the region of eastern Anatolia and northern Syria has religion for its focus (Janowski, Koch and Wilhelm 1993), and there have been many articles comparing aspects of Anatolian and Aegean religion, such as Masson (1950) on military rituals, Steiner (1971) on the Luwian ritual of Zarpiya and the Odyssey, Hutter (1995) on the Luwian deity Pihassassi and the Greek Pegasos; Bremmer (2001) on scapegoat rituals, Tassignon (2001) on the Anatolian deities Telepinu and Dionysus, Collins (2002) on the connection between Demeter and the Sun-goddess of the Earth, and Morgan (2005) on the iconography of the cult center at Mycenae and the sword deity Ugur in Chamber B at Yazılıkaya. (Occasional attempts have been made to compare the economics of Mycenaean cults with those of the Near East; Ventris and Chadwick 1973; Sucharski 2003). It is harder to find good comparative work on aspects of culture distinct from religion for two reasons: first, because in Late Bronze Age cultures of this type, religion is everywhere and anything of importance takes place within a framework of religious symbols and, second, because those parts of the operation of society that are distinct from the religious sphere are not well understood. Fifty years ago, the linguist Leonard Palmer suggested general parallels between the political structures of Mycenaean Greece and Near Eastern societies, including Hittite Anatolia, but these have generally not been accepted (see the critique by Jasink 1981). Melas has suggested that aspects of Late Bronze Age funeral practice in Greece, specifically the increase in the incidence of cremation, might reflect imitation of Anatolian and Hittite practice (Melas 1984; Testart 2005). And, Finkelberg (2005) has postulated the practice of matrilineal descent for both Anatolia and Late Bronze Age Greece, suggested that this be seen as an "areal" feature. Other scholars have explored common patterns of language that might suggest bilingualism or linguistic areas: e.g., Watkins (1986) on bilingual naming patterns in the Late Bronze Age Troad, or Catsanicos (1991) on the vocabulary of sin and fault.

Nevertheless, the amount of work that has been done is less than might have been expected. There are perhaps three reasons for this. First, academic specialization, in particular the fact that the evidence for Anatolian society and religion remains largely unknown to classicists in the Anglo-Saxon world, may be a factor. Even the works that address the problem of cultural interaction between the Aegean and the Near East tend to leave out Anatolia (e.g., in West's discussion of cultural interaction between Greece and the Near East [1997], Anatolia plays little part).

Another reason may be that people are reluctant to speculate when the make-up of societies like this and their languages are imperfectly understood. We should remember that it is only recently that the geography of western Asia Minor has been more or less established (Hawkins 1998), and our knowledge of some of the cultures, such as those of the Hurrians and Luwians (Melchert 2003), is still increasing.

Finally, in archaeology, the idea of cultural interaction has been out of fashion for many decades now, thanks to the dominance of the approaches of processualism and postprocessualism, which tend to require that cultures be interpreted on their own terms (see the useful survey in Kristiansen ad Larson 2005). This factor as well as others may well have inhibited the development of tools and paradigms for explaining cultural change.

There remain four general issues:

1. How much cultural interaction went on in the region, and how can we establish that it did? Things are easiest when we have explicit written sources and/or iconography, but often we do not. And, given that we have established that a significant parallel exists between two cultures, how can we establish that it is the result of interaction and movement between them, and not an independent development in each?
2. When does it happen? Given that we can observe parallels between two cultures, the question remains when they came about. Some contact may have happened in the Late Bronze Age; but some of it could have been much earlier. And in some cases (as in the cases of presumed influence of Near Eastern poetry on Homer and Hesiod), it is difficult to decide whether the contact that resulted in these is Bronze Age or Iron Age (i.e., the "Orientalizing Epoch" of the eighth century BC).
3. Why does it happen? In particular, is it the result of migration and military conquest? Dynastic marriage between royal powers? Trade? Or is it a general process of general (and possibly low-level) diffusion? Or do political and religious authorities deliberately adopt foreign customs for reasons of prestige, as has recently been argued by Kristiansen and Larsson (2005)? Put abstractly, the transmission of one meme from culture A to culture B can be thought of either as i) culture A "influencing" culture B (by conquest, colonization, trade, or as ii) culture B actively selecting features from other cultures, including culture A. Some interactions could be almost unconscious, others are explicit and formalized, for example, one religious system may take over a deity or a ritual from somewhere else, acknowledging the provenance.
4. How do these borrowings work out in practice? For example, are borrowings from Mesopotamia in Anatolia a thin veneer confined to royal and religious institutions, or do they permeate through the culture? What is the relationship between Hittite and Hattic and Luwian culture "on the ground" in Anatolia of the Late Bronze Age? Is the "cultural identity" of southwestern Asia Minor in the Late Bronze Age predominantly Greek or Anatolian? And can we talk about "cultural identity" at all in societies like this?

Anatolia's geographical position made it a key player in the eastern Mediterranean network, while at the same time its diverse topography helped to develop a distinctive role within that network for each region (Sherratt and Sherratt 1998, 336). As a result, the inhabitants of Anatolia were exposed to cultural contacts of many kinds. But geography played another key role in Anatolia, for nowhere did it have a greater impact on shaping cultural identity, and identity is, after all, at the core of cross-cultural interaction, since without an "us" there can be no "them."

Cultural identity can be maintained for economic and political reasons as well as psychological ones (Banks 1996, 33). In this vein, Hall has argued that the Ionian and Aiolian Greeks developed identities for themselves out of a desire for *inclusion* within a wider world of multiple ethnic groups with economic advantage as the goal rather than seeing an oppositional situation in which the Greeks defined themselves against other groups (Hall 2002, 71–73). If this is so, then what can we learn, or relearn, about Greek attitudes toward their neighbors and the nature of interaction in western Anatolia? For example, was conflict the inevitable outgrowth of contact? There are certainly ample examples of this pattern in Hittite dealings with foreign and contiguous states, in particular the Mycenaeans. In part 1, "History, Archaeology and the Anatolian-Mycenaean Interface," Eric Cline takes up this issue effectively in his article on "Troy as a 'Contested Periphery.'" Caught between the Mycenaeans on the one hand and the Hittites on the other, Troy lacked the necessary hinterland and natural resources to become a core territory itself, but as a key entrepôt on the periphery of other major powers, it experienced intense military activity and constantly changing political alliances. Cline offers the intriguing suggestion that Troy's status as a contested periphery is the root of the Trojan War tradition, which may have collapsed centuries of military conflict between Trojans and Mycenaeans into the story of a single prolonged war.

With new evidence for pushing further back in time the onset of Anatolian-Aegean contacts (see Yener 2002, 2–3), not to mention the possibilities of bilingualism (Hall 2002, 7; Watkins 1986) and an Anatolian provenance for pre-Greek Aegean languages, it is clear that nowhere did cross-cultural contacts play out more dramatically than in western Anatolia in the second millennium. Models suggest that conflict arises in particular when vital economic interests are at stake. Itamar Singer adds a new dimension to this discussion in suggesting purple dye as a possible bone of contention along the western interface. Drawing on evidence of the purple-dye manufacturing in the eastern Mediterranean from Ugarit to Troy, Singer sheds new light on a tense episode in the politics of exchange involving the Hittites, Mycenaeans, and purple-dyers on the island of Lesbos.

The Anatolian purple-dyers who visited Lesbos on this occassion represent but one of many groups or individuals who crossed borders carrying innovation with them; others included physicians, ritualists, merchants, musicians, sailors and diplomats. Still others were not transients, but immigrants. Stavroula Nikoloudis describes the diversity in Mycenaean society that resulted in the exchange of personnel at the lowest levels of societies. She lays out the evidence for the presence of immigrant workers or settlers from Anatolia, for example, textile workers, agricultural laborers, and rowers, whose integration into Mycenaean society may have been overseen by an offical with the title *lāwāgetās*. But these individuals and groups, the ones undergoing the process of change, must be distinguished from those who controlled the patterns of interaction. Interregional exchanges were monopolized by an elite in the Late Bronze Age who had a common interest in restricting access to luxury goods and so developed a language of gift exchange between brothers in the negotiation of high-level transfers of commodities (Sherratt and Sherratt 1998, 341).

Returning again to Lesbos, the only Aegean island referred to by name in the Hittite texts, Hugh Mason looks for evidence of Hittites in order to test the theory that the island was under Hittite control in the Late Bronze Age. He finds possible evidence of Anatolian connections in the names of the island of Lazpa and its chief city, Mytilene, and in the Greek traditions about Makar, king of Lesbos, Mytilene, the Amazon who founded Lesbos's chief city, and Pelops.

Adding to the body of comparative work on religion discussed above, the articles in part 2, "Sacred Interactions," take on some key issues in the transmission of mythological and religious elements between cultures. Norbert Oettinger follows the journey of the legendary Mopsos through myth and history alike, casting him as a Greek adventurer who founded a new dynasty in Cilicia some time during the dark ages following the collapse of the Hittite Empire and in the process built a reputation as a seer that bought him a permanent place in Greek myth.

The means by which one state or culture imported a deity from another is something of a mystery. We know that one way the Hittites did this was by "splitting" the deity's identity. Jared Miller examines this phenomenon for the cult of the "Deity of the Night," who was transferred from Kizzuwatna to Hittite Samuha in the fifteenth century BC. Miller's careful analysis of this deity's cult offers a unique view of a cult imported from Kizzuwatna to the Hittite heartland with all of the ramifications stemming therefrom, and in particular offering the opportunity to view the end result of prolonged religious interaction within a single cult.

One important aspect of ritual, documented both in Anatolia and the Aegean, is the performance of choral song. Ian Rutherford explores this area, focusing particularly on the song culture of the Hattic stratum. As he shows, striking parallels exist between the song-cultures of Bronze Age Hatti and Iron Age Greece, and the likeliest explanation for these is some sort of cultural diffusion happening in the region over a long period.

The correspondences between literary texts from the Near East and Greece have been studied most carefully by classical scholars, especially Walter Burkert and Martin L. West. While the focus has been on the similarities that demonstrate that Greece, like North Syria and Anatolia, took part in an eastern Mediterranean cultural area, equally interesting is the change across time and space in motifs as they are adapted to new milieus, in part to respond to the particular interests of new audiences, in part in a conscious effort to differentiate one culture and people from another by making idiosyncratic use of a common fund of myth and legend. Thus, Haubold (2002) has argued that the various cosmogonic myths found in Kumarbi, Hesiod and other writers work in counterpoint to each other. In part 3, "Identity and Literary Traditions," Trevor Bryce explores the ways in which the story of the fall of Troy and its aftermath was made to appeal to successive audiences, first to those aristocrats of mixed heritage in Anatolia, then to the Greek *poleis* who were fighting a common eastern enemy, the Persians, then to the Romans who wished to establish a legendary past equal to that of the Greeks.

Mary Bachvarova also traces the evolution in an epic motif, that of the ruler who refuses to accept the omens of the gods and thus dooms his city, moving from the earliest version of the fall of Akkade in Sumerian to the Cuthean Legend of Naram-Sin to the Hurro-Hittite Song of Release to the story of Hector in the *Iliad*. She argues that winners and losers in a conflict can choose to tell the same story in very different ways, hypothesizing that the sympathetic treatment of the Trojan prince's delusion may indicate that a pro-Trojan version of the story of the destruction of Troy, perhaps preserved in lament rather than epic, was merged with one told from the Greek point of view, a theory that, like Bryce's, assumes a mixed audience in the eighth century for Homer's *magnum opus*.

Amir Gilan focuses on an earlier stage in ethnogenesis, showing how the upper echelon of Hittite society forged a collective identity for the residents of Anatolia, no matter what language they spoke or what their ethnic origin was, by a conscious selection and adaptation of foreign cultural artifacts, specifically, the literature concerning the Akkadian kings, in their legends and mythopoetic historiographical texts.

The documents of ancient Anatolia offer to linguists a wealth of data on language contact and its results. In turn, current theories that correlate specific types of changes to particular linguistic ecologies (Thomason and Kaufman 1988; Thomason 2000, 2001; Mufwene 2001) provide scholars of ancient Anatolia the ability to delve beyond what the texts say about interpersonal and intercultural interactions and to flesh out and modify the data provided by the artifacts to understand better how people perceived and reacted to their contacts with other population groups. The concept of a linguistic area has been applied productively to the Balkans and South Asia, the former including, besides various Slavic languages, Greek, Turkish, Romani and Albanian, the latter encompassing Indo-Aryan languages and Dravidian languages such as Tamil and

Kannada, and to a lesser extent Munda languages such as Santali (Thomason and Kaufman 1988; Thomason 2001). It has recently been applied to Anatolia by Watkins (2001), and the chapters grouped in part 5, "Identity and Language Change," use linguistic data to refine our understanding of the interrelations between the various peoples who lived in Anatolia, including native Anatolians, speakers of Indo-Hittite languages, Greek-speakers and Hurrians.

Annick Payne offers the intriguing suggestion that the hieroglyphic script was introduced to reinforce a collective Anatolian identity, in counterpoint to the wider collective identity provided by cuneiform. While the cuneiform script fulfilled the empire's external economic and communication needs, the visual nature of the monumental hieroglyphic inscriptions provided an internal form of power display comparable to, and perhaps even modeled on, Egypt's hieroglyphic script, for the benefit of Hittite subject states.

Ilya Yakubovitch looks at the ways that Luwian speakers left their mark on the extant written documents, such as borrowings into Greek from Luwian and Lydian, and the onomastics of texts from the Old Assyrian merchant colony Kanes, to place the second-millennium homeland of the Luwians (without prejudice to the original homeland of the Proto-Anatolians) in central Anatolia (the Konya plain), thus rejecting the popular view of a Luwian eastward expansion from western Anatolia in the Middle Bronze Age.

Calvert Watkins examines a particular type of borrowing, in which the target language mimics the phonological shape of a source language's morpheme or compound member, which he labels a "hermit crab," following J. Heath. As is characteristic of his work, Watkins links language to culture, looking across time as well as space and searching poetry for linguistic evidence of cultural contact in his discussion of the nomenclature for *stelae* in Anatolia, especially the Lycian type, which is topped by a tomb, noting that such a tomb is specifically mentioned in the *Iliad* as proper for the Lycian Sarpedon, whose memorialization is expressed with a verb borrowed from an Anatolian language (*tarkhuô*).

It will be interesting to see if new research bears out the "maintenance/change" model put forward by Milroy and Milroy, which predicts that the more cohesive the social group, the greater will be the resistance to linguistic changes originating outside the group (Milroy and Milroy 1997, 75). In situations of massive upheaval and abrupt social change, the model predicts that pre-existing strong networks will be disrupted and weak-tie situations will predominate. In such a situation, there may be quite a rapid language shift (one language replacing another). Conversely, in periods of social stability, social networks remain relatively strong and linguistic change within a language is relatively slow. It is these weak ties that form the channels through which innovations flow (Granovetter 1973 apud Milroy 1997, 78). With this in mind it is notable that Yener writes of the flexible organizational structure of the Hittite and Mitanni kingdom facilitating the flow of goods and people in the Late Bronze Age even as "shared ethnic identities, prestige definitions, and status markers also promoted coherence and intensified interregional interaction" (Yener 1998, 275). In other words, the condition was right, especially in the area of Kizzuwatna, for rapid linguistic innovation. Silvia Luraghi looks at a possible example of such an innovation, the phenomenon of case attraction, which, Luraghi argues, ultimately came into the Anatolian languages from Hurrian. Because this kind of borrowing requires intensive contact (bilingualism in fact), and because of the differential occurrence of genitival adjectives, which only completely substituted for the Indo-European genitive in Cuneiform Luwian, and penetrated least into Hittite, Luraghi suggest that Hurrians in Kizzuwatna were in close contact with speakers of the Cuneiform Luwian dialect, and the innovation then spread from one Anatolian language to another.

H. Craig Melchert examines what seems to be a fairly straightforward example of the results of a different, less-intense type of contact. Trade contacts typically induce the borrowing of the name for an item with the item itself, in this case, the metal lead, attested first on the Greek side in Linear B (*mo-ri-wo-do*) and found in Lydian in the meaning "dark" (*mariwda*). The linguistic evidence however runs counter to the archaeological evidence, which indicates that Mycenaean Greeks were exploiting local sources of lead rather than importing it from Anatolia.

The papers presented in part 5, "Anatolia as Intermediary: The First Millennium," share a common theme, that of the Anatolian kingdoms of the first millennium as cultural filters and conduits through which North Syrian or Near Eastern ideas or materials were transmitted to the Greeks. In particular, the role of Phrygia in conveying Neo-Hittite religious symbols to the west is visited by Mark Munn, who restores a long-standing, but recently challenged, theory equating Neo-Hittite Kubaba with the Phrygian Mother and Greek Cybele.

Maya Vassileva argues that Phrygian involvement in southeastern Anatolia was far more extensive and of longer duration than generally assumed. A sustained Phrygian presence in the region, evident, for example, in the inscribed Black Stones erected in Tyana (a Tabalian state) and in apparent Phrygian influences on Tyana's material culture, facilitated not only Phrygia's absorption of certain Neo-Hittite religious and cultural traditions, but also the transmission of Near Eastern ideas to the west.

Patrick Taylor finds a missing link in the Hittite sources between the *kalu* (Sumerian *gala*), a class of Babylonian priests, and the *gallos*, devotees of Cybele known from Hellenistic Greece and Rome among the "Men of Lallupiya," functionaries in the Istanuwian cult of the Lower Land in south-central Anatolia. Like their counterparts in Mesopotamia and the Greek and Roman worlds, these cultic personnel engaged in bloodletting and transgendered behavior, suggesting either the regional diffusion of a cultic institution of Mesopotamian origin or the inheritance of a transgendered institution developed in common with the Near Eastern region.

Susanne Ebbinghaus attributes to Phrygian elites the transmission of certain stylistic traits, specifically of the animal-headed situlae that were a part of the Assyrian-dominated court culture of the eighth century BC. Ebbinghaus also explores not only the means by which such objects moved from east to west, but the modifications in use that they underwent in their new cultural contexts.

According to John Franklin, beginning with the court of Gyges there was a detectable increase in Mesopotamian influence on the culture of the Lydian elite resulting from the Mermnads's emulation of Assyrian court life. This influence is especially apparent in the musical arts, where, Franklin argues, Lydian musicians cultivated a taste for Mesopotamian music, perhaps with the encouragement of the Assyrian kings. Sardis was thus able to make a unique contribution to Archaic Greek orientalism through a continuous, focused infusion of classical Mesopotamian art and learning into the Greco-Lydian and thence, the wider Greek world.

Thus, the papers in this collection cover an impressive range of issues relating to the complex cultural interactions that took place on Anatolian soil over the course of two millennia, in the process highlighting the difficulties inherent in studying societies that are multi-cultural in their make-up and outlook, as well as the role that cultural identity played in shaping those interactions.

REFERENCES

Algaze, G. (1993) *The Uruk World System: The Dynamics of Expansion of Early Mesopotamian Civilisation*. Chicago, University of Chicago.

Anthony, D. (1997) Prehistoric Migration as Social Process. In J. Chapman and H. Hamerow (eds.) *Migration and Invasions in Archaeological Explanation*, 21–31. BAR International Series 664. Oxford, BAR.

Banks, M. (1996) *Ethnicity: Anthropological Constructions*. New York, Routledge.

Bergquist, B. Bronze-Age Sacrificial Koine in the Eastern Mediterranean? A Study of Animal Sacrifice in the Ancient Near East. In J. Quaegebeur (ed.), *Ritual and Sacrifice in the Ancient Near East*, 11–43. OLA 55. Leuven, Peeters.

Bochner, S., ed. (1982) *Cultures in Contact: Studies in Cross-Cultural Interaction*. Oxford, Pergamon Press.

Bremmer, J. (2001) The Scapegoat Between Hittites, Greeks, Israelites and Christians. In R. Albertz (ed.), *Kult, Konflikt und Versöhnung*, 175–86. Münster, Ugarit-Verlag.

Catsancicos, J. (1991) *Recherches sur le vocabulaire de la faute. Apports du Hittite a l' étude de a phraseologie ind-européenne.* Paris, Société pour l'Étude du Proche-Orient Ancien.

Collins, B. J. (2002) Necromancy, Fertility and the Dark Earth: The Use of Ritual Pits in Hittite Cult. In P. Mirecki and M. Meyer (eds.) *Magic and Ritual in the Ancient World*, 224–42. Leiden, Brill.

Crossland, R. A. and A. Birchall (1974) *Bronze Age Migrations in the Aegean.* Sheffield, Noyes Press.

Finkelberg, M. (2005) *Greeks and Pre-Greeks. Aegean Prehistory and Greek Heroic Tradition.* Cambridge, Cambridge University.

Granovetter, M. (1973) The Strength of Weak Ties. *American Journal of Sociology* 78, 1360–80.

Hägg, R. (1985) Mycenaean Religion: The Helladic and the Minoan Components. In A. Morpurgo Davies and Y. Duhous (eds.) *Linear B: A 1984 Survey*, 203–25. Louvain, Peeters.

Hall, J. M. (2002) *Hellenicity: Between Ethnicity and Culture.* Chicago: University of Chicago.

Haubold, J. (2002) Greek Epic: A Near Eastern Genre? *Proceedings of the Cambridge Philological Society* 48, 1–19.

Hawkins, J. D. (1998) Tarkasnawa King of Mira: "Tarkondemos," Bogazköy Sealings and Karabel. *Anatolian Studies* 48, 1–31.

Hutter, M. (1995) Der luwische Wettergott piyassassi und der friechsche Pegasos. In M. Ofitisch and C. Zinko (eds.) *Studia Onomastica et Indogermanica. Festschrift für Fritz Lochner von Hüttenbach.* Graz, Leykam.

Jasink, A. M. (1981) Methodologcal Problems in the Comparison of Hittite and Mycenaean Institutions. *Rivista di Filologia e di Istruzione Classica* 109, 88–105.

—— (1983) *Movimenti di popoli nell' area egeo-anatolica (III–II millennio a.C.).* Florence, Lettere.

Janowski, B., K. Koch, and G. Wilhelm, (1993) *Religionsgeschichtliche Beziehungen zwischen Kleinasien, Nordsyrien und dem Alten Testament.* OBO 129. Fribourg, Academic Press.

Lévêque, P. (1975) Le syncrétisme créto-mycénien. In F. Dunand and P. Lévêque (eds.), *Les syncrétismes dans les religions de l'antiquité*, 19–73. Leiden, Brill.

Masson, O. (1950) À propos d'un rituel hittite pour la lustration d'une armée. Le rite de purification par le passage entre les deux parties d'une victime. *Revue de l'histoire des religions* 137, 5–25.

Melas, E. M. (1984) The Origins of Aegean Cremation. *Anthropologika* 5, 21–36.

Melchert, H. C. (ed.) (2003) *The Luwians.* Leiden. HbOr I/68. Brill.

Milroy, J. and L. Milroy (1997) Social Network and Patterns of Language Change. In J. Chapman and H. Hamerow (eds.) *Migrations and Invasions in Archaeological Explanation*, 73–81. BAR International Series 664. Oxford, BAR.

Morgan, L. (2005) The Cult Centre at Mycenae and the Duality of Life and Death. In L. Morgan ed., *Aegean Wall Painting. A Tribute to Mark Cameron*, 159–71. London, British School at Athens.

Morris, S. (2001) Potnia Aswiya: Anatolian Contrubutions to Greek Religion. In R. Laffineur and R. Hägg (eds.) *Potnia. Deities and Religion in the Aegean Bronze Age*, 423–34. Aegaeum 22. Liège, Université de Liège.

Mountjoy, P. (1998) The East Aegean–West Anatolian Interface in the Late Bronze Age: Mycenaeans and the Kingdom of Ahhiyawa. *Anatolian Studies* 48, 33–67.

Mufwene, S. S. (2001) *The Ecology of Language Evolution.* Cambridge, Cambridge University.

Ramsay, W. M. (1928) *Asianic Elements in Greek Civilisation.* Second edition. London, Murray.

Renfrew, C. (1987) *Archaeology and Language: The Puzzle of Indo-European Origins.* Cambridge, Cambridge University.

Sherratt, A. and S. Sherratt (1998) Small Worlds: Interaction and Identity in the Ancient Mediterranean. In E. H. Cline and D. Harris-Cline (eds.) *The Aegean and the Orient in the Second Millennium*, 329–42. Aegeum 18. Liège, Université de Liège.

Stein, G. (1999) *Rethinking World Systems: Diasporas, Colonies and Interaction in Uruk Mesopotamia.* Tucson, University of Arizona.

—— (2002) Colonies without Colonialism: A Trade Diaspora Model of Fourth Millennium BC Mesopotamian Enclaves in Anatolia. In C. L. Lyons and J. K. Paradopoulos (eds.) *The Archaeology of Colonialism*, 27–64. Los Angeles, Getty.

Steiner, G. (1971) Die Unterweltsbeschwörung des Odysseus im Lichte hethitischer Texte. *Ugarit-Forschungen* 3, 265–83.

Sucharski, R. A. (2003) A Gloss on Three "Olive-Oil Tablets" (Ugarit, Pylos) Connected with Fertility Rites. In F. M. Stepniowski (ed.) *The Orient and the Aegean. Papers Presented at the Warsaw Symposium, 9th April 1999*, 143–48. Warsaw, Warsaw University Institute of Archaeology.

Tassignon, I. (2001) Les éléments anatoliens du mythe et de la personalité de Dionysos. *Revue de l'histoire des religions* 218, 307–37.

Testart, A. (2005) Le texte hittite des funérailles royals au risue du comparatisme. *Ktêma* 30, 29–36.
Thomason, S. G. (2000) Linguistic Areas and Language History. In D. G. Gilbers, J. Nerbonne and J. Schaeken (eds.) *Languages in Contact*, 311–27. Amsterdam, Rodopi.
___ (2001) *Language Contact*. Washington, D. C., Georgetown University.
___ and T. Kaufman (1988) *Language Contact, Creolization and Genetic Linguistics*. Berkeley, University of California.
Van Brock, N. (1959) Substitution rituelle. *Revue hittite et asianique* 65, 117–46
Ventris, M. and J. Chadwick (1973) *Documents in Mycenaean Greek*. Second edition. Cambridge, Cambridge University.
Wallenstein, I. (1974) *The Modern World System I: Capitalist Agriculture and the Origins of the European World-Economy in the Sixteenth Century*. New York, Academic Press.
Watkins, C. (1986) The Language of the Trojans. In *Troy and the Trojan War*, 45–62
___ (2001) An Indo-European Linguistic Area and its Characteristics: Ancient Anatolia. Areal Diffusion as a Challenge to the Comparative Method? In A. Y. Aikhenvald and R. M. W. Dixon (eds.) *A real Diffusion and Genetic Inheritance: Problems in Comparative Linguistics*, 44–63. Oxford, Oxford University.
Weingarten, J. (1991) *The Transformation of Egyptian Taweret into Minoan Genius: A Study in Cultural Transmission in the Middle Bronze Age*. SIMA 99. Jonsered, Åströms.
West, M. L. (1997) *The East Face of Helicon: West Asiatic Elements in Greek Poetry and Myth*. Oxford, Clarendon.
Yener, K. A. (1998) A View from the Amuq in South-Central Turkey: Societies in Transformation in the Second Millennium BC. In Eric H. Cline and Diane Harris-Cline (eds.) *The Aegean and the Orient in the Second Millennium*, 273–80. Aegeum 18. Liège, Université de Liège.
___ (2002) Excavations in Hittite Heartlands: Recent Investigations in Late Bronze Age Anatolia. In K. Aslihan Yener and Harry A. Hoffner, Jr. (eds.) *Recent Developments in Hittite Archaeology and History: Papers in Memory of Hans G. Güterbock*, 1–9. Winona Lake, IN, Eisenbrauns.
Zatelli, I. (1998) The Origin of the Biblical Scapegoat Ritual: The Evidence of Two Eblaite Texts. *Vetus Testamentum* 48, 254–63.

1

TROY AS A "CONTESTED PERIPHERY": ARCHAEOLOGICAL PERSPECTIVES ON CROSS-CULTURAL AND CROSS-DISCIPLINARY INTERACTIONS CONCERNING BRONZE AGE ANATOLIA

Eric H. Cline

Achilles, Agamemnon, Menelaus, and Helen. Hector, Paris, Priam, Cassandra and Andromache.... These names have resonated down through the ages to us today, courtesy of Homer's *Iliad* and *Odyssey*, the epic stories of the Trojan War.

Even for those who had never heard of Troy and its story before, the plot and the names of those involved are now familiar territory, courtesy of Brad Pitt, Peter O'Toole, Orlando Bloom, Eric Bana, Sean Bean and Diane Kruger. They appeared in an epic of their own – the movie *Troy*, made by Warner Brothers and released during the summer of 2004. The film was neither particularly accurate nor faithful to the original story, but occasionally it stumbled close to the truth. "I've fought many wars in my time," says Priam at one point. "Some are fought for land, some for power, some for glory. I suppose fighting for love makes more sense than all the rest." Later, however, Agamemnon disputes this point. "This war is not being fought because of love for a woman; it is being fought for power, wealth, glory, and territory, as such wars always are," he says. I agreed with Agamemnon so much that I stood up and cheered in the theater, to the great embarrassment of my students sitting around me.

But was there really a Trojan War? Did Homer exist? Did Hector? Did Helen really have a face that launched a thousand ships? How much truth is there behind Homer's story? Was the Trojan War fought because of one man's love for a woman ... or was that merely the excuse for a war fought for other reasons – land, power, glory?

POSITION OVERVIEW

First and foremost, during the Late Bronze Age Troy was a "contested periphery" located between the Mycenaeans to the west and the Hittites to the east. There is both direct and indirect evidence that each group regarded the Troad as lying on the periphery of its own territory and attempted to claim it for itself. As I have argued in previous articles, whereas the Hittite king Tudhaliya II sent troops to quell the Assuwa rebellion in the late-fifteenth century and later Hittite kings left their mark as well, Ahhiyawan warriors apparently also fought on occasion in this region from the fifteenth through the thirteenth centuries BC (Cline 1996, 1997).

Second, perhaps because of its status as a "contested periphery," the city of Troy itself, and possibly also surrounding communities, such as Beşiktepe, were likely to have been home, or at least played host, to a variety of people of different cultures and ethnicities during the Late Bronze Age, whether permanent inhabitants, traveling merchants, sailors or warriors. The archaeological remains should reflect this diversity to a certain extent, as indeed they do in some cases (see the various finds in the Beşiktepe cemetery, for example; Basedow 2000, 2001).

However, I suggest that early excavators, such as Heinrich Schliemann with his hordes of workmen, will not have been nuanced enough in their approach necessarily to have discerned such diversity. Fortunately, the manner in which archaeology has been conducted in Anatolia has changed dramatically over the past century, in part because of the new questions being asked, in part because of the increasingly multidisciplinary nature of the new projects, and in part because of the new approaches being undertaken – particularly the cross-disciplinary efforts between archaeologists, historians, linguists, anthropologists, and other scholars. The recent efforts of Manfred Korfmann, with his integrated team of archaeologists and scientists, have sent us in new and interesting directions since the late 1980s and allow us to study the excavated material more carefully than ever before.

As my third and final point, I will suggest that Troy may be used as a specific case study not only of a "contested periphery" in terms of its geographical location in Anatolia during the Late Bronze Age but also as a "contested periphery" today in terms of its scholarly location, for the study of Troy and the Trojan War is positioned on the periphery between academic and popular scholarship. As Professor Spyros Iakovides, one of my original dissertation advisors with whom I have stayed in contact, wrote to me recently: "Be careful about the Trojan War. It is a slippery slope on which much has been said and written" (personal communication, 31 July 2004).

TROY AND THE TROAD AS A "CONTESTED PERIPHERY"

Several years ago I published an article in which I argued that Megiddo and the Jezreel Valley in Israel could be viewed as a "contested periphery" throughout history. The term "contested periphery" was first coined by Mitchell Allen for use in his 1997 UCLA dissertation concerned with Philistia, the Neo-Assyrians, and World Systems Theory. Allen identified "contested peripheries" as "border zones where different systems intersect." Chase-Dunn and Hall immediately adopted this term and defined it more formally as "a peripheral region for which one or more core regions compete" (Allen 1997, 49–51, 320–21, fig. 1.4; cf. also Berquist 1995a, 1995b; Chase-Dunn and Hall 1997, 37; Cline 2000).

In my original article on Megiddo, which appeared in the *Journal of World-Systems Research* in 2000, I said that if this concept of a "contested periphery" is to become a viable part of World Systems Theory, it must be able to explain more than a single case. Now I will suggest that it can. Back then, I suggested that additional areas in the world that might also qualify as "contested peripheries" were the area of Troy and the Troad, Dilmun in the Persian Gulf region, areas in the North American Midwest or Southwest, perhaps various regions in Mesoamerica, and the Kephissos River Valley commanded by Boeotian Thebes in central Greece. I have not yet had time to investigate the other suggestions, but I would now argue that the region of Troy and the Troad does indeed qualify as a "contested periphery" (Cline 2000).[1]

As I have argued previously, the term "contested periphery" has geographical, political and economic implications, since such a region will almost always lie between two larger empires, kingdoms or polities established to either side of it. Moreover, I would still argue that "contested peripheries" are also likely to be areas of intense military activity, precisely because of their geographical locations and constantly changing political affiliations. Thus, Mitchell Allen's phrase is not only applicable to the area of Megiddo and the Jezreel Valley in northern Israel, which has seen thirty-four battles during the past 4,000 years, but is also, I would argue, applicable to the area of Troy and the Troad. This region has similarly been the focus of battles during the past 3,500 years or more, from at least the time of the Trojan War in the Late

Bronze Age right up to the infamous battle at Gallipoli across the Hellespont during World War I. (The Hellespont is, of course, also known as the Dardanelles and is the strait leading from the Aegean Sea into the Sea of Marmara, which then connects with the Black Sea.)

Like Megiddo in Israel, which commands the Jezreel Valley, the region of Troy and the Troad in Anatolia, commanding the Hellespont was always a major crossroads, controlling routes leading south to north, west to east, and vice versa. Whoever controlled Troy and the Troad, and thus the entrance to the Hellespont, by default also controlled the entire region both economically and politically, vis á vis the trade and traffic through the area, whether sailors, warriors, or merchants. As "a thriving centre of ... commerce at a strategic point in shipping between the Aegean and Black seas," it is not difficult to see why this region was so desirable for so many centuries to so many different peoples.[2]

In the specific case of the Trojan War, I would argue that Troy and the Troad region was caught between the Mycenaeans, located to the west but interested in expanding ever eastward, and the Hittites, located to the east and interested in expanding ever westward.[3] Moreover, I would argue that it was the Trojan War itself that partially gave this region its geographical *je ne sais quoi* from then on, bringing great conquerors together through time and space in a way that no other circumstance has or can. Xerxes, the Persian king, stopped by in 480 BC, while en route to his invasion of Greece. Alexander the Great came to visit the site in 334 BC, making sacrifices to Athena and dedicating his armor in a temple there, before continuing on to conquer Egypt and much of the ancient Near East. Later, Julius Caesar, Caracalla, Constantine, and Mehmet II (the conqueror of Constantinople) all went out of their way to visit the site and pay their respects (Sage 2000). Like Megiddo in Israel, Troy and the Troad is among the elite sites and areas of the world that can claim to have seen many different armies and many famous leaders march through their lands during a sustained period from the Bronze Age to the Nuclear Age.

A continuous stream of armies should actually be expected as a natural occurrence in a region such as the Troad or the Jezreel Valley, which sit astride important routes where different geographical, economic, and political world-systems came into frequent contact, and which may have grown wealthy in part by exploiting international connections. Such desirable peripheral regions would likely gain the covetous gaze of rulers in one or more neighboring cores and thus would be highly contested. Like Megiddo, Troy may have had insufficient hinterland and natural resources to become a true core on its own, but it certainly became a major entrepôt and an important periphery, waxing and waning in a complex series of cycles with the nearby major players and world-systems who competed for control of this lucrative region each time they pulsed outward and bumped into each other (cf. Hall 1999, 9–10).

If an area is truly a "contested periphery," I would expect to find shifts in key trading partners, particularly if the region changed hands or political affiliations every so often. Such changes can also take place even if the region doesn't change hands or political affiliations, especially if the area, like the Jezreel Valley or the Troad, is located on a major trade route. Indeed, both regions fit the definition of an entrêpot or a crossroads area, providing a zone of cross-fertilization for the ideas, technology, and material goods that came into and passed through the region (cf. Teggart 1918, 1925; Bronson 1978; Bentley 1993).

As a perfect example of such cross-fertilization, I would offer the bronze sword from the time of the Hittite king Tudhaliya II, dating to about 1430 BC, which was found in 1991 by a bulldozer operator working near ancient Hattusa's famous Lion Gate. The sword, which has generated much publicity and many publications concerning its origin, looks suspiciously like a Mycenaean Type B sword generally manufactured and used in mainland Greece – by Mycenaeans – during this period. As I have suggested in two previously published and related articles, if this sword is not actually a product of a Mycenaean workshop, then it is an extremely good imitation of such a Type B sword, perhaps manufactured on the western coast of Anatolia. Either way, this sword is an excellent example of the transmission of either actual material goods, or ideas about such goods, during the Late Bronze Age in the region of the Troad.[4]

Even more importantly, inscribed on the blade of the sword is a single line in Akkadian, which reads in translation: "As Duthaliya [Tudhaliya] the Great King shattered the Assuwa-Country, he dedicated these swords to the Storm-God, his Lord." The inscription thus confirms other accounts written during Tudhaliya's reign concerning a rebellion by a group of twenty-two small vassal kingdoms, collectively known as Assuwa, along the northwestern coast of Anatolia. Tudhaliya, the accounts tell us, marched west to crush this so-called Assuwa Rebellion. This is potentially extremely important for the history of Troy, for it seems that the city was a member of this Assuwa coalition that rebelled against the Hitttites – the last two named polities of this coalition are Wilusiya and Taruisa.[5]

The literary texts from Tudhaliya's reign suggest that one of the allies of the Assuwa league were men from "Ahhiyawa." This place name comes up frequently in Hittite documents. It has been the cause of debates among Hittitologists since the 1920s, when the Swiss scholar Emil Forrer claimed that "Ahhiyawa" was a Hittite transliteration of the Greek "Achaea," the word Homer uses to refer to mainland (or Mycenaean) Greece. Initially, identification of the Ahhiyawans with the Mycenaeans won little support; but today more and more scholars believe that the Ahhiyawans were in fact either people from the Greek mainland or Mycenaean settlers along Anatolia's Aegean coast (see now Niemeier 1998).

So here, in the Hittite texts, which are augmented by a bronze sword of possible Mycenaean origin, we may well meet the Achaeans who, according to Homer, crossed the Aegean and fought at the city of Troy. However, this event was two hundred years before Homer's Trojan War ... and the evidence suggests that in this conflict the Mycenaeans and the Trojans were allies, not enemies, fighting together against the Hittites.

Confusing as this may seem, it leads to the intriguing possibility that the Trojan War may not have been simply a one-time conflict. Instead, it might have been the consummation of centuries-long contacts, sometimes friendly and sometimes hostile, between the Mycenaeans and the Trojans. We know, from both archaeological and literary evidence, that the Mycenaeans were involved in both peaceful and military expeditions to the region of Troy during the period from the fifteenth to the thirteenth century BC, that is, for nearly two hundred years up to and including the time of the Trojan War. It may well be that Homer telescoped these two centuries of on-again, off-again running conflicts into a single, ten-year-long battle fought for Helen. At the very least, I would argue that both the literary and the archaeological data may be used as evidence that Troy and the Troad was a contested periphery situated between the Mycenaeans to the west and the Hittites to the east during the Late Bronze Age and that the story of the Trojan War can be seen as a conflict fought precisely because this region was a contested periphery.

ARCHAEOLOGY AND ETHNICITY AT TROY

The city of Troy itself, and probably surrounding communities such as the harbor town of Beşiktepe as well, were likely to have been home, or at least played host, to a variety of people of different cultures and ethnicities during the Late Bronze Age, whether permanent inhabitants, traveling merchants, sailors, or warriors, in part because of its status as a "contested periphery" and its commanding position along a major trade route. The archaeological remains should reflect this diversity to a certain extent.

Considering that archaeologists have now been excavating at Troy for more than 120 years, it is perhaps surprising that of all three groups probably or possibly involved in the Trojan War – Mycenaeans, Hittites and Trojans – we know the least about the daily life of the Trojans. The problem is simple: whereas in the cases of both the Mycenaean and the Hittite civilizations we have entire countries in which to search and many different sites where we can excavate, in the case of the Trojans, we have only a single site, plus perhaps the nearby harbor city of Beşiktepe, that can provide evidence for their way of life.

Moreover, Heinrich Schliemann with his hordes of workmen will not have been nuanced enough in his approach to have necessarily discerned the diversity and ethnicity of the Trojan culture during the Late Bronze Age, particularly since he plunged right on through the levels of Troy VI and VII during his frenzied hunt for the Trojan War. Fortunately, the actual practice of doing archaeology in Anatolia has changed dramatically over the past century and we are now able to discern the diversity present at Troy during the Late Bronze Age.

Goods found by archaeologists in the ruins of Troy VI – dating between 1700 and 1250 BC – provide evidence of the city's wealth and of the diverse ethnicity of the visitors to this international emporium. Imported objects were discovered at Troy during the careful excavations by Dörpfeld in the years after Schliemann's death, again during the excavations conducted at the site during the 1930s by Carl Blegen and the University of Cincinnati, and, since 1988, by the excavations being conducted today by the University of Tübingen at both Troy and Beşiktepe directed until recently by the late Manfred Korfmann.[6]

As an aside, I would note that the reciprocal goods recorded in Late Bronze Age texts as probably exported from Troy and the surrounding Troad region include commodities that originated, or would have been available, in northwestern Anatolia: horses, copper, lead, ivory and lapis lazuli. These are items commonly found in high-level gift-exchanges across the Bronze Age Near East. However, with the exception of so-called Trojan grey ware, the majority (if not all) of these goods presumably exported from Troy are perishable in nature and would not have left any remains behind in the material record, and so would not be readily identified by any of the archaeologists who have excavated on the Greek Mainland, in Egypt, or elsewhere in the eastern Mediterranean.[7]

Since 1988, Manfred Korfmann and his team have been re-excavating the Bronze Age levels at Troy, with amazing results. Their archaeological excavations at the site have revealed a city far larger than previously thought to exist, including a new lower city surrounded by a ditch and supplied by an underground water system originally constructed during the Early Bronze Age and used for the next thousand years.[8]

This recent archaeological evidence supports Homer's description that Troy was a large, wealthy and quite probably multi-ethnic city that could have resisted a prolonged siege by a Greek army. Korfmann has also found evidence of destruction of the city by fire and war. Arrowheads, slingstones and bodies have been discovered in the streets of the citadel and the lower city that are clear indications of fierce fighting in the city. However, it is not yet clear whether this assault should be dated to Troy VI or to Troy VIIa; in his publications, Korfmann has taken to calling the remains Troy VI/VIIa.[9]

Korfmann is the first to admit that his data are open to interpretation. However, his own colleague at the University of Tübingen, Frank Kolb, went one step further several years ago and accused Korfmann of exaggeration, misleading statements, and shoddy scholarship. This eventually led to a symposium entitled "The Importance of Troia in the Late Bronze Age," held at the university on February 15/16, 2002, which ended in "an unseemly bout of fisticuffs" between Korfmann and Kolb – a new Trojan War, if you will.[10] And this, in turn, brings us to my third and final interrelated point.

TROY AND THE TROJAN WAR AS A "CONTESTED PERIPHERY" IN ACADEMIC AND PUBLIC PERCEPTION

I would like to introduce a variation on my initial discussion, for the search for Troy and the Trojan War continues today to be a "contested periphery," not in a geographical sense but rather in both academic and public perception. That is to say, while it is possible to discuss Troy as a "contested periphery" not only in terms of its physical and geographic location, as we have already done, it is also possible to discuss Troy and the Trojan War in terms of its acceptable position within academia.

At first, back in the mid-nineteenth century when Schliemann set out to prove that the academics of that time were wrong and that Troy did exist, the search for Troy and the Trojan War lay firmly on the periphery of academic scholarship. Now, in today's world of the early twenty-first century, the search for Troy and the Trojan War has been charged once again with being on the periphery of academic scholarship, according to the very public accusations of Frank Kolb that Troy was not a major player in the Late Bronze Age world, that it was in fact "a trivial nest of pirates at the margin of civilization," and that Manfred Korfmann is the equivalent of "the batty Erich von Däniken," in both exaggerating and distorting the importance of Troy and his own findings (see Howard 2002, 12; Wilford 2002, F1).

I personally disagree completely with Frank Kolb and am firmly on the side of Manfred Korfmann in this ridiculous controversy, as are most other practicing Late Bronze Age archaeologists, historians, and epigraphers. Indeed, Donald Easton, J. D. Hawkins, and Andrew and Susan Sherratt published an article in *Anatolian Studies* (2002) entitled "Troy in Recent Perspective," in which they addressed the accusations made by Frank Kolb and concluded that his criticisms of Korfmann "are themselves considerably exaggerated" (see Easton et al. 2002).

However, I would suggest that, particularly in the case of Troy and the Trojan War, it has become clear that we are now faced with numerous meanings and connotations of a "contested periphery," not just the rarified geographic and academic definition that I gave at the beginning of this chapter. Moreover, I would argue that while, on the one hand, excavating at Troy and studying what happened there over the millennia is very much in the mainstream of archaeology and Bronze Age studies, especially in terms of public consciousness of the site (because everyone has heard of it), on the other hand, the topic of Troy and the Trojan War runs the risk of being seen as very much on the periphery of serious archaeology and of being labeled by some as "pseudo-archaeology."

I say this not because Troy and the Trojan War is viewed by many academics to be a "popularizing" topic (horror of horrors!), but because the topic is frequently lumped into a larger category by the general public and the television documentary makers and is considered by them as part-and-parcel with searches for other events and ideas that are indeed on the outer fringes of believability, such as Atlantis and Noah's Ark. We here today know that some or all of these topics may well have had some kernel of truth around which the later epic, myth or legend is wrapped – for instance the story of Atlantis might have the eruption of Santorini as its origin – but a chemist, physicist or nuclear scientist undoubtedly regards the study of Troy and the search for the Trojan War as lying much more on the periphery of real science than, say, the study of the human genetic code or the ongoing attempt to find a cure for cancer.

And yet, I would challenge those who would place the study of Troy and the Trojan War on the fringe of serious academia, for studying such topics can frequently serve a far more mainstream purpose than the pursuers of other much more esoteric topics would ever deign to believe, particularly if one feels that part of our responsibility as scholars is to bring a distilled and understandable version of our research back to the public.

Thus, I would consider this topic to be very much a "contested periphery" today, in terms of its acceptability to the scholarly establishment on the one hand and the general public on the other. It is on the periphery of acceptability for some in the academy (viz. Frank Kolb) who prefer more hard science and less speculation. It is on the opposite periphery of acceptability for those in the general public, who are quick to embrace the concept of aliens building the pyramids or a vanished civilization building the Sphinx, yet who are a bit more reluctant to tackle a topic that requires actual reading (i.e., the *Iliad* and the *Odyssey*) and at least a minimal amount of intellectual comprehension.

SUMMARY AND CONCLUSIONS

In the end, what do we know and what do we believe? Much nonsense has been written about Troy and the Trojan War in both the distant and the recent past. Assertions that Troy was located in England and/or Scandinavia, that the story was actually a garbled version of the legend of Atlantis, and other flights of fantasy have found their way into print within the past decade alone.[11] But are there any historical "facts" to support Homer, or is his tale simply a good yarn?

In my opinion, although many questions remain that have ignited scholarly controversies and even most-unscholarly fist-fights, conservatively one can conclude that there is a kernel of truth in Homer's story. A Trojan War did take place. Further, I believe that we can now say with confidence that we know the site of ancient Troy, and that its location has been known for nearly 150 years, ever since the days of Frank Calvert and Heinrich Schliemann. It lies in northwestern Turkey, well placed to command the Hellespont (Dardanelles) and the maritime route leading from the Aegean Sea to the Black Sea, a route that has been of continued importance to shipping ventures for millennia.

I believe that of the nine cities that lie one on top of another at the site of Troy, it is most likely the sixth city – Troy VI – that belonged to Priam and that the Mycenaean Greeks besieged in approximately 1250 BC. Troy VIIa, the city subsequently built upon the ruins of the city destroyed by the Mycenaeans, was – I believe – destroyed in turn some seventy-five years later by the marauding Sea Peoples, who not only brought an end to Bronze Age Troy but also to virtually all of the Late Bronze Age civilizations around the Mediterranean.

For now, I remain convinced that Helen's abduction makes a nice story and served as a good excuse for the Mycenaeans to besiege Troy, in the same way that the murder of the Hittite prince Zannanza may have begun a war between the Hittites and the Egyptians a century earlier and the assassination of Archduke Ferdinand served to begin World War I three thousand years later.[12] However, there were far more compelling economic reasons and political motives to go to war in this "contested periphery" more than three thousand years ago. And that, I would argue, is perhaps the most important point. Beyond simply providing a convenient (and common-sense) term by which to describe the region of Troy and the Troad, in designating Late Bronze Age Troy and the Troad as a geographical "contested periphery," we enable researchers to begin the next steps in comparing this areas with the other sites and areas in the world with similar geographical definitions and similar bloody military histories, such as Megiddo and the Jezreel Valley in Israel or Boeotian Thebes and the Kephissos River Valley in Greece. Future cross-disciplinary efforts between archaeologists, historians, linguists, anthropologists, political scientists and other scholars should be able to unearth additional, and even more fruitful, comparisons with various sites and areas in other parts of the world and other moments in time. Such cross-disciplinary efforts are indeed possible and could yield important results in the future.

NOTES

1 Much of the following section reiterates what I said in that original paper, since I am now confident that my comments there about Megiddo apply equally well to Troy. See also Allen (2001, 265), which was presented as a follow up to my published suggestion but which itself never appeared in print beyond this short Abstract (at least to my knowledge).

2 See now discussion in Guzowska (2002). For the description of Troy as "a thriving centre of ... commerce...," see Wilford (2002, F1).

3 See now also Korfmann (2000).

4 See Cline (1996, 1997), with further references and bibliography. In addition to the literature on the sword cited in those articles, see now also Taracha (2003).

5 See again Cline (1996, 1997), with further references and bibliography; now also Bryce (2003).

6 See now the discussions in Kolb (2004) and Jablonka and Rose (2004).
7 See references in Cline (1997). On Trojan grey ware, see Allen (1994).
8 See the publications in the *Studia Troica* volumes, as well as Korfmann (2000, 2003, 2004) and Basedow (2000, 2001).
9 See, for instance, the popularizing article in *Archaeology* magazine, Korfmann (2004).
10 See now the discussions in Kolb (2004) and Jablonka and Rose (2004), with a subsequent rejoinder by Kolb posted on the Online Forum of the *American Journal of Archaeology* (http://www.ajaonline.org/forum/viewtopic.php?t=9). See previously Heimlich (2002), Howard (2002, 12), Wilford (2002, F1).
11 See recent publications, including those by Wilkens (1991), Zangger (1992, 1993).
12 On the death of Zannanza and its consequences, see Bryce (1998, 193–98) with further references.

REFERENCES

Allen, M. J. (1997) Contested Peripheries: Philistia in the Neo-Assyrian World-System. Ph.D. diss., University of California, Los Angeles.

Allen, S. H. (1994) Trojan Grey Ware at Tell Miqne-Ekron. *Bulletin of the American Schools of Oriental Research* 293, 39–51.

___ (2001) The Hellespont as a "Contested Periphery." *American Journal of Archaeology* 105/2, 265.

Basedow, M. A. (2000) *Beşik-Tepe: Das Spätbronzezeitliche Gräberfeld.* Mainz, von Zabern.

___ (2001) Der spätbronzezeitliche Friedhof am Beşiktepe: Geschichte und Landschaft. In J. Latacz, P. Blome, J. Luckhardt, H. Brunner, M. Korfmann, and G. Biegel (eds.) *Troia: Traum und Wirklichkeit*, 415–18. Stuttgart, Konrad Theiss.

Bentley, J. H. (1993) *Old World Encounters: Cross-Cultural Contacts and Exchanges in Pre-Modern Times.* Oxford, Oxford University.

Berquist, J. L. (1995a) *Judaism in Persia's Shadow: A Social and Historical Approach.* Minneapolis, Fortress.

___ (1995b) The Shifting Frontier: The Achaemenid Empire's Treatment of Western Colonies. *Journal of World-Systems Research* 1, 1–38.

Bronson, B. (1978) Exchange at the Upstream and Downstream Ends: Notes Toward a Functional Model of the Coastal State in Southeast Asia. In K. L. Hutterer (ed.) *Economic Exchange and Social Interaction in Southeast Asia: Perspectives from Prehistory, History, and Ethnography*, 39–52. Ann Arbor, University of Michigan.

Bryce, T. (1998) *The Kingdom of the Hittites.* Oxford, Clarendon.

___ (2003) Relations between Hatti and Ahhiyawa in the Last Decades of the Bronze Age. In G. Beckman, R. Beal, and G. McMahon (eds.) *Hittite Studies in Honor of Harry A. Hoffner Jr. on the Occasion of His 65th Birthday*, 59–72. Winona Lake, IN, Eisenbrauns.

Chase-Dunn, C. and Hall, T. D. (1997) *Rise and Demise: Comparing World-Systems.* Boulder CO, Westview Press.

Cline, E. H. (1996) Aššuwa and the Achaeans: The "Mycenaean" Sword at Hattušas and its Possible Implications. *Annual of the British School at Athens* 91, 137–51.

___ (1997) Achilles in Anatolia: Myth, History, and the Aššuwa Rebellion. In G. D. Young, M. W. Chavalas, and R. E. Averbeck (eds.) *Crossing Boundaries and Linking Horizons: Studies in Honor of Michael Astour on His 80th Birthday*, 189–210. Bethesda, MD, CDL Press.

___ (2000) "Contested Peripheries" in World Systems Theory: Megiddo and the Jezreel Valley as a Test Case. *Journal of World-Systems Research* 6, 8–17.

Easton, D. F. et al. (2002) Troy in Recent Perspective. *Anatolian Studies* 52, 75–109.

Guzowska, M. (2002) The Trojan Connection or Mycenaeans, Penteconters, and the Black Sea. In K. Jones-Bley and D. G. Zdanovich (eds.) *Complex Societies of Central Eurasia from the 3rd to the 1st Millennium BC*, Vol. II, 504–17. Washington, DC, Institute for the Study of Man.

Hall, T. D. (1999) World-Systems and Evolution: An Appraisal. In P. Nick Kardulias (ed.) *World-Systems Theory in Practice: Leadership, Production, and Exchange*, 1–23. Lanham, MD, Rowman & Littlefield.

Heimlich, R. (2002) The New Trojan Wars. *Archaeology Odyssey* 5/4, 16–23, 55–56.

Howard, P. (2002) Troy Ignites Modern-Day Passions. *The Australian*, February 26, 2002, 12.

Jablonka, P., and Rose, C. B. (2004) Late Bronze Age Troy: A Response to Frank Kolb. *American Journal of Archaeology* 108/4, 615–30.

Kolb, F. (2004) Troy VI: A Trading Center and Commercial City? *American Journal of Archaeology* 108/4, 577–613.

Korfmann, M. (2000) Homers Troia: Griechischer Außenposten oder hethitischer Vasall? *Spektrum der Wissenschaft*, July 2000, 64–70.

— (2003) Troia im Lichte der neuen Forschungsergebnisse. In *Festvortrag am Dies academicus 2003 der Universität Trier*, 9–70. Trier, Universität Trier.

— (2004) Was There a Trojan War? *Archaeology* 57/3, 36–41.

Niemeier, W.-D. (1998) The Mycenaeans in Western Anatolia and the Problem of the Origins of the Sea Peoples. In S. Gitin, A. Mazar, and E. Stern (eds.) *Mediterranean Peoples in Transition: Thirteenth to Early Tenth Centuries BCE*, 17–65. Jerusalem, Israel Exploration Society.

Sage, M. (2000) Roman Visitors to Ilium in the Roman Imperial and Late Antique Period: The Symbolic Functions of a Landscape. *Studia Troica* 10, 211–31.

Taracha, P. (2003) Is Tuthaliya's Sword Really Aegean? In G. Beckman, R. Beal, and G. McMahon (eds.) *Hittite Studies in Honor of Harry A. Hoffner Jr. on the Occasion of His 65th Birthday*, 367–76. Winona Lake, IN, Eisenbrauns.

Teggart, F. J. (1918) *The Processes of History*. New Haven, Yale University.

— (1925) *Theory of History*. New Haven, Yale University.

Wilford, J. N. (2002) Was Troy a Metropolis? Homer Isn't Talking. *New York Times*, October 22, F1.

Wilkens, I. (1991) *Where Troy Once Stood*. New York, St. Martin's.

Zangger, E. (1992) *The Flood from Heaven*. New York, William Morrow.

— (1993) Plato's Atlantis Account – A Distorted Recollection of the Trojan War. *Oxford Journal of Archaeology* 12, 77–87.

2

PURPLE-DYERS IN LAZPA

Itamar Singer

The organizers of this conference should be acclaimed for bringing together scholars dealing with a broad scope of subjects from both sides of the Aegean. It is increasingly recognized (though not in all scholarly circles, regrettably) that an interdisciplinary approach, with a fruitful cooperation between Hittitologists and Mycenologists, archaeologists and philologists, can yield important advances in our comprehension of the complex relationships between Anatolian and Aegean cultures.[1] This paper aims at introducing a previously unsuspected economic factor in the strained Hittite-Ahhiyawan contacts in western Anatolia and the offshore islands.

ṢĀRIPŪTU-MEN IN THE MANAPA-TARHUNTA LETTER

The Manapa-Tarhunta Letter (*CTH* 191) is a large one-column tablet, the reverse of which is uninscribed.[2] The main fragment, *KUB* 19.5 (VAT 7454 + Bo 2561), was augmented by Laroche (*CTH* suppl.) with the small join *KBo* 19.79 (1481/u), which was found in the dump of Temple I. Parts of the text were discussed in early studies (Forrer 1926, 90–91; Sommer 1932, 170, n. 1), but the first comprehensive treatment was presented by Houwink ten Cate (1983–84, 38–64), and this served as the basis for all subsequent studies.

The letter was sent by Manapa-Tarhunta, king of the Seha River Land, to his Lord, either Mursili II, or, more probably, Muwatalli II.[3] After a surprisingly short greeting, Manapa-Tarhunta presents his reasons (or perhaps pretexts) for failing to participate in a Hittite military expedition to the Land of Wilusa. This important historical reference has attracted the attention of most commentators, but will not be discussed in this paper.

The next paragraph takes up the rest of the obverse, some thirty partly preserved lines. Here we encounter the notorious troublemaker Piyamaradu and his son-in-law Atpa, the ruler of Millawata/Millawanda/Miletos. The two, who acted as the main proxies of Ahhiyawa in Anatolia, humiliated Manapa-Tarhunta by conducting an attack on the Land of Lazpa and carrying away some prisoners.[4] This could indicate that the island of Lesbos[5] belonged to the Seha River Land, situated on the opposite coast, in the valley of the Caicos, the Hermos, or both.[6]

In Lazpa, two groups of *ṢĀRIPŪTU* -men were forced to "join up"[7] and were brought by Piyamaradu's men before Atpa. One group consisted of Manapa-Tarhunta's *ṢĀRIPŪTU* and the other of His Majesty's (the Hittite king). The latter, or perhaps both groups, were headed by their *chief*,[8] a man whose name ends with [...]*ḫuḫa*.[9] After their abduction, these persons appealed to Atpa, probably in Millawata, with the following significant words (ll. 15–18): "We are *tributaries* (*arkammanaliuš*) and we came o[ve]r the sea. Let us [render] our *tribute* (*arkamman*)! Šigauna may have committed a crime, but we have done nothing."[10] Who the "criminal" Šigauna might be we do not know.[11] It seems that Atpa was willing at first to set free the

ṢĀRIPŪTU-men, but he was then persuaded by this Šigauna to take advantage of the golden opportunity presented by the Storm-god,[12] and ultimately refused to let them go. At this stage Kupanta-Kurunta, probably the well-known king of Mira, intervened in the matter, and "the ṢĀRIPŪTU-men of the gods who (belong) to His Majesty" (l. 27) were released. In the remaining text we only have the ends of lines, which do not provide a context.[13]

Various questions are raised by this intriguing episode, but all depend on the identity of the ṢĀRIPŪTU-men,[14] who are otherwise not attested in the Boğazköy tablets. They do appear, however, in the Ras Shamra tablets, and these may provide the right answer.

ṢĀRIPŪTU-MEN IN THE TEXTS FROM UGARIT

Ugaritica 5. 26 (RS 20.03) is a letter sent by the Hittite prince Šukur-Tešub to the king of Ugarit, Ammištamru II, in the mid-thirteenth century BC (Nougayrol 1968, 91–93). The prince had just been appointed as governor in Alalah and he appeals to his southern neighbor in an important matter: The ṢĀRIPŪTU-men of Panešta will be sent over the border to Ba'alat-rimi[15] in order to máš.da.a.ri *ana epeši*, rendered by Nougayrol (without commentary) as "to perform the regular offerings" ("pour faire les offrandes perpétuelles"). After completing their mission they should be sent back to the "mayor" (*ḫazannu*) of Šalmiya. They should be protected on their way through the mountains and should be provided for all their needs.

In his *editio princeps*, J. Nougayrol associated ṢĀRIPŪTU with the Semitic verb *ṣarāpu*, which has a wide range of meanings, all of them associated with the processing of some material through high temperatures: "to smelt and refine" metals, "to fire or bake" pottery, bricks or tablets, "to dye" textiles and leather, etc.[16] Nougrayrol opted for "smelters" ("fondeurs") and was followed by Houwink ten Cate.[17] A different interpretation, far more fruitful, was put forward by S. Lackenbacher in her recent anthology of Akkadian texts from Ugarit (2002, 95–96, with n. 276). Drawing from other texts, some still unpublished, she concluded that the ṢĀRIPŪTU were "purple-dyers." Another letter, already indicated by Nougayrol (1968, 93, n. 15), mentions the "ṢĀRIPŪTU of the king" (Lackenbacher 1989, 317–18; 2002, 97). Piha-ziti, a leading official from Carchemish (Singer 1999, 653, n. 142), complains that these had been subjected to custom duties in Ugarit. He threatens to file a complaint with "the king" (of Carchemish). Finally, in an unpublished letter from the Urtenu archive, the Hittite king is explicitly mentioned as sending wool to Ugarit *a-na ṣa-ra-pi*, "for dyeing" (Lackenbacher 2002, 96 n. 276).

Concerning the mission of the ṢĀRIPŪTU in Ugaritica 5. 26 (máš.da.a.ri *ana epeši*), Lackenbacher pointed to a strand of evidence in a lexical text from Boghazköy in which Sumerian máš.da.a.ri is equated with Akkadian *irbu* and Hittite *arkammaš*, "income" or "tribute."[18] But, according to Lackenbacher, "to make/perform the tribute" does not provide a satisfactory sense in this text, and she therefore substituted a related Akkadian term, *argamannu*, which in later texts means "purple wool."[19] In other words, what the ṢĀRIPŪTU-men were supposed to do in Ugarit is to dye their wool in purple, a well-known industry of the Levantine coast. From all the references cited above, it is obvious that representatives of the Hittite crown closely supervised the movements of these itinerant craftsmen and controlled their lucrative revenues.[20]

PURPLE IN THE ANCIENT NEAR EAST

Lackenbacher's ingenious solution opens new vistas in the interpretation of the Manapa-Tarhunta letter and its relevance to eastern Aegean economy and politics. However, this solution, concisely indicated in her lengthy footnote, needs some further consideration and bolstering in a broader context of what is presently known about the purple-dye industry and its terminology in the Near East and the Aegean.[21]

The meaning of *argamannu* may serve as a good point of departure. As first recognized by Albright (1933,

15), Luwian/Hittite *arkamma(n)*-[22] is etymologically related to Akkadian *argamannu* and its West Semitic cognates (Ugaritic *ʾargmn/irgmn*, Hebrew *ʾargaman*, Aramaic *ʾargwan*, Arabic *arjawan*, etc.).[23] A vast literature has been dedicated to the problem of etymology, Semitic, Indo-European, or other, and to the circuitous question of what was the primary sense, "tribute" or "purple."[24] Either way, the semantic shift is easily comprehensible. Since the most conspicuous component of the Ugaritic tribute to Hatti (and of the Phoenician tribute to Assur) was purple-dyed fabrics, the two meanings became conflated. The difficult question remains whether this semantic shift had already occurred in the second millennium,[25] or only in the first.[26] With the new data from Ugarit adduced by Lackenbacher an early semantic shift seems preferable.

Akkadian *argamannu* was not the only Akkadian designation for purple-dyed fabrics. It is well known that the terminology for colors in cuneiform literature is notoriously complex. Landsberger's seminal study of Sumerian-Akkadian colors (1967) still serves as the best starting point. The Mesopotamian color palette consists of five basic colors—white (BABBAR=*peṣû*), black (GE$_6$=*ṣalmu*), red (SA$_5$=*sāmu*), yellow/green (SIG$_7$(.SIG$_7$)=(*w*)*arqu*), and multicolored (GÙN(.GÙN)=*burrumu*). "Blue" is expressed only by comparison to the color of lapis lazuli (ZA.GÌN=*uqnû*). Hence, "blue wool" is simply designated as *šīpātu uqnû* or *uqnâtu* (SÍG.ZA.GÌN).[27] Blue fabrics are already mentioned in Early Dynastic times (Biggs 1966), long before the advent of the purple dye. With the invention of the new technology sometime during the second millennium BC (see below), SÍG.ZA.GÌN (occasionally SÍG.ZA.GÌN.GE$_6$) became the standard designation for wool dyed "blue purple." At the same time, SÍG.ZA.GÌN, without additional specifications, continued to designate blue fabrics in general, including those tinted with other dyestuffs, of mineral or vegetal origin. For "red purple" the ideogram SÍG.ZA.GÌN.SA$_5$ was reserved. This chromatic division must be situated within the range of light-red to dark-blue, but the exact hue of each of the two designations is not easy to establish.[28] Another problem is the correspondence between the above logograms and their phonetic spellings. Without delving into the various problems involved, it may summarily be concluded that only the terms *argamannu*, *ḫašmānu* and *takiltu* are related to the purple-dye industry, whereas other designations for reddish and bluish shades have probably nothing to do with the dye produced from the marine snails.[29] To these three terms for purple colors we must add a fourth, *ṣirpu*, which relates to the industrial process involving high temperatures. Although the verb *ṣarāpu* may denote the heating of various substances (see above), when *ṣirpu* is associated with dyed fabrics it usually denotes red or purple colors. The same root also generated the professional designation of the purple-dyers, *ṢĀRIPŪTU*.

There might be some scattered earlier attestations,[30] but the best evidence for second-millennium purple comes from Ugarit, which also supplied the first archaeological evidence for the industry in the Levant (see below).[31] The lexical correspondence between the Akkadian and the Ugaritic terms is notoriously difficult and controversial.[32] We follow here the conclusions reached by W. van Soldt in his 1990 study on "Fabrics and Dyes at Ugarit."

The two main categories are "blue (or violet) purple," SÍG(.ZA.GÌN) *takiltu*, which corresponds to Ugaritic *iqnu* (lit. the color of lapis lazuli), and "red purple," SÍG(.ZA.GÌN) *ḫašmānu*, corresponding to alphabetic *pḥm* (lit. the color of glowing charcoal).[33] As already mentioned, the generic term for "purple-dyed wool" is SÍG.ZA.GÌN, and in order to specify its color as either "blue" or "red" one had to add the specification *takiltu* or *ḫašmānu*, respectively. The ideogram ZA.GÌN was gradually dropped, leaving only the phonetic spellings.

These designations from Ugarit are matched with Neo-Assyrian *takiltu* and *argamannu*, and with Hebrew *tekhelet* and *argaman*.[34] Clearly, the terms *ḫašmānu* and *argamannu* were interchangeable, both referring to "red purple" (SÍG ZA.GÌN SA$_5$).[35] It is regrettable that, relying on some late lexicographical equations, the main Akkadian dictionaries define *ḫa/ušmānu* as "blue-green" (*CAD Ḫ*, 142) or "bläulich" (*AHw*, 334b), and these translations have been followed by most Assyriologists and Hittitologists.[36] The expression "*ḫašmānu* of the sea" in a fragmentary Akkadian text from Boghaköy does not help in solving the problem.[37] Does it refer to the color of the sea (whatever that is), or does it rather refer to the murex shells coming from the sea? Either way, it strikingly recalls Homer's *halipórphyros*, "purple of the sea."[38]

Ugarit supplies some valuable data on the prices of purple-dyed wools.[39] One talent (ca. 30 kilos) of red purple costed on the average four shekels of silver, and one talent of blue purple more than five silver shekels. A comparison with the prices of untreated wool shows that the dyeing process more than doubled its value. Although these prices are but a far cry from the exorbitant prices paid for Tyrian purple in Classical times,[40] they were a major source for the prosperity of Ugarit and other Levantine cities. Naturally, the great demand for the genuine substance generated cheaper imitations of inferior quality produced from plant and mineral sources (Blum 1998, 31 with notes 51–52).

The Ugaritic information on the textile production is quite limited.[41] The palace personnel (*bnš mlk*) included "shearers" (*gzzm*), "spinners" (*ǵzlm*), "weavers" (*mḫṣm*; cf. Akk. *mūḫiṣu* and *ušparu*) and "fullers" or "dyers" (*kbsm/kbśm*). The last term may be the Ugaritic designation for the craftsmen involved in the purple-dye industry. A text published by Thureau-Dangin (1934) lists twenty-nine persons along with[42] various quantities (from one to four hundred shekels) of purple-dyed wool (SÍG.ZA.GÌN), altogether two talents and six hundred shekels of wool (ca. 66 kilos). No further details are provided about these men, but we may perhaps see in them subcontractors allotted with small quantities of dyed wool for the production of fabrics and garments, either for themselves or for export. This could show that as in many other places around the world, dyeing was applied to the yarn before being woven ("dyed-in-the-wool"). Rather surprisingly, female workers are not mentioned in the Ugaritic texts, unlike other places where they constitute the main labor force in the textile industry.[43] Unless Ugarit was exceptional in this regard (which is hard to believe), one may assume that at least some of the men mentioned in the texts in relation with the production of fabrics were in fact the heads of households or guilds who managed the transactions, while the actual manufacture was performed by women.

Evidence for the consumption of purple-dyed fabrics at Ugarit is quite limited. There is no direct evidence on the apparel worn by the king and his family, but there are several references to the presentation of purple to deities (Ribichini and Xella 1985, 17). The most interesting is a letter of Takuhli(nu), governor of Ugarit, in which he implores his king to send him a large quantity of blue purple wool for a thanksgiving offering to the deity who saved his life.[44] He concludes his letter by exclaiming (rev. 43–46): "If my master does not send me blue purple wool, who else would give me blue purple wool?" Is this simply a figure of speech, or may it be conceived as an indication for a royal monopoly on the purple-dye industry? Ugarit must have exported large quantities of purple-dyed fabrics abroad, besides the annual tribute given to her Hittite overlords (see below), but the evidence for this is surprisingly meager.[45]

Perhaps the scarcity of evidence for purple exports from the Levant to Mesopotamia in the late-second millennium BC may partly be explained by the discovery of alternative supplies in the Persian/Arabian Gulf.[46] A French mission exploring the archaeology of Qatar discovered in the early 1980s clear evidence for a purple-dye industry on a small island in the Bay of Khor (Edens 1986; 1987; 1994; 1999). The site consists of small structures and a shell midden dominated by a single species of marine gastropod (*Thais savignyi*). The breakage pattern of the shells proves that the site was specialized in the production of purple-dye with techniques similar to those developed in the Mediterranean. The pottery assemblage dates the site to the thirteenth–twelfth centuries BC, contemporary to the late-Kassite materials of southern Mesopotamia and the islands of Failaka and Bahrain (Edens 1999, 80). Edens assumes that the purple technology, oriented towards provisioning elite consumption, was transferred from the Mediterranean to Kassite Babylonia and it was controlled by government officials. The logistic effort was worthwhile considering the high price of purple and especially its symbolic association with political power among the elite (Edens 1987; 1994).

PURPLE-DYE PRODUCTION AND CONSUMPTION THROUGH THE AGES

In view of the detailed descriptions, including recipes, of the production of some materials in cuneiform literature,[47] it is somewhat disappointing that not a single hint can be found in the ancient Near Eastern sources about the actual processing methods of the purple dye. For this we have to consult the Classical sources and the archaeological evidence. There is a vast literature on "purpurology," including scientific studies on the chemical processes involved.[48] Nevertheless, it might be worthwhile to provide the readers with a brief abstract on the technical background and on the later history of purple, including some bibliographical references.

According to legend, the discovery of purple dye is closely tied to the Phoenician coast. A late Greek tale recounts how the dog of Melqart-Herakles (or according to another version, the dog of Helen of Troy) started to chew on a murex shell and his mouth turned purple red.[49] The Tyrian hero disclosed his discovery to King Phoenix (brother of Kadmos and Europa) who decreed that the rulers of Phoenicia should wear this color as a royal symbol.

The first concrete descriptions on the methods of production of "Tyrian purple," later known as "Royal purple," are found in Aristotle (*Historia Animalium* 5.15.22–25), Pliny the Elder (*Historia Naturalis* 9.62.133) and Vitruvius (*De architectura* 7.13.1–3).[50] The purpura marine snails (or mollusks) live in shallow waters of warm seas around the world. Two main varieties are found along the Mediterranean coasts: *Murex trunculus*, which produces the red or violet purple, and *Murex brandaris*, which produces the blue purple.

The raw material of the purple-dye industry was produced from the secretion of a small bladder, the hypobranchial gland of the molluscs. The secreted fluid is yellowish, but in contact with air and light it undergoes a photochemical reaction and gradually turns into purple in various hues, from purple red or scarlet (*purpura*) to deep blue violet (*pelagia*).[51] The snails were collected by hand from the shallow seafloor or by lowering baited wicker baskets into the depths. Then, they were collected into metal or pottery tanks. The larger snails were broken open to extract the dye-producing gland, whereas the smaller ones were simply crushed. Salt was added and the mass was exposed to the sun for three days. Then it was slowly boiled for another week or so in a vat (which explains the association with the Semitic root *ṣrp*). Eventually, the costly liquid was extracted and the wool yarn was dyed in it ("dyed-in-the-wool") before being woven. This resulted in an incomparably color-fast fabric, produced in a wide range of shades, from pale pink to dark violet and black purple. According to the traditional view, the end product was only transported in the form of dyed fabric, but one cannot entirely exclude the possibility that dye dissolved in an alkaline solution allowed transportation in the form of an soluble pigment to be redissolved at the point of destination (Lowe 2004, 47).

The shining iridescent quality of ancient purple explains the confusion in translating the terms used by the ancients to designate the different shades of scarlet, purple and crimson. Some were puzzled, for example, by Homer's striking array of figures employing the term "purple"—"purple sea," "purple blood," "purple rainbow" and even "purple death."[52] Obviously, color terminology varies within the same language, not to mention through translation. We should better give up our modern notion of a "purple" hue and work instead with the ancient concept of a "purple" dyestuff and the technology for its production.[53]

Usually, the only archaeological evidence for a purple-dye industry is the broken or crushed shells discarded in large quantities, sometimes in separate heaps for each kind of shell. A huge amount of snails was needed to dye a single piece of fabric.[54] Enormous mounds of discarded murex shells were located in the vicinity of Phoenician cities, disclosing the location of their industrial quarters (Reese 1987, 206 with notes 49–50).

One must consider carefully this evidence, since snails were also eaten and the empty shells were used for lime production, pottery temper and construction fill.[55] Beautiful shells were also used for decoration, especially in landlocked places, where they were considered a rarity.[56] A meticulous examination of the shells in their archaeological context is therefore essential, and such information is often missing from excavation reports. A good clue to determine whether the shells belong to a purple-dye industry or are merely kitchen refuse is their location within the site. Since the industry was notorious for producing repulsive smells,[57] the installations were usually located at some distance from the habitation, taking into account the prevailing wind directions. In any case, contrary to other perishable goods, which seldom leave any archaeological trace,[58] a purple-dye industry may at least be suspected in murex-rich coastal areas, and a careful examination of discarded shells, rarely performed in the past, may prove its actual existence and extent.

The purple-dye industry of Ugarit was situated at the port of Minet el Beida, where Schaeffer found huge heaps of punctured and crushed murex shells and also pottery vessels stained with purple (1951, 188–89 with fig. 1). Other Late Bronze Age evidence, and much better recorded, comes from Sarepta, biblical Ṣarfat, an important Phoenician city situated between Tyre and Sidon, whose very name is probably derived from its purple-dye industry.[59] Further south, purple-dyeing installations were excavated at Akko, Tel Keisan, Shikmona, Dor, and Tel Mor near Ashdod.[60] Some of these sites also produced pottery vessels with traces of purple color inside them (Karmon and Spanier 1987, 149, fig. 2; 150, fig. 4; 155, fig. 9). Scattered evidence for purple-dyeing was also found in Cyprus.[61]

The Phoenicians spread their skill throughout the Mediterranean, and, in fact, the search for new sources of murex may well have been one of the motives for their expansion.[62] With the Assyrian conquest of the Levant, purple tribute streamed in large quantities to the east and soon became one of the notorious symbols of imperial power.[63] Babylonians, Medes, Lydians, Phrygians and Jews[64] also indulged in the splendor of purple, but it reached its unrivalled apex under the Achaemenid emperors.[65]

In Greece there was first a fierce resistance to anything Persian or oriental and purple was boycotted for a long time.[66] According to legend, Alexander the Great refused to wear purple when he conquered and destroyed Tyre, and Darius of Persia exclaimed his astonishment over the Macedonian who only dressed in white. But eventually the Greeks adopted the Persian imperial insignia, which brought a new world-wide expansion of the prestigious color.

The Romans were among the last to adopt purple for status display, but it was in their times that it enjoyed its greatest vogue in antiquity.[67] First to wear a *toga picta* was Julius Caesar, and consequently, a strong Republican hostility developed to the excessive or even immoral elite display of purple (designated by Seneca as *color improbus*). But, despite repeated attempts to regulate the wearing of purple and restrict it to official and ecclesiastical uses, as the Empire aged, more and more influential groups were permitted to wear stripes or even entire garments of "Royal purple."[68]

Only under Diocletian, the highest quality Tyrian purple became reserved as a privilege of emperors, with the epithet Porphyrogenitus appended to their name. Its extraction and preparation became a royal monopoly and the manufacturing methods were closely guarded. Unauthorized possession of "Imperial purple" became a capital offense.[69] With Constantine, purple was institutionalized by the Christian church and purple became an essential symbol in the sacerdotal vestments of both Oriental church patriarchs and Latin cardinals.

With the Turkish conquest of Constantinople in AD 1453, the purple-dyeing craft ceased to be practiced in the Mediterranean basin. Here and there purple-dyeing was continued on a small scale at various places in the world, as distant as Britain and Mexico (Jensen 1963, 117; Spanier 1987, 171), but the three-millennia-long predominance of "the most long-lived status symbol of antiquity" (Reinhold 1970, 6) was gone forever.

Before we continue to the Aegean challenge to the Levantine origin of the purple-dye industry, it is well to note that the chromatic qualities of some marine snails were independently discovered in various parts of the world. For example, on the Pacific coast of Mexico, since ancient times, people used to rub the

Plicopurpura pansa snails on wet cotton mops and then return them to the sea.[70] This way multiple "milkings" of the snails could be obtained every couple of weeks. There has even been a recent revival of the method in Mexico to support a Japanese market for expensive kimonos, and the dye is also used to trim some Mexican basketware.

PURPLE IN THE AEGEAN

The ancient belief in the Levantine origins of purple-dyeing has been adopted, almost unanimously, in modern scholarship as well.[71] Still, some nineteenth-century scholars had the right instinct to doubt this truism and to suggest the existence of a more universal practice of purple-dyeing. George Tyron (quoted in Herzog 1987, 39) wrote in his *Manual of Conchology* in 1880: "It is probable that all ancient peoples inhabiting sea-shores have become accidentally acquainted with this property common to so many molluscs at a very early date." So, in dealing with the origins of purple-dyeing, the question is less about who invented it, but rather who developed it into a large-scale industry with extensive exports abroad. The Levantine origin of the industry has seriously been challenged in recent years by discoveries in the Aegean, notably on Crete and adjacent islands.[72]

Already at the beginning of the last century, large quantities of murex shells were found at a Middle Minoan site on the small island of Kouphonisi (ancient Leuke), southeast of Crete, and at Palaikastro in eastern Crete. In 1904, Bosanquet explicitly stated that "it is clear that the Minoan Cretans had anticipated the Phoenicians in the manufacture of purple-dye" and that "sponges as well as purple-juice were among the wares shipped from Crete to her markets in the East" (Bosanquet 1904, 321).

More conclusive evidence turned up recently in Crete, notably at Kommos,[73] and elsewhere in the Aegean, including the islands of Kythera (also known as Porphyroussa), Keos and Thera.[74] At Akrotiri, besides large quantities of shells,[75] a small ball of pigment was recently found and laboratory tests prove that it was produced from murex shells (Aloupi et al. 1990). Purple was also used in the magnificent wall paintings, as recently shown by Raman spectroscopy on samples taken from Xeste 3, a public building with evident religious character (Sotiropoulou et al. 2003).

In short, until other evidence turns up, we must get used to the idea that large-scale purple-dyeing started on Crete in the first half of the second millennium BC, and thence it spread to other areas under strong Minoan influence in the Aegean, and also to the Levant, to major port towns such as Ugarit and Byblos.[76] To the growing list of Cretan export items, including itinerant artists, we should now add purple-dyed textiles, typical luxury objects of high value and very low bulk.[77] These dyed textiles may have been traded in exchange for Anatolian and Near Eastern metals.[78]

The archaeological evidence may be supplemented with some valuable, though scarce, philological data from the Linear B tablets. Already Ventris and Chadwick (1959: 321, 405) called attention to the adjective *porphyrea* (*po-pu-re-ja*) in the Knossos tablets, corresponding to Homer's *porphyreos*, "purple."[79] The evidence has recently been reexamined by Palaima (1991, 289–91; 1997, 407–12). There are only four Mycenaean occurrences related to *porphyra* and all come from Knossos. One of them modifies a type of cloth (*pu-ka-ta-ri-ja*). Another intriguing occurrence is unfortunately incomplete (KN X 976 + 8263). It has the adjectival forms *po-pu-re-jo* and *wa-na-ka-te-ro* "of the wanax," i.e., "royal," in proximity to each other. However, it is uncertain whether the two refer to a cloth. *po-pu-re-jo* could also refer in this context to "purple-dye workers" or to "a purple-dye workshop" (Palaima 1991, 291; 1997, 407). In any case, the attribute *wanakteros*, "royal," suggests that the purple-dyeing considerably enhanced the value of the fabrics, and it curiously recalls the millennium-later Roman designation "royal purple."

In his 1997 article dealing with the "royal" products, possessions and personnel in the Linear B tablets, Palaima draws an interesting parallel to the Hittite ^{GIŠ}TUKUL-men, specialist craftsmen who performed services for royal and religious institutions in Hatti, and were rewarded with land grants (Beal 1988, 410). The Mycenaean "royal" specialists included the "potter" and certain cloth-working specialists, namely, the "fuller," the "cloth finisher," and the "purple-dye worker" (Palaima 1997, 412).

As for the etymology of *porphyra* (Latin *purpura*), various proposals have been put forward, but neither the Greek (Faure 1991, 311; cf. Blum 1998, 28), nor the Semitic (Astour 1965, 349–59) ones are sufficiently convincing. Therefore, an argument could be made for a Minoan (Linear A) source, especially since another dying substance, *pa-ra-ku* ("blue, bluish green"), seems to be of Minoan origin (Palaima 1991, 289).

From the eastern Aegean, the evidence is less adequate, but still meaningful. The most abundant evidence comes from Troy. Already Schliemann (1881, 318) reported that he found "a whole layer formed exclusively of cut or crushed murex-shells." In his chapter on the "Zoology of the Troad" (1881, 115) he explicitly states that the "*Murex trunculus* and *Purpura haemastoma* [found at Troy] have probably served for the manufacture of purple." To this archaeological evidence he appended the information from Aristotle (*Historia Animalium* 5.15.547) on the purple-dyeing industry that flourished near Sigeion on the coast of the Troad.

The American excavations produced more accurate information pertaining to periods VIf and VIg (Reese 1987, 205). According to Blegen (1937, 582), "several of the layers so clearly differentiated were composed almost wholly of crushed murex shells by the thousands, and these strata can be traced continuously some twenty or thirty meters northward into square J 6. There can be little doubt that the passage between the Sixth City wall and the large houses VI E, VI F, and VI G was treated as a repository for rubbish from a purple-factory. Indeed, the establishment may have occupied this open space itself, and it is possible that the diminutive 'wells' had some function in connection with the purple industry. Numerous stone grinders and pounders and fragments of worn millstones recovered here were doubtless used to crush the shells."

Fresh evidence for the purple-dyeing industry of Troy was found in the latest excavations, notably at the edge of the lower-city area (Korfmann 1997, 59; 1998, 9; 2001, 503). Some ten kilograms of crushed murex have been recovered in proximity to an installation that may have served for the boiling of the shells (1996, 59). They belong to the middle phase of Troy VI ("Troia VI-Mitte") dated to the Late Bronze Age.

Except for Troy, archaeological evidence for a purple-dyeing industry in western Anatolia is ephemeral.[80] Perhaps Miletos with its numerous Minoan-type discoid loomweights (Niemeier 1999a, 548) will fill the gap one day.[81]

The situation on the offshore islands is unfortunately even less clear. There is abundant evidence in Classical sources on purple-dyeing in most of the Aegean islands (for references see Reese 2000, 645), but very limited archaeological information has turned up so far proving Bronze Age industries. One must take into account, of course, that the northeastern islands have been barely explored, except for their large Early Bronze Age settlements. Recently, however, some new investigations have been launched into second-millennium strata, especially on Lemnos (at Hephaistia, Koukonisi and Poliochni), and these may provide some new information.[82] So far, large quantities of *Murex brandaris* were found in the Early Bronze Age levels at Poliochni[83] and in a Hellenistic industrial zone at Mytilene (Williams and Williams 1987, 11).

In anticipation of more archaeological evidence from early western Anatolia and the offshore islands, it may be of interest to underline the fame of the first-millennium purple-dye industries of Lydia, Phrygia, and the Greek cities of Ionia.[84] The appropriate juncture to begin with is Homer's *porphyreos* (Blum 1998, 68–71, with refs.). The only persons actually to wear purple robes are Agamemnon in the *Iliad*, and Odysseus and his son in the *Odyssey*. There are also other purple fabrics used on special occasions, such as the rugs in the tent of Achylles and the *peploi* enshrouding the urn of Hektor. It is important to note that Homer's royal women (Helen, Andromache, Arete) do not wear purple clothes, but only weave them. What kind of reality is reflected in Homer is of course a much-discussed question, but it is well to note that purple is associated with royalty and prestige, as in Near Eastern and Mycenaean prototypes (Blum 1998, 75).

The first "historical" Greek man attested to have worn purple attire is the poet Magnes from Smyrna in the seventh century BC, and it is perhaps not coincidental that he professed his art mainly at the court of Gyges king of Lydia (Blum 1998, 143). Perhaps he received his attire in Sardis, whose purple industry was known to have inspired the Greek cities of Ionia. King Kroisos dedicated purple coats and tunics to the Delphian Apollo. Xenophanes reports that the inhabitants of his native town of Colophon learned to wear purple garments from the Lydians, and similar statements were later made by Strabo and by Democritus of Ephesos (Blum 1998, 144). The Ionian fashion came to mainland Greece much later and to a lesser extent. For almost a century (490–420 BC), the use of the luxury color was interdicted in Greece as a result of nationalistic anti-Persian feelings, but after this interlude purple returned to its full vigor in Athens.

The first "historical" Greek woman associated with purple is – how appropriate – Sappho of Lesbos (Blum 1998, 86, 91) at the turn of the sixth century BC. The context is not without interest for our topic. She presented purple veils to her goddess Aphrodite, and this *doron* is considered by experts to be the first attestation of an *anathema*, a "dedication" to a deity.[85] The custom of dressing up Greek cult statues with purple garments became quite popular from the fourth century on, but the earliest examples again point towards the east, notably Lydia, as the source of influence. As mentioned above, this practice has deep roots in Near Eastern cult. Takuhlinu of Ugarit vows to present purple-dyed offerings to Apšukka of Irhanda (RS 17.383, 37–41) and the same purpose may have been served by the visit of the *ṢĀRIPŪTU*-men in Ugarit and in Lazpa. But before we return to our point of departure from this detour after the origins of purple, let us first throw a glance on the Hittite evidence, which is regrettably quite limited.

PURPLE IN HATTI

The best point of departure is the yearly tribute sent by Ugarit to the Hittite court.[86] The original list was appended to the Suppiluliuma-Niqmaddu treaty and it was repeated, with slight emendations, in the Mursili-Niqmepa treaty. Besides the Akkadian versions, there is also an Ugaritic one and, as mentioned before, the terminological equation between the two languages has long been debated until its present resolution (van Soldt 1990, 341).

Besides a yearly tribute of five hundred shekels of gold, Ugarit was required to send golden cups, linen garments and purple-dyed wool to the Great King, to the queen, to the crown prince and to five other Hittite dignataries. The king received five hundred shekels of blue-purple wool (SÍG.ZA.GÌN [*takiltu*]) = *iqnu*)[87] and five hundred shekels of red-purple wool (SÍG.ZA.GÌN *ḫašmānu* = *pḫm*). All the others received only one hundred shekels of each. It should be emphasized that the present consisted of dyed wool and not of ready-made garments. Therefore, it is not known whether the colored wool was used by its recipients for their own wardrobe, or whether it was presented as an offering to their gods, as in the above-mentioned case of Takuhlinu of Ugarit.[88]

In Hittite texts, dyed fabrics are mentioned in rituals, festivals, descriptions of cult images, and mostly in inventories, which have been studied by Goetze (1955; 1956), Košak (1982) and Siegelová (1986). These lists usually provide the weight of the catalogued objects, their color, and occasionally some indications about their place of origin. The Hittite color palette is unusually well understood, and, as pointed out by Landsberger (1967, 159), the Hittite names are not dependent on the Syro-Mesopotamian terminology.[89] Hittite "blue" is *antara-*, but most occurrences refer to ZA.GÌN, which, as already noted, is rather ambiguous. It may refer to "regular" blue, produced from some mineral or plant dye, or to the far more expensive "blue-purple," which is produced from marine snails (*Schneckenpurpur*).[90] Except for rare cases in which this distinction may be fathomed from the context (see below), the texts leave us in the dark (or rather in the generic "blue"). Surprisingly, *takiltu* is not attested in the Boghazköy tablets, whereas *argamma(n)* means "tribute" (but see below). Only the third Akkadian designation for purple, *ḫašmānu*, is well attested. Its

Hittite reading is unknown, unless the term was borrowed from Akkadian.[91] As mentioned above, the color of *ḫašmānu* has been intensely debated, but "red purple" is preferable, in my opionion,[92] than the obscure "blue-green" (*CAD*) or "bläulich" (*AHw*).[93]

The items made of *ḫašmānu* include "tunics" (TÚGE.ÍB), "long gowns" (TÚGBAR.DUL$_5$), "waist bands" (TÚG*maššiaš*), "luxurious garments" (TÚG*mazagānniš*), "diadems" (TÚG*lupani*), "Hurrian shirts" (TÚG.GÚ.È.A *Ḫurri*), and an "Ikkuwaniya garment" (TÚG *Ikkuwaniya*). In short, many accessories in the Hittite wardrobe were red-purple or at least were trimmed with purple hems. Perhaps some of the SÍG.ZA.GÌN items were blue-purple, but, as mentioned before, there is no way to tell which was tinted by marine dye and which by some cheaper substitute made of minerals or plants. There is one context, though, in which the former option is clearly preferable.

The price list in the Hittite Laws dedicates a separate paragraph to cloth and garments (§182; Hoffner 1997, 145–46). The prices range from thirty shekels of silver for a "fine garment" (TÚG.SIG) to one shekel for a "sackcloth" (TÚG.BÁR).[94] The second-most-expensive garment, with the price tag of twenty silver shekels, is TÚG.SÍG ZA.GÌN. I doubt that a simple "blue wool garment" (Hoffner 1997, 146) would justify this price, and therefore I prefer Goetze's (1955, 51) "blue purple-dyed garment." A comparison with prices at Ugarit and other Near Eastern lands (see Heltzer 1978, 38–50, 90–91) supports this conclusion: clothing items cost no more than a few shekels, unless they were made of expensive purple-dyed fabrics. Also, the fact that there are no other color designations in this price list may indicate that the author was referring to the quality of the material rather than its color.

Regarding the origin of purple, there is one explicit source besides the tribute lists from Ugarit. The Middle Hittite *taknaz dā-* ("take from the earth") ritual of Tunnawiya provides the following significant passage on the source of different kinds of wool.[95] Unfortunately, a crucial piece is missing: "They brought white wool (SÍG BABBAR) from Hurma; they brought [red wool (?) from ...]; they brought blu[e(-purple) wool] ([SÍG ZA.]GÌN) from Ura." Without delving into complicated issues of magical color symbolism,[96] the important information for our purposes is the origin of blue-purple in Ura, the well-known port on the Mediterranean coast (probably at Silifke). Does this mean that there was an independent dyeing industry on the Mediterranean coast of Anatolia, or is it simply an indication that Ura was the port of entry for purple-dyed fabrics produced elsewhere, or perhaps both? In any case, the marine location of SÍG ZA.GÌN lends strong support to the rendering "blue purple-dyed wool" (Otten 1967, 59) in this context.

The production and processing mode of the Hittite textile industry can only cursorily be perceived through some of the inventory texts.[97] Bo 6489 (Siegelová 1986, 324–27) is a poorly preserved late text listing large quantities of wool (SÍG)[98] presented to various persons, some identified by their place of residence, others apparently managers of central storehouses of the kingdom (É.GAL *tupp[aš*, É Gazz]imara). The type of color of the wool is not defined, which could mean that these were allotments of unprocessed material collected in regional depots, perhaps in anticipation of further processing, dyeing and fitting. Another fragmentary list, with smaller allotments, has women's names only, perhaps the weavers who would turn the wool into fabric.[99]

Much has been written about the symbolism of red, blue and purple as the colors of gods and kings throughout the ages.[100] Can we detect anything comparable in the status of these colors in the Hittite world? Before we delve into an intensive search for the putative prerogatives of the Hittite *purpurati*, I should add in passing that I did not investigate the premises on which the alleged exclusivity of purple raiment in other ancient Near Eastern societies rests. Such an enterprise would require an in-depth investigation of the entire cuneiform documentation, which is far beyond the scope of this study. Nevertheless, I would tentatively remark that even in my cursory browsing through the primary and secondary sources, I found ample evidence to the effect that red, blue and purple garments[101] were owned not only by gods, kings and conjurers fighting against demons,[102] but also by important officials and dignitaries, not necessarily of royal descent.[103] In other words, purple clothing, like gold,[104] was definitely designated for elite consumption, but, as far as I can see, there was nothing in the ancient Near East even remotely resembling the strict imperial monopolies imposed on Tyrian purple in Late Roman and Byzantine times, neither in legislation nor in practice.[105] Although the association between color and social rank is certainly valid for oriental cultures as well, one should refrain from automatically replicating concepts and conducts from the Classical world to the ancient Near East. A completely different question is whether the lucrative purple industry and trade was closely supervised by the crown, as was the case with other strategic commodities.

In any case, I could not find any evidence for purple as a prerogative of Hittite kings and their families. The purple tribute from Ugarit, for example, is given not only to the king, the queen and the crown prince, but also to five leading state officials. One can argue, of course, that the entire higher echelons of the Hittite administration consisted of princes of various ranks, but this is hardly the point here. Anyone who could afford to buy these luxury items could do so, and I suppose that not only dignitaries of royal blood, but also wealthy merchants, diplomats and others had the necessary means.[106] This is quite a different situation than the one prevailing in Byzantium, where an unauthorized person could lose his head for wearing Imperial purple.

BACK TO LAZPA

Equipped with the diverse information about purple that we have gathered from various sources, we should now return to the mission of the *ṢĀRIPŪTU* -men in Lazpa. The Ugaritic parallels solved the question of their profession: they were itinerant purple-dyers in the service of the Hittite king and of the king of the Seha River Land. In fact, the parallel between the two cases, both of them in coastline provinces of the Hittite Empire, may go further than apparent at first sight.

Let us reconsider the highly significant plea of the abducted *ṢĀRIPŪTU*-men before Atpa: "We are *arkammanaliuš* and we came over the sea. Let us [perform[107]] our *arkamman*!" What exactly are they pleading? Do they simply state their status as tributaries, but then, tributaries to whom? And what kind of tribute were they bringing to Lazpa? Or might their explanation be more specific and accurate?

One has to admit that the clear references to *arkamma(n)* in Hittite texts are indeed to "tribute,"[108] and the few references to *arkammanali-* are probably to "tributaries" ("tributpflichtig").[109] Nevertheless, in view of the parallels from Ugarit, I would tentatively suggest that what we have here is actually a rare reference to the other meaning of the Kulturwort *argamman*, "purple-dyed wool," and that *arkammanaliuš* could simply be the Hittite reading of LÚ.MEŠ *ṢĀRIPŪTU*. It must have been in such concrete circumstances, the preparation and presentation of purple offerings, that the semantic shift from "purple" to "tribute" (or vice versa) developed. And, considering the strong Luwian connections, perhaps even origins of *arkamman*,[110] this incident in western Anatolia could very well span the transition from one meaning to the other.

If so, the plea of the *ṢĀRIPŪTU*-men before their capturers becomes more intelligible. They simply state their profession and mission, the preparation and/or presentation of purple in Lazpa. They further emphasize that, unlike the mysterious Šigauna who had "sinned" (*waštaš*), they were not involved in any way in this affair and should therefore be released. Manapa-Tarhunta, who is quoting their speech, must have received his information from these very purple-dyers who were eventually released.

This new interpretation of the Lazpa incident remains tentative until corroborated by further evidence. Even so, it makes more sense, in my opinion, than an undesignated expedition of tribute-bringers who carried their tribute to the distant Land of Lazpa. Their identification as purple-dyers opens new vistas in our understanding of the interface between the Hittite and the Mycenaean orbits in the eastern Aegean. In Classical antiquity this region was renowned for its purple-dye industry, and unsurprisingly, it turns out that this lucrative trade has much earlier origins. The actual remains of the purple-dye industry of Lesbos and the opposite coast of western Anatolia in the late-second millennium BC have yet to be discovered, but in view of the clear evidence from Bronze Age Troy, this endeavor should not be impossible.

Regarding the origins of the purple-dyers who came "over the sea" to Lazpa, the ready answer should be somewhere on the western Anatolian coast.[111] Still, I would mention in passing another, more distant, possibility. The texts from Pylos provided the much-discussed reference to western Anatolian women from Miletos (*Mi-ra-ti-ja*), Knidos (*Ki-ni-di-ja*), Lemnos (*Ra-mi-ni-ja*), etc.[112] It is usually assumed that these women-workers were slaves who were either purchased or abducted during razzias to the western Anatolian coasts and were then employed in the Aegean textile industry. Stimulating as this may seem, I do not think that the foreign women in Pylos had anything to do with the purple-dyers in our text. But of course, both episodes may be viewed in the general context of the intense Hittite-Ahhiyawan competition over territories, resources and markets in the Aegean realm.

Indeed, the question must be raised whether Lazpa was just another island among many, or does this incident relate to some special role this island played in the eastern Aegean orbit. Once again the text from Ugarit may serve as a springboard. The purple-dyers who cross over the border from Alalah to Ugarit are expected to perform their duty at Belet-remi, creatively rendered by Nougayrol as "Notre-Dame-de-Grâce." May we assume that the mission of the "purple-dyers of the gods of his Majesty" in the Manapa-Tarhunta letter (l. 27) had a similar purpose, the dedication of purple-dyed *anathemata* to some important deity of Lazpa? Fortunately, this assumption is supported not only by Sappho's purple veils dedicated to Aphrodite half a millennium later, but also by a contemporary Hittite text. In a well-known oracular inquiry, an ailing Hittite king (probably Hattusili III) consults the Deity of Ahhiyawa and the Deity of Lazpa.[113] This unique reference shows that Lazpa, the only eastern Aegean island explicitly mentioned in the Hittite texts, was the abode of some important deity, perhaps an early hypostasis of Aphrodite.[114] Incidentally, the same text also refers to oracular consultations at the other end of the Hittite Empire, at Aštata on the Middle Euphrates (*KUB* 5.6 I 6–13; Laroche 1980, 240). Here too, the name of the deity involved is not specified, but from other references we know that she must have been the goddess Ishara.[115]

Whoever the Deity of Lazpa was in the Bronze Age, I wonder whether the visit of the purple-dyers on the island, with the postulated mission of presenting their offerings at the local shrine, was simply an act of piety initiated by the Hittite king and the king of the Seha River Land. Since, from time immemorial, religion and politics go hand in hand, I doubt it. It does not take too much imagination to attribute a political purpose to this visit, a statement of the Hittite claim on the off-shore islands, and on Lazpa in particular. This issue is ardently debated in *KUB* 26.91, an important letter in the Hittite-Ahhiyawan correspondence (Taracha 2001; Starke, forthcoming). Great, and also lesser, kings were in the habit of marking the limits of their authority by sending official expeditions, sometimes disguised under peaceful religious or cultural intents. If indeed such were the circumstances of the Lazpa incident, the result was a resounding fiasco for the Hittite king and his western vassal. He barely saved face by obtaining a negotiated release of his purple-dyers.

The "Lazpa incident," which apparently stirred up the entire western Anatolian milieu, provides a rare glimpse into yet another economic facet of the strained Hittite-Ahhiyawan relations. It was perhaps "the tip of a purple iceberg" in an intense competition over a lucrative and prestigious industry of the Aegean.[116]

NOTES

1 For recent surveys on "Homer and the East" see, e.g., Burkert (1991), Morris (1997), Watkins (1998).

2 Except for two lines incised deeply in the middle of the tablet at an angle of 60° to each other. I am grateful to Prof. Gernot Wilhelm, Director of the research program *Hethitische Forschungen* at the Akademie der Wissenschaften

und der Literatur, Mainz, for permission to study the photographs of the tablet. Dr. Jared Miller kindly collated the text for me in 2004 and I had the occasion to examine the photographs in June 2005.

3 Sommer (1932, 33ff.) and Garstang and Gurney (1959, 95) hesitated between the two datings. For Mursili II, see Forrer (1926, 22), Stefanini (1964, 27), Cornelius (1973, 217–18). For Muwatalli II, see Heinhold-Krahmer (1977, 174, 221), Houwink ten Cate (1983–84, 50, 58–64), Singer (1983a, 210), Güterbock (1986, 37, n. 11), Freu (1990, 25; 1998, 103), Starke (1997, 453), Bryce (1998, 246; 2003, 70), Taracha (2001, 419).

4 In my opinion, the formulation implies a direct connection between Manapa-Tarhunta's humiliation and the attack on Lazpa, but cf. Houwink ten Cate (1983–84, 50; but cf. p. 55 n. 48), who assumes that the humiliation refers to a military defeat of the past.

5 The identification of Lazpa with Lesbos, first suggested by Forrer, is now universally accepted. For the conflict between Hatti and Ahhiyawa over the northeastern Aegean islands, see Taracha 2001 (with earlier literature) and Starke (forthcoming). As noted by Houwink ten Cate (1983–84, 55, n. 48), according to Homeric tradition, Lesbos was the furthest outpost of the Trojans and it was assailed by the Greeks who took human spoils (*Il.* 9.270–276, 663–665).

6 For the choice between the Caicos (Bakir) or the Hermos (Gediz) valleys as the Seha River Land, see Starke (1997, 451), Hawkins (1998, 23–24), Niemeier (1999b, 143), Bryce (2003, 38–39).

7 For *anda ḫandai-*, see Sommer (1932, 348–49; "mit jemandem paktieren," "sich jemandem anschliessen"); Garstang and Gurney (1959, 95; "make common cause with"); Houwink ten Cate (1983–84, 44–45; "join in"); *HED* 3, 100. I do not see any grounds for Houwink ten Cate's assumption (1983–84, 47) that the *ṢĀRIPŪTU*-men "joined in of their own accord and thus voluntarily." On the contrary, according to their own testimony, they did not share the guilt of Šigauna, Piyamaradu's proxy.

8 The reading and rendering of the logographic compound LÚ.AMA.A.TU LÚ.BANŠUR(?) is not clear. Houwink ten Cate's (1983–84, 40) literal translation "domestic and table man" is not very convincing. The first component, LÚ.AMA.A.TU, corresponds to Akkadian *illatu*, "band, (family) group, clan" (Friedrich 1926, 79, "Hausgenosse"). The second component lacks the GIŠ determinative and should probably be read differently, but I cannot suggest how.

9 Heinhold-Krahmer (1977, 222) suggested *ḫuḫa-* "grandfather," but this appelative also appears in personal names (Laroche 1966, 70); for the correspondence between Hittite/Luwian *Ḫuḫḫas* and Lydian *Gyges*, see Carruba (2003, 151). Another possible restoration could include the theophoric element *[Kar]-ḫu-ḫa-aš* (l. 14), a deity that is already attested in second-millennium cuneiform texts (Singer 2001, 638–39). A king named Maza-Karhuha appears in the Luwian hieroglyphic inscription inscribed on a silver bowl in the Ankara Museum (Hawkins 1997).

10 (15) ... *an-za-aš-wa-an-na-aš ar-kam-ma-na-al-l[i-u]š* (16) *[nu-wa-kán(?)]*⌜A⌝.AB.BA *p[ár-ra]-an-ta ú-wa-u-en* ⌜*nu-wa-an-na-aš ar-kam-ma*⌝*-an* (17) *[i-ua-u]-e-ni(?)* ⌜*nu-wa* ^{m}⌝*Ši-ig-ga-ú-na-aš wa-aš-ta-aš* (18) *[an-za-aš-ma-w]a(?) Ụ́-U[L] ku-ịt-ki i-[y]a-u-en....* For parallels to *-kan aruni parranta pai-*, see Houwink ten Cate (1983–84, 47).

11 For the possible role of Šigauna in the affair, see Houwink ten Cate (1983–84, 53–54). Could he perhaps be the ruler of Lazpa who betrayed his Anatolian overlord and collaborated with Piyamaradu?

12 Lines 22–23: "The Storm-god [ga]ve (them) to you, (so) why should you [give] them back?" Houwink ten Cate (1983–84, 39–40, 49) read ^{D}U-*ta[r*, which he rendered as "a ty[pe of] Storm god." The sign after ^{D}U is not clear. Jared Miller suggests a simple ^{D}U-*aš* with a superfluous lower horizontal.

13 Houwink ten Cate (1983–84, 52) suggests that the remainder of the letter dealt with the fate of Manapa-Tarhunta's *ṢARIPŪTU*-men. Worth noting is ^{LÚ}AD.KID-*ta-ra-aš(-wa-aš-kán)*, "basket-weaver" (l. 33). For *atkuppu*, "a craftsman making objects of reeds," see *CAD A/II*, 494–95; sometimes these craftsmen prepared reed boats and reed containers coated with bitumen to make them watertight. The Hittite reading is unknown, but the suffix *-tara* is found in professional terms, such as ^{LÚ}*akuttara-*, ^{LÚ}*weštara-*, ^{SAL}*taptara-*. See further below on the method of collecting sea snails by lowering baited wicker baskets into the sea.

14 The word is variously spelled as *ṢA-RI-PU-TI* (l. 9), *ṢÍ-RI-PU-TE* (l. 12) and *ṢÍ-RI-PU-TI* (l. 14). Early renderings of the vocable include Forrer's "Metöken" (1926, 90) and Cornelius's "Feuerleute" (1973, 217). Sommer and other commentators have refrained from suggesting an exact translation; see, e.g., Heinhold-Krahmer (1977, 223), Starke (1997, 453; 2001, 346, "Handwerker"). The Akkadian dictionaries leave open the exact occupation of the *ṣāripu*-men: *AHw* 1085b: "eine Art von Hofleuten"; *CAD/Ṣ*, 111a: "a class of persons"; *CDA*, 334: "a kind of court personnel." See further below.

15 ^{URU}NIN-*ri-mi* is not otherwise attested (Belmonte Marín 2001, 51). Is this indeed the name of a town, or perhaps just the sanctuary of a goddess bearing the epithet.

16 *AHw*, 1083b–84b; *CAD Ṣ*, 102–3. When referring to fabrics, *ṣe/irpu* (from OB on) is usually defined as "red dyed wool (or fabric)"; see *CAD Ṣ*, 208–9; *CDA*, 336; *AHw*, 1092a; Cassin (1968, 115). Some references, however, show that it may also refer to dyed fabrics in general. For Ugaritic *ṣrp*, see *DLU*, 421; for *abn ṣrp*, "alum," see van Soldt (1990, 321–25). In Mari, NA_4 *ṣirpum* denotes an imitation of lapis lazuli (Guichard *apud* Durand 1997, 275).

17 Who added that their occupational activities may have also included basket-weaving (Houwink ten Cate 1983–84, 45). He also suggested (1983–84, 50) that they were "workers of a relatively low social standing."

18 *KBo* 1.42 v 17–22 = MSL XIII, p. 143 (Izi Bogh. A, l. 317): *e/irbu* is rendered in the Akkadian dictionaries as "income" (*AHw*, 233; *CAD I*, 174; *CDA*, 76). The next entry (l. 318) equates máš.da.a.ri with Akk. *iš-di$_{12}$-ḫu*, "profit" (*CDA*, 133), but the Hittite equivalent is not sufficiently preserved (*iš-x-x-x-a-u-wa-ar*).

19 Lackenbacher does not indicate that the meaning "purple wool" for *argamannu* is attested (until now) only in first-millennium texts, whereas in Hattusa and Ugarit, Akkadian *argamannu* means "tribute" (*AHw*, 67; *CAD A/2*, 253). However, this apparent difficulty can now be overhauled in view of the new interpretation of the evidence from Ugarit and Hatti.

20 On mobile artisans in the ancient Near East who were highly valued palace dependants, see Zaccagnini (1983). Their intentional or forced flight into foreign territory prompted immediate search expeditions in order to bring them back, often bound and chained (1983, 247). The case of the *ṢĀRIPŪTU*-men seems to fall within the first, so-called redistributive category, of the mobility pattern in Zaccagnini's model.

21 For a recent summary on purple in the ancient Near East, see Fales (1992–93; 1998).

22 For which see Friedrich (1942, 483); *HW*, 30; *HW*², 302–4; *HED* 1, 143–46; *HEG* I, 59–60; *CLL*, 28.

23 See, e.g., Rabin (1963, 116–18; with refs. to earlier literature on the subject).

24 For references, see Goetze (1968, 18); *DLL*, 31; *DLU*, 48–49; *HED* 1, 145–46; Mankowski (2000, 38–39).

25 E.g., Pardee (1974, 277–78) and Dijkstra (1989, 144).

26 E.g., Dietrich and Loretz (1964–66, 218–19), Sanmartín (1978, 455–56), van Soldt (1990, 344–45).

27 For details and references, see Borger, *MesZL*, p. 440 (no. 851). When the determinative is not indicated, as occasionally happens in peripheral Akkadian, there remains an ambiguity between the precious stone and the dyed wool.

28 The occasional confusion between blue and red purple in the texts has been appropriately explained by Cassin (1968, 115–16): the quality of shininess and iridescence (Akk. *namru*) shared by both fabrics was more eye-catching for the ancients than the exact chromatic divisions appreciated by us.

29 This includes *tabarru* (SÍG.HÉ.ME.DA), *ḫašḫūru* (SÍG.ḪAŠḪUR), *ruššu* (ḪUŠ.A), *ḫûratu* (GIŠ.ḪAB), *inzaḫurētu*, *kinaḫḫu*, etc., which are probably dyes produced from plants and insects (see, e.g., Oppenheim 1967, 242–43). Occasionally, some confusion was introduced in the terminology, which distinguished between purple dyes of marine origin and other dyestuffs.

30 The designation "cloth of lapis lazuli color" appears in an Old Assyrian text, (Kt 93/k 779, 8': 2 TÚG *ḫu-sà-ru-um*; Michel 2001, 344, n. 19), but it is very unlikely that this should refer to a purple-dyed fabric. The same applies to the isolated occurrence of SÍG *uqniati ta-ak-la-tim* in an Old Babylonian letter (Kraus 1964, 50–51, no. 60). On the other hand, *takiltu* in some Amarna tablets (e.g., in Tušratta's dowry list in EA 22) may already refer to blue-purple, although this cannot be proven.

31 For relatively recent studies on dyed fabrics in Ugarit, see Heltzer (1978, 38–41, 81–82), Ribichini and Xella (1985), van Soldt (1990).

32 See, *inter alia*, Goetze (1956, 34–35), Dietrich and Loretz (1964–66, 288–91), Landsberger (1967), Ribichini and Xella (1985, 32), van Soldt (1990), Knoppers (1993, 88).

33 Other, rarely attested, kinds of SÍG.ZA.GÌN are *ḫandalatu*, *ḫasertu* and *dupašši* (RS 20.19: 9–10 = *Ugaritica* 5, 136, n. 1; van Soldt 1990, 344).

34 Translated in the Septuagint as *hyakinthos* and *porphyra*, respectively. For the color of biblical *tekhelet*, see Ziderman (1987; 2004).

35 Cf. Faist (2001, 71, n. 86, with refs.) for the reading of SÍG ZA.GÌN SA_5 (in Middle Assyrian texts) as either *argamannu* or *ḫašmānu*.

36 But cf. *CDA*, 111, which abstains from defining the color of *ḫa/ušmānu*. Landsberger (1967, 156–57) distinguished between a Mesopotamian and an Ugaritic meaning of *ḫa/ušmānu*, which is hardly a satisfactory solution.

37 *KUB* 4.90 i 9′, 16′: *ḫašmani ša* A.AB.BA. Note also the appearance of "slave girls [who manufacture(?)] *ḫašmanu* garments" in an Akkadian Gilgamesh fragment from Boghazköy (*KUB* 4.12 rev. 7; *CAD H*, 142).

38 Blum (1998, 31, with refs). It also recalls the Greek designation *alourges/alourgos*, "made of the sea," refering to purple-dyed fabrics (1998, 25–27).

39 Stieglitz (1979, 19), Ribichini and Xella (1985, 16), van Soldt (1990, 345).

40 Jensen (1963, 115). By the sixth century BC, purple dye was worth its weight in silver in Greece (*Athenaeus* 12.526). In Caesar's time Tyrian purple wool cost above one thousand denarii, and by the time of Diocletian it was literally worth its weight in gold (Stieglitz 1994, 46). Even though some of the prices indicated in classical sources may be exaggerated (Blum 1998, 24 with n. 18), there is no doubt that purple-dyed garments were among the most expensive luxury items of antiquity.

41 Ribichini and Xella (1985, 18), Heltzer (1982, 80–102, esp. n. 64 on pp. 97–98; 1999, 452). There may be some references to sea molluscs in literary texts, but the evidence is quite obscure and inconclusive (de Moor 1968; van Soldt 1990, 346).

42 The laconic formula has only *eli* (UGU), "on, on to, on behalf of," which is rendered by Thureau-Dangin as "due" ("dus"). He further suggests (p. 140) that these persons were artisans who were given the wool in order to dye it.

43 For the Aegean region, see Barber (1991; 1994; 1997). For Late Bronze Age Cyprus, see Smith (2002). For Mesopotamia, see Van De Mieroop (1989), Donbaz (1998, 183). For Latin America, see Brumfiel (1991), Uchitel (2002).

44 RS 17.383: 32–47 = PRU 4: 223. For Takuhlinu, the author of a letter sent to Aphek in Canaan, see Owen (1981), Singer (1983b, 6–18; 1999, 655). He sends to the Egyptian governor of Canaan a present consisting of 100 (shekels of) blue wool (SÍG ZA.GÌN) and ten (shekels of) red wool ($SÍG.SA_5$ *tabari*). The word *tabari* (preceded by a double Glossenkeil) is a gloss providing additional clarification for the color of the wool. For *tabarru* (SÍG.ḪÉ.ME.DA), see *AHw*, 1298.

45 For Ugarit's foreign trade, with occasional references to purple-dyed wool or fabrics, see Singer (1999, 653–78).

46 One may also mention in this connection the relatively small quantities of purple-dyed wool and fabric imported from the west in the Neo-Babylonian period (Oppenheim 1967, 246). Perhaps in this period, too, purple was produced for the Babylonian market in the Gulf, at some yet undiscovered site.

47 E.g., colored glass, for which see Oppenheim (1970).

48 For recent studies on the purple-dye industry in general (with refs. to the primary sources), see Jensen (1963), Forbes (1964, 114–22), Bruin (1966), Doumet (1980), Steirgerwald (1986), Spanier (1987), Ziderman (1990, 2004), Edmonds (2000). For a literary portrait of the history of purple (violet), see Finlay (2004, ch. 10).

49 Pollux, *Onomasticon* 1.45–49; Palaephatus, *De incredibilibus*, 62.

50 For the Classical sources on purple see, recently, Steigerwald (1986), Blum (1998), Longo (1998).

51 On the chemistry of the purple-dye industry, see McGovern and Michel (1984; 1985), Michel and McGovern (1987), Spanier and Karmon (1987), McGovern (1990b), Ballio (1998).

52 Blum (1998, 28–29). One of Homer's figurative phrases about purple was already explained by Pliny (*Historia Naturalis* 9.124–141): "Its highest glory consists in the color of congealed blood, blackish at first glance when held up to the light; this is the origin of Homer's phrase, 'blood of purple hue'." On the image of "purple blood," cf. Longo (1998).

53 Blum (1998, 31), Ziderman (2004, 40–41).

54 For the various figures suggested, see Burke (1999, 81, with n. 42).

55 Reese (1979–1980). Purple snails are still considered as a culinary delicacy in some parts of the Adriatic. Since the shell is cooked whole and the snail is removed without breaking it, a deposit of broken or crushed shells usually indicates a dyeing site (Ziderman 1990, 100).

56 Various Mediterranean shells were found at Mesopotamian sites, and these were probably used as personal ornaments or for ritual purposes (Oppenheim 1963; Aynard 1966; Moorey 1994, 131, 137–38).

57 Tyre became notorious for its smell, as noted by Strabo (*Geog.* 16.2.23, *cap.* 575): "Tyre purple has proved itself by far the most beautiful of all.... But the great number of dye-works makes the city unpleasant to live in. Yet, it makes the city rich through the superior skill of its inhabitants."

58 For trade in perishable goods see, recently, Palmer (2003). The accumulation of remarkably rich data on organic goods from the Uluburun shipwreck are of course a rare exception to the rule. Incidentally, in early descriptions of this unique discovery it was erroneously reported that the ship carried murex shells or even murex dye. The confusion resulted from the discovery of murex opercula trapped between copper ingots on the Uluburun ship (Pulak 2001, 32–33). This horn or shell-like plate, which is attached to the foot of the gastropod, was probably used for the production of medicines or incense, but has no connection to the purple-dye industry.

59 For the history of the city, see Pritchard (1972); for its purple-dye industry, see Pritchard (1978, 126–27), Reese (1987, 206).

60 In Pharaonic Egypt, dyed textiles were quite rare, probably because linen, the most common Egyptian textile, is difficult to dye (Germer 1992, 95–96; Nicholson and Shaw 2000, 278). Some of the dyed fabrics and garments discovered in Egypt were probably imported from the Aegean and the Levant (Barber 1991, 224, 351; Burke 1999, 78–79). On the Hellenistic dyeing traditions in Egypt, see Brunello (1973, passim).

61 In Late Bronze Age Hala Sultan Tekke (Reese 1987, 205) and in Iron Age Polis-Peristeries (Smith 1997, 90–91; Reese 2000, 645).

62 Ziderman (1990, 98), Faure (1991, 312). For the Phoenician and Punic purple-dye industry, see Acquaro (1998, with refs.). For purple-dye production in the western Mediterranean and the Atlantic, see Lowe (2004, with refs.). For the naval trade of Tyre as reflected in Ezek 27, see Liverani (1991), Diakonoff (1992); the reference to "the islands of Elisha" as the origin of *tekhelet w'rgmn* garments (Ezek 27:7) is generally related to Alasia/Cyprus, but cf. Diakonoff (1992, 176), who pleads for the identification of Elisha with Carthage and its dependencies in Sicily and Sardinia.

63 For purple-dyed fabrics and trimmings entering Assyria from the west, both as booty and as tribute, see Oppenheim (1967, 246–48), Edens (1987, 286–88), Elat (1991), Moorey (1994, 138). It should be noted, however, that *takiltu* and *argamannu* were captured by the Assyrians in large quantities not only in western lands, but also in Babylonia, Urartu, and elsewhere. This should probably represent accumulation of these luxury items by import or capture rather than a local production of purple-dyed fabrics.

64 The origin and dating of the biblical sources relating to the use *tekhelet* and *argaman* in the decoration of the tabernacle (Exod 26:1, 31, 36; 27:16; 36:8), in the ceremonial apparel of the high priest (Exod 28: 5–8; 39: 1–5), and in the *tallit* garment (Num 15:38–40), which later became the Jewish prayer shawl, cannot be discussed here (see Danker 1992). The later prophets castigated the use of purple as a foreign symbol of tyranny and sin (Jer 10:9; Ezek 23:6; 27:24), as did the early Christians. On Hebrew and Jewish "purpurology" throughout the ages, see Herzog (1987; reviewed by McGovern 1990a).

65 For a post-Assyrian tribute list specifying large amounts of *takiltu* and *argamannu*, see Wiseman (1967). Cf. also Weisberg (1982) for Neo-Babylonian disbursements of colored wool from the temple. For Achaemenid imports of purple-dyed wool from the West, see Elat (1991, 34–35).

66 On purple in Greece, see Blum (1998).

67 For Roman purple, see Bessone (1998).

68 The earliest use of the term is attributed to Cicero (for refs. see Reinhold 1970, 8, n. 2). In the fourth century AD, the term "Imperial purple" was introduced.

69 For Late Roman and Byzantine purple, see Bridgeman (1987), Carile (1998).

70 Michel-Morfín and Chavez (2000); Michel-Morfín, Chavez, and Landa (2000). According to various accounts, the children at Tyre and Sidon were still using the same method in recent times (see, e.g., Schaeffer 1951, 189, n. 1).

71 Herzog (1987, 39–42), Blum (1998, 42 with further refs.) The thorny problem of the origin of the Greek name of Phoenicia (*Phoinikê*) cannot be discussed here (see Speiser 1936, 123; Astour 1965, 348). In any case, the meaning of Greek *phoinix* is "red" (Blum 1998, 32–35), not purple, and is therefore unrelated to our topic. The same applies to the the term *kinaḫḫu*, of Hurrian origin, from which the name of Canaan (*Kinaḫḫi*) is probably derived.

72 Reese (1987), Karali-Yannacopoulou (1989), Faure (1991), Stieglitz (1994).

73 For the Middle Minoan evidence from Kommos on the southern coast, see Ruscillo (1998, 392), Burke (1999, 81). Maria C. Shaw reported on the Aegeanet ("murex," May 13, 1999) that she had "excavated part of what seems to be an installation for extracting purple in a MM IIB context at Kommos.... In the area involved [she] found crushed murex and some channels carved in the ground filled with murex shells."

74 For the Bronze Age evidence, see Reese (1987); for the Iron Age and later evidence, see Reese (2000).

75 Murex shells are particularly abundant at Akrotiri, but the excavators justly warn of the temptation to identify a purple-dye production wherever one finds a larger concentration of shells, pointing out that shellfish are still an important part of the local diet (Karali-Yannacopoulou 1990, 413–14). Industrial installations have not been found as yet, but then, because of the noxious odor, these would have been situated far from the inhabited area of Akrotiri and may still turn up in the future.

76 This would then be an opposite perspective to the one suggested by Morris (1992, 162), namely, that the rich murex deposits might have been one of the things that attracted Levantines to eastern Crete, where they founded cities named "Phoinix."

77 Palmer (2003, 134). For the Aegean textile industry see, e.g., Killen (1964), Wiener (1987), and the papers on Aegean craftsmanship assembled in Laffineur and Betancourt (1997).

78 As recently suggested by Burke (1999, 82). For the metal trade and the Minoan/Mycenaean presence in the southeastern Aegean, see references cited in Niemeier (1999b, 148–49).
79 For the Greek evidence on *porphyra*, see Blum (1998, 28).
80 A large mound of *murex trunculus* shells and rectangular brick tanks have been discovered near the Early Roman-Byzantine site of Aperlae in Lycia (Reese 2000, 645). Other concentrations of murex shells are known from the Classical sites of Pergamon, Didyma, Aphrodisias and other sites, but most of these were food debris rather than the refuse of dye extraction (for references, see De Cupere 2001, 16–17). Note also Aristotle's witness (*Historia Animalium* 5.15.547) that the sea shores of Sigeion, Lekton and Caria were rich in purple shells.
81 Meanwhile, however, as Wolf-Dietrich Niemeyer informed me (28 May 2004), a lot of purple shells were found in the Minoan and Mycenaean levels at Miletos, but no other evidence as yet for the purple-dye industry.
82 Yasur-Landau and Guzowska (2003); see also the papers of M. Cultraro, and E. Greco and S. Privitera at the 10th International Aegean Conference of the Italian School of Archaeology in Athens, 14–18 April 2004, entitled *Emporia, Aegeans in Central and Eastern Mediterranean*.
83 Information courtesy of Massimo Cultraro, who is working on the Italian finds from Poliochni.
84 Forbes (1964, 119), Reinhold (1970, 22–25), Blum (1998, 45–48) For a large quantity of blue wool from Ionia (4 1/2 MA.NA SÍG ZA.GÌN.KUR.[RA] šá KUR *Iamanu*) figuring in a Neo-Babylonian text, see Weisberg (1982, 220; YOS 17253: 1–2).
85 Note also the embroidered Sidonian garments presented by the Trojan women to Athena (*Il.* 6.86-98, 288–310) and the purple garments dedicated to Artemis Brauronia by women after childbirth (Blum 1998, 87–88).
86 Beckman (1996, 152–54), Singer (1999, 635 with biblio., refs. in n. 96; 698).
87 One version provides the full designation SÍG.ZA.GÌN *takiltu*, whereas another has only SÍG.ZA.GÌN (van Soldt 1990, 335).
88 In the preserved descriptions of the ceremonial dress worn by the Hittite king on festive occasions, I could not find any reference to purple-dyed garments. See Goetze (1947; 1955, 50ff.), Singer (1983c, 58). For colored garments mentioned in other contexts, see Siegelová (1986, 77–79).
89 On Hittite colors see also Košak (1982, 201), Siegelová (1986, 313), Haas (2003, 638–49).
90 A similar situation exists in the Greek usage of *porphyreos*, which denotes not only "sea purple" (Homer's *halipórphyros*), but also various imitations thereof (Blum 1998, 31–32).
91 It is quite often spelled *ḫaš-man*, and this can hardly be an omission of the final *-nu*. I wonder whether this (Hittitized?) spelling came about following the model of the *-n* stem *argamman*.
92 Following Goetze (1956, 34–35) and Košak (1982, 201)
93 Followed by Siegelová (1986, 78–79) and others. Note, e.g., the first entry in the inventory *IBoT* 1.31 (Goetze 1956; Košak 1982: 4–10), which juxtaposes "blue wool" (SÍG ZA.GÌN), "red wool" (SÍG SA_5) and SÍG *ḫašmanu*. This implies that *ḫašmanu* was clearly distinguished from both blue and red.
94 I wonder what TÚG*ḫappušandaš*, which opens the list, might be. It is a participle in gen. sg. of *ḫappuš-*, "reclaim, resume, make up for," but a "reclaimed, previously used" garment (*HED* 3, 134) would hardly justify the high price of twelve silver shekels. Could it rather refer to a "double-dyed" garment, similar to the highly praised Tyrian *dibapha* of the Classical world?
95 *KUB* 9.34 I 3′–7′ (with dupls.); Hutter (1988, 24), Haas (2003, 650, n. 241).
96 For which see now Haas (2003, 657–62)
97 Cf. Beckman (1988, 5 with notes 18–23).
98 The largest preserved quantity is 78 MA(.NA) in l. 2′.
99 *KBo* 18.199(+)*KBo* 2.22; Košak (1982, 157–59), Siegelová (1986, 310–12). The descriptive designations *ašara* and *gaši(š)* could refer to the fair color of unprocessed wool; *HED* 4, 119–20 suggests "bright white" and "off white, grey," respectively.
100 For Mesopotamia, see, e.g., Cassin (1968, 103–19), Waetzoldt (1972, 50–51), Edens (1987, 258–389).
101 Actually, the use of purple wool is usually not for the entire garment, but only for a hem or trimming (*sūnu*) attached to the bottom of the garment, for which see Dalley (1980, 72–73), Donbaz (1991, 78–79).
102 For the "red wrap of *puluḫtu*" worn by the conjurer-priest for his fight against demons, see Oppenheim (1943, 33).
103 For some references to colored garments in "private" contexts, see Edens (1987, 296–99). Cf. also van Soldt (1997, 97–98), for belts of red wool given to messengers in a Middle Babylonian administrative text, and Donbaz (1991, 75–76), for blue-purple hems given to a certain Tukulti-Ninurta (who can hardly be the Assyrian king). Note also Ezekiel's description of Assyrian dignitaries wearing *tekhelet* garments (Ezek 23:6). Even the Achaemenid rulers,

renowned for their extravagant purple apparel (see Xenophon's description of the royal dress of Cyrus in *Cyropaedia* 8.2.8, 8.3.13), distributed purple robes to their functionaries and to allied monarchs, a tradition also reflected in Esth 8:15.

104 For the parallel restriction of golden garments to the wardrobe of gods and kings, see Oppenheim (1949). Isolated exceptions are admitted though (1949, 191, n. 31).

105 Reinhold (1970, 8) reached the same conclusion: "purple was valued and displayed in many societies as a symbol of economic capability, social status, and official rank (both political and sacerdotal)—but it was never in antiquity, as a color, sequestered and reserved as an exclusive prerogative of noble or royal status."

106 It might be well to recall in this connection Palmer's pointed statement, still valid nowadays, that "connoisseurship of imported exotic wines, perfumes and textiles was the mark of the true aristocrat" (Palmer 2003, 134).

107 Houwink ten Cate (1983–84, 39–40) restores the verb [*pid-da-u*]-*e-ni*, "let us render (our tribute)," but in view of the clear parallel with máš.da.a.ri *ana epeši* at Ugarit, I would rather opt for a verb expressing performance, such as [*iyau*]*eni*, or [*eššau*]*eni*.

108 Note, however, the association with "cloth, garment" in a Middle Hittite text, unfortunately in fragmentary context: *KBo* 3.23 rev. 2: *ma-a-an* TÚG.ḪI.A *ar-ga-ma*[-.

109 Hatt. iii 51′: *na-at-za ar-kam-ma-na-al-li-uš* [*iyanun*], "and [made] them tributaries"; *KUB* 19.8 iii 24: *na-aš-za ar-kam-ma-na-li-uš* [... (Riemschneider 1962, 117). Both references (in acc. pl.) are dated to Hattusili III. Note also the Luwian denominative *arkammanalla-* "make tribute-bearing" (Melchert *CLL*, 28).

110 *HW* 30; Starke 1990, 260–62; *CLL*, 28. For other etymological assessments, see *HW*², 303; *HED* 1, 145–46. For the postulated connection with Greek *argemone*, "agrimony, wild poppy," see Rabin (1963, 117); *HED* 1, 145.

111 Houwink ten Cate (1983–84, 46) assumes that they came from the Seha River Land.

112 See Chadwick (1988), Parker (1999, 499), and the contribution of S. Nikoloudis in this volume.

113 *KUB* 5.6 + *KUB* 18.54 ii 57′–65′; Sommer (1937, 282–83, 289–91), Houwink ten Cate (1983–84, 44 with n. 26, 53), Taracha (2001, 420–21).

114 For Aphrodite's oriental origins, see Burkert (1977, 238). If we take at face value Piyamaradu's quotation in the letter, namely that a storm-god gave the *ṢĀRIPŪTU*-men to Atpa (l. 22), the Deity of Lazpa could be a storm-god-like deity, perhaps Zeus (Freu 1990, 21). However, this could simply be a common expression without any relevance to the actual deity of Lazpa.

115 E.g., *KUB* 14.4 iv 10-23; Laroche (1966); Singer (2002, 73–75, no. 17).

116 For a possible Hittite embargo on Ahhiyawan trade (which could explain the scarcity of Mycenaean objects in Anatolia), see Cline (1991); cf. also Yakar (1976, 126–27). For a concealed reference to the prestigious purple-dye trade in the Argonaut Myth, see Silver (1991, with updates on the Internet). Silver claims that "the 'golden fleece' signifies wool or cloth of woolen garments that are dyed with murex-purple and then exchanged for gold." He finds support in Simonides (sixth–fifth century BC), an interpreter of Euripides's *Medea*, who in his *Hymn to Poseidon* stated that the "golden fleece" was dyed with sea purple. In view of this and similar evidence, he maintains that "it is possible to entertain the hypothesis that the underlying meaning of the Argonaut myth is that the *Argo* arrived in Kolchis with a cargo of purple-dyed cloth and returned to Iolkos with their price in gold."

REFERENCES

Acquaro, E. (1998) I Fenici, Cartagine e l'archeologia della porpora. In Longo (ed.), 99–110.

Albright, W. F. (1933) More Light on the Canaanite Epic of Aleyan Baal and Mot. *Bulletin of the American Schools of Oriental Research* 50, 13–20.

Aloupi, E., et al. (1990) Analysis of a Purple Material found at Akrotiri. In D. A. Hardy, et al. (eds.) *Thera and the Aegean World III*, Vol. 1, 488–90. London, The Thera Foundation.

Astour, M. C. (1965) The Origin of the Terms "Canaan," "Phoenician," and "Purple." *Journal of Near Eastern Studies* 24, 346–50.

Aynard, J. M. (1966) Coquillages Mésopotamiens. *Syria* 43, 21–37.

Baker, J. T. (1974) Tyrian Purple: An Ancient Dye, a Modern Problem. *Endeavour* 32, 11–17.

Ballio, A. (1998) Chimica della porpora: una sintesi che inizia nel mare e si completa sulla terra. In Longo (ed.), 41–52.

Barber, E. J. (1991) *Prehistoric Textiles: The Development of Cloth in the Neolithic and Bronze Ages, with Special Reference to the Aegean.* Princeton, Princeton University.

___ (1994) *Women's Work: The First 20,000 Years, Women, Cloth, and Society in Early Times.* New York, Norton.

___ (1997) Minoan Women and the Challenge of Weaving for Home, Trade, and Shrine. In R. Laffineur and P. Betancourt (eds.) *TEXNH. Craftsmen, Craftswomen and Crafsmanship in the Aegean Bronze Age*, 515–19. Aegaeum 16. Liège, Universitè de Liège and University of Texas at Austin.

Beal, R. H. (1988) The ^{GIŠ}TUKUL-Institution in Second Millennium Hatti. *Altorientalische Forschungen* 15, 269–305.

Beckman, G. (1988) Herding and Herdsmen in Hittite Culture. In E. Neu and Ch. Rüster (eds.) *Documentum Asiae Minoris Antiquae. Festschrift für Heinrich Otten zum 75. Geburtstag*, 33–44. Wiesbaden, Harrassowitz.

Belmonte Marín, J. A. (2001) *Die Orts- und Gewässernamen der Texte aus Syrien im 2. Jt. v. Chr.* Wiesbaden, Reichert.

Bessone, L. (1998) La porpora a Roma. In Longo, ed., 149–202.

Biggs, R. (1966) Le lapis lazuli dans les textes sumèriens archaiques. *Revue d'Assyriologie* 60, 175–76.

Blegen, C. W. (1937) Excavations at Troy, 1937. *American Journal of Archaeology* 41, 553–97.

Blum, H. (1998) *Purpur als Statussymbol in der griechischen Welt.* Bonn, Habelt.

Bosanquet, R. C. (1904) Some "Late Minoan" Vases found in Greece. *Journal of Hellenic Society* 24, 317–29.

Bridgeman, J. (1987) Purple Dye in Late Antiquity and Byzantium. In Spanier, ed., 159–65.

Bruin, F. (1966) Royal Purple and the Dye Industries of the Mycenaeans and Phoenicians. In M. Mollat (ed.) *Sociétés et compagnies de commerce en orient et dans l'Océan Indien (Actes du huitième colloque international d'histoire maritime, Beyrouth 5-10 Septembre, 1966)*, 73–90. Paris, S.E.V.P.E.N.

Brumfiel, E. M. (1991) Weaving and Cooking: Women's Production in Aztec Mexico. In J. M. Gero and M. W. Conkey (eds.) *Engendering Archaeology: Women and Prehistory*, 224–51. Oxford, Blackwell.

Brunello, F. (1973) *The Art of Dyeing in the History of Mankind.* Vicenza, Neri Pozza.

Bryce, T. (1998) *The Kingdom of the Hittites.* Oxford, Oxford University.

___ (2003) History. In H. C. Melchert (ed.) *The Luwians*, 27–127. Leiden, Brill.

Burke, B. (1999) Purple and Aegean Textile Trade in the Early Second Millennium B.C. In P. P. Betancourt, et al. (eds.) *Meletemata. Studies in Aegean Archaeology Presented to Malcolm H. Wiener as he Enters his 65th Year*, 75–82. Aegaeum 20. Liège and Austin, Universitè de Liège and University of Texas at Austin.

Burkert, W. (1977) *Griechische Religion der archaischen und klassischen Epoche.* Stuttgart, Kohlhammer.

___ (1991) Homerstudien und Orient. In J. Latacz (ed.) *Zweihundert Jahre Homer-Forschung, Rückblick und Ausblick*, 155–81. Stuttgart, Teubner.

Carile, A. (1998) Produzione e usi della porpora nell'impero bizantino. In Longo, ed., 243–75.

Carruba, O. (2003) La Lidia fra II e I millennio. In M. Giorgieri et al. (eds.) *Licia e Lidia prima dell'Ellenizzazione*, 145-69. Roma, Consiglio Nazionale delle Ricerche.

Cassin, E. (1968) *La splendeur divine.* Paris, Mouton.

Chadwick, J. (1988) The Women of Pylos. In J.-P. Olivier and T. G. Palaima (eds.) *Texts, Tablets and Scribes: Studies in Mycenaean Epigraphy and Economy*, 43–95. Minos Supplement 10. Salamanca, Universidad de Salamanca.

Cline, E.H. (1991) A Possible Hittite Embargo against the Mycenaeans. *Historia* 40, 1–9.

Cornelius, F. (1973) *Geschichte der Hethiter.* Darmstadt, Wissenschaftliche Buchgesellschaft.

Dalley, S. (1980) Old Babylonian Dowries. *Iraq* 42, 53–74.

Danker, F. W. (1992) Purple. In *Anchor Bible Dictionary*, Vol. 5, 557–61. New York, Doubleday.

De Cupere, B. (2001) *Animals at Ancient Sagalassos. Evidence of the Faunal Remains.* Turnhout, Brepols.

Diakonoff, I. M. (1992) The Naval Power and Trade of Tyre. *Israel Exploration Journal* 42, 168–93.

Dietrich, M., and Loretz, O. (1964–66) Der Vertrag zwischen Šuppiluliuma und Niqmandu. *Welt des Orients* 3, 206–45.

Dijkstra, M. (1989) Marginalia to the Ugarit Letters in KTU (II). *Ugarit-Forschungen* 21, 141–52.

Donbaz, V. (1991) The Date of the Eponym Nabû-bela-usur. In D. Charpin and F. Joannès (eds.) *Marchands, diplomates et empereurs. Études sur la civilisation Mésopotamienne offertes à Paul Garelli*, 73–80. Paris, Cerf.

___ (1998) Assur Collections Housed in Istanbul, General Outlines. In S. Alp and A. Süel (eds.) *Acts of the IIIrd International Congress of Hittitology*, 177–88. Ankara, Uyum Ajans.

Doumet, J. (1980) *A Study on the Ancient Purple Colour.* Beirut, Imprimerie Catholique.

Durand, J.-M. (1997) *Les documents épistolaires du palais de Mari.* Tome I. Paris, Cerf.

Edens, C. (1986) Bahrain and the Arabian Gulf during the Second Millennium B.C.: Urban Crisis and Colonialism. In H. A. al-Khalifa and M. Rice (eds.) *Bahrain through the Ages: The Archaeology*, 195–216. London, KPI.

___ (1987) A Late Second Millennium B.C. Purple Dye Industry in Qatar (Arabian Gulf): Archaeological and Historical Interpretations. Ph.D. diss., Boston, MA, Harvard University.

___ (1994) On the Complexity of Complex Societies: Structure, Power and Legitimation in Kassite Babylonia. In G. Stein and M. Rothman (eds.) *Chiefdoms and Early States in the Near East: the Organizational Systematics of Complexity*, 209–33. Madison, WI, Prehistory Press.

___ (1999) Khor Ile-Sud, Qatar: The Archaeology of Late Bronze Age Purple-Dye Production in the Arabian Gulf. *Iraq* 61, 71–88.

Edmonds, J. (2000) *The Mystery of Imperial Purple Dye*. Little Chalfont, John Edmonds Publisher.

Elat, M. (1991) Phoenician Overland Trade within the Mesopotamian Empires. In M. Cogan and I. Eph'al (eds.) *Ah, Assyria... Studies in Assyrian History and Ancient Near Eastern Historiography Presented to Hayim Tadmor*, 21–35. Jerusalem, Magnes.

Faist, B. (2001) *Der Fernhandel des assyrischen Reiches zwischen dem 14. und 11. Jh. v. Chr.* AOAT 265. Münster, Ugarit-Verlag.

Fales, F. M. (1992–93) La porpora nel Vicino Oriente. In F. M. Fales, O. Longo, and F. Ghiretti (eds.) *La porpora degli antichi e la sua riscoperta ad opera di Bartolomeo Bizio*, 826–41. Atti dell'Istituto Veneto di Scienze, Lettere ed Arti, Classe di scienze morali, lettere ed arti 151.

___ (1998) Archeologia della porpora nel Vicino Oriente antico. In Longo, ed., 91–98.

Faure, P. (1991) La pourpre, invention égéenne. In R. Laffineur and L. Basch (eds.) *Thalassa. L'Egée préhistorique et la mer*, 311–13. Aegaeum 7. Liège, Universitè de Liège.

Finlay, V. (2004) *Color: A Natural History of the Palette*. New York, Random House.

Forbes, R. J. (1964) Dyes and Dyeing. Pp. 98–142 in *Studies in Ancient Technology*, Vol. 4. Leiden, Brill.

Forrer, E. (1926) *Forschungen I.1*. Berlin, Selbstverlag.

Freu, J. (1990) KUB XIX 5 + KBo XIX 79: le pays du fleuve Seha, le Wilusa et Lazpa. *Centre de recherches comparatives sur les langues de la Mediterranée ancienne* 11, 15–28.

Friedrich, J. (1926) *Staatsverträge des Hatti-Reiches in hethitischer Sprache I*. Leipzig, Hinrichs.

___ (1942) Hethitisch-Ugaritisches. *Zeitschrift der deutschen Morgenländischen Gesellschaft* 96, 471–84.

Garstang, J., and Gurney, O. R. (1959) *The Geography of the Hittite Empire*. London, British Institute of Archaeology at Ankara.

Germer, R. (1992) *Die Textilfärberei und die Verwendung gefärbter Textilien im Alten Ägypten*. Wiesbaden, Harrassowitz.

Goetze, A. (1947) The Priestly Dress of the Hittite King. *Journal of Cuneiform Studies* 1, 176–85.

___ (1955) Hittite Dress. In *Corolla Linguistica (Festschrift Ferdinand Sommer)*, 48–62. Wiesbaden, Harrassowitz.

___ (1956) The Inventory IBoT I 31. *Journal of Cuneiform Studies* 13, 32–38.

___ (1968) Review of J. Friedrich, *Hethitisches Wörterbuch. 3. Ergänzungsheft*. *Journal of Cuneiform Studies* 22, 16–24.

Haas, V. (2003) *Materia Magica et Medica Hethitica: Ein Beitrag zur Heilkunde im Alten Orient*. Berlin, De Gruyter.

Hawkins, J. D. (1997) A Hieroglyphic Luwian Inscription on a Silver Bowl in the Museum of Anatolian Civilizations, Ankara. *Anadolu Medeniyetleri Müzesi, 1996 Yilliği*. Ankara.

___ (1998) Tarkasnawa King of Mira. "Tarkondemos," Boğazköy Sealings and Karabel. *Anatolian Studies* 48, 1–31.

Heinhold-Krahmer, S. (1977) *Arzawa. Untersuchung zu seiner Geschichte nach den hethitischen Quellen*. Heidelberg, Carl Winter.

Heltzer, M. (1978) *Goods, Prices and the Organization of Trade in Ugarit*. Wiesbaden, Reichert.

___ (1982) *The Internal Organization of the Kingdom of Ugarit*. Wiesbaden, Reichert.

___ (1999) The Economy of Ugarit. In W. G. E. Watson and N. Wyatt (eds.) *Handbook of Ugaritic Studies*, 423–54. Leiden, Brill

Herzog, I. (1987) Hebrew Porphyrology. In Spanier (ed.), 17–145.

Houwink ten Cate, P. H. J. (1983–84) Sidelights on the Aḫḫiyawa Question from Hittite Vassal and Royal Correspondence. *Jaarbericht Ex Oriente Lux* 28, 33–79.

Hutter, M. (1988) *Behexung, Entsühnung und Heilung*. Göttingen, Vandenhoeck and Ruprecht.

Jensen, L. B. (1963) Royal Purple of Tyre. *Journal of Near Eastern Studies* 22, 104–18.

Karali-Yannacopoulou, L. (1989) Purpura: A Valuable Ancient Dye. *Greek Anthropological Annals* 1989, 92–96.

___ (1990) Sea Shells, Land Snails and other Marine Remains from Akrotiri. In D. A. Hardy, et al. (eds.) *Thera and the Aegean World III*, Vol. II, 410–15. London, The Thera Foundation.

Karmon, N., and Spanier, E. (1987) Archaeological Evidence of the Purple Dye Industry from Israel. In Spanier, ed. 1987, 147–58.

Knoppers, G. N. (1993) Treaty, Tribute List, or Diplomatic Letter: KTU 3.1 Reexamined. *Bulletin of the American Schools of Oriental Research* 289, 81–94.

Korfmann, M. (1997) Troia-Ausgrabungen 1996. *Studia Troica* 7, 1–71.

___ (1998) Troia-Ausgrabungen 1997. *Studia Troica* 8, 1–70.

___ (2001) Troy (Troia) in A. M. Greaves and B. Helwing, Archaeology in Turkey, The Stone, Bronze, and Iron Ages, 1997–1999. *American Journal of Archaeology* 105, 463–511.

Košak, S. (1982) *Hittite Inventory Texts (CTH 241-250)*, Heidelberg, Carl Winter.

Krauss, F. R. (1964) *Altbabylonische Briefe I: Briefe aus dem British Museum (CT 43 und 44)*. Leiden, Brill.

Lackenbacher, S. (1989) Trois lettres d'Ugarit. In H. Behrens, D. Loding, M. T. Roth (eds.) *dumu-é-dub-ba-a. Studies in Honor of Åke W. Sjöberg*, 317–20. Philadelphia, Samuel Noah Kramer Fund.

___ (2002) *Textes akkadiens d'Ugarit. Textes provenant des vingt-cinq premières campagnes*. Paris, Cerf.

Landsberger, B. (1967) Über Farben im Sumerisch-Akkadischen. *Journal of Cuneiform Studies* 21, 139–73.

Laroche, E. (1966) *Les noms des Hittites*. Paris, Klincksieck.

___ (1980) Emar, étape entre Babylone et le Hatti. In J. C. Margueron (ed.) *Le Moyen Euphrate*, 235–44. Leiden, Brill.

Liverani, M. (1991) The Trade Network of Tyre According to Ezek. 27. In M. Cogan and I. Ephʿal (eds.) *Ah, Assyria... Studies in Assyrian History and Ancient Near Eastern Historiography Presented to Hayim Tadmor*, 65–79. Jerusalem, Magnes.

Longo, O. (1992–93) La porpora nell'antichità greco-romana. Conoscenze zoologiche e pratiche di tintura. In F. M. Fales, O. Longo, and F. Ghiretti (eds.) *La porpora degli antichi e la sua riscoperta ad opera di Bartolomeo Bizio*, 843–67. Atti dell'Istituto Veneto di Scienze, Lettere ed Arti, Classe di scienze morali, lettere ed arti 151.

___ (1998) Porpora e sangue. Da Omero a Shakespeare. In Longo, ed., 125–31.

Longo, O. ed. (1998) *La porpora. Realtà e immaginario di un colore simbolico (Atti del convegno di studio, Venezia 1996)*. Venezia, Istituto Veneto di Scienze, Lettere ed Arti.

Lowe, B. (2004) The Industrial Exploitation of Murex: Purple Dye Production in the Western Mediterranean. In L. Cleland and K. Stears (eds.) *Colour in the Ancient Mediterranean World*, 46–48. BAR International Series 1267. Oxford, John and Erica Hedges.

Mankowski, P. V. (2000) *Akkadian Loanwords in Biblical Hebrew*. Winona Lake, Eisenbrauns.

McGovern, P. E., (1990a) Review of Spanier 1987. *Isis* 81, 563–65.

___ (1990b) Royal Purple Dye: The Chemical Reconstruction of the Ancient Mediterranean Industry. *Accounts of Chemical Research* 23, 152–58.

McGovern, P. E., and Michel, R. H. (1984) Royal Purple and the Pre-Phoenician Dye Industry of Lebanon. *MASCA Journal* 3, 67–70.

___ (1985) Royal Purple Dye: Tracing Chemical Origins of the Industry. *Analytical Chemistry* 57, 1515–22.

___ (1988) Has Authentic *Tekelet* Been Identified? (Including Responses). *Bulletin of the American Schools of Oriental Research* 269, 81–90.

Michel, C. (2001) Le lapis-lazuli des Assyriens au début du IIe millénaire av. J.-C. In W. H. van Soldt et al. (eds.) *Veenhof Anniversary Volume*, 341–59. Leiden, Nederlands Instituut voor het Nabije Oosten.

Michel, R. H., and McGovern, P. E. (1987) The Chemical Processing of Royal Purple Dye: Ancient Descriptions as Elucidated by Modern Science. *Archaeometry* 1, 135–43.

Michel-Morfín, J. E., and Chávez, E. A. (2000) Effect of Repetitive Dye Extraction over Yield and Survival Rate of the Purple snail Plicopurpura Pansa (Gould, 1853). *Journal of Shellfish Research* 19, 913–17.

Michel-Morfín, J. E., Chávez, E. A., and Landa, V. (2000) Population Parameters and Dye Yield of the Purple Snail Plicopurpura Pansa (Gould, 1853) of West Central Mexico. *Journal of Shellfish Research* 19, 919–25.

De Moor, J. C. (1968) Murices in Ugaritic Mythology. *Orientalia* 37, 212–15.

Moorey, P. R. S. (1994) *Ancient Mesopotamian Materials*. Oxford, Clarendon.

Morris, S. P. (1992) *Daidalos and the Origins of Greek Art*. Princeton, Princeton University.

___ (1997) Homer and the Near East. In I. Morris and B. Powell (eds.) *A New Companion to Homer*, 599–623. Leiden, Brill.

Nicholson, P. T. and Shaw, I. (2000) *Ancient Egyptian Materials and Technology*. Cambridge, Cambridge University.

Niemeier, B., and W.-D. Niemeier (1999a) The Minoans of Miletus. In P. P. Betancourt, et al. (eds.) *Meletemata. Studies in Aegean Archaeology Presented to Malcolm H. Wiener as he Enters his 65th Year (Aegaeum 20)*, 543–54 and pls. cxvii–cxx. Liège and Austin, Université de Liège and University of Texas at Austin.

Niemeier, W.-D. (1999b) Mycenaeans and Hittites in War in Western Asia Minor. In R. Laffineur (ed.) *Polemos. Le contexte guerrier en Égée à l'Âge du Bronze*, 141–55 and pl. xv. Liège, Université de Liège.

Nougayrol, J. (1968) Textes Suméro-Accadiens des archives et bibliothèques privées d'Ugarit. *Ugaritica* 5, 1–446.

Oppenheim, A. L. (1943) Akkadian *pul(u)ḫ(t)u* and *melammu*. *Journal of the American Oriental Society* 63, 31–34.

___ (1949) The Golden Garments of the Gods. *Journal of Near Eastern Studies* 8, 172–93.

___ (1963) Mesopotamian Conchology. *Orientalia* 32, 401–12.

___ (1967) Essay on Overland Trade in the First Millennium B.C. *Journal of Cuneiform Studies* 21, 263–54.

___ (1970) *Glass and Glassmaking in Ancient Mesopotamia*. Corning, NY, Corning Museum of Glass.

Otten, H. (1967) Ein hethitischer Vertrag aus dem 15./14. Jahrhundert v. Chr. *Istanbuler Mitteilungen* 17, 55–62.

Owen, D. I. (1981) An Akkadian Letter from Ugarit at Tel Aphek. *Tel Aviv* 8, 1–17.

Palaima, T.G. (1991) Maritime Matters in the Linear B Tablets. In R. Laffineur and L. Basch (eds.) *Thalassa. L'Egée préhistorique et la mer*, 273–310. Aegaeum 7. Liège, Université de Liège.

___ (1997) Potter and Fuller: The Royal Craftsmen. In R. Laffineur and P. Betancourt (eds.) *TEXNH. Craftsmen, Craftswomen and Crafsmanship in the Aegean Bronze Age*, 407–12. Aegaeum 16. Liège, Universitè de Liège and University of Texas at Austin.

Palmer, R. (2003) Trade in Wine, Perfumed Oil and Foodstuffs: The Linear B Evidence and Beyond. In N. C. Stampolidis and V. Karageorghis (eds.) *Sea Routes... Interconnections in the Mediterranean 16th-6th c. BC*, 125–40. Athens, Leventis Foundation.

Pardee, D. (1974) The Ugaritic Text 147(90). *Ugarit-Forschungen* 6, 275–82.

Parker, V. (1999) Die Aktivitäten der Mykenäer in der Ostägäis im Lichte der Linear B Tafeln. In S. Deger-Jalkotzy, et al. (eds.) *Floreant Studia Mycenaea*, Band II, 495–502. Wien, Österreichische Akademie der Wissenschaften.

Pulak, C. (2001) The Cargo of the Uluburun Ship and Evidence for Trade with the Aegean and Beyond. In L. Bonfante and V. Karageorghis (eds.) *Italy and Cyprus in Antiquity: 1500-450 BC*, 13–60. Nicosia, Costakis and Leto Severis Foundation.

Pritchard, J. B. (1972) Sarepta in History and Tradition. In J. Reumann (ed.) *Understanding the Sacred Text; Essays in honor of Morton S. Enslin on the Hebrew Bible and Christian Beginnings*, 101–14. Valley Forge, Judson Press.

___ (1978) *Recovering Sarepta, a Phoenician City*. Princeton, Princeton University.

Rabin, C. (1963) Hittite Words in Hebrew. *Orientalia* 32, 113–39.

Reese, D. S. (1979–80) Industrial Exploitation of Murex Shells: Purple-Dye and Lime Production at Sidi Khrebish, Benghazi (Berenice). *Society for Lybian Studies Annual Report* 11, 79–83.

___ (1987) Palaikastro Shells and Bronze Age Purple-Dye Production in the Mediterranean Basin. *Annual of the British School of Archaeology at Athens* 82, 201–6.

___ (2000) Iron Age Shell Purple-Dye Production in the Aegean. In J. W. Shaw and M. C. Shaw, *Kommos IV. The Greek Sanctuary*, Part 1, 643–46. Princeton, Princeton University.

Reinhold, M. (1970) *History of Purple as a Status Symbol in Antiquity*. Bruxelles, Latomus.

Ribichini, S., and Xella, P. (1985) *La terminologia dei tessili nei testi di Ugarit*. Roma, Consiglio Nazionale di Ricerche.

Riemschneider, K. K. (1962) Hethitische Fragmente historischen Inhalts aus der Zeit Hattušilis III. *Journal of Cuneiform Studies* 16, 110–21.

Ruscillo, D. (1998) Working Double Tides: The Marine Molluscs from Kommos, Crete. *American Journal of Archaeology* 102, 392.

Sanmartín, J. (1978) *Riš argmn* in den Ug. Ritualen. *Ugarit-Forschungen* 10, 455–56.

Schaeffer, C. F.-A. (1951) Une industrie d'Ugarit: La pourpre. *Annales Archéologiques de Syrie* 1, 188–92.

Schliemann, H. (1881) *Ilios: The City and Country of the Trojans*. London, Harper and Bros.

Siegelová, J. (1986) *Hethitische Verwaltungspraxis im Lichte der Wirtschafts- und Inventardokumente*. Prague, Národní Muzeum v Praze.

Silver, M. (1991) The Commodity Composition of Trade in the Argonaut Myth. In M. Silver (ed.) *Ancient Economy in Mythology: East and West*, 241–82. Savage, MD, Rowman and Littlefield.

Singer, I. (1983a) Western Anatolia in the Thirteenth Century B.C. according to the Hittite Sources. *Anatolian Studies* 33, 205–17.

___ (1983b) Takuḫlinu and Ḫaya: Two Governors in the Ugarit Letter from Tel Aphek. *Tel Aviv* 10, 3–25.

___ (1983c) *The Hittite KI.LAM Festival*. Wiesbaden, Harrassowitz.

___ (1999) A Political History of Ugarit. In W. G. E. Watson and N. Wyatt (eds.) *Handbook of Ugaritic Studies*, 603–733. Leiden, Brill.

___ (2001) The Treaties between Karkamis and Hatti. In G. Wilhelm (ed.), *Akten des IV. Internationalen Kongresses für Hethitologie*, 635–41. Wiesbaden, Harrassowitz.

___ (2002) *Hittite Prayers*. Atlanta, Society of Biblical Literature.

Smith, J. S. (1997) Preliminary Comments on a Rural Cypro-Archaic Sanctuary in Polis-Peristeries. *Bulletin of the American Schools of Oriental Research* 308, 77–98.

___ (2002) Changes in the Workplace: Women and Textile Production on Late Bronze Age Cyprus. In D. Bolger and N.

Serwint (eds.) *Engendering Aphrodite. Women and Society in Ancient Cyprus*, 281–312. Boston, American Schools of Oriental Research.

Sommer, F. (1932) *Die Aḫḫijavā-Urkunden*. München, Gerstenberg.

Sotiropoulou, S., Andrikopoulos, K., and Chryssikopoulou, E. (2003) The Use of Tyrian Purple in the Wall Paintings of Thera. 4th Symposium of Archaeometry (Athens, May 28–31, 2003). Hellenic Society of Archaeometry (http://www.archaeometry.gr/eae/HSA.htm).

Spanier, E., and Karmon, N. (1987) Muricid Snails and the Ancient Dye Industries. In Spanier, ed. 1987, 179–92.

Spanier, E., ed. (1987) The Royal Purple and the Biblical *Tekhelet. The Study of Chief Rabbi Dr. Isaac Herzog on the Dye Industries in Ancient Israel and Recent Scientific Contributions*. Jerusalem, Keter.

Speiser, E. A. (1936) The Name Phoinikes. *Language* 12, 121–26.

Starke, F. (1997) Troia im Kontext des historisch-politischen und sprachlichen Umfeldes Kleinasiens im 2. Jahrtausend. *Studia Troica* 7, 448–55.

___(2001) Sēḫa. *Der Neue Pauly. Enzyklopädie der Antike, Band II*, 345–47.

___ (forthcoming) Wilusa im Lichte der schriftlichen überlieferung des 2. Jt. v. Chr.

Stefanini, R. (1964) *KUB* XXI 33 (Bo 487): Mursili's Sins. *Journal of the American Oriental Society* 84, 22–30.

Steigerwald, G. (1986) Die antike Purpurfärberei nach dem Bericht Plinius' des Älteren in seiner "Naturalis Historia." *Traditio* 42, 1–57.

Stieglietz, R. R. (1979) Commodity Prices at Ugarit. *Journal of the American Oriental Society* 99, 15–23.

___ (1994) The Minoan Origin of Tyrian Purple. *Biblical Archaeologist* 57, 46–54.

Taracha, P. (2001) Mycenaeans, Ahhiyawa and Hittite Imperial Policy in the West: A Note on KUB 26.91. In Th. Richter, D. Prechel, J. Klinger (eds.) *Kulturgeschichten: Altorientalische Studien für Volkert Haas*, 417–22. Saarbrücken, Saarbrücker Druckerei.

Thureau-Dangin, F. (1934) Un comptoir de laine pourpre á Ugarit d'après une tablette de Ras-Shamra. *Syria* 15, 137–46.

Uchitel, A. (2002) Women at Work: Weavers of Lagash and Spinners of San Luis Gonzaga. In S. Parpola and R. M. Whiting (eds.) *Sex and Gender in the Ancient Near East*, Part II, 621–31. Helsinki.

Van De Mieroop, M. (1989) Women in the Economy of Sumer. In B. S. Lesko (ed.) *Women's Earliest Records from Ancient Egypt and Western Asia*, 53–69. Atlanta, Scholars Press.

Van Soldt, W. H., (1990) Fabrics and Dyes at Ugarit. *Ugarit-Forschungen* 22, 321–57.

___ (1997) Kassite Textiles for Enlil-Nērāru's Messenger. *Altorientalische Forschungen* 24, 97–104.

Ventris, M. and Chadwick, J. (1959) *Documents in Mycenaean Greek*. Cambridge, Cambridge University.

Waetzoldt, H. (1972) *Untersuchungen zur neusumerischen Textilindustrie*. Roma, Centro per le antiquità e la storia dell'arte del Vicino Oriente.

Watkins, C. (1998) Homer and Hittite Revisited. In P. Knox and C. Foss (eds.) *Style and Tradition. Studies in Honor of Wendell Clausen*, 201–11. Stuttgart, Teubner.

Weisberg, D. B. (1982) Wool and Linen Material in Texts from the Time of Nebuchadnezzar. *Eretz-Israel* 16, 218–26.

Wiener, M. H. (1987) Trade and Rule in Palatial Crete. In R. Hägg and N. Marinatos (eds.) *The Function of the Minoan Palaces*, 261–68. Stockholm, Svenska Institutet i Athen.

Williams, C. and Williams, H. (1987) Excavations at Mytilene, 1987. *Canadian Mediterranean Institute Bulletin* 1987, 10–11.

Wiseman, D. J. (1967) A Late Babylonian Tribute List? *Bulletin of the School of Oriental and African Studies* 30, 495–504.

Yakar, J. (1976) Hittite Involvement in Western Anatolia. *Anatolian Studies* 26, 117–28.

Yasur-Landau, A., and Guzowska, M. (2003) Before the Aeolians. Prolegomena to the Study of Interactions with the North-East Aegean Islands in the 13th and 12th Centuries BC. In N. Kyparissi-Apostolika and M. Papakonstantinou (eds.) *The 2nd International Interdisciplinary Colloquium "The Periphery of the Mycenaean World" (Lamia 26-30 Sept. 1999)*, 471–86. Athens, Ministry of Culture and the 14th Ephorate of Prehistoric and Classical Antiquities.

Zaccagnini, C. (1983) Patterns of Mobility among Ancient Near Eastern Craftsmen. *Journal of Near Eastern Studies* 42, 245–64.

Ziderman, I. I. (1987) First Identification of Authentic Tekelet. *Bulletin of the American Schools of Oriental Research* 265, 25–33.

___ (1990) Seashells and Ancient Purple Dyeing. *Biblical Archaeologist* 1990, 98–101.

___ (2004) Purple Dyeing in the Mediterranean World: Characteristics of Biblical Tekhelet. In L. Cleland and K. Stears (eds.) *Colour in the Ancient Mediterranean World*, 40–45. BAR International Series 1267. Oxford, John and Erica Hedges.

3

MULTICULTURALISM IN THE MYCENAEAN WORLD

Stavroula Nikoloudis

The form of cross-cultural interaction examined in this paper is the physical presence and interaction of culturally diverse population groups and individuals in the Mycenaean world, as indicated by the information contained in the Greek Linear B texts (ca. 1400–1200 BC). Davis and Bennet (1999) have emphasized the ability of the Mycenaean palatial systems to absorb distinct populations. At the Greek mainland site of Pylos, for instance, the initial consolidation of the kingdom, or "Hither Province," in the LH IIIA period (fourteenth century BC) and the addition of the "Further Province" early in the LH IIIB period (thirteenth century BC), would have involved reconfiguring the relationships between the various inhabitants of the region. Feasting and palatial iconography depicting military conquests were media through which overall group identity could be reinforced. The Linear B texts provide evidence of this inherent cultural pluralism, which is worth investigating in spite of the challenges involved in retrieving such information from tablets that are often fragmentary, written in a proto-literate stage of Greek, and used entirely for economic purposes.

Multiculturalism is defined as the existence of "several cultural or ethnic groups within a society" (Oxford Dictionary 1996). While it is the former kind of identity group that is primarily addressed here, a word on each of these occasionally overlapping social constructs is warranted. A *cultural group* is taken to be an aggregate of people generally sharing the same life-style, adaptive strategies within their ecological setting, and symbolic systems of communication. As Eriksen (2000, 202) puts it, "people who live in the same place and interact intensively get a lot of shared experiences." As Rapoport (1980, 287) explains,

> culture is about a group of people who have a set of values and beliefs which embody ideals and which are transmitted to members of the group through enculturation.... These beliefs lead to a world view – the characteristic way of looking at the world and ... of shaping the world. These ideals also create a system of habits and consistent choices. These rules, therefore, both reflect an ideal and create life-styles....

These life-styles, or behavioral similarities, may leave traces in the material record. While cultural features such as language, religion and customs, including dress and diet, can often serve as "surface pointers" or "markers" of a particular ethnic identity, the defining criteria of an *ethnic group* are, instead, as outlined by Hall (2002, 9–24), a shared myth of common kinship and descent (whether real or imagined), an association with a specific territory, and a shared sense of history. Not all cultural groups are ethnic groups. To take a modern example, not all Arabic-speaking people consider themselves to be one ethnic group (Renfrew 1987, 216).

An ethnic group is self-ascribing. It is fluid in its capacity to assimilate with, or differentiate itself from, other groups (whether they share the same material *culture* or not). There may exist varying degrees of ethnicity (e.g., local and supra-local units). Ethnic group membership becomes especially critical when the integrity of the group is threatened, and ethnicity itself "often emerges in the context of migration, conquest or the appropriation of resources by one group at the expense of another" (Hall 2002, 10; also Renfrew 1987, 214–18). The most fruitful starting point for studying ancient ethnic affiliations is the textual record, where self-conscious group identifications and testimonies about kinship and territorial ties are preserved (Hall 2002, 23–24; Shennan 1989, 14).[1] The Mycenaean accounting records, however, lack the rich ethnic discourse articulated in Classical Greek literature. The term "Mycenaean" is itself a modern coinage (Davis and Bennet 1999, 112), applied to the *relatively* homogeneous material culture found on mainland Greece and the southern Aegean in the Late Bronze Age, as well as to the inhabitants of these regions. That some members of these *cultural* groups spoke Greek is reasonably certain (Linear B documents), but whether they identified themselves as an *ethnic* group (and if so, by what name) is not.

THE LINEAR B TOPONYMICS

The most compelling textual evidence *related* to the theme of ethnicity consists of toponymics. In Mycenaean scholarship, these adjectival descriptions of people are often, and probably erroneously, called "ethnics." As far as we can tell, they often refer simply to the geographical origins of groups and individuals (as understood and identified by the Mycenaean administrators). These people would have brought cultural baggage from their homelands (some similar and some different beliefs and practices). Lifestyles may subsequently have undergone changes due to processes of acculturation and *degrees* of assimilation. Still, the use of these toponymics reflects the multicultural (awareness) and composition of the "Mycenaean" population.

At a local level (Fig. 1), in terms of geography, at the mainland site of Pylos, the texts of the A-series, recording personnel who seem to be dependent on the Palace for their rations, feature female workers grouped by toponymics, including women from the nearby island of Kythera, to the south. Tablet An 610 records some five- to six-hundred male rowers, including about seven from the island of Zakynthos, to the northwest. In the *o-ka* set of tablets, the contingents of about eight hundred men in total guarding the coast of the kingdom of Pylos are occasionally described by toponymics clearly associated with local place names. Some toponymics, given their position in the entries, appear to serve as personal names, e.g., in the land tenure series at Pylos, *te-qa-ja* "Theban woman" who is a *te-o-jo do-e-ra* "servant of the god" (PY Ep 539) and *ka-pa-ti-ja* "woman from the island of Karpathos" (near Crete) who is a "key-bearer" (PY Ep 704). Both these job descriptions seem to belong to the religious sphere. At Knossos, there is a Theban woman involved in the Cretan cloth production industry (KN Ap 5864), and a group of men from the mainland site of Nauplia, or Tiryns (KN Fh 5432).[2] At Mycenae, a Zakynthian man is recorded alongside assessments or allocations of wool (MY Oe 122). At Thebes, a name "Lakedaimonios" or "son of Lakedaimon," alluding to the toponym used at least in later times for Sparta or the region of Laconia, in the Peloponnese, appears on a number of tablets, e.g., the TH Fq series (Palaima 2002b, 483). These textual details attest to an intermingling of different groups and individuals between the Mycenaean centers of the mainland and Crete.

Beyond the immediate geographical sphere, an interesting *pattern* of distribution of toponymic adjectives seems to corroborate the archaeological picture provided by the ceramic evidence, indicating that while, thanks largely to the Minoans, the fourteenth century BC was the time of greatest contact between the Aegean and Egypt (in the reign of Amenhotep III), a shift in focus occurred in the thirteenth century BC, as the Mycenaeans became prominent, with closer ties developing between the Aegean and Anatolia (Shelmerdine 1998, 296). Male individuals listed as Egyptian are restricted to Knossos, Crete. These Knossos tablets may reflect contacts previously established by the Minoans as they are relatively earlier in date [LM IIIA2 or IIIB] than the mainland texts [end of LH IIIB] (294–96). In contrast, toponymics referring to

Local:

PY A- series (Aa, Ab, Ad) series of dependent female workers, including:

ku-te-ra$_3$ /*Kuthērrai*/ (nom.pl.) "women of Kythera"

PY An 610 *ẓạ-ku-si-jo* male rowers from island "of Zakynthos"

PY *o-ka* set: e.g., *u-ru-pi-ja-jo* (nom.pl.) An 519,etc. "men of Olympia"(?)

PY Ep 539 *te-qa-ja* /*Thēbaiā*/ (nom.sg.) "woman of Thebes"

PY Ep 704 *ka-pa-ti-ja* (nom.sg.) "woman of Karpathos"

KN Fh 5432 *ṇạ-u-pi-ri-jọ-ị* /*Nauplioihi*/ (dat.pl.) "men of Nauplia" (=Tiryns?)

KN Ap 5864 *te-qa-ja* (nom.sg.) "woman of Thebes"

(and other women have names derived from known Cretan toponyms (e.g. *pa-i-ta* "of Phaistos" and *e-ra* "of *e-ra*")

MY Oe 122 *za-ku-si-jo* /*Dzakunsios*/ (or dat.) "man of Zakynthos"

TH Gp 227 ra-]ke-da-mi-ni-jo-u-jo /*Lakedaimonios huios*/ & Fq series (in dat.sg.) "son of Lakedaimon" or "Lakedaimnios, son"

Further afield:

Egypt: these occur on texts from Crete.

KN Db 1105 *a*$_{3}$-*ku-pi-ti-jo* /*Aiguptios*/ (nom.sg.) "Memphite" or "Egyptian" [shepherd]

KN F(2)841 *mi-sa-ra-jo* /*Misraios*/ (nom.sg.) "Egyptian" [recipient of figs & olives]

Western Anatolia: these are especially common on mainland texts.

PY A- series of dependent women-workers, incl.:

*a-*64-ja* /*Aswiai*/ "women of Asia (Lydia)"

[Hittite "Assuwa" = *a-swi-ja*? = Lin.B *a-*64-ja* = "Asia"]

ki-ni-di-ja /*Knidiai*/ "Knidians" (& on PY An 292)

ze-pu$_{2}$-*ra*$_3$ /*Dzephurai*/ "Halikarnassos"(Strabo 14.2.16)

mi-ra-ti-ja /*Milātiai*/ "Milesians"

ki-si-wi-ja /*Kswiai*/ "Khians"

ra-mi-ni-ja /*Lāmniai*/ "Lemnians"

ra-wi-ja-ja <**lāwiā* (λεία "war-plunder") "captives"

a-si-wi-jo shepherd's name, PY Cn 285; landholder's name, PY Eq 146

*a-*64-jo* name, PY Cn 1287, Fn 324, Jn 832

ra-mi-ni-jo PY An 209, Cn 328, Cn 719

ze-pu$_{2}$-*ro* stitcher ([*ra-*]*pte*) who holds land, PY Ea 56

MY *a-si-wi-jo* MY Au 653, Au 657 (personnel lists)

TH *mi-ra-ti-jo* references to "Milesian" individual(s?) in Fq series

KN *a-si-wi-jo* KN Df 1469 shepherd

*a-*64-jo* KN Sc 261 (from RCT: LM II date -i.e., earlier)

ki-si-wi-jo[KN V(2) 60 [+]151 (from RCT)

Cyprus: these are found equally on Crete and mainland sites.

KN *a-ra-si-jo* /*Alasios*/ KN Df 1229, Fh 369, X1463: human(s)

ku-pi-ri-jo /*Kuprios*/ -KN Od 667: adjective modifying wool (i.e., *ḳụ-pi-ri-jạ* "Cypriot"& *ke-*[*re-si*]*-ja* "Cretan"), esp. in KN Fh (oil) series: toponymic (or adjective describing the oil)

PY *ku-pi-ri-jo* shepherd Cn 131, Cn 719; bronzesmith Jn 320; "collector" Un 443 (-wool, cloth, alum)

Fig. 1 Sample of Toponymics attested in the Linear B tablets.
(Crete KN: Knossos, Mainland PY: Pylos; MY: Mycenae; TH: Thebes)

western Anatolia are especially common on tablets from the mainland Mycenaean sites: at Pylos, the A-series personnel lists (which, as stated above, include local women) also feature groups of working women with toponymics linking them to the eastern Aegean (Chadwick 1988, 79), for example, women from Knidos, Halikarnassos, Miletos, and from the islands of Khios and Lemnos off the Anatolian coast, as well as women from "Aswia," that is, Hittite *Assuwa* > **Asswiya*- "(land) of Assuwa" (Melchert 2003, 7 n. 10), possibly referring to the area of later Lydia (Chadwick 1988, 79).[3] The A-series deals with some 750 women and their children (a total of about 1500 individuals). The tablets record the location of these groups of women in the palatial territory of Pylos and the rations allocated to them. The women are described either by toponymic or occupation. They include corn-grinders, bath-pourers/attendants and, predominantly, textile-workers, namely, weavers, distaff women, sewing women, flax or linen workers, cloth finishers and headband makers (Chadwick 1988). They are not described as "slaves" (*do-e-ra*), but usually tablets dealing with issues of rations are irregular and in the nature of ad hoc payments for services, whereas the comprehensiveness of the A-series could imply that the Palace was solely responsible for these women's livelihood (Chadwick 1988, 90–93). Whether the women were captives or refugees, i.e., slaves or free, is debatable. One group of these women (Aa 807) is specifically called *ra-wi-ja-ja* "war-captives," a derivative of **lāwiā* "war-plunder" (attested as Attic λεία, Ionic ληίη). In Chadwick's opinion, the rest of the women were *bought* in the slave markets of the eastern Aegean coastal sites for exploitation as a labor force. Each group, which may have shared a mother tongue and perhaps even expertise in a particular craft activity, would have been kept together for effective communication and maximum productivity. Their toponymic designations may have in fact specified the trading-posts from which they were bought (Chadwick 1988, 92) or, like ethnics, they may have been hereditary and the women designated by them actually born in Pylos (Carlier 1983, 17). In two cases, there is a connection between these women and the male rowers of the PY An texts, but it is unclear if casual sexual encounters (ensuring for the Palace another generation of dependent workers) or more stable family bonds are implied.[4] The rest of the examples in fig. 1 from Pylos, Mycenae, Thebes and Knossos seem to be names of individuals. Where details exist, they do not appear to be restricted to a specific occupation or status. Open to interpretation are a few relating to Syria-Palestine (in Cline 1994, 129). The toponymics relating to Cyprus occur in fairly equal amounts on Crete and the mainland, with the peculiar distribution of *a-ra-si-jo* and *ku-pi-ri-jo* potentially reflecting the enduring contact between Cyprus and the Aegean over time (Shelmerdine 1998, 296).[5] The term *ku-pi-ri-jo* "Cypriot" may modify commodities or people (295). At Pylos, *ku-pi-ri-jo* designates or names individuals associated with sheep-herding, bronze-working and mixed commodities, including wool, cloth and alum (a dye mordant).

The individual *ku-pi-ri-jo* "Cypriot" on PY Un 443 is interpreted by Killen as a "collector" – a term that refers to "prominent members of the palace élite who have been allocated part of the productive capacity of the kingdom for their own benefit" in return for services rendered by their workgroups or in return for commodities acquired (Killen 1995, 218). One of the functions of "collectors" may have been to organize external trade, either personally conducting it or arranging it through a third party. Given that perfumed olive oil is known to have been exported from Crete and that Cyprus happens to be one of the Mediterranean sources of alum, Killen suggests that the individual called *ku-pi-ri-jo* in the Knossos Fh oil-series and the *ku-pi-ri-jo* who provided the palace at Pylos with alum were both given their names because "they (or their fathers or grandfathers) were members of the palace élite, one at Knossos and the other at Pylos, who had a particular involvement in the trade with Cyprus" (Killen 1995, 221). This system of royal trade agents is thought to have resembled the Near Eastern *tamkar* system, involving semi-independent merchants who were accountable to the palace (Killen 1995, 220–21).

It should be reiterated that, in many cases where individuals are concerned, it is difficult to determine if these terms served as true toponymics or if they had come to be used as actual personal names (Palaima 1991, 280). Also, in the case of toponymics, identifying a person as "Egyptian" does not necessarily imply that (s)he is of Egyptian birth. Instead, it may be the result of an individual's taste for things Egyptian or dealings (e.g., trade) with that country or an extended stay there. Even today, for instance, an expatriate Greek returning to Greece from Australia is regularly identified as "So-and-so, the Australian." Nevertheless, in spite of the variety of ways that toponymics can be used, they reveal the cultures with which the Mycenaeans interacted, either directly or indirectly (Shelmerdine 1998, 296).

ONOMASTICS

If handled cautiously, onomastics may also be useful in exploring cultural diversity. While we lack the rules that may have operated in the Mycenaean transmission of names, a particular *pattern* of distribution may prove meaningful. This is precisely the case with the numerous studies carried out on the personal names from Knossos (Crete), which have found that non-Greek personal names appear (a) in larger numbers among the individuals of the lower classes of Mycenaean society, and (b) more frequently in the Knossos archive than on the mainland. For example, most of the twenty-five high-status collectors' names at Knossos can be identified as Greek, whereas most of the shepherds' names are non-Greek (Ilievski 1992, 337–38). The non-Greek names on Crete (such as those with the "pre-Greek" suffix -σσος,-σσα represented in the Linear B script by the endings *-so*, *-sa*) are thought to belong, for the most part, to the population groups that the Mycenaeans encountered when they arrived there. Some features of the non-Greek names are characteristic of Anatolian languages, as seen in names such as *pi-ja-mu-nu* (KN L 5901), *wa-du-na-ro* (KN C 912), *ku-ka-da-ro* (KN Uf 836).[6]

Confirmation of the multicultural character of Mycenaean society is provided by the names of the divinities worshipped. On Crete, the non-Greek name of the (Minoan) divinity *pi-pi-tu-na*, on KN Fp 13 (Gulizio, Pluta and Palaima 2001, 458), suggests that the Mycenaeans, like the Hittites, were open to the idea of integrating foreign gods into their pantheon. Similarly, on the Greek mainland, the popular Mycenaean goddess *Potnia*, "Mistress" (derived from the Indo-European root **pot-* relating to "power"), is accompanied on a tablet from Pylos by the epithet *a-si-wi-ja* : *po-ti-ni-ja a-si-wi-ja* (PY Fr 1206) "Asian *Potnia*" (see note 3).

THE TAWAGALAWA LETTER AND THE MYCENAEAN EVIDENCE: HITTITES, LUWIANS, MYCENAEANS

A striking piece of evidence for the interaction of Mycenaeans and western Anatolians in the thirteenth century BC is found in the Hittite Tawagalawa Letter (discussed in Bryce 2003), now generally ascribed to Hattusili III (1264–1239 BC). In this letter, originally comprising three tablets, only the last of which survives, the Hittite king complains to the king of Ahhiyawa (whose name is not preserved) about the transplantation of Hittite subjects to Ahhiyawa (*KUB* XIV 3 iii 7–17). Ahhiyawa is taken to refer to the Mycenaean world or some component of it.[7]

In the Tawagalawa Letter, the Hittite king complains about the rebel Piyamaradu's practice of raiding Hittite subject territory and removing large numbers of Hittite subjects from it. In this case, about seven thousand people from the Lukka Lands (referring either specifically to the southwestern Anatolian homeland of Luwian speakers [later Lycia] or to the broader region inhabited by them) had been transplanted to Ahhiyawa. Some had apparently gone willingly (as refugees), while others had been taken by force. The Hittite king wanted them to be returned (Bryce 2003, 76–78, 85).

There were probably two main incentives for Ahhiyawa's interest in western Anatolia, namely, the acquisition of raw materials, lacking or rare in the Greek world (e.g., timber, gold, copper), and the recruitment of labor from the Luwian regions. Workers were needed for the palaces' large-scale textile industries and massive construction projects. When Strabo later wrote that the fortification walls of Tiryns were built by Cyclopes from Lycia (Strabo, *Geog.* 8.6.11), he could have been drawing on a tradition that recognized the input of the Bronze Age Lukka people (Bryce 2003, 85–86). The recruitment of labor through the forced resettlement of conquered people was common practice in Anatolia. Beginning in the fifteenth century, the Hittites regularly raided Luwian territory in the west and transported people and livestock back to the Hittite homeland (Bryce 2003, 84). The dependent working women of the A-series at Pylos recruited from western Anatolia might reflect a similar practice in the Mycenaean world.

The "rower" texts from Pylos (PY An 1, An 610, An 724) are also suggestive in this regard. They record male rowers who seem to provide their services in return for the use of land. The relevant lines of PY An 724 (ll. 3–4) read *ki-ti-ta o-pe-ro-ta e-re-e ktitān ophēlonta ereen* "settler/landholder owing service as a rower." Tablet PY An 610 (fig. 2) refers to "settlers" *ki-ti-ta* (l. 2), "after-settlers" *me-ta-ki-ti-ta* (l. 5), and "immigrants" *po-si-ke-te-re* (l. 6). This terminology could suggest that the settling of/access to the land takes place in stages. The thirty rowers listed in An 1 are sailing off for duty to a site called Pleuron (perhaps north of the Peloponnese). The status of these men is unclear, but they seem to possess a degree of independence from the palace uncharacteristic of mere slaves. Slaves do not typically need to fulfill obligations; they are simply put to work. Could it be that these rowers included foreign refugees seeking asylum with the rulers of Pylos as a means of escaping political or economic hardship at home? Seeking refuge with another leader was a regular phenomenon in Anatolia, where alliances were constantly shifting between individuals and between states (Bryce 2003, 51–59). Some of the western Anatolian states may in fact have preferred to cultivate commerical and other links with Ahhiyawa than to continue their relationship with the Hittites whose treaties with them typically banned them from dealing directly with foreign powers (Bryce 2003, 80).[8]

It is also worth considering whether the Linear B texts provide evidence for the kind of (voluntary or forced) relocation of entire communities alluded to in the Tawagalawa Letter. It is tentatively proposed that Tablet PY Un 718 might refer to an enclave of such foreign inhabitants. This tablet is one of a set of three texts (PY Un 718, Er 312, Er 880) written by a single tablet-writer (Hand 24) dealing with the site of *sa-ra-pe-da* (translation in Palaima 2004).[9] It records the anticipated contributions of food and drink for a banquet in honor of the god Poseidon. Four contributors are listed (fig. 3): *e-ke-ra$_2$-wo* (l. 2), generally (but not universally) taken to be the name of the king of Pylos, who "will give" (*do-se*) barley, wine, a bull, cheese, a sheepskin and honey; the *da-mo* (l. 7), the established group of landholders and administrators, expected to give barley, wine, two sheep, cheese, anointing oil and a sheepskin; the *ra-wa-ke-ta*, i.e., *lāwāge(r)tās* (l. 9), "the one who leads (<*agō*) or assembles (<*ageirō*) the **lāwos*," traditionally viewed as the military commander, who will give two sheep, flour and wine; and the enigmatic *wo-ro-ki-jo-ne-jo ka-ma* (l. 11), appearing only in this set of texts, expected to contribute barley, wine, cheese and honey.[10] In this tablet, just as *e-ke-ra$_2$-wo* (l. 2) may be viewed as the symbolic head of the (privileged) group following him, the *da-mo* (l. 7), so the *lāwāge(r)tās* may be seen as the representative of the *wo-ro-ki-jo-ne-jo ka-ma*, possibly a group of agricultural laborers. The syntax strengthens these associations: in ll. 7 and 11, the adverbial *o-da-a$_2$* (= "thus also") links each group to the individual recorded before it, while in l. 9 (Palaima, personal communication) the *-de* of *to-so-de* ("*and* so much [the *lāwāge(r)tās* will give]") effectively separates the two sets of information. Could this reflect an underlying division between "rulers" (palace and *da-mo*) and "ruled"? In my dissertation I argue that the *lāwāge(r)tās* served as a liaison officer between the privileged, landholding members of Mycenaean society and the less privileged, landless individuals and groups, including foreigners. He seems to have played a key role through such avenues as military service and agricultural labor in mediating the incorporation of outsiders into the Mycenaean community.

PY Un 718 offers three pieces of evidence for the settlement of immigrant groups: (1) As Palaima (2002a) has observed, the Special (=unusual) dative ending in *-i* in the word *po-se-da-o-ni* "[contribution(s)] to/for Poseidon" (l. 1) instead of the Standard Mycenaean dative ending in *-e* [in the Linear B script], and the form *pe-ma* (=*sperma* "seed grain") in related tablets PY Er 312 and Er 880 instead of the regular *pe-mo*, may reflect

PY An 610 (S1 H1)

.1	me-za-[ ]ne , e-re-ta [ ]*vacat* [			
.2	*vestigia*[ ] , ki-ti-ta	VIR 46 [		
.3	me-]ṭạ-ki-ti-ta	VIR 19 [	]*vac.*	
.4	]wa , ki-ti-ta	VIR 36 [	]*vac.*	
.5	ṃẹ-ta-ki-ti-ta	[ ] VIR 3 [		
.6	e-wi-ri-po	VIR 9	po-si-ke-te-re [	VIR
.7	a-ke-re-wa	VIR 25	wo-qe-we [	VIR
.8	ri-jo	VIR 24	wi-nu-ri-jo [	VIR
.9	te-ta-ra-ne	VIR 31	me-ta-ḳị[-ti-ta	VIR
.10	a-po-ne-we	VIR 37	me-ta[-ki-ti-ta]*v.*	[VIR *qs*
.11	ma-ra-ne-nu-we	VIR 40	po-ti-ja-ke-e	VIR 6[
.12	ẓạ-ku-si-jo	VIR 7̣	za-e-to-ro	VIR 3
.13	da-mi-ni-jo[ ]	VIR 40	e-ke-ra$_{2}$-wo-no	VIR 40
.14	we-da-ne-wo	VIR 20	ko-ni-jo 126 me-ta-ki-ti-ta	VIR 26
.15	po-ku-ta	VIR 10	we-re-ka-ra , te-qa-ta-q̣ẹ	VIR 20
.16	*vacat*		[	
.17	*vacat*		[	
.18	] *vacat*		[	
.19	] *vacat*		[	

NB:

l.1 e-re-ta	ἐρέται "rowers"
l.2 ki-ti-ta	κτίται "inhabitants" (Classical κτίτης, κτίζω "I occupy")
l.5 ṃẹ-ta-ki-ti-ta	μετακτιται "after-settlers"
l.6 po-si-ke-te-re	<ποσ-hικτήρ (< ποτί (Doric for πρός) "to" + ἵκω "I come"): *pos-ik-tēres* "immigrants, newcomers"

Fig. 2 Linear B tablet PY An 610 (from Palace of Nestor Vol. IV edition in progress, by Melena, Palaima et al.)

PY Un 718 (S312 H24)

.1	sa-ra-pe-da , po-se-da-o-ni , do-so-mo
.2	o-wi-de-ta-i , do-so-mo , to-so , **e-ke-ra$_{2}$-wo**
.3	do-se , GRA 4 VIN 3 BOS^{m} 1
.4	tu-ro$_{2}$, *TURO$_{2}$* 10 ko-wo , **153* 1
.5	me-ri-to , v 3
.6	*vacat*
.7	o-da-a$_{2}$, **da-mo** , GRA 2 VIN 3
.8	OVIS^{m} 2 *TURO$_{2}$* 5 a-re-ro , *AREPA* V 2 **153* 1
.9	to-so-de , **ra-wa-ke-ta** , do-se ,
.10	OVIS^{m} 2 me-re-u-ro , FAR T 6
.a	**-ma**
.11	VIN S 2 o-da-a$_{2}$, **wo-ro-ki-jo-ne-jo** , k̲a̲-
.12	GRA T 6 VIN S 1 *TURO$_{2}$* 5 me-ri[
.13	*vacat* [me-]ṛị-ṭọ v 1

NB:
l.1 "Special" (i.e., unusual) dative ending in *-i* (instead of *-e*) in: po-se-da-o-ni

Fig. 3 Linear B tablet PY Un 718 (from Palace of Nestor Vol. IV edition in progress, by Palaima, Melena et al.)

a different dialect – perhaps that of the scribe or of the people from whom the recorded information was obtained at *sa-ra-pe-da*. If so, could it be that the speakers of a foreign mother tongue were producing this peculiar pronunciation? (2) The *wo-ro-ki-jo-ne-jo* group will contribute the least amount of all the contributors, probably reflecting its inferior status, possibly due to the foreign origin of (some of) its members. (3) One wonders whether the place name *sa-ra-pe-da,* which appears only in this set of texts, and seems to be a nominative neuter plural in Un 718, could have been formed from the Hittite adverb *šarā* "up, upwards" and noun *peda-* "place, spot, location" meaning something like "grounds/plains high up." This would be an appropriate place name for a site near the mountain range separating the Hither (west) and Further (east) Provinces of the kingdom of Pylos. The Further Province was incorporated into the kingdom by/early in the thirteenth century (Davis and Bennet 1999, 115), perhaps some decades before the Tawagalawa Letter was written, but it is unlikely that the large-scale population movement reported in this letter was an isolated incident. The Further Province would have been a logical place for the Pylian administrators to settle newcomers from overseas. A plural for the word *peda-* (n.) "place" is not attested in Hittite, but the ending of *sa-ra-pe-da* could be explained as a grammatically integrated lexical transfer whereby Greek speakers normalized the ending to their own neuter plural *-a* when they adopted it into Greek. A Luwian origin can also be posited, given the existence of Cuneiform Luwian *sarra* "up(on)" and Hieroglyphic Luwian *sara* "on, above; over, up," *pida-* (n.) "place, precinct" (Melchert 1993; Payne 2004). Indeed, the Greek mainland and Crete furnish a number of Luwian-related names, including that of mainland Mt. Parnassos (Luwian *parna-* (n.) "house"; García Ramón 1998, 932). It is tempting to view the form *sa-ra-pe-da* as originally coined for an uninhabited area on the mainland by Hittite or Luwian settlers or by Greek-speaking officials overseeing these settlers' migration to the Greek mainland from Anatolia.

The name of another site in the Further Province of Pylos possibly tied to that part of the world is *a-si-ja-ti-ja* (PY Jn 829, On 300). It could perhaps refer to the area of Assuwa, if borrowed directly from the Egyptian rendering of Assuwa, which also lacks a *-w-* (digamma): in fifteenth-century BC Egyptian texts, "Assuwa" is recorded as *J-s-jj* (=*Isy*) or as *A-si*$_x$*-ja* (Cline 1997, 193). Otherwise, and more likely given that the digamma is in fact rendered in Linear B toponymics referring to Assuwa (see fig. 1), Mycenaean *a-si-ja-ti-ja* could be a derivative of "Assos" (Melchert, personal communication), a site located in Classical times on the Anatolian coast, north of Lesbos. Adding *-ijo-* to the base **Assa/o-* would give "(the land) of Assos." The derivation of Greek place name Βοιωτία < Βοιωτός [< Βοῖον (ὄρος)] (García Ramón 2002, 276) is instructive: Mycenaean *a-si-ja-ti-ja* could, in a similar fashion, mean "the place of – the person from – the land of Assos." Perhaps then, *a-si-ja-ti-ja,* located in the Further Province of Pylos, was named after an Anatolian homeland site by/for settlers relocated on the Greek mainland.

CONCLUDING REMARKS

In comparison with the Classical Greek evidence of Athenians who were of Ionian ethnicity (at least according to some versions) and Spartans who were Dorian, the Linear B corpus could be said to preserve the toponymics corresponding to the Classical Greek "Athenians" and "Spartans" but not the ethnic groupings. We do not know the ethnicity of the Milesian women of the PY A-series, for instance, or of the Lemnians, or the Khians.[11] Regarding the fluidity of ethnic identity, it is not difficult to imagine that migrants arriving in Mycenaean regions would initially feel like outsiders, especially if attached to a territory elsewhere, while their children and grandchildren might feel ties of allegiance with both the land of their ancestors and, increasingly so, with the land of their own birth. In terms of degrees of identity, the toponymics – we have no certain "ethnics" to work with – suggest that the (people whom *we* call) Mycenaeans generally thought and operated on the basis of small-scale, local-level identity groups.[12] Lacking the rich discourse of foundation myths and genealogies through which ethnicity may have been constructed and manipulated, the Mycenaean textual evidence does not permit the fine-tuned analysis of ethnicity possible for the Classical Greek world. Yet, it has the advantage of constituting *real* data. These real economic documents strongly suggest that the arrival of groups, whether from nearby or further afield, like the female workers from the Anatolian coastline and the "settlers" on the rower texts, would have produced the *conditions* (e.g., migration and the accompanying competition between groups over land, food and other resources) in which ethnic consciousness is known to emerge or intensify. Mycenaean society, like any other, was created through complicated and perhaps at times contradictory strategies of inclusion and exclusion. Its members had varied cultural pasts and quite likely varying ethnic allegiances.

As it stands, the Linear B evidence attests to the physical presence and interaction in the Mycenaean world of culturally diverse population groups and individuals. The toponymics surveyed in this paper relate to local, nearby and overseas place names, and the individuals and groups designated by them include seemingly dependent female workers, as well as high-status individuals probably acting as semi-independent merchants, and a range of other members of Mycenaean society including shepherds, bronzesmiths, rowers and landholders. The non-Greek form of some personal names also suggests mixed populations. The rowers described as "settlers" and "immigrants" point to the arrival of newcomers. The cultural diversity of the Mycenaean world was created in part by importing to it the labor forces, from the Lukka Lands and elsewhere, required to sustain the Mycenaean palatial systems. The acquisition of such human resources from western Anatolia, in particular, whether by force or invitation, or both, is highlighted by the Luwian connection in the Tawagalawa Letter and may have been the underlying reason, at Pylos, for the existence of a settlement called *sa-ra-pe-da* and for naming a Further Province site *a-si-ja-ti-ja*. The mention of "foreign" divinities, such as "Minoan" *pi-pi-tu-na* and "Anatolian" *po-ti-ni-ja a-si-wi-ja*, hints at an acceptance, even celebration, of "otherness" or diversity. The Linear B tablets, fragmentary though they are, offer us valuable glimpses of the multicultural character of Mycenaean society resulting from its interaction with, and input from, its Aegean and Anatolian neighbors.

NOTES

This paper deals specifically with the textual evidence pertaining to multicultural, direct *human* interaction in the Mycenaean world. A study of the relevant archaeological evidence is under way. Textual and archaeological data concerning items of *trade* are discussed, with references, in Niemeier (1998), Shelmerdine (1998), Cline (1994), and Palaima (1991). I thank T. Burnes, P. Carlier, C. Justus, S. Kimball, T. Palaima, C. Shelmerdine, M. Southern, and J. Wright for their comments, C. Melchert for generously answering my linguistic queries on the terms *sa-ra-pe-da* and *a-si-ja-ti-ja*, and J. L. García Ramón for all his help with *wo-ro-ki-jo-ne-jo*. Any shortcomings in any argumentations are entirely my own.

1 Based on his study of the textual corpus, Hall proposes a distinction between the *aggregate* nature of ethnic composition in the late Archaic Greek period and an *oppositional* mode of ethnic consciousness in the Classical period (2002, 179–80). In the former case, he cites examples of genealogies being manipulated by influential players, like the Thessalians, who could *add* an eponymous figure of their own, or attach themselves to an existing one, in a key position in the family tree of a given descent group, as a means of legitimizing their emerging power and territorial claims in a particular region. The main ethnic groups at the time were the Dorians, Ionians, Akhaians and Aiolians. In the Classical period, an overarching Hellenic ethnic consciousness was forged in *opposition* to the external threat of the barbarian Persians.

2 The identification of Nauplia as Tiryns is supported by the inscription on the Kom el-Hetan statue base of Amenhotep III of the four major mainland palatial sites: Mycenae, Dikte (=Boiotian Thebes), Messana (=Pylos) and Nauplia (=Tiryns) (Shelmerdine 1998, 292; Palaima 1991, 280).

3 As Cline (1997, 190–92) explains, while the coalition of western Anatolian states known as Assuwa in the Hittite texts had ceased to exist before the time of most of the Linear B tablets, "it is now fairly certain that the name 'Assuwa' gave rise to the Greek name 'Asia' ('*Assuwa*' = Hittite *A-as-su-wa* > '*Aswia*' = Linear B *A-si-wi-ja* and other variations > Greek Ἀσία = '*Asia*')" (1997, 192). While eventually applied to most of western Anatolia, the term

'Asia' was first used by later Greek authors to refer only to the west-central region of Lydia (1997, 192). Thus, whether Assuwa itself was originally restricted to the northwest is not entirely clear (Melchert 2003, 7).

4 (1) A note added on PY Ad 684 describes the children in question as *a-pu-ne-we e-re-ta-o ko-wo* "sons of the rowers at *a-pu-ne-we*" (=variant spelling of *a-po-ne-we*, a site known from PY An 1 and An 610 to provide rowers). (2) The boys on PY Ad 697 are said to be *e-re[-ta] qe-ro-me-no* "serving as rowers" (Chadwick 1988, 55, 58, 87–88; Carlier 1983, 14–20; Palaima 1991, 286). Del Freo (2001–2002) persuasively argues that *ko-wo* could mean "apprentice" instead of "son."

5 The toponyms *a-ra-si-jo* and *ku-pi-ri-jo* coexist at Knossos, but the former is absent from Pylos, leading Shelmerdine to wonder whether *Alasija* may have been "a designation (perhaps earlier, perhaps in a different language) for all or part of Cyprus ... that the Pylian scribes rejected" preferring the alternative Greek form *Kupros* (Shelmerdine 1998, 296). In the case of the Egyptian toponymics preserved at Knossos, distinct language sources or degrees of identification may suffice to explain the presence of both *a$_3$-ku-pi-ti-jo* and *mi-sa-ra-jo* (Cline 1994, 128) in contemporary contexts.

6 According to Billigmeier (1970, 179), Anatolian features include a tendency to vowel harmony, prefixes such as *a-ra-*, *da-ra*, *ku-ka-*, *wa-du-*, *pi-ja-*, and suffixes such as *-da-ro*, *ma-ro*, *na-ro*, *na-to*, in which the *-o* is explained as "possibly the result of the Hellenization of these names."

7 If Ahhiyawa does *not* refer to a Mycenaean power, then (a) there is no identifiable reference to the Mycenaeans in the Hittite texts, in spite of the material evidence for Mycenaean contact with western Anatolia and the eastern Aegean, and (b) only it (i.e., textually attested Ahhiyawa) has left no trace of its existence in the archaeological record (Bryce 1989, 3–4). Perhaps the most serious problem with the identification is that Ahhiyawa appears in the Hittite texts as a single entity, whereas the Mycenaean states definitely operated as independent palatial territories (Niemeier 1998, 44; Bryce 1989, 5). It is quite possible, however, as Bryce points out, that one center could occasionally take the lead (as Mycenae is said to have done in Homer's *Iliad* during the Trojan War). Alternatively, perhaps the center with closest ties to the Hittites presented itself as the leader and/or the Hittites perceived and portrayed one center as such. Linguistically, Finkelberg argues that a descendant of the form *Ahhiyawa* could in fact correspond to the Greek *Akhaia* (*Akhaioi*, *Argeioi* and *Danaoi* being the three collectives that Homer uses, interchangeably, to refer to the Greeks). Her study presents "the Greek stem **Akhaiw-* as derivative of the stem *Ahhiyaw-* by the application of phonetic regularities attested for the Greek language": *Ahhiyaw-* > **Ahhiaw-* > **Ahhyaw-* > **Akhaw-* > **Akhaiw-* > Ἀχαι- (Finkelberg 1988, 133–34; also Hall 2002, 49–55).

8 Tablet An 610 is fragmentary and difficult to interpret. Expert treatments of the "rower" series of texts include Chadwick (1987); Killen (1983a); Perpillou (1968). Helpful Ugaritic parallels show them to be recruitment records or registers of naval personnel, supplied by communities for a fleet controlled by the Palace, levied according to the normal principles of Mycenaean taxation (Palaima 1991, 285–86). For an alternative view of these documents as a call-up for an overseas migration, i.e., an expedition of men sent to colonize a site off the mainland, see Wachsmann (1998, 126–27, 159–61) and Yasur-Landau (2002). Yasur-Landau suggests that since the terms *ki-ti-ta*, *me-ta-ki-ti-ta*, *po-si-ke-te-re* do not appear in the main landholding texts dealing with the Pylian kingdom (PY E-series), they may point to individuals settling *outside* the boundaries of the Pylian polity. Chadwick (1987, 82) nevertheless links the *ki-ti-me-na* lands of the E-series with precisely these *ki-ti-ta*. An alternative (speculative) explanation for these terms' absence from the E-series is that they designated relatively marginalized members of society and not the landholders and leasers with whom the palace authorities were directly concerned in the E-series. The rowers might have used/worked on (some of) the lands mentioned in the E-series which were "held" by others.

9 For an excellent discussion in support of the interpretation of *sa-ra-pe-da* as a place name as opposed to a land tenure term, see R. Palmer (1994, 66–72).

10 The noun *ka-ma* is known from the PY land-tenure texts (E series) to designate a particular kind of land plot. It seems that it may refer both to the land and to the group of people working it. Here, its animate nature is indicated by the verb "will give" (ll. 3, 9), implied for each of the four parties. The accompanying term, *wo-ro-ki-jo-ne-jo*, is either a possessive adjective built to a man's name resulting in "**Wroikiōn's ka-ma*," according to Killen (1983b, 83–88), or a toponymic adjective built to the word for "break," *ϝρώξ, such as a natural or artificial break in the earth's surface, with **Wrōgiōn* being the "Place of the Breaks," as outlined by Heubeck (1966). For the alternative view that the term was built to the IE root **werg-* "to do, work" (ἔργον, etc.), see the reservations of Palmer (1963, 27, 214): in particular, the "*r*" of **werg-* is typically not rendered in the Linear B Script, e.g., *we-ka-ta* *ϝεργάται "workers" (referring to plough oxen on KN Ce 59).

11 Given the fluidity and varying degrees of ethnicity, the Classical Athenians, who are known to have been intensely

loyal to their city, could be thought of "as in some sense ethnic groups" (Renfrew 1987, 217). Perhaps the same applied to (some of) the population groups recorded in the Linear B texts. Two ethnic groups known from the Classical period, Ionians and Akhaians, *might* be alluded to in the texts from Knossos (the names seem to match, but whether they had ethnic value at this time is simply unknown): a fragmentary record of men, KN B (4) 164, includes a viable nominative plural form *i-ja-wo-ne* (*Iawones* > *Iōnes*) but the reading is uncertain (e.g., Hall 2002, 71 n. 74), while on KN C (2) 914, the allative form *a-ka-wi-ja-de* ("to *a-ka-wi-ja*") might refer to a site (of Akhaians?) on Crete, or the mainland, or elsewhere, to which fifty sheep and fifty goats are being sent or, hypothetically (Killen 1994, 78), to a religious festival, the Akhaia.

12 *ke-re-te* (*Krētes*) "Cretans" appear on a list of (crafts?)men on PY An 128 and, apparently as a personal name in the singular, *ke-re* (*Krēs*), on the list of men on KN As 1516 (l.17), but it is unclear if, in the Bronze Age, the term referred to the inhabitants of Crete at a supra-local level or to a specific subset of the island's population (cf. Hall 2002, 70–71 and Bryce 2003, 43–44).

REFERENCES

Aura Jorro, F. (1985) *Diccionario Micénico* I. Madrid, C.S.I.S.

___ (1993) *Diccionario Micénico* II. Madrid, C.S.I.S.

Billigmeier, J. C. (1970) An Inquiry into the Non-Greek Names on the Linear B Tablets from Knossos and their Relationship to Languages of Asia Minor. *Minos* 10, 177–83.

Bryce, T. R. (1989) The Nature of Mycenaean Involvement in Western Anatolia. *Historia* 38, 1–21.

___ (2003) History. In H. C. Melchert (ed.) *The Luwians*, 27–127. Leiden, Brill.

Carlier, P. (1983) La femme dans la société mycénienne d'après les archives en linéaire B. In E. Lévy (ed.) *La femme dans les sociétés antiques*, 9–32. Strasbourg, Université des Sciences Humaines de Strasbourg.

Chadwick, J. (1987) The Muster of the Pylian Fleet. In P. Ilievski and L. Crepajac (eds.) *Tractata Mycenaea*, 75–84. Skopje, Macedonian Academy of Sciences and Arts - Skopje.

___ (1988) The Women of Pylos. In J.-P. Olivier and T. G. Palaima (eds.) *Texts, Tablets and Scribes. Studies in Mycenaean Epigraphy and Economy*, 43–95. Minos Supplement 10. Salamanca, Ediciones Universidad de Salamanca Servicio Editorial.

Cline, E. H. (1994) *Sailing the Wine-Dark Sea. International Trade and the Late Bronze Age Aegean.* BAR International Series 591. Oxford, Tempus Reparatum.

___ (1997) Achilles in Anatolia: Myth, History, and the Assuwa Rebellion. In G. D. Young, M. W. Chavalas and R. E. Averbeck (eds.) *Crossing Boundaries and Linking Horizons. Studies in Honor of Michael C. Astour on His 80th Birthday*, 189–210. Bethesda, CDL.

Davis, J. L., and Bennet, J. (1999) Making Mycenaeans: Warfare, Territorial Expansion and Representations of the Other in the Pylian Kingdom. In R. Laffineur (ed.) *Polemos. Le Contexte guerrier en Égée à l'Âge du Bronze*, 105–20. Aegaeum 19. Liège-Austin, Université de Liège and UT-PASP.

Del Freo, M. (2001–2002) Les Rameurs d'A-PO-NE-WE. *Studia Minora Facultatis Philosophicae Universitatis Brunensis* 6–7: 83–90.

Driessen, J. M. (1985) Quelques Remarques sur la "grande tablette' (As1516) de Cnossos. *Minos* 19, 169–93.

Eriksen, T. H. (2000) Ethnicity and Culture: A Second Look. In R. Bendix and H. Roodenburg, (eds.) *Managing Ethnicity*, 185–205. Amsterdam, Het Spinhuis.

Finkelberg, M. (1988) From Ahhiyawa to Ἀχαιοί. *Glotta* 66, 127–34.

García Ramón, J. L. (1998) Geographische Namen. *Der Neue Pauly* 4, 930–34.

___ (2002) Völker- und Stammesnamen. *Der Neue Pauly* 12/2, 276–78.

Gulizio, J., Pluta, K., and Palaima, T. G. (2001) Religion in the Room of the Chariot Tablets. In R. Laffineur and R. Hägg (eds.) *Potnia: Deities and Religion in the Aegean Bronze Age*, 453–61. Aegaeum 22. Liège-Austin, Université de Liège and UT-PASP.

Hall, J. M. (1997) *Ethnic Identity in Greek Antiquity.* Cambridge, Cambridge University.

___ (2002) *Hellenicity: Between Ethnicity and Culture.* Chicago, University of Chicago.

Heubeck, A. (1966) Myk. *wo-ro-ki-jo-ne-jo ka-ma. živa Antika* 15, 267–70.

Hock, H. H., and Joseph, B. D. (1995) *Language History, Language Change, and Language Relationship.* Berlin, de Gruyter.

Ilievski, P. H. (1992) Observations on the Personal Names from the Knossos D Tablets. In J.-P. Olivier (ed.) *Mykenaïka*, 321–49. BCH Supplement 25. Paris, Diffusion de Boccard.

Killen, J. T. (1983a) PY An 1. *Minos* 18, 71–79.

___ (1983b) Mycenaean Possessive Adjectives in -E-JO. *Transactions of the Philological Society*, 66–99.

___ (1994) Thebes Sealings, Knossos Tablets and Mycenaean Banquets. *Bulletin of the Institute of Classical Studies* 39: 67–84.

___ (1995) Some Further Thoughts on "Collectors." In R. Laffineur and W.-D. Niemeier (eds.) *Politeia. Society and State in the Aegean Bronze Age*, 213–26. Aegaeum 12. Liège-Austin, Université de Liège and UT-PASP.

Luraghi, N. (2002) Becoming Messenian. *Journal of Hellenic Studies*, 45–69.

Melchert, H. C. (1993) *Cuneiform Luvian Lexicon.* Chapel Hill, self-published.

___ (2003) Introduction. In H. C. Melchert (ed.) *The Luwians*, 1–7. Leiden, Brill.

Niemeier, W.-D. (1998) The Mycenaeans in Western Anatolia and the Problem of the Origin of the Sea Peoples. In S. Gitin, A. Mazar and E. Stern (eds.) *Mediterranean Peoples in Transition. Thirteenth to Early Tenth Centuries BCE*, 17–65. Jerusalem, Israel Exploration Society.

Nikoloudis, S. (2006) The *lāwāge(r)tās*, Ministerial Authority and Mycenaean Cultural Identity. Unpublished Ph.D.diss., Austin, The University of Texas at Austin.

Palaima, T. G. (1991) Maritime Matters in the Linear B Tablets. In R. Laffineur and L. Basch (eds.) *Thalassa: l'Égée préhistorique et la mer*, 273–310. Aegaeum 7. Liège, Université de Liège.

___ (2002a) Special vs. Normal Mycenaean: Hand 24 and Writing in the Service of the King? In J. Bennet and J. Driessen (eds.) *A-NA-QO-TA. Studies Presented to J. T. Killen*, 205–21. *Minos* 33–34. Salamanca, Ediciones Universidad de Salamanca.

___ (2002b) Review of V. Aravantinos, L. Godart and A. Sacconi (eds.) *Thèbes. Fouilles de la Cadmée. I. Les tablettes en linéaire B de la Odos Pelopidou. Édition et commentaire.* Rome: Istituti Editoriali Poligrafici Internazionali, 2001. *Minos* 35–36, 475–86.

___ (2004) Sacrificial Feasting in the Linear B Documents. In J. C. Wright (ed.) *The Mycenaean Feast*, 217–46. Princeton, American School of Classical Studies at Athens.

Palaima, T. G., Melena, J.-L. et al. (forthcoming) *The Palace of Nestor at Pylos in Western Messenia.* Vol. IV *The Inscribed Documents.* Princeton, Princeton University.

Palmer, L. R. (1963) *The Interpretation of Mycenaean Greek Texts.* Oxford, Oxford University.

Palmer, R. (1994) *Wine in the Mycenaean Palace Economy*. Aegaeum 10. Liège-Austin, Université de Liège and UT-PASP.

Payne, A. (2004) *Hieroglyphic Luwian.* Elementa Linguarum Orientis 3. Wiesbaden, Harrassowitz.

Perpillou, J.-L. (1968) La Tablette PY An 724 et la Flotte Pylienne. *Minos* 9, 205–18.

Rapoport, A. (1980) Vernacular Architecture and the Cultural Determinants of Form. In A. D. King (ed.) *Buildings and Society: Essays on the Social Development of the Built Environment*, 283–305. London, Routledge and Kegan Paul.

Renfrew, C. (1987) *Archaeology and Language: The Puzzle of Indo-European Origins.* Cambridge, Cambridge University.

Shelmerdine, C. W. (1998) Where Do We Go from Here? And How Can the Linear B Tablets Help Us Get There? In E. H. Cline and D. Harris-Cline (eds.) *The Aegean and the Orient in the Second Millennium*, 291–99. Aegeum 18. Liège-Austin, Université de Liège and UT-PASP.

Shennan, S. (1989) Introduction: Archaeological Approaches to Cultural Identity. In S. Shennan (ed.) *Archaeological Approaches to Cultural Identity*, 1–32. London, Unwin Hyman.

Southern, M. R. V. (forthcoming) War and Captivity in the Greco-Anatolian Bronze Age: Hittite *zahh-* "fight," Homeric *daï*, Indo-Iranian *dāsa-* "enemy, slave," Mycenaean *do-e-ro* "captive." *Historische Sprachforschung.*

Ventris, M. and Chadwick, J. (1973) *Documents in Mycenaean Greek.* 2nd ed. Cambridge, Cambridge University.

Voutsaki, S., and Killen, J. eds. (2001) *Economy and Politics in the Mycenaean Palace States.* Cambridge, Cambridge Philological Society.

Wachsmann, S. (1998) *Seagoing Ships and Seamanship in the Bronze Age Levant.* London, Chatham.

Watkins, C. ed. (2000) *American Heritage Dictionary of Indo-European Roots.* Boston, Houghton Mifflin.

Yasur-Landau, A. (2002) Social Aspects of Aegean Settlement in the Southern Levant in the End of the 2nd Millenium BCE. Unpublished Ph.D.diss., Tel Aviv, Tel Aviv University.

4

HITTITE LESBOS?

Hugh J. Mason

Two texts from Hattusa refer to *la-az-pa,* which is identified as a place name by the determinatives URU and KUR (*KUB* 5.6 ii 57, 60 and *KUB* 19.5 + *KBo* 19.79, ed. Houwink ten Cate 1983–84: 38–40; Texts 1 and 2 below). The first is an oracle text from the reign of Mursili II (1321–1295 BC), while the second deals with the misadventures of Manapa-Tarhunta, king of a state called the "Seha River Land," and vassal of the next Hittite king, Muwatalli II (1295–1271 BC).

In Text 1, the Hittite king consults the Deity of Lazpa (DINGIR-*LUM* ^{URU}*la-az-pa-ia*), which an Anatolian would have understood as addressing a statuette or other representation of the god physically present in Hattusa, and more likely to have been acquired by conquest than diplomacy. Text 2 descibes the capture and removal from Lazpa of persons called by the Akkadian word *ṣāripūtu* ($^{LÚ.MEŠ}$*ṢA-RI-PU-TI*), some of whom belonged to the (Hittite) king and some to "the god." Both passages suggest that Lazpa was well integrated into the Hittite sphere of influence, and probably part of the empire ruled from Hattusa. According to text 1, the sacrifices used for its deity resemble those employed for the household deities of the king, while the *ṣāripūtu*-men of text 2, known also from a Hittite context in Ugarit (Nougayrol 1968), as specialized workers, possibly dyers responsible for ceremonial apparel,[1] who are owned by the king and/or attached to a temple, appear entirely Anatolian in culture.

Most Hittite scholars accept the equation of Lazpa with the island that the Greeks later called Lesbos. Classicists have described "Lazpa" as an Anatolian spelling of Greek *Lesbos* (Huxley 1961, 12–13), but the Anatolian form is attested four centuries before the Greek, and conforms to the familiar correspondence of second-millennium Luwian /a/ to first-millennium Greek /e/ found, for example, in *Apasa/Ephesos* and *Parha/Perge.* Whatever its origin, the name *Lazpa* occurs around 1300 BC in a Luwian form. For the use of Luwian in the region, note the possible example of Troy/Wilusa (Starke 1997, 456–59; Watkins 1998, 204; Hawkins and Easton 1996, 111–13), and Stephanos of Byzantium's observation that the Aeolic town of *Elaia* ("Olive-oil"), near the mouth of the Kaikos, had the alternative name *Dainis* which corresponds to the *Luwian* adjective *tāini,* "oily" (*DLL* 89; Starke 1990, 241, n. 827a; 1997, 475, n. 101).

Lazpa incorporates the highly productive Anatolian place-name suffix *-pa/ba,*[2] and finds an exact phonetic match in *Gazpa,* a variant spelling of Kazapa, a city on the northern border with Kaska territory.[3] In contrast, words ending in -βα, -βη, and –βος, including place names, are not very common in Greek;[4] besides the Boeotian *Thebai* and *Thisbe*, we should note, significantly, *Arisba/Arisbe*, the name of cities in Lesbos and the Troad (Herodotus, *Hist.* 1.151; Homer, *Il.* 2.836).

In line 16 of Text 2, we learn that the *ṣāripūtu*-men were taken "over sea" (A.AB.BA *p*[*ar-ra*]*-an-ta*),[5] suggesting that Lazpa, like Lesbos, was an island.[6] Manapa-Tarhunta, king of the "Seha River Land," a state located between Mira (whose capital was Apasa/Ephesos) and Wilusa/Troy, claimed it. Manapa-Tarhunta also controlled a realm called *Apawiya,* presumably the district that the Greeks called *Abaeitis* (Strabo, *Geogr.* 12.8.11, 13.4.4), located at the headwaters of the river Makestos, northeast of the Kaikos River. Thus, Anatolian

Seha was located in the same region as Greek Kaikos, and Manapa-Tarhunta's realm corresponded to the region that Greeks in the first millennium called *Aeolis,* which extended from the Hermos to Cape Lekton, and whose cities acknowledged Lesbos as their *metropolis* (Strabo, *Geog.* 13.1.8, 13.2.1). All of this strongly supports the identification of Lazpa with Lesbos.

While those who look at these texts from an Anatolian perspective have concluded that Lazpa or Lesbos was under Hittite control around 1300, classical scholars, although interested in Hittite texts as evidence of the "reality" of the Trojan War or as comparanda for Greek mythology, do not, as Calvert Watkins has said, "seem to be trampling each other in their haste to get at [them]" for other purposes (1998, 201). There certainly has been little discussion of the implications of these two documents for the history of Lesbos, either by classicists[7] or by local historians.[8]

What evidence might there be for a Hittite or Luwian Lesbos beyond the two Hittite texts under consideration? The material evidence is inconclusive. In the Early Bronze Age, Lesbian ceramic traditions find their closest affinities in (northwest) Anatolia, in a northeast Aegean culture with close parallels at Troy and on Lemnos (Axiotis 2001). In the Late Bronze Age, there is more emphasis on the increased presence of "Mycenean" or mainland material, but the evidence on Lesbos is very incomplete. Only Thermi, a site north of Mytilene, has systematically been published (Lamb 1936); results from the Bronze Age sites at Kourtir on the Gulf of Kalloni (Spencer 1995a, 20, site 91) and Chalakies/Perama on the Gulf of Yera (Spencer 1995a, 13, site 54, and informal reports of recent excavations) are not yet in the public realm. Nonetheless, the consensus position is that Lesbos belongs to a "northern" interface of the Aegean and Anatolian world, less Aegean-influenced than the "southern" region centered on Rhodes and Miletos/ Millawanda (Mountjoy 1998).

Lesbos' ties to any of the mainland Greek kingdoms are difficult to demonstrate. There do not seem to be any women from Lesbos, along with the Chians and Milesians, identified among the foreign workers on tablets from Pylos. Scafa proposed that *a-ri-qa* (PY Jn 832,14) might be interpreted as *Arisba,* but assigned it to the town in the Troad (1999, 271–77); the vowel of the third syllable excludes the possibility that *Mu-ti-ri* (PY Ep 212.6, Eb 858.1) could have anything to do with *Mytilena.*

In terms of material culture, what is striking about Lesbos is the continued production of a local tradition of pottery, Lesbian Grey "bucchero" ware, right through the end of the Bronze Age and into the Archaic Greek period, as though there had been no major population shift of Greeks into the island (Spencer 1995b, 301–6). The Aeolian Greeks are supposed to have arrived four generations after the fall of Troy, but it is hard to find evidence of their presence so early; there are, significantly, no local traditions of an expelled or conquered allophone population. When we do have usable Greek cultural material from the island, in the poetry of Sappho and Alcaeus, the Lesbians have especially close ties with Sardis. All of this suggests a mixed Achaean/Anatolian population in the Late Bronze Age finally assimilated to Greek only in the Archaic period.

There may be some support for a period of Anatolian influence on Lesbos in the toponymy. It is very tempting to see in *laz-pa* the presence of the Hittite root *lazzi-* ("auspicious, desirable"); Pliny the Elder (Text 5: *HN* 5.139) lists a number of alternative names for Lesbos including *Himerte* (ἱμερτή), "desirable," and *Lasia* (Λασία), which is usually understood to mean "shaggy" and refer to the island's tree cover, but also represents a fairly accurate phonetic treatment of the Hittite adjective. We should, however, be cautious; very few Anatolian place names have clear Indo-European etymologies. If the name was Anatolian, it ought to be Luwian in form; the *lazzi-* stem is not attested in Cuneiform Luwian, but should be closer to the hieroglyphic *lata* (*HED* 5, 73).[9]

On the other hand, the city name *Mytilene* (in local dialect *mu-ti-le-na*) does appear to have an Anatolian etymology, based on the noun *muwa,* "might, " if not the royal and divine name Muwatalli. For the treatment of *muwa* in Greek as *my-*, compare Anatolian Tu-wa-na/ Greek Tyana; the syncopation of *mu-wa-ti* to *mu-ti* is observed in a Luwian text *KBo* 7.68 ii 13 (Melchert 1993, 152). *-il* is a recognizably Anatolian way of forming a personal name ("he who has power"), while the ending *-ena* suggests the common Greek place name adjective suffix –ηνος, as in Λαμψακηνός "from Lampsacus" and Παλαιστήνη. If *Mytilena* means something like "the land associated with the powerful one," we may find a dim echo of this meaning in Pliny the Elder (text 5), who called Mytilene *per MD annos potens, "powerful* for 1500 years."

In the Hittite texts, Lazpa is labeled as both KUR "land" and URU "city." This is normal in cuneiform documents and highly appropriate for the Mespotamian city-states for whom the writing system developed; but it is quite inappropriate for Greek, first-millennium, Lesbos, which had neither a unified government nor a city called Lesbos. However, the earliest Greek references to Lesbos, in the Homeric poems (Text 3), do describe Lesbos in the same way as our Hittite texts, both as "well-built" *(euktimene)* like a city (*Il.* 9. 129), and as the realm or "seat" of a single king, called Makar (*Il.* 24.544). Although the island's Bronze Age sites are desperately under-investigated, we should be looking for an appropriate location for an Anatolian fortified palace; Thermi had defensive walls in the Late Bronze Age, but one might want to look at more citadel-like locations, in Mytilene, Methymna or Antissa.

Homer referred to Lesbos as the land of *Makar.* Although the narrative recorded by Diodorus Siculus (text 4) made Makar a Greek from the Peloponnese (5.81.4), it ascribed to him (5.82.3) a law code called "Lion." A king as an author of a written law code is entirely plausible in a Hittite context, but does not fit either what the Greeks ascribed to their Heroic-Age Kings, nor what we know from Linear B evidence about Bronze Age Mycenean rulers. Furthermore, the name of the law code, "of the Lion," does not make much sense in Greek, despite Diodorus' comment about the "strength and courage of the beast;" but in an Anatolian context, it would clearly memorialize *Muwawalwi,* "Might of a Lion," the Luwian name of Manapa-Tarhunta's father, the founder of the Seha dynasty (Starke 2001).

Given these Anatolian associations for Makar, one would like to find Anatolian associations for the name. The word *makar,* an adjective of the third declension, with the meaning "blessed," has no recognized Indo-European etymology. By the time of Hesiod (*Op.* 171), it was applied to the heroized dead, believed to dwell in the "Islands of the Blessed;" both the concept and the term have been traced to Egyptian *m3-ʿḫrw* (Griffith 2001, 214, n. 2). After Homer, the adjective was reformed to first/second declension *makarios,* and the eponymous King became "Makareus" with a productive agent-suffix ("making *makar*"). The alternative name for the island, *Makaria,* was interpreted as both "Makar's land" and "Blessed Land."

Makara also occurs as a place-name for a settlement at the entrance to the Bay of Kalloni (Spencer 1995a, 28, site 131); there is a Bronze Age tomb at the site, but it was found empty, so there is no ceramic evidence to confirm the dating or suggest Achaean or Anatolian connections (Papadimitriou 2001, 146–48). The name, a neuter plural in the earlier third-declension form, appears ancient,[10] but "happy things" or "heroized dead things" does not make much sense as a place name. Apart from religious and church names, most small places on the island whose name can be interpreted are named (either in Greek or Turkish) for concrete features that define them, such as trees or rocks.[11] It would be desirable therefore to find a meaning for *makar* that would be appropriate to a physical feature of the island as a whole and to *Ta Makara* in particular. If *makar* could be shown to be Anatolian in origin, it would enhance the case for a Hittite Lesbos.

There is indeed a very similar-looking place-name in Hittite, [URU]*ma-kar-ua-an-da* (*KUB* 31.44 i 7), which should mean "region of *makar,*" "place rich in *makar,*" formally corresponding to Greek *Makara* and *Makaria.* However, in both Hittite and Luwian, a form written in cuneiform as *makar* with one *-k-* would be pronounced *magar,* and Greek names for Anatolian places which have a single internal *-k-* in Greek have a geminate in their cuneiform spelling, as in Greek *Ikonion*/Hittite *Ikkuwanya* and Greek *Lykia*/Anatolian *Lukka.* The stem *makari/magari* occurs in only one text (*KUB* 34.89) and has no generally accepted meaning; it is associated with silver and copper, and seems to refer to a part of a chariot, such as a wheel (*HED* 6, 17). None of this has any obvious application to Lesbos, and *magari* and *makaruanda* must regretfully be discarded as possible

Anatolian equivalents of *Makaria.* There is an agental form *makkuya* "churner" (*KUB* 29.45 rev. 10–12, *HED* 6:20) which could be derived from an Anatolian stem in *makk-,* but there is no evidence of it having an extension in *-ar-* and its meaning does not shed much light on the Greek name.

There are, however, two Greek mythical traditions that may connect Lesbos with the Hittites. One is a legend about Mytilene, the eponymous founder of Lesbos' chief city. In one narrative, recounted by Diodorus (3.55, see text 4), she is an Amazon, sister of Myrina, and both came to the Aegean from central Anatolia. In modern times, representations of kilted Hittites were (mis)taken for Amazons (Gurney 1954, 199–200), and it is possible that first-millennium Greeks made the same mistake in interpreting reliefs in western Anatolia. Greek myths and fantasies about the Amazons have their own complex history far removed from what we know about Anatolian culture, but there is a case to be made that legends of the foundation of many cities on the Aegean coast of Anatolia may ultimately reflect a Hittite or Luwian stage in their history. Since Mytilene does appear to have a Luwian etymology, the tradition in this case may possibly have some connection with reality.

Finally, there is the myth of Pelops, founder of the Olympic games, who gave his name to the Peloponnese. Pelops is the figure in Greek myth most likely to have a Hittite connection. He is always identified as an Anatolian, either from Lydia or Phrygia; his father Tantalus and sister Niobe, are especially connected with Mt. Sipylos, near Magnesia; the figure of Niobe turned into stone (Pausanias 1.21.3) may in fact have been a Hittite rock-cut relief (Bean 1966, 93–95). Pelops won the hand of Hippodameia, the daughter of Oinomaos, in a chariot-race, through the treachery of Oinomaos' charioteer, Myrsilos or Myrtilos. If anything in Mycenean Greek culture can be traced to the Hittites, it is the military use of chariots (Lorimer 1950, 320–23), and Oinomaos' charioteer bears the unmistakably Hittite name Mursili. In the canonical version of the myth, Myrsilos is a Peloponnesian, like Oinomaos; but there is an alternative version that connects him to Lesbos. In the Lesbian version of the Pelops/Myrsilos myth, noted in a scholion to Euripides' *Orestes* 990, Oinomaos was King of Lesbos, and the whole narrative probably took place on Lesbos (Scherling 1933, 115). The other two bearers of the name Myrsilos in Greek history were both Lesbians; the first a tyrant of Mytilene in the seventh century named by Alkaios, and the second a third-century historian from Methymna (*FGrH* 477).

All of these pieces – the Anatolian appearance of the name *Lazpa,* a possible Hittite etymology for *Mytilene,* the association of Makar's law code with King *Muwa-walwi,* and possible connections of the Pelops/Myrsilis myth with Lesbos – do not add up to very much. But regardless of classical Greece's ignorance of its Bronze Age predecessors in Anatolia, these pieces of evidence probably do provide reasonable support for the Hittite texts that suggest that Lesbos was under Hittite control in the Late Bronze Age.

APPENDIX: TEXTS

1. *KUB* 5.6 ii 57–60 (Sommer 1932, 282–91): With reference to the Deity of Ahhiyawa (DINGIR-*LUM* ^{URU}*aḫ-ḫi-ia-ua-kán*) and the Deity of Lazpa (DINGIR-*LUM* ^{URU}*la-az-pa-ia*) and the Deity of Persons (DINGIR-*LUM* NÍ.TE^{ni}*-ia*), which are identified as belonging to My Sun: Should we consult those also in the way we consult the Deities of the King's Person, and carry out the three-day cult performance also for the Deities of Ahhiyawa and Lazpa as for those (i.e., the personal gods)? Or should the performances be carried out as in the pure distributions made on the *šaknuwant* dishes of My Sun, and as in the libations made by the rite of Hattusa? Should one ask about the sacrifice from the Deity through the oracle? In the same manner? Then can they be valid? Oracular answer: Valid.

2. *KUB* 19.5 + *KBo* 19.79 (Houwink ten Cate 1983–84, 38–40): To his majesty speak! Thus Manapa-Tarhunta, your servant. Behold, within the country everything is in order. Gassus arrived and brought along the Hittite troops. When they set out again to attack the country of Wilusa, I became ill. When Piyamaradu had humiliated me, he set Atpas against me. He attacked the country of Lazpa (^{KUR}*La-az-pa-an* GUL-*aḫ-ta*). All without exception joined in and whichever *ṣāripūtu*-men belonged to His Majesty ... [xxx]-*ahuhas* made those too join in. However the *ṣāripūtu*-men made a petition to Atpas, "We are tributaries and we came over the sea. Let us pay our tribute. Šigauna committed a crime, but we did nothing." When they made their petition, Atpas did not transport them. He would have sent them home, but Piyamaradu

sent Šigauna and spoke to him .... When Atpas heard the word of Piyamaradu, he did not return them. But when Gassus arrived, Kupanta-Kurunta sent a message to Atpa: "The *ṣāripūtu*-men of His Majesty who are there, let them go home." And he let the *ṣariputu*-men who belong to the God and those who belong to His Majesty ... go home.

3. Iliad

9.128–130:

I will give seven Lesbian women, skillful at their tasks
whom I picked when he (Achilles) took well-built Lesbos,
women who surpassed the tribes of women in beauty.

24. 543–545:

Old man, we learned that you too once were prosperous.
All that Lesbos above, the seat of Makar, encloses
and Phrygia below, and the boundless Hellespont,
of these, old man, they say you excelled in wealth and sons.

4. Diodorus of Sicily

3.55.5–7: (The Amazon Myrina) conquered the races in the region of the Taurus and descended through Greater Phrygia to the sea; then she won over the land lying along the coast and fixed the bounds of her campaign at the River Kaikos. Selecting in the territory sites well suited for cities, she built a considerable number of them, and founded one which bore her own name; others she named after women who held the most important commands, such as Kyme, Pitana and Priene. She seized also some of the islands and Lesbos in particular, on which she founded the city of Mytilene, which was named after her sister who took part in the campaign.

5.81.2–7: The first people to seize [Lesbos] were Pelasgians. Xanthus crossed over to Lesbos, which was uninhabited and divided the land among the folk, and he named the island, which had formerly been called Issa, Pelasgia. And seven generations later ... Lesbos was also laid desolate by the deluge (of Deucalion) ... and after these events Makareus came to the island and recognizing the beauty of the land, he made his home in it. This Makareus was the son of Krinakos the son of Zeus, and was a native of Olenos in what is now called Achaia. The folk with him had been gathered from here and there, some being Ionians ... Makareus' power increased because of the fertility of the island and his own fairness, and he won for himself the neighboring islands. And during this time, Lesbos, the son of Lapithes, the son of Aeolus, sailed with colonists to the island, and marrying Methymna, the daughter of Macareus, made his home there ... and named the island Lesbos after himself ... And there was born to Makareus, in addition to other daughters, Mytilene and Methymna, from whom the cities in the island got their names.

5.82.2–4: The islands supplied the inhabitants with wholesome air and ... were filled with greater and greater abundance, and have been called the Islands of the Blessed (*Makaron)* ... but some say that they were called Islands of the Blessed after Makareus. And the islands are in truth blessed. And Makareus, while King of Lesbos, issued a law which contributed much to the common good, and he called the law "Lion" giving it the name after the strength and courage of that beast.

5. Pliny, *Natural History* 5.39.139: The most famous island is Lesbos, 65 miles from Chios. It was formerly called Himerte, Lasia, Pelasgia, Aegira, Aethiope, Macaria. It had nine noteworthy towns ... Pyrrha, Arisbe, Antissa, Methymna, Agamede, Hiera, Eressos and Mytilene, powerful for 1500 years.

NOTES

1 They are not found in Pecchioli Daddi (1982), a study of Hittite crafts and professions. For the *ṣāripūtu*-men as dyers or colorers, see Starke (1990, 556, §325; Luwian *ašharnumman*, Hittite *išharnumai-* "blütig machen"). Itamar Singer argues convincingly in this volume that they were purple-dyers.

2 Jie lists ninety-nine examples (1994, 90–91). For names found only in Hieroglyphic texts, see Savaş (1998, 172–224).

3 ^{URU}*ga-az-pa-as, KUB* 19.10.I.21; *RGTC* 6.1: 204, *NH* 269.

4 Kretschmer and Locker (1963, 3, 75, 329). Note that all -βος words listed by Kretschmer and Locker are oxytone, while Λέσβος is paroxytone.

5 *HZL* 274, §364, A.AB.BA, "Meer;" *CHD* 4, 135, *parranda*, "across, over."

6 *RGTC* 6, 27; Garstang and Gurney (1959, 97), Hawkins (1998, 23).

7 Even Spencer (1995b), a discussion of Lesbos' Anatolian connections, mentions only briefly the Hittite texts that name *Lazpa* (274 and n. 24), and does not explore their content.

8 The standard history of Lesbos used in the island's schools (Tzimis et al. 2001) makes no reference to the Hittites.
9 Thanks to Craig Melchert for advice on both Luwian and Hittite phonetics.
10 For the preservation of ancient place names on Lesbos, see Mantzouranis (1951).
11 Lesbos has places named prosaically after pear trees (Ἀχλαδερή), a plain (Πεδή), a rock (Πέτρα), and small springs (Πηγαδάκια).

REFERENCES

Axiotis, M. (2000) Η συμμετοχή της Λέσβου στον λεγόμενο πολιτισμό του ΒΑ Αιγαίου. *Λεσβιακά* (Δελτίον της Εταιρείας Λεσβιακών μελετών) 18, 88–114.

Bean, G. (1967) *Aegean Turkey: An Archaeological Guide.* London, Benn.

Garstang, J., and Gurney, O. R. (1959) *The Geography of the Hittite Empire*, Occasional Papers, 5. London, British Institute of Archaeology in Ankara.

Griffith, R. D. (2001) Sailing to Elysium: Menelaus' Afterlife (*Odyssey* 4.561–569). *Phoenix* 55, 213–43.

Gurney, O. R. (1954) *The Hittites*, 2nd ed. Harmondsworth: Penguin.

Hawkins, J. D. (1998) Tarkasnawa, King of Mira. *Anatolian Studies* 48, 1–32.

Hawkins, J. D., and Easton, D. F. (1996) A Hieroglyphic Seal from Troia. *Studia Troica* 6, 111–18.

Houwink ten Cate, Ph. H. J. (1983–1984) Sidelights on the Ahhiyawa Question from Hittite Vassal and Royal Correspondence. *Jaarbericht ex Oriente Lux* 28, 33–79.

Huxley, G. L. (1961) *Crete and the Luwians.* Oxford, Oxford University.

Jie, J. (1994) *A Complete Retrograde Dictionary of the Hittite Language.* Istanbul, Nederlands Historisch-Archaeologisch Instituut.

Kretschmer, P., and Locker, E. (1963) *Rückläufiges Wörterbuch der griechischen Sprache*, 2nd ed. Göttingen, Vandenhoeck und Ruprecht.

Lamb, W. (1936) *Excavations at Thermi in Lesbos.* Cambridge, Cambridge University.

Lorimer, H. L. (1950) *Homer and the Monuments.* London, MacMillan.

Mantzouranis, D. P. (1951) Σωζόμενα τοπονύμια τοῦ ἀρχαίου κτηματολογίου τῆς Λέσβου. *Byzantinische Zeitschrift* 44, 412.

Melchert, H. C. (1993) *Cuneiform Luvian Lexicon.* Chapel Hill, University of North Carolina.

Mountjoy, P. A. (1998) The East Aegean-West Anatolian Interface in the Late Bronze Age: Myceneans and the Kingdom of Ahhiyawa. *Anatolian Studies* 48, 33–69.

Nougayrol, J. (1968) Textes Suméro-Accadiens des archives et bibliothèques privées d' Ugarit. *Ugaritica* 5, 1–100.

Papadimitriou, N. (2001) *Built Chamber Tombs of Middle and Late Bronze Age Date in Mainland Greece and the Islands.* BAR International Series 925. Oxford, BAR.

Pecchioli Daddi, F. (1982) *Mestieri, professioni e dignità nell' Anatolia ittita.* Rome, Edizioni dell'Ateneo.

Savaş, Ö. S. (1998) *Divine, Personal and Geographical Names in the Anatolian (Hittite-Luwian) Hieroglyphic Inscriptions.* Istanbul, Eskiçağ Bilimleri Enstitütü.

Scafa, E. (1999) Le relazioni esterne dei regni micenei: i testi in Lineare B. In V. La Rosa, D. Palermo, L. Vagnetti (eds.) ἐπὶ πόντον πλαζόμενοι: *Simposio Italiano di Studi Egei*, 269–83. Rome, Scuola archeologica italiana di Atene.

Scherling, K. (1933) Myrtilos. *Paulys Realencyclopaedie der Classischen Altertumswisssenschaft, neue Bearbeitung*, 16.1, 1152–64. Munich, Druckenmuller.

Sommer, F. (1932) *Die Aḫḫijavā-Urkunden.* Abh. Bay. Akad. Wiss., Ph.-Hist. Abt., n.f. 6.

Spencer, N. (1995a) *Gazetteer of Archaeological Sites in Lesbos.* Oxford, BAR International Series 623.

___ (1995b) Early Lesbos between East and West: A "Grey Area" of Aegean Archaeology. *Annual of the British School at Athens* 90, 269–306.

Starke, F. (1990) *Untersuchungen zur Stammbildung des keilschrift-luwischen Nomens.* Studien zu den Boğazköy-Texten, 31. Wiesbaden, Harrassowitz.

___ (1997) Troia im Kontext des Historisch-Politischen und Sprachlichen Umfeldes Kleinasiens im 2. Jahtrtausend. *Studia Troica* 7, 447–87.

___ (2001) Sēḫa. *Neue Pauly* 11, 345–47.

Tzimis, S. et al. (2001) Ιστορία της Λέσβου. 5th edition. Mytilene, Syndesmos Philologon N. Lesvou.

Watkins, C. (1998) Homer and Hittite Revisited. In P. Knox and C. Fox (eds.) *Style and Tradition: Studies in Honor of Wendell Clausen*, 201–11. Stuttgart, Teubner.

5

THE SEER MOPSOS (MUKSAS) AS A HISTORICAL FIGURE

Norbert Oettinger

1. Many Anatolian influences on Greek have been brought to light, especially during the last two decades.[1] The direction of the borrowing, however, has to be checked in every single case. A further example of this need is the case of the Greek seer Mopsos.[2] It has long been supposed that there is a connection between Mopsos, who, according to tradition, founded cities and oracles in the plain of Cilicia, and Muksas, the Luwian founder of a dynasty, attested in the very same area. A detailed review of the problem from a recent perspective can be found in Vanschoonwinkel (1990). Hence, there is no need to recapitulate all of the arguments here, and we can instead refer to the material provided by the work cited.

1.1. A new point of view to be considered though takes into account the recently discovered Hieroglyphic Luwian inscription of Çineköy, situated south of Adana. Its editors, Tekoğlu and Lemaire (2000, 983–85), have expressed the view that the Muksu- mentioned in the Hittite letter to Madduwattas might be the same historical figure as Muksa-, the dynasty founder known from Çineköy and Karatepe:[3] "Il est possible que le Muksus du texte de Madduwattas ait été mentionné comme une personne liée à *Ahhiyawa*. Si cette relation était confirmée, elle pourrait être significative et la relation entre Muk(a)sas et *Hiyawa* pourrait correspondre à celle entre Muksus et *Ahhiyawa*." This is the first hypothesis we will have to discuss.

1.2. Heubeck was of the opinion that the Greek seer Mopsos is not to be identified with the ruler Muksa- named in the Hieroglyphic Luwian inscription of Karatepe: "Wenn Perge den Seher Mopsos als mythischen Gründer beansprucht und wenn in Kilikien die Orte Mópsou hestía und Mópsou Kréne entstehen, so bergen diese Tatsachen keineswegs die Erinnerung an eine griechische Besiedlung Südkleinasiens etwa in submykenisch-vorhistorischer Zeit, sie beruhen vielmehr auf nach-homerischer Sagenklitterung, die letztlich politischen Zwecken ihr Dasein verdankt" (1961, 74). This is the second hypothesis that shall concern us in the following.

1.3 The idea that the name Mopsos has its origin in the Anatolian languages and was thence borrowed into Greek is a notion that was put forward already early on and that has since won general acceptance (thus Landau 1959, 85, 185, 272; Astour 1967, 61–62; Zgusta 1964, 331; Vanschoonwinkel 1990, 197 [referring to phonological considerations by E. Forrer]). This is the third hypothesis to be discussed.

2. Firstly, about the representation of the name. It appears in the following forms (cf. Vanschoonwinkel 1990; except for Çineköy):

2.1. Mycenean Greek *Mo-qo-so* (Knossos and Pylos), rendering /*Mok^{w}so-*/.

2.2. Greek *Mópsos* (Μόψος) is attested as the name of several different persons. For one, we have Mópsos, son of Ampyx, from Thessaly, who took part in the expedition of the Argonauts. Being a member of this expedition usually implies being an early intrinsic part of Greek tradition.[4]

2.3. He first appears in Hesiod, *Aspis* 181. The Thessalian city of *Mopsion* belongs here.

2.4. Furthermore, the name is attested in Thrace, and there were various bearers of the name in Anatolia, lending their name to places in Phrygia and Armenia.

2.5. Nicolaus of Damascus mentions a Lydian named *Moxos*, this certainly is the Greek rendering of the native-Anatolian name-form *Muksu-/Muksa-* (otherwise Vanschoonwinkel 1990, 193).

3. The most famous bearer of the name Mopsos was, according to tradition, a Greek seer, son of the god Apollo and of Manto, daughter of the seer Teiresias (Pausanias 7.3.1). Connected with this Mopsos are numerous accounts of foundations of cities and oracles. He founded the oracle at Klaros, where he defeated Kalchas in a contest between seers (Hesiod fr. 278). Then he emigrated to Cilicia, where the city of *Mopsuestia* is named after him. He is also held to be the founder of *Perge* in Pamphylia, a place already attested in Hittite times (around 1200 BC) as *Parha* (for *Parha-* see Otten 1988, 35–37).

4. In the Hittite letter to Madduwatta, which is to be dated to shortly before 1400 BC, a man named *Muksu-* is mentioned, as noted above.

4.1. A *Muksa-* is found in the Hieroglyphic-Luwian inscriptions of Karatepe (early-seventh century) and Çineköy (late-seventh century). In Karatepe 1, §XXI, the text reads, "(wherein were bad men, robbers,) who had not served under Muksas' house" (*mu-ka-sa-sa-na* DOMUS-*ní-i*), and in §LVIII: "and much let them be in service to Azatiwatas and to Muksas' house (*mu-ka-sa-sá-há-´* DOMUS-*ní-i*) by Tarhunzas and the gods!" (see Hawkins 2000, 51, 56). In the Phoenician translation the name appears as *MPŠ*, that is, with a *p* as in Greek. In our opinion, this may indicate that, in the Near East, the Greek form, as opposed to the Anatolian one, was considered to be the proper form of the name.

4.2. The recently found Hieroglyphic-Luwian inscription of Çineköy begins as follows: "[I am] Warikas, son of [...], descendant of [Muka]sas ([*mu-ka-*]*sa-sa* INFANS.NEPOS-*si-sà*), king of Hiyawa...." (cf. Tekoğlu and Lemaire 2000, 968, 970). Thus, the authors of these inscriptions located in the Cilician plain both name Muksa- as the first ancestor of the ruling dynasty. Accordingly, Muksa- must have lived at least several and at most many generations before the beginning of the seventh century. He ruled over *Hiya(wa)-*, which had developed from *Ahhiya(wa)-*, showing the typical aphaeresis of certain Luwian dialects. Cf. PN *Tawagalawa-* from Gk. *Etewaklewēs. In the Çineköy inscription, the Phoenician translation has *Adana-* in place of Hiya(wa)-, the kingdom of Hiya(wa)- is consequently identical with the kingdom of Adana.

5. Is *Mopsos* (*Muksu-*, *Muksa-*) a name of Anatolian origin, as is normally assumed (see 1.4. above) or not? At any rate the form **Mok^{w}so-* or **Muk^{w}so-* is original. If this form had already existed in Anatolian in early times, in Hittite and Luwian it would have been written **Mukussa-* or **Mukussu-* and not /Muksa-/ and *Muksu-* as it is in our documents. There is no phonetically acceptable way from a **Mukkussa-* or **Mukkussu-* to the attested forms.[5] On the other hand, if we assume the name *Mok^{w}so-* to be of Greek origin, then the phonological correspondences are easy to explain: the labiovelar was delabialized before *s* in the transmission from Greek to Anatolian.[6] And the Hittite language treated the word as a *u*-stem: cf. Hittite nominative singular *Muksus* (see sect. 4 above) from Mycenean /Mok^{w}sos/ like Hittite *Alaksandus* from Mycenean **Alexandros*. Perhaps this bearer of the name *Muksus* was a Greek. If so, he would not have been the only Greek involved in the political affairs of the Anatolian west coast; cf. *Tawagalawa-* and *Attar(is)siya-*. Later there was a tendency to adapt Greek *o*-stems to the most common *a*-stem class, hence Hieroglypic-Luwian /Muksa-/. In Greek, however, the development from /Mók^{w}sos/ to later *Mópsos* is in accordance with the sound laws. From this follows that *Mok^{w}sos* was a loanword passing from Greece to Anatolia[7] and not the other way round; contra above 1.3.

6. This has the following historical consequences: The Name *Mók^{w}sos* (*Mópsos*) was originally only Greek, this claim is also supported by 2.2. above. The *Muksus* living in the late-fifteenth century and mentioned in the Hittite letter to Madduwattas could have been a Greek. In any case we find here the Greek name for the first time in a Hittite phonological adaptation. Thus, whereas we cannot exclude an earlier date, it is possible that not before the appearance of Mopsos, son of Apollo and Manto, did native Anatolians begin to bear this name as well.

7. Who then was Mopsos, son of Apollo and Manto? The linguistic examination confirms in fact the claim of the myth. Mopsos was of Greek origin, only later did he go to Cilicia. We have seen that in the seventh century kingdom of Hiya(wa), a certain Muksa- was regarded as the dynasty founder. The kingdom of Hiya(wa) was identical with the kingdom of Adana and perhaps included parts of the old kingdom of Tarhuntassa.[8] Tarhuntassa was an appanage of the Hittite Empire during the late-thirteenth century (Otten 1988, 3–9; Dinçol et al. 2000). I do not believe though in an unbroken continuity. Rather, I would assume that during the so-called Dark Ages a change of dynasty occurred, brought about by a Greek conquest under the leadership of our Greek Mok^{w}sos (Mopsos), whom legend held to be the son of Apollo and Manto. Therefore, he is referred to as the dynasty founder by his successors, the rulers of Hiya(wa) = Adana. The conquest took place at a time when the Greeks were still called Ahhiya and Ahhiyawa (Achaioi) by the Luwians. That is the reason why the kingdom of Mopsos (Muksa-) was called Hiya(wa) by them (see above). They are the very same Achaeans of Cilicia who were called Hypachaioi by Herodotus.[9]

8. To the west, the kingdom of Tarhuntassa stretched as far as the city of Perge on the river Kestros, which was called Parha on the river Kastayara by the Hittites (cf. Otten 1988, 37–39). It seems likely that after the conquest, Mopsos fortified his western frontier. This would be the reason why in the Greek tradition Perge still honored Mopsos as its founder, even though it had already existed under the very same name in Hittite times.[10] In Cilicia proper, the conqueror Mopsos refounded his capital. As a ruler, he was in his Anatolian environment simultaneously a priest-king. This may have led or contributed to his designation as a "seer" in the Greek tradition.[11] With regard to chronology, our Mok^{w}sos (Mopsos) probably lived in the twelfth or eleventh century, at the latest in the ninth century BC. After only a short time, the Luwian language of the population presumably prevailed over the Greek of the ruling class.

9. Let me draw attention to a second mythological figure who made a journey similar to that of Mopsos. The Corinthian prince Bellerophon (Bellerophontes) is the possessor of the divine winged horse Pegasos, whose name is a loan from Luwian *piḫaššašša-*, *piḫaššašši-*, surname of the storm-god.[12] He is sent to Lycia, because he has been calumniated. From Greece the Lycian king receives the order to kill him. For this reason, he orders him to perform several virtually impossible tasks, among them the killing of the monster Chimera. But the hero is successful in fulfilling these tasks, so that the king finally gives his daughter to him. He becomes the founder of a dynasty of Lycian rulers. In view of these parallels, it is possible that behind the mythological figure of Bellerophontes, whose name is definitely Greek,[13] there is a historical figure similar to that of Mopsos, namely a Greek conqueror of a coastal plain of Lycia during the "Dark Ages."

NOTES

1 For examples of Anatolian influence on early Greek, see for instance Hutter (1995; Greek *pégasos*); Melchert (1998; Greek *tolýpe*); Oettinger (2002; psilosis in Greek); Starke (1997, 462–64; Greek *demogérontes*).

2 I am indebted to Peter Högemann and Craig Melchert for very useful comments and to David Heath for correcting my English.

3 See already Heubeck (1961, 75). Before Otten (1969, 33) the Hittite letter to Madduwattas was believed to have been written in the late-thirteenth century and not, as nowadays, in the late-fifteenth century.

4 He is called seer. The reason could be a contamination with the second Mopsos, son of Apollo and Manto.

5 Cf. Hittite *nekumant-* "naked" from Proto-Anatolian **neg^{w}-mo(-nt)-* (Melchert 1994, 96). There is no variant **nekmant-* beside *nekumant-*. Hittite *tekkussiye-* "to appear" contains no labiovelar (Oettinger 1998, 106).

6 I am grateful to Craig Melchert for important advice in this matter.

7 Heubeck (1961, 75) had suggested that the name Mopsos/Muksus came independently into the Indo-European Anatolian languages and into Greek from a common non-Indo-European substratum of Anatolia and Greece. It may well be that Mopsos and his troops belonged to the Sea People.

8 For interesting news about Hiyawa see now Singer (2006, 257–58).

9 A connection between Hiyawa and the Hypachaioi of Herodotus (*Hist.* 7.91) has been suggested also by Tekoğlu and Lemaire (2000, 981–83). Hajnal (2003, 39–42) identifies this Hiyawa of Cilicia geographically with the Ahhiya(wa) of the Hittite texts and supposes that Greeks founded the kingdom of Ahhiyawa in Cilicia during the Hittite period. But I think that there was a first Ahhiyawa in the Greek mainland during the Hittite period and a second Hiyawa (*Ahhiyawa) in the plain of Cilicia after the Hittite period. If, during the Hittite period, a kingdom had been founded by Greek invaders in Cilicia, the geographical center of the Hittite empire, we would know of it from the Hittite texts. Tekoğlu and Lemaire suggest that the Muksu- of the late-fifteenth century is identical with the Muksa- of the seventh century. This is not plausible either.

10 For this reason the hypothesis of Heubeck (see above) cannot be upheld any longer.

11 It is possible that Mopsos in some way promoted the influence of (post-)Hittite oracle techniques on Greece.

12 For *Pegasos* see Hutter (1995).

13 For the name of *(B)ellerophon(tes)* see Watkins (1995, 383–86); Katz (1998, 325–28); and Oettinger (in press, §3.2) with literature.

REFERENCES

Astour, M. (1967) *Hellenosemitica*. Leiden, Brill.

Dinçol, A. M., Yakar, J., Dinçol, B., and Taffet, A. (2000) The Borders of the Appanage Kingdom of Tarhuntassa. *Anatolica* 26, 1–29.

Hajnal. I. (2003) *Troia aus sprachwissenschaftlicher Sicht: Die Struktur einer Argumentation*. Innsbruck, Institut für Sprachen und Literaturen, Abteilung Sprachwissenschaft.

Hawkins, J. D. (2000) *Corpus of Hieroglyphic Luwian Inscriptions*, Vol. I,2, Berlin, de Gruyter.

Heubeck, A. (1961) *Praegraeca: Sprachliche Untersuchungen zum vorgriechisch-indogermanischen Substrat*. Erlangen, Universität Erlangen.

Hutter, M. (1995) Der luwische Wettergott *pihassassi* und der griechische Pegasos. In M. Ofitsch and C. Zinko (eds.) *Studia Onomastica et Indogermanica. Festschrift für Fritz Lochner von Hüttenbach zum 65. Geburtstag*, 79–97. Graz, Leykam.

Katz, J. T. (1998) How to be a Dragon in Indo-European: Hittite *illuyankas* and its Linguistic and Cultural Congeners in Latin, Greek and Germanic. In J. Jasanoff et al. (eds.), *Mír Curad: Studies in Honour of Calvert Watkins*, 317–34. Innsbruck, Innsbrücker Beiträge zur Sprachwissenschaft.

Landau, O. (1959) *Mykenisch-griechische Personennamen*. Göteborg, Almquist & Wiksell.

Melchert. H. C. (1994) *Anatolian Historical Phonology*. Leiden Studies in Indo-European 3. Amsterdam, Rodopi.

___ (1998) Once More Greek *tolúpē*. *Orpheus* 8 (Memorial volume for V. Georgiev), 47–51.

Oettinger, N. (1998) Review of H. C. Melchert, *Anatolian Historical Phonology*. Amsterdam, Rodopi. *Kratylos* 43, 96–108.

___ (2002) *Die griechische Psilose als Kontaktphänomen*, 95–101. Münchener Studien zur Sprachwissenschaft 62. München.

___ (in press) Überlegungen zu gr. äol. *ámphen* „Nacken", lat. *anguis* „Schlange" und heth. *illuyanka-*. In Festschrift for J. J. S. Weitenberg.

Otten, H. (1967) *Sprachliche Stellung und Datierung des Madduwatta-Textes*. Wiesbaden, Harrassowitz.

___ (1988) *Die Bronzetafel aus Boğazköy. Ein Staatsvertrag Tuthalijas IV.* Wiesbaden, Harrassowitz.

Singer, I. (2006) Ships Bound for Lukka: A New Interpretation of the Companion Letters RS 94.2530 and RS 94.2523. *Altorientalische Forschungen* 33, 242–62.

Starke, F. (1997) Troia im Kontext des historisch-politischen und sprachlichen Umfeldes Kleinasiens im 2. Jahrtausend. *Studia Troica* 7, 447–87.

Tekoğlu, R. et al. (2000) La bilingue royale louvito-phénicienne de Çineköy. In *Comptes rendus des scéances de l'année* 2000, 961–1007. Paris, Académie des inscriptions et belles-lettres.

Vanschoonwinkel, J. (1990) Mopsos: légendes et réalité. *Hethitica* 10, 185–211.

Watkins, C. (1995) *How to Kill a Dragon: Aspects of Indo-European Poetics*. Oxford, Oxford University.

Zgusta, L. (1964) *Kleinasiatische Personennamen*. Prague, Tschechoslowakischen Akademie der Wissenschaften.

6

SETTING UP THE GODDESS OF THE NIGHT SEPARATELY

Jared L. Miller

Local hypostases of supra-regional deities are well known to any student of the ancient Near East; so well known, in fact, that this rather remarkable phenomenon is seldom the topic of further inquiry. It is not often asked, for example, perhaps because the answers seem self-evident, how there could be an Ishtar of Nineveh and an Ishtar of Hattusa? Were these two hypostases essentially the same deity, worshipped at two different places, or two distinct personalities? How did the two forms come into being? If a single entity, how did the deity reside in two distinct temples? And perhaps most importantly: How did the worshippers perceive their deities and the processes by which they became differentiated?

Fortunately for the researcher interested in the answers to such questions, there exists a passage that is, to the best of my knowledge, unique in ancient Near Eastern literature, an incantation that provides much insight into a process of differentiation that presumably would have happened repeatedly in polytheistic cultures such as those of the ancient Near East, Anatolia and Greece. The passage occurs in a composition commonly known, after Heinz Kronasser's 1963 edition, as *Die Umsiedelung der schwarzen Gottheit*, but more appropriately described as the Expansion or "Adlocation" of the Goddess of the Night.[1] This remarkable composition is, to paraphrase its incipit, intended for when a man takes it upon himself to build a second temple for the Goddess of the Night (DINGIR GE_6) and for setting up the Goddess of the Night herself separately.

The rites consist mainly of preparing all the paraphernalia needed for the new temple, which are exhaustively listed, then evoking the "old" deity, as she is called, into the "old" temple so that she can be worshipped and sacrificed to in a manner to which she is accustomed. Once the deity is comfortable and content, then comes the crucial incantation (§22):

> Honored deity! Preserve your being, but divide your divinity! Come to that new temple, too, and take yourself the honored place! And when you make your way, then take yourself only that place!

This "new deity" is then afforded in her new temple all the customary rites that the old deity received in her original temple.

This splitting of the deity and her relocation seems not to have been without some risk in the mind of the person(s) composing the incantation. The deity is explicitly asked to preserve her being while dividing her divinity, and she is admonished to come specifically to the place intended, that is, to the new temple built for her, perhaps to ward off the possibility that she might wander off to some other location, in the worst case, to some enemy land, a constant fear among the Hittites. This incantation seems to imply that the deity was conceived of as a single entity, a distinct personality, which, however, could divide herself into two parts that would each retain the qualities of the original singularity.[2]

Since Beal has recently devoted an article to splitting deities (2002), I will concentrate rather on the development and wanderings of the Goddess of the Night, as an attempt to trace her steps may help us better understand the processes of syncretization and differentiation seen in the polytheistic religions of the ancient Near East and beyond.

In the modern secondary literature, the Goddess of the Night is normally associated, even identified, with Ishtar,[3] who of course is at least typologically related to Aphrodite.[4] More specifically, it is generally accepted that the Goddess of the Night is Ishtar's Venus aspect, even if, as we shall see, the evidence for this equation is less than robust and not without its difficulties. As Beckman wrote in his study of Ishtar of Nineveh, "any special features of the (Ishtar) varieties will become apparent only if each is initially studied in isolation" (1998, 4–5), an approach that clearly bore fruit for Beckman. In keeping with this principle, this paper will attempt to arrive at a more differentiated picture of the Goddess of the Night.

In the Expansion of the Goddess of the Night composition just mentioned (henceforth Expansion), it cannot be ascertained where the original temple and deity was located or where the new home of the new deity was established, and the event can only be dated roughly to perhaps the late-Middle or early-New Hittite period at the latest, that is, some time in the first part of the fourteenth century.

In another text, however, the Great King Mursili II (last third of the fourteenth century) makes reference to a time when his forefather, Tudhaliya I (I/II),[5] split the Goddess of the Night from her temple in Kizzuwatna, that is, approximately classical Cilicia, and worshipped her separately in Samuha,[6] to be sought on the upper Kızılırmak, perhaps near Sivas. Tudhaliya I (I/II) thereby established a temple for this Kizzuwatnean deity in Hittite territory, and the rites that must have been carried out on this occasion presumably would have had much in common with those detailed in the Expansion. This event during the reign of Tudhaliya I (I/II) – which must be kept distinct from the events of the strictly local Expansion[7] – is thus dated to that period of time that sees the start of a deluge of Hurrian and Syrian influence in practically all aspects of religion and culture in Hattusa, and the "adlocation" of the cult from Kizzuwatna to Samuha can be seen as part of this process, which in turn was presumably due to the subjugation and subsequent annexation of Kizzuwatna to Hatti under Tudhaliya I (I/II) and Arnuwanda I toward the end of the Middle Hittite period. It is this Goddess of the Night brought from Kizzuwatna to Samuha who is generally assumed to be identical with Ishtar of Samuha, a deity who plays an important role in later Hittite history, and to whom we shall return in a moment.

This Kizzuwatnean deity, as far as can be judged by the available documentation, which, it should be noted, originates exclusively from Hattusa, seems to have been an autochthonous Kizzuwatnean entity, with no Mesopotamian precursors. No "Deity of the Night" (DINGIR GE_6) is known from Mesopotamia or Syria. There one finds only a general description "gods of the night" (*ilū/ilānī mušīti*) used as a poetic epithet for the stars and/or planets and the various gods associated with them.[8] This is practically all that one can say about the Goddess of the Night as she existed in Kizzuwatna before her importation into Hatti. Much of what will be said in the remainder of this chapter *may* also have applied to the deity in Kizzuwatna, but is known only concerning the deity as witnessed in Hatti.

As mentioned, the Goddess of the Night is generally identified with Ishtar or considered to be her Venus aspect. The earliest, and among the best, evidence for the association of the Goddess of the Night with Ishtar is a passage from a Middle Hittite oracle investigation, in which two local hypostases of the Goddess of the Night are the subject of inquiry immediately following an inquiry concerning one Ishtar hypostasis and immediately preceding an inquiry concerning four more Ishtars, and finally, an inquiry aimed at ascertaining if any Ishtar at all is angry.[9]

A further support for the association is the fact that the Goddess of the Night and a deity named Pirinkir are worshipped as a dyad of sorts in the Expansion, while the names Ishtar and Pirinkir are used seemingly interchangeably in a set of rituals in which the incantations are set down in *babilili*, that is, in the language of Babylon, Akkadian.[10] This fits nicely with an incantation found in the Expansion in which the Goddess of the Night, apparently along with Pirinkir, is evoked (§25) "from Akkade, from Babylon, from Susa, from Elam (and) from the Ḫur.sağ.kalam.ma in the city that you[(fem. sg.)] love." Akkade, Babylon and the temple precinct Ḫur.sağ.kalam.ma in Kish are of course well-known cult centers of Ishtar, while Susa in Elam was the original place of worship during the second half of the third millennium of Pinenkir, the progenitor of the Anatolian Pirinkir.[11]

Also supporting the association between the Goddess of the Night and Ishtar is the hermaphroditic character of both. This trait for the Goddess of the Night is best seen, again, in the Expansion, in which she is provided with sets of clothing and utensils of both genders (§8), and in which she is addressed as essentially female.[12] The hermaphroditic character of Ishtar need not be further detailed.[13]

Hence, if one considers only the evidence mentioned thus far, one could confidently assert that the Goddess of the Night in Kizzuwatna and Hatti is to be identified with Ishtar, and to what aspect of Ishtar could the epithet "Deity of the Night" refer if not the Venus star? However, this ignores some evidence that might cause one to temper, though not necessarily reject, these conclusions.

First, it is actually quite uncertain that the epithet "Deity of the Night" refers to the Venus star, an assumption based solely on the association of the Goddess of the Night with Ishtar,[14] who indeed is known in Mesopotamia to be seen in the Venus star.[15] The Venus aspect is actually nowhere attested for Ishtar, the Goddess of the Night or Pirinkir in Anatolia, except in the list of oath deities in the Suppiluliuma-Shattiwaza Treaty. Here, however, a closer look suggests that the usage ^{d}*Ištar* ^{MUL}*Dil-bat*, "Ishtar, the Venus star," may be rather Mittannian than Hittite.[16] Further, the Sumerogram DINGIR GE$_6$, when found in Anatolian personal names, represents not a star, but the moon, and alternates with ^{d}30, generally indicating in Anatolian context the Luwian name of the moon-god, Arma.[17] This evidence should not be neglected when considering the nature of the Goddess of the Night, as odd as it may seem for a deity apparently associated with Ishtar.

Second, the Goddess of the Night shows one feature that Ishtar, at least as she is known in Mesopotamia, never elicits, namely an infernal aspect.[18] This is seen from the fact that she is evoked up out of the netherworld through an offering pit dug in the earth, a rite typical of, though not restricted to, the heterogeneous religious culture of Kizzuwatna. Interestingly, Ishtar is also attested in one text passage of Kizzuwatnean ilk as being evoked up from the underworld in similar fashion,[19] and hence, while this feature does not exclude an association or identity of the Goddess of the Night and Ishtar, she would certainly be a deity who possesses some unique characteristics in comparison with Ishtar known from Mesopotamia.

Further insight into the nature and development of the Goddess of the Night and her relationship to Ishtar is gained by a diachronic analysis of the texts concerning her and Ishtar of Samuha.[20] It will be remembered that the Goddess of the Night divided in Kizzuwatna and "adplanted" in Samuha by Tudhaliya I (I/II) is often taken by modern researchers as the progenitor of, or identical with, Ishtar of Samuha.

The first result yielded by a diachronic analysis is that the Goddess of the Night is well attested in the mid to late Middle Hittite period, with an active cult relating to her, while Ishtar of Samuha is absent from the textual sources.[21] At the same time there is evidence, in the form of the Middle Hittite oracle investigation mentioned above, that the Goddess of the Night of Samuha was grouped with the Ishtar deities even during this early period. Still, she seems to have maintained a separate identity, never being confused with, or subsumed by, Ishtar, and in the oracular investigation she is referred to by her epithet "Deity of the Night" even while listed among the other Ishtars. The scribe could, after all, simply have written "Ishtar of Samuha" if there were no difference between the two deities.

Moreover, there is already at this point in the latter part of the Middle Hittite period an Ishtar to be found in Samuha, but this is Ishtar of Tamininga,[22] who was worshipped in Samuha, perhaps because there was no hypostasis there who was considered a real Ishtar deity. Was it this deity, rather than the Goddess of the Night, who eventually became Ishtar of Samuha? When exactly in the latter part of the Middle Hittite period Ishtar of Tamininga was brought to Samuha is impossible to ascertain, but if she were already there during the reign of Tudhaliya I (I/II), why would he have brought the Goddess of the Night to Samuha from Kizzuwatna if she were simply another Ishtar or some aspect thereof? Conversely, if the Goddess of the

Night was the first to have been imported to Samuha, why would Ishtar of Tamininga have then been brought to Samuha if there were already an Ishtar resident there? This seems to suggest that there was sufficient distinction during this period between Ishtar and the Goddess of the Night to warrant both being worshipped separately in the same town.

The Middle Hittite period thus provides ample data, as well as unanswered questions, concerning the Goddess of the Night. In the New Hittite period, in contrast, there is little evidence for further worship of the Goddess of the Night. Most of the activity concerned with her consists of copying and cataloguing the Middle Hittite texts already extant. Ishtar of the Field and Ishtar of Samuha, in contrast, experience a flurry of cult activity during the reigns of Mursili II and his son Hattusili III, respectively, who venerated these Ishtar hypostases as their patron deities. Hattusili III even further "split" Ishtar of Samuha in order to found an additional cult for her in the town of Urikina.[23] The copying and cataloguing activity relating to the Goddess of the Night during the reigns of Mursili II and Hattusili III seems to be connected to the rise in prominence of Ishtar of the Field and Ishtar of Samuha and may have been part of some kind of "background research" into the nature and history of these Ishtar hypostases.

This activity even included a reform of the cult of the Goddess of the Night in Samuha by Mursili II, who felt that the worship of the deity had become corrupted since the days of his forefather, Tudhaliya I (I/II). In the incipit of Mursili's Reform we read: [24]

> When my forefather, Tudhaliya, Great King, split the Goddess of the Night from the temple of the Goddess of the Night in Kizzuwatna and worshipped her separately in a temple in Samuha, those rituals and obligations which he determined in the temple of the Goddess of the Night – it came about, however, that the wooden tablet scribes and the temple personnel began incessantly to alter them – I, Mursili, Great King, have re-edited them from the tablets.

This text thus gives the impression that the cult of the Goddess of the Night received new impetus at this point during the reign of Mursili II, if, that is, she is not simply to be equated by this time with his Ishtar of the Field. If indeed Mursili's Reform indicates a reinvigorated cult, it may have been a last gasp of sorts for the active and separate cult of the Goddess of the Night, for in the great offering lists for Ishtar of Samuha dating to the time of Hattusili III,[25] the Goddess of the Night is not even mentioned, though the entire entourage of Ishtar is listed, including Pirinkir, along with many deities who can hardly be said to have belonged to Ishtar's inner circle. It is difficult to imagine that the Goddess of the Night, who had formerly enjoyed such prominence, would not even have been mentioned if indeed she maintained a separate identity and cult. Hence, the "revival" of interest in the Goddess of the Night during this period might be largely a scribal phenomenon related to the interest in the Ishtar deities of Mursili and Hattusili rather than a genuine revival of an active cult.

It is also during this period, and up to the end of the Empire – and only during this late period – that the signs DINGIR GE_6 are used in personal names to represent the Luwian Moon-god, Arma.[26] How this is to be explained remains a mystery. No known Ishtar hypostasis, to the best of my knowledge, has a real lunar aspect. Neither would it otherwise be conceivable for a sign/signs representing Ishtar to be used in personal names to signify the Moon-god, especially since Ishtar is essentially female, the Moon-god male. Yet the epithet "Deity of the Night" would clearly be a more apt description of the moon than any other nocturnal body, and this should be remembered when considering whether or not the Goddess of the Night might be the Venus aspect of Ishtar. Are we to assume that the Goddess of the Night really was a lunar deity, despite her obvious affiliation with Ishtar, but that this aspect remained undetectable throughout the Middle Hittite and early New Hittite periods, only to surface in personal names so late in Hittite history? This seems somehow unlikely. Did the Goddess of the Night at this late stage of her evolution begin to develop a lunar aspect? This seems no more probable than the first suggestion. Does, then, the alternation signify no more than a playful graphic innovation, by which the scribes sought to represent in a descriptive manner the moon-god, the dominant deity of the night sky, without intending to transfer with the graphic representation the person and nature of the Goddess of the Night? Were the New Hittite scribes who employed the grapheme DINGIR GE_6 to represent the moon-god Arma completely unaware of the existence of a Goddess of the Night associated with Ishtar? If so, perhaps no further theological implications need be derived from the phenomenon. Unfortunately, this explanation is no more convincing than the others, especially since at least one scribe responsible for the writing of the personal names was a scribe of Puduhepa, queen of Hattusili, and hence, presumably would have been aware of the nature and history of the Goddess of the Night.

In conclusion, the dividing and "adplanting" of the Goddess of the Night from one cultural sphere to another represent just one stage in the development and evolution of this deity, much of which should perhaps be left open for debate rather than glossed over by a hasty identification with Ishtar or an aspect thereof.

NOTES

1 See the most recent edition in Miller (2004, 272–312) as well as the translation by Collins (1997).

2 This may be contrasted with the oft-quoted passage in which Puduhepa, in her prayer to the Sun-goddess of Arinna, seems to imply that the "Sun-goddess of Arinna" and "Hebat" are simply two names for the same deity (*KUB* 21.27 i 4–6; see Singer 2002, 102): "In Hatti you have given yourself the name Sun-goddess of Arinna; but the land which you made, that of the cedar, there you gave yourself the name Hebat."

3 E.g., Lebrun (1976, 16); Wegner (1981, 163–65); Haas (1994, 352–53); similarly, Beckman (1999, 30).

4 The most thorough study to of Ishtar as known from Anatolia is that of Wegner (1981).

5 For argumentation in favor of Tudhaliya I (I/II) being the one referred to in Mursili's Reform, see Miller (2004, 350–56).

6 For this text, which could be dubbed "Mursili's Reform of the Cult of the Goddess of the Night" (henceforth "Mursili's Reform"), see Miller (2004, 312–19).

7 For the argumentation concerning this point, see Miller (2004, 357–62).

8 For an alternative opinion, see Mouton (2004, 88).

9 *KBo* 16.97+*KBo* 40.48 rev. 12–32. The deities in the order of their appearance are: *IŠTAR* of Nineveh; the Goddess of the Night of Samuha; the Goddess of the Night of Lahhurama; *IŠTAR* of Nineveh; *IŠTAR* of Hattarina; *IŠTAR* of his mother; *IŠTAR* of his father; any other *IŠTAR*. (The pronoun of "his mother/father" in the second and third to last inquiries presumably refers to the king who instigated the oracle inquiry.) See edition and involved discussion of terminology in Schuol (1994, 73–124, 247–304) and evaluation of its historical contents and setting by de Martino (1992) and Klinger (1998, 108–111); see also Miller (2004, 355, 365, 379–80).

10 No edition of the *babilili* texts has yet been published, a desideratum that Beckman (2002, 35), in his discussion of the texts, has announced he plans to fulfill.

11 See Beckman (1999); Kühne (1993, 245–46).

12 See discussion in Wegner (1981, 163–64).

13 See, e.g., the various contributions in *NIN: Journal of Gender Studies in Antiquity* 1 (2000); Groneberg (1986); Wegner (1981, 46–55).

14 It should be noted here that the inclusion of a *wannupattalla/i*-"star" symbol among the accoutrements of the Deity of the Night in the Expansion text (§§2, 17) cannot necessarily be used as support for the equation since the exact meaning of the word *wannupattalla/i*- is yet to be determined. See discussion in Riemschneider (2004, 279); cf. Kronasser (1969, 313), Kümmel (1967, 370). It should in any case be noted that mul.á.gú.zi.ga in RS 25.421, 13′ (Ug. V, No. 169) is fully restored, and therefore cannot lend any credence to the equation, as implied in *HW* 3. Erg., s.v., and followed elsewhere.

15 Pirinkir is also associated with the Venus star at Emar; see Beckman (1999, 27–28).

16 See *KBo* 1.1 rev. 45′, 57′, *KBo* 1.2 rev. 22′–23′, 33′, *KBo* 1.3(+)*KUB* 3.17 rev. 42′; for the distribution of the attestations and further discussion, see Miller (2004, 391 n. 622).

17 See Miller (2004, 370–73).

18 The possibility exists that this feature might have accrued to Ishtar already in northern Syria, judging from the entry "*a-na* ᵈINANNA *ša a-bi* ..." in the *zukru*-festival text from Emar (see Emar VI/3, No. 373, 92'; Fleming 2000, 186–87 and n. 200, with references), but the meaning of *abi* in this context is disputed. I wish to thank Yori Cohen, Tel Aviv, for directing my attention to this attestation and to his discussion of it (2003, 271).

19 *KUB* 15.35+*KBo* 2.9 i 21–55; see Miller (2004, 374–76).
20 See Miller (2004, 378–90).
21 For a discussion of the one possible exception, *KUB* 32.130, see Miller (2004, 385–87), where it is maintained that this text should likely be dated to the early New Hittite period.
22 See ChS I/3-1, No. 12 and discussion in Miller (2004, 384, n. 600).
23 *KUB* 21.17 ii 5–8; see Miller (2004, 360, n. 514).
24 *KUB* 32.133 i 1-7; see Miller (2004, 312).
25 E.g., *KUB* 27.1 (ChS I/3-1, Nr. 1); see also *KUB* 6.45++ i 43–45 (see Singer 1996, 10, 33, 54).
26 See Miller (2004, 370–73).

REFERENCES

Beal, R. H. (2002) Dividing a God. In P. Mirecki and M. Meyer (eds.) *Magic and Ritual in the Ancient World*. Religions in the Graeco-Roman World 141. Leiden, Brill.

Beckman, G. M. (1998) Ishtar of Nineveh Reconsidered. *Journal of Cuneiform Studies* 50, 1–10.

___ (1999) The Goddess Pirinkir and Her Ritual from Ḫattuša (CTH 644). *Ktêma* 24, 25–39.

___ (2002) Babyloniaca Hethitica: The "babilili-Ritual" from Boğazköy (CTH 718). In K. A. Yener and H. A. Hoffner, Jr. (eds.) *Recent Developments in Hittite Archaeology and History. Papers in Memory of Hans G. Güterbock*, 35–41. Winona Lake, IN, Eisenbrauns.

Cohen, Y. (2003) Review of D. E. Fleming, *Time at Emar*. *Orientalia NS* 72, 267–74.

Collins, B. J. (1997) Rituals. In W. W. Hallo (ed.) *The Context of Scripture. Vol. I. Canonical Compositions from the Biblical World*, 160–77. Leiden, Brill.

de Martino, S. (1992) Personaggi e riferimenti storici nel testo oracolare ittito KBo XVI 97. *Studi micenaei ed egeo-anatolici* 29, 33–46.

Fleming, D. E. (2000) *Time at Emar: The Cultic Calendar and the Rituals from the Diviner's Archive*. Mesopotamian Civilizations 11. Winona Lake, IN, Eisenbrauns.

Groneberg, B. (1986) Die sumerisch-akkadische Inanna/Ishtar: Hermaphroditos? *Die Welt des Orients* 17, 25–46.

Haas, V. (1994) *Geschichte der hethitischen Religion*. Handbuch der Orientalistik I/15. Leiden, Brill.

Klinger, J. (1998) Zur Historizität einiger hethitischer Omina. *Altorientalische Forschungen* 25, 104–11.

Kronasser, H. (1963) *Die Umsiedelung der schwarzen Gottheit. Das hethitische Ritual KUB XXIX 4 (des Ulippi)*. Österreichische Akademie der Wissenschaften, Philosophische-Historische Klasse, Sitzungsberichte, 241. Band, 3. Abhandlung. Wien, Hermann Böhlaus.

___ (1969) Review of J. Friedrich, HW, 3. Erg. *Wiener Zeitschrift für die Kunde des Morgenlands* 62, 311–14.

Kühne, C. (1993) Zum Vor-Opfer im alten Anatolien. In B. Janowski, K. Koch and G. Wilhelm (eds.) *Religionsgeschichtliche Beziehungen zwischen Kleinasien, Nordsyrien und dem Alten Testament. Internationales Symposion Hamburg 17.-21. März 1990*, 225–85. Orbis Biblicus et Orientalis 129. Freiburg/Göttingen, Universitätsverlag/Vandenhoeck & Ruprecht.

Kümmel, H. M. (1967) Review of J. Friedrich, *HW*, 3. Erg. *Orientalia NS* 36, 365–72.

Lebrun, R. (1976) *Samuha. Foyer religieux de l'empire Hittite*. Publications de l'Institut Orientaliste de Louvain 11. Louvain-la-Neuve, Institut Orientaliste de l'Université Catholique de Louvain.

Miller, J. L. (2004) *Studies in the Origins, Development and Interpretation of the Kizzuwatna Rituals*, StBoT 46. Wiesbaden, Harrassowitz.

Mouton, A. (2004) Le rituel hittite de Walkui (*KBo* 32.176): quelques réflexions sur la deesse de la nuit et l'image du porc dans le monde hittite. *Zeitschrift für Assyriologie* 94, 85–105.

Riemschneider, K. K. (2004) *Die akkadischen und hethitischen Omentexte aus Boğazköy*, Dresdner Beiträge zur Hethitologie 12. Dresden, Verlag der Technischen Universität Dresden.

Schuol, M. (1994) Die Terminologie des hethitischen ŠU-Orakels. Eine Untersuchung auf der Grundlage des mittelhethitischen Textes KBo XVI 97 unter vergleichender Berücksichtigung akkadischer Orakeltexte und Lebermodelle. *Altorientalische Forschungen* 21, 73–124, 247–304.

Singer, I. (1996) *Muwatalli's Prayer to the Assembly of Gods through the Storm-God of Lightning (CTH 381)*. Atlanta, Scholars Press.

___ (2002) *Hittite Prayers*, WAW 11. Atlanta, GA, Society of Biblical Literature.

Wegner, I. (1981) *Gestalt und Kult der Ishtar-Šawuška in Kleinasien*, AOAT 36. Neukirchen-Vluyn, Neukirchener/Butzon and Bercker.

7

THE SONGS OF THE *ZINTUḪIS*: CHORUS AND RITUAL IN ANATOLIA AND GREECE

Ian C. Rutherford

GREEK AND ANATOLIAN SONG CULTURES[1]

Considering that our knowledge of Anatolian religion in the Late Bronze Age is so extensive, it is surprising that no systematic attempt has yet been made to compare and contrast it with Aegean religion.[2] This broader project would have two parts: a) a comparison of Late Bronze Age Anatolian religion with what we know of Aegean religion in the same period; b) a comparison of it with what we know of the much better-attested Greek religion in the Iron Age, i.e., the "Archaic" and "Classical" periods, using this to reconstruct what might have been the relationship between the two cultures in the Bronze Age. In the case of a), the absence is partly to be explained by the fact that the sources for Aegean religion in the Late Bronze Age are somewhat inferior to those we have for Anatolia of the same period; those that we do have are different in kind: archaeological and iconographical rather than textual, and Linear B sources provide at best only a very oblique perspective into Mycenaean religion. As for b), the problem here is perhaps partly one of disciplinarity: Anatolian sources are not ones that most students of classical Greek religion have a familiarity with, and the high volume of the evidence, as well as its inaccessibility, may well have been off-putting.

As a contribution towards getting this project started, this paper sets out to examine one often-neglected aspect of ritual performance in Anatolia and the Aegean, namely, the use of the choral performance of song to accompany ritual. The performance of choral song is familiar from Archaic and Classical Greece, which has been described as a "song culture" (Herington 1985; see more recently Habinek 2005). Performances seem generally to have taken place in social and religious contexts, particularly festivals. We can perhaps distinguish three modes of performance (on choral performance in ancient Greece, see Calame 1977; Herington 1985; Rutherford 2001a, 2001b):

a. performances that accompanied a ritual action whose primary performers were distinct from the singers;

b. performances that were ritual acts in themselves, not simply accompanying someone else's ritual act, though they may well have been part of a ritual complex; examples here would include hymns to the gods, with the purpose of praising them or invoking an epiphany;

c. performances that took place at religious festivals, although they were neither ritual actions themselves, nor closely accompanied by ritual actions; here belongs the use of choral songs in poetic competitions, such as the use of the dithyramb at the Athenian Dionysia festival.

Performers were generally ordinary members of society, male or female, adult or children; more rarely they were members of specialized religious or political groups. The point of choral performance may have varied: the aesthetic effect of synchronized musicality may have been part of it, and most of it in the context of festival competitions, but in most cases the main purpose was probably to enhance the effect of the ritual: in choral performance the message of the song is amplified by the unison voices of the singers and by their synchronised movements. For members of an age group, the performance of choral song may have had the effect of generating a sense of social cohesion, "communitas," in Victor Turner's language, and it may also have been used by ruling elites as a medium to convey traditional authority, either to the performers or to the audience (Bloch 1974).

In Minoan Crete and Mycenaean Greece, song is likely to have played a considerable role. Oblique support for this hypothesis has been found in the poetic language of the Greek language in the first millennium BCE, which seems in some respects to reflect Mycenaean Greek (Trümpy 1986). The Bronze Age evidence for choral performance is mostly material culture and iconography. Many fragments of musical instruments have been found in Aegean tombs, including *phorminxes*, wind instruments, and percussion instruments (Younger 1998, 63–65). Musical performance is also a common subject in Mycenaean and Minoan frescoes, some of the more important examples of which are (Kontorli-Papadopoulou 1996, 151–53):

K-P29 (i.e., n. 29 in the catalogue in Kontorli-Papadopoulou 1996): grand staircase Knossos, musician leads procession of men with offerings
K-P37: Ayia Triadha, procession with lyre-player
K-P98: Pylos, lyre player and bird, together with male figures at a banquet

In each of these cases there are other figures in the fresco who could be taking part in song. Among frescoes that could illustrate dance is, most importantly, K-P9 from Knossos, the "sacred grove and dance festival," which seems to have a grove of trees in the upper band and in the lower band a group of women who are generally interpreted as dancing; if they are dancing, they could be singing as well. Related to this are certain seal rings from Crete and mainland Greece that seem to illustrate groups of people expecting or reacting to divine epiphany (Matz 1958, 388–89). Finally, we should mention the painted *larnakes* found at Tanagra in Boeotia, some of which portray groups of women, who are likely to be mourning (to make a reasonable inference from the funerary context) and could possibly be singing lamentations as well (Immerwahr 1995). On the other hand, texts make virtually no contribution. We have no references to performers in Mycenaean texts, except for the recently published text from Thebes mentioning lyre-players (*ru-ra-te-a* in Thebes Av106.7; Aravantinos, Goddart, Sacconi 2001, 177–79), and certainly no accounts of performances or texts of songs. This is not necessarily evidence of absence: the surviving Linear B texts are simply the wrong medium.

For song in Bronze Age Anatolia, the evidence is much better, at least the textual evidence. Three sorts of texts are relevant: first, we have accounts of Anatolian festivals, particularly festivals that involve the king and queen, and these contain many references to song; second, we have texts of the songs themselves, or at least a few of them, and thirdly, we have library catalogues that mention texts of songs. If you put all this together, we have quite a good picture, recently synthesized in Monika Schuol's monograph on the subject (Schuol 2004).

In order to understand the Anatolian evidence, we have to take account of the complex and layered nature of Anatolian society, in which four cultures and religious traditions played a particularly important role[3]: first the culture and religion of the Indo-European speaking Hittites themselves who seem to have migrated into central Anatolia, perhaps about the eighteenth century BC; second, the culture of the non-Indo-European-speaking "Hattic" people, who were probably the main local culture in central Anatolia before the arrival of the Hittites; third, the Indo-European Luwian culture, which existed in the west and south of Anatolia; and fourth, the Hurrian culture of Mitanni in northern Syria, whose culture and religion were adopted by the Hittites, especially from the fifteenth century BC.

Each of these cultures had its own traditions of song, known almost entirely through the Hittite state archives. The *modus operandi* of the Hittite kingdom, like that of many ancient empires, was not to impose its own religion on the peoples whose territory it came to control, but rather to make use of the religious traditions that it found, drawing the gods of its subject peoples to itself. Any deity the Hittites appropriated had to be worshipped exactly as in its home country, which meant performing songs in the original language.[4]

Ironically, the song culture of the Hittites themselves is the one we know least about. Hittite texts refer to "singers of Kanes," who are likely to have sung in the Hittite or "Nesite" language, but there is little evidence about the nature of the songs they sang.[5]

HATTIC CHORAL SONG

In this paper, I will concentrate on the song culture of the "Hattic" stratum, which is comparatively well documented, though poorly understood (because our understanding of the Hattic language remains very basic), and almost wholly neglected when it comes to comparative work (see Klinger 1996; Soysal 2004). Most of our evidence for these comes from texts that give a running order for festival or rituals. Embedded in these we find many Hattic songs, usually just a few lines, and always anonymous; it is likely that in some cases fuller versions of the songs were recorded in separate tablets, as in the case of the "Songs of the Women of Tissaruliya" (see Ex. 5 below). The performers are generally groups of singers, choirs or "choruses," we might say. Many of them are composed of girls, called by the Hittite word "*zintuḫis*," which is sometimes written with the sumerogram KI.SIKIL (on *zintuḫis*, see Jian 1994; Schuol 2004, 147–48; Soysal 2004, 328, who doubts whether the word is Hattic); we also find choruses of men and women, though generally not boys.

Some of the key points that can be made about the performance of the songs and their performers are these:

- The context for all or almost all of our evidence is rituals and festivals (e.g., the *purulli* or the KI.LAM), which were deemed to be importance to the Hittite state and in which the Hittite royal family took part. Thus, we see the Hattic data from the point of view of Hittite hegemony (see Gilan this volume).
- Various modes of performance are described; the singers usually process or stand; they are not said to dance as they sing, with a few exceptions (see Ex. 10 below). They may prostrate themselves (cf. Popko 1994, 159).
- Performance often accompanies and supports a ritual action, and is not the main focus of attention in itself; i.e., it falls into the second of the three modes of performance distinguished in section 1.
- Performance is often antiphonal. The leader of the chorus is generally said to "shout" (*ḫalzai-*), while the chorus chant in response ("*kattan arku*"; the verb *arku* seems to be related to Vedic *ṛc*, as in "*Ṛg Veda*"). The antiphonal performance as a whole is referred to by the verb "*išḫamai*" ("sing"), an Indo-European word, which seems to be connected to Vedic *saman*, as in "Sama-Veda."[6] So too some Luwian performances were antiphonal (for antiphonal performance and Wechselgesänge, see Klinger 1996, 277–84).
- Performers are sometimes specified as being affiliated with a certain town. This may in some cases have amounted to a temple, but in some cases it may have been just that, namely, a town.

The nature of the material is best understood by looking at some examples. I begin with texts that show performers processing. In the first of these, a priestess called the *entu* makes a ritual journey to two towns, Tawinia and Wargatawi, and to a shrine of the goddess Teteshapi situated in a wood, and the *zintuḫis* sing at various points along the way.

Ex. 1: The priest lifts the goddess Teteshapi ... and they turn the *ḫuluganni*-wagon. The *entu*-priestess sits down and goes to the town of Tawinia. The "lords of speech" march.

The *zintuḫis* sing this song: *talaya talayata*. And they answer. Further, the chief of the *zintuḫis* shouts: *emamurišta iyanni wurella*, and they answer.

When the *entu*-priestess approaches the city of Wargatawi, they offer a drink to the *entu*.

The *zintuḫis* ...

The priest lifts the goddess and brings her into the tents. The *entu*-priestess goes in, and sits down in the *ḫuluganni*-wagon. The man of the staff rushes forward.

She goes to the wood, to the *uḫuruš*-tree, and the *zintuḫis* behind her sing: "*talaya talayata*." When she reaches the wood, leaving the tent there(?), the *entu*-priestess comes down from the *ḫuluganni*-wagon. And the priest brings the god of the tent. The *entu*-pristess and the AMA.DINGIR-*LIM* (another priestess) go in.

(*KUB* 20.17 = *KUB* 11.32 cols. ii, iii, iv, v)

Here, then, antiphonal song of the *zintuḫis* accompanies ritual action, "walking behind" the procession, and singing when it approaches a point of significance.

The Gatehouse, or KI.LAM, festival is one of the best-documented festivals in the Hittite calendar (Singer 1986; Rutherford 2005). A fragmentary library catalogue refers to *zintuḫis* singing the "songs of the KI.LAM" (*KUB* 30.68; Singer 1983–1984, 1.48; Dardano 2006, 194–95), and we have fragments of a "liturgy" for the festival, comprising the words that people sang. One of the central sections of the KI.LAM-festival was a spectacular procession, involving all sorts of cult functionaries and religious symbols. There were dancers (LÚ.MEŠ.ḪUB.BI), a reciter (*palwatala-*), and a group of singers called "the men of Anunuwa" (Singer 1983–1984, 2.15 [text]; 1.90 [analysis]; also Klinger 1996, 237–38):

Ex. 2: They strike the Inanna-instrument.
the men of Anunuwa sing like this:
[ ]*zu wamaniya*
[ ]*izuwatueš*
[ ] *kanewa*
[ ] *šaliu*
And they clash their spears

Notice that in this case the performance is not antiphonal. Interestingly, there are indications that the men of Anunuwa performed in a similar way, singing and clashing their spears in other festivals also, so that it would be reasonable to think of them as a group with a well-defined performance style in rituals (for references, see Rutherford 2005).

Another example of procession are a group of songs performed by a chorus who ascend "Mount Daha," a sacred peak in the vicinity of Zippalanda. Our fragment seems to come at the end of the sequence (*KUB* 48.21; Popko.1994, 156–58; Kllinger 1996, 7–15):

Ex. 3: *ma*[?]*-a-a-ša* [ ] *maizzi-x* [ ] *waḫga-x-za x-x-x-x* [
Seventh song of the ascent of Mt. Daha
ma wiulla wiulla wiulla maizzi wiulla wiulla šaḫapuna wiulla
Eighth song of the ascent of Mt. Daha

In this case, the performance does not, as far as we can tell, accompany another ritual activity, although if we had the full context things might look different,

A fourth example of procession comes from a text describing a six-say festival concerning the deity Telepinu in the towns of Kasha and Hanhana (Haas and Jakob-Rost 1984). On day three, the statue of Telepinu is taken to a river and purified. This seems to have been performed to the accompaniment of song. One text mentions an *arraš išḫamai* "song of washing" (text 8 in H/J-R),[7] another describes how on the return journey girls sing (p.46J/J–R).

Ex4: The four priests of Kasha turn their eyes to the river, sit. Then they take livers and hearts, and stand up. Then they speak to the lord of Hanhana like this: "O lord of Hanhana you have vanished into the river."
Then they set the god (Telepinu) on the wagon, and his priest accompanies him and holds the god in place. The equipment of the god and the deities they raise up behind him. They strike cymbals and tambourines before the god, and behind him the girls sing ($^{munus.meš}$KI.SIKIL). In front of the god are the people, three oxen and sheep.

The girls of Kasha are also mentioned in the description of day five of the ritual, when they sing on the roof of the temple of Telepinu at Kasha while the priests perform a ritual there.

Another common mode of performance is to accompany a ritual action, particularly arrival, departure or movement. For example the performances of the "women of Tissaruliya" were described in a special edition in the Hittite archives, which specified the songs performed when the king left the palace to go to "the *huwaši*-shrine." When the king went down from the palace, this chorus sang an antiphonal song, of which we have the beginning and the end (*CTH* 741; see Klinger 1996, 719–26). This is the last verse, which happens to be completely preserved; only the first line changes between verses:

Ex. 5 leader: *zišdu panuela lalankašandyu ailina*
chorus: *alinaiu linaiu ilina muwalina*
leader: *anteggaḫuli*
chorus: *teggaḫuli teka tekaḫuli*

The text states that the king went to the *huwasi*-shrine to swear an oath, they sang a different song, but this one again when he returned to the palace. Again the choral performance accompanies a ritual movement, this time movement by the king, though in this case the singers themselves do not process.

Similarly, according to the archives relating to the Hittite temple at Zippalanda, the local chorus of girls performed songs when the king visited festivals there (*KBo* 23.103).

Ex. 6: When the king goes from Hattusa to Zippalanda, and when the king shows himself, the girls of Zippalanda sing as follows. The first ones cry out: *maiya lula taie taie luwaiu*. And they answer: Tabarna ^{uru}Ḫattuš Tabarna *tuḫanu*. The first ones cry out: *itaš tawarnu šetanu ešta arnu še takaḫziiš* And they answer: *maya lula taie taie luwaiu*

They perform similarly when he drinks to the storm-god of Zippalanda, when he sits on the wagon and when, after a lacuna, "he goes through the great gate of the *ḫalentuwa*." The colophon of this text says: "Tablet One: If the King comes to Zippalanda for the ordinary festival, the girls sing these songs. If the king ever comes to the *purulli*-festival, they sing the same songs on the first day" (*KUB* 23.103; Popko 1994: 154–55).

Another case of performance while a procession takes place is described in a fragment from an unknown ritual where salt is brought from the town of Durmitta; the text says that the *zintuḫis* of the town Tahurpa, through which this procession must have passed, "[sing] in Hattic" (*KBo* 11.73; on salt in Hittite rituals, see Haas 2003, 1, 225–27).

Rarely, singers go round something. In part of the festival for renewing the hunting bags (*kuršaš*), an old hunting bag is taken from Hattusa to the town of Durmitta and there renamed "tutelary deity of Zapatiskuwa." At the ritual in honor of this deity, the singers of Hattusa sing, and the "dog men" bark; then:

Ex. 7: "the singers of the place" (which must be Durmitta) "come in, go once around the hearth and sing." (McMahon 1991, 155 and 179)

Notice that ritual interaction between Hattusa and Durmitta is expressed here via successive performances by two choruses. A hearth also figures in a ritual described in the tablet of the men of Tuhumiyara, probably part of one of the major Hittite festivals, involving the king, various officials and "men of Tuhumiyara" (*CTH* 739 = *KUB* 12.8+). At two points in the ritual, we find the formula:

Ex. 8: The men of Tuhumiyara arrive at the hearth and three men shout, and the *panku* sings thus:
kiruša mai tuḫašta
lammaškai wurum katte
tabarna warak
warašib zuruš iera
kiyaruša
tiltililiaš
tiltililibuš
And they go on

We recognize in the Hattic song reference to the king (*tabarna*) as ruler (*katte*) of the land (*wurum*). Later on, the men of Tuhumiyara are twice themselves said to sing. The word "*panku*" means "totality," and it denotes unison utterance, the chorus complementing the three shouters. The reference may either be to "all the (other) men of Tuhumiyara," or to all persons present, i.e., the congregation (Melchert 1998). Analogy with Ex. 6 suggests that the three men who shout and the *panku* are distinct from the men of Tuhumiyara, whose arrival they celebrate in song.

Elsewhere, no form of movement is mentioned. For example, in a ritual from the sacred city of Nerik (*KUB* 20.10 iv; Haas 1970, 63 and 94),

Ex. 9: a sacred cowherd drives bulls and they lock them in the courtyard. The women of Nerik sing the song of the bulls: "*awan kaitgaḫilu* *ᴰTaru leli lipḫaippin.*"

The theonym Taru seems to be the Hattic name of the local weather-god, and the song of the bulls seems to have begun with an appeal to him (Haas 1970, 63, suggests that *kaitgaḫilu* means "grain"; Soysal 2004, 284 is less certain).

Singing is rarely combined with dancing in the Anatolian song culture, but such combination performances are found occasionally, for example in this festival fragment, which describes the behavior of *zintuḫi*-girls and a group of men called *zinḫuris* (*KBo* 20.40; de Martino 1989; on the *zinḫuri*-men, see Pecchioli-Daddi 1982):

Ex. 10: The *zinḫuri* men come and dance three times. The *zinhuri* men and the girls (*zintuḫis*) sing and for the second time all dance; the girls do not sing; for the third time they take the rope;[8] they sound the Inanna-instruments, and they strike the *argami* instrument. The *zinhuri* men continue to shout out "*zinḫuriya, zinḫuriya.*"

Many of these choirs are being associated with specific places. In the examples above we had:

the women of Tissaruliya (men of Tissaruliya are also singers)
the women of Nerik
the girls of Zippalanda
the girls of Tahurpa
the girls of Kasha
the men of Tuhumiyara
the men of Anunuwa
the singers of "the place" (i.e., Durmitta)

More could be added to this list (see Schuol 2004, 145) for the men of Hursamma and the men of Taggalmuha; from the Luwian tradition we have the men of Istanuwa and the men of Lallupiya). It is quite uncertain how to interpret these, and it is possible that they should not all be interpreted in the same way. Some, such as the women of Nerik and the girls of Zippalanda, may represent permanent or semi-permanent choirs attached to temples (see Rutherford 2004). Others could be a specialized group within the population of a town (the girls of Kasha? the singers of "the place" [i.e., Durmitta]?). Possibly in some cases we should think of the citizens of a town as a whole, for example in the case of the men of Tuhumiyara? (although the surviving evidence does not suggest that every one of the hundreds of towns attested in Hittite texts provided its own choir). Common descriptions such as "women of Tissaruliya" and "men of Anunuwa" pose a special problem for interpretation: are we to suppose that some towns specialized in providing singers for common festivals? Or are such names ways of referring to groups of singers, without reference to any real place?

PARALLELS BETWEEN ANATOLIA AND THE AEGEAN

Attempts to compare the song culture of Late Bronze Age Anatolia and Late Bronze Age or Iron Age Greece have hitherto tended to concentrate on Hurrian and to a lesser extent Luwian. The most-discussed cases are without a doubt the mythological poems that make up the so-called Kingship in Heaven cycle of Hurrian poetry, which have long been believed to have influenced Hesiod's Theogony. The more-recently published Hurrian "Song of Liberation" has been shown to have parallels with Greek epic (see most recently Bachvarova 2005). As far as the Luwian material is concerned, one thinks of Calvert Watkins' argument that one of the "songs of thunder," whose first lines are cited in a ritual text connected with the town of Istanuwa, may have been the opening line of a Luwian poem about the city of Wilusa, and therefore a sort of Luwian correlate to Homer's *Iliad* (Watkins 1986).[9]

Comparison between Hattic choral song and its Greek counterpart, or indeed comparison between any part of the "Hattic" stratum in Anatolian religion and Greece, has not, so far as I am aware, been attempted.[10] Lack of evidence precludes saying anything substantial about song-dance in Greece or Crete in the Late Bronze Age; one might argue that the "sacred grove and dance" fresco from Knossos (K-P9) could be interpreted as an illustration of a ritual rather like that of the *zintuḫis* and the *entu*-priestess who enters the wood in Ex. 1, but it might be a lot of other things as well. If we turn to Greece in the Iron Age, we have complete or fragmentary texts by a number of poets (Pindar and Bacchylides in particular), and since these texts are composed in ancient Greek, they can be understood, more or less, but we know comparatively little about the detailed performance context of individual poems: the poems were transmitted without the rituals in which they were originally embedded. In that respect, the Bronze Age Anatolian evidence is much richer; on the other hand, the content of the Hattic songs is almost entirely obscure, except for isolated references to the king and to deities. One of the songs of the KI.LAM seems to have included a reference to "the queen bee," and that suggests what would on other grounds have seemed reasonable, that the content of some Hattic poems was mythological, and overlapped with Hattic myths known in Hittite translations, such as the myth of the vanishing god Telepinu (Singer 1983–1984, 1.49; 2.100; for the myths, see Hoffner 1998). Even if we were able to understand Hattic, and if we had the full text of the songs, there would be the further problem of a difference in artistic ambition between songs in the two cultures: the Hattic songs are likely to have been traditional and anonymous cult songs, and, whereas the song culture certainly had traditional poems of this type, those that survive tend to be elaborate virtuoso pieces (such as those of Pindar and Bacchylides). Thus, relatively few extant ancient Greek cult songs have a regular refrain, and we virtually never find the true "Wechselgesang" structure with leader and chorus exchanging lines, but it is likely that simple antiphonal structures of that sort were a feature of ordinary cult song (see Moritz 1979; Rutherford 2001a, 69–72).

Obviously there are a few *prima facie* differences between the two systems. First, the surviving Hattic material is focused on the king (though that is to be expected, since all the evidence we have concerns the uses Hittite royal authority made of this material). Second, choral song in ancient Greece is never sung in any language other than Greek, as far as I am aware. Third, Anatolian song culture did not, as far as we know, have competitions for singers or choruses (on competitions, see Gilan 2001; Schuol 2004, 205), nor does Hattic choral song usually involve dance, or at least dance is rarely mentioned as part of the performance (with occasional exceptions such as Ex. 10 above), whereas Greek choral performance often combined song and dance ("molpe"; Schuol 2004). Finally, in Iron Age Greece, it is unusual for a chorus to be permanently attached to a temple. The only well-documented exception is that of the "Delian Maidens" who seem to have been a chorus permanently attached to the temple of Apollo on Delos (for Delian Maidens see Bruneau 1970).

Nevertheless, there are some striking similarities between the two traditions, and I will mention three. First, in the Greek song culture, a common class of performers are choruses of girls ("parthenoi"), attested at least as early as the poet Alcman in Sparta in the seventh century BC, In fact, a whole genre of choral lyric was named after them, the "partheneion" ("maiden-song"). The Swiss scholar Claude Calame argued three decades ago that participation in such performances fulfilled an important social role in early Greek society, functioning as part of a "rite of passage" for young women (Calame 1977). Adult women singers are also attested, though more rarely, for example in a ritual in honor of Dionysus in Elis described by Plutarch (*Greek Questions* 36, 1962, n. 871).

> Why do the women of Elis when singing their hymn to Dionysus invite him to come to them "with ox foot"? The hymn runs as follows: "*Come hero Dionysus, to the holy temple of the Eleans ... To the temple, raging with your ox foot*" Then they add the double refrain: "*Worthy bull, worthy bull.*"

The reference to the bull reminds us of the "song of the bulls" sung by the women of Nerik in honor of Taru (Ex. 9), and there does seem to be reason to think that the name "Taru" was related to the word for "bull" (Haas 2004, 285: "angerufen zu sein scheint *daaru*, vielleicht eine variante zu *taru* "Stiere").

A second point of comparison is affiliation of performers to towns, In discussing the Anatolian song-culture above, I noticed that, although some of the Hattic choirs were probably linked to major temples, there seems also to have been a tendency for groups of singers to be associated with ordinary towns. This observation is worth setting against two things that we know about the song culture of classical Greece. First, a high degree of civic participation in choral performances staged at civic festivals seems to have been normal; in classical Athens five hundred boys and five hundred men participated in the dithyrambic competitions at the Dionysia every year, and it has even argued that choral activity became an important part of the political process. Secondly, partly as a result of that, it was common for cities participating in common festivals at sanctuaries outside their territory to send delegations accompanied by choruses of citizens whose performances would amount to propaganda on its behalf. These civic uses of choruses has sometimes been seen as a characteristic feature of the political structure of Iron Age Greece, which consisted of a large number of more-or-less autonomous city-states without any major central authority. Given that Bronze Age societies are supposed to have been much more centralized, it seems surprising to find signs that there too communal song was used as a medium for articulating the religious identity of towns.

A third point of comparison is mode of performance and relation to ritual context. Procession was always a common mode of choral performance in the Greek world; songs performed in this way were sometimes referred to by the generic descriptor "prosodion" (Rutherford 2001b). A particularly well-documented example of the use of song in procession is that of the so-called Molpoi of the city Miletus, a guild of singers who doubled as magistrates, and who each year walked from their home city to the oracle of Apollo at Didyma, stopping at points of religious significance *en route* and singing paeans (Sokolowski 1955, n. 50; Rutherford 2001a, 60).

Relation to ritual context is harder to demonstrate because the texts of Greek songs tend to be preserved on their own without metatextual descriptions of context. It is probably easiest to approach this from the point of view of cases where the ritual takes the form of a procession. We saw in the Hattic material cases in which a ritual actor makes a cultic journey (Ex. 1) or an object of religious significance is transported (Ex. 7) or a divine statue is transported to a river to be washed, and all of these were accompanied by choral singing (Ex. 4). There are parallels for all of these from ancient Greece. For the cultic journey of ritual actors, consider the case of the the Daphnephoria ("laurel-carrying")-festival at Thebes, where a procession was led by two focal performers, both young men, while a chorus of girls walked behind and sang (see Schachter 1981–1994, 1.83–85). For the transportation of ritual objects, a relavant parallel is the Tripodephoria ritual, in which tripods were transported from Thebes to Dodona in northwestern Greece, again to the accompaniment of song (Proclus apud Photius, *Bibliotheca* 239, 321b, 32).

Procession in the context of statue-washing has a rich set of parallels in the Greek song culture, for example some processional songs (i.e., "prosodia") by the poet Pindar of Thebes (fifth century BC) were performed in a context of the washing a statue of the deity, and the ritual washing of a statue is also the theme of the Hymn to Athena by the third-century BC poet Callimachus of Cyrene (D'Alessio 1997, 36–37).

The match between the two cultures is by no means exact: in the Hattic song culture, song performance marks the movements of the king, a practice alien to Greek mentality. And there is no parallel in Hittite sources for the transportation of sacrificial victims to the altar that frequently accompanies Greek choral song (though notice that animals are involved in Exx. 8 and 9). Still, there exists a basic core of correspondences between the two song cultures.

It is one thing to collect parallels of this sort, and quite another to ask what they might signify. There are three approaches we might take.

1. First, it could be argued that these parallels are insignificant: choral performance, while not a universal in human cultures, is nevertheless so widespread that it could be predicted that any two given ancient societies would probably develop traditions of choral song that would show some general similarities in terms of performance and performers.[11]

2. Second, these parallels are significant (in the sense that they are much closer than we would expect from any two randomly selected ancient societies), and the most reasonable way to explain it is to assert that "influence" or "imitation" must have taken place in one direction or another; and here one would mention all the evidence usually cited to support the hypothesis of cultural contact between Anatolian and the Mycenaean world (see the introduction to this volume). One factor that seems to support this is that there is already some reason to posit that Greek poetry was influenced by Hurrian poetry, and that the latter reached the former through Anatolia.

3. Somewhere between 1 and 2 is the idea that resemblance between these two cultures can be explained *via* a deep-rooted cultural homogeneity in the Aegeo-Anatolian region, an areal *koiné*, which could have originated through cultural diffusion over several centuries or even millennia. What we see in our data are the same types of ritual practice being adapted to different purposes (and different ideologies) in the different cultures: in Late Bronze Age Anatolia the determining factor are festivals involving the Hittite king, whereas in Iron Age Greece the crucial thing is the city-state culture. This model of areal diffusion could be seen as a special version of the model of "borrowing" or "imitation," but it differs from it in so far as the process is not a simple one between two cultures, but a more complex one involving multiple cultures and a much longer time period.

It is impossible at this stage in the investigation of these cultures to say which of these approaches is right. The hypothesis of direct borrowing seems unsupported on present evidence. If it is ever going to be possible to decide whether parallels like this are significant indications of an areal *koiné*, or ultimately insignificant, it will be necessary to develop a much more nuanced understanding of the general relationship between Anatolian religion (especially the Hattic stratum) and the religion of Iron Age Greece. NB: it would be helpful if we had good data for the Luwian cultures of western Anatolia that were close to the interface.

NOTES

1 Earlier versions of this paper were given at Tel Aviv in 2003 and Emory and Messina in 2006.

2 See the introduction to this volume. Morris (2001) is the most recent survey.

3 Other languages may have been used as well. For example, in *KUB* 58.5 i 6, a group of women sing in the *taggurka* language, whatever that was.

4 On taking over, see Gilan, this volume; on importing song with religion, see Bachvarova, in press, on how this process might have facilitated the transmission of song from one culture to another.

5 Archi (2004). A possible example of singing in Hittite comes in the cult inventory for the goddess of the night, *KBo* 2.8 ii 2; Hazenbos (2003, 138). The main text known in Hittite is the "shirt of Nesa" text; Schuol (2004, 208); Watkins (1995, 248).

6 The original meaning may be "stitch," which is reminiscent of the Greek "rhapsōdos," which means a "stitch singer," and possibly *humnos*, which could be from the "weave" root.

7 Haas and Jakob-Rost write *arraš* with a question mark, because we would expect a longer word, e.g., *arramaš*. We have a song of washing also in *IBoT* 3.115 (De Martino 1989, 26), where they wash the feet of a deity and sing the "song of washing" (*arumaš* SIR). There is a song of washing of feet in *KUB* 45.5 ii 22 (Salvini and Wegner 1986, n. 10).

8 *išḫimana*; so De Martino (1984, 66, n. 29). Schuol (2004, 177) translates "take up the song."

9 For other parallels between Luwian traditions and Greco-Roman religion, see Taylor, this volume.

10 One exception is the dossier of Hattic-Hittite texts that distinguish two names of the same deity, identifying one as the mortal name and the other the divine one; see Laroche (1947); as Watkins (1970) points out, there is an analogy with a Homeric idiom. Mention here should also be made of Collins's (1995) argument that Hittite *palwai* in ritual contexts ("recite, shout out") corresponds to Greek *ololuzo*.

11 Cf. *Les Danses sacrees: Egypte ancienne, Israel, Islam, Asie centrale, Inde, Cambodge, Bali, Java, Chine, Japon*. Sources orientales 6. Paris, Editions du Seuil, 1963.

REFERENCES

Archi, A. (2004) The Singer of Kanes and His Gods. In M. Hutter and S. Hutter-Braunsar (eds.) *Offizielle Religion, lokale Kulte und individualle Religiosität. Akten des religionsgeschichtlichen Symposiums "Kleinasien und angrenzende Gebiete vom Beginn des 2. bis zur Mitte des 1. Jahrtausends v. Chr." (Bonn, 20–22. Februar 2003)*, 11–26. Münster, Ugarit-Verlag.

Aravantinos, V. L., Godart, L. and Sacconi, A. (2001) *Thèbes. Fouilles de la Cadmée I. Les tablettes en linéaire B de la Odos Pelopidou. Édiion et commentaire*. Pisa, Istituti editoriali e poligrafici internazionali.

Bachvarova, M. R. (2005) The Mediterranean Epic Tradition from *Atrahasis* to the *Song of Release* to the *Iliad*. *Greek, Roman and Byzantine Studies* 45, 131–53.

___ (in press) Local Word-Smiths and Supra-Local Audiences: Hittite Perspectives. In R. Hunter and I. C. Rutherford (eds.) *Poeti Vaganti*. Cambridge, Cambridge University Press.

Bloch, M. (1974) Symbols, Songs, Dance and Features of Articulation: Is Religion a Form of Traditional Authority. *Archives Européennes Sociologiques* 15, 155–81 = id. *Ritual, History and Power: Selected Papers in Anthropology*, 19–45. London, Athlone Press, 1989.

Bruneau, P. (1970) *Recherches sur les cultes de Délos à l'époque hellénistique et à l' époque impériale*. Paris, Boccard.

Calame, C. (1977) *Les choeurs de jeunes filles en Grèce archaique*. Two volumes. Rome, Edizioni dell'Ateneo & Bizzarri.

Collins, B. J. (1995) Greek *ololuzo* and Hittite *palwai-*: Exultation in the Ritual Slaughter of Animals. *Greek, Roman, and Byzantine Studies* 36, 319–25.

D'Alessio, G. B. (1997) Pindar's Prosodia and the Classification of Pindaric Papyrus Fragments. *Zeitschrift für Papyrologie und Epigraphik* 118, 23–60.

Dardano, P. (2006) *Die hethitische Tontafelkataloge aus Hattusa* (CTH 276–282). StBoT 47. Wiesbaden, Harrassowitz.

De Martino, S. (1989) *La danza nella cultura ittita. Espressioni filologiche e formali*. Florence, Elite.

Gilan, A. (2001) Kampfspiele in hethitischen Festritualen – eine Interpretation. In D. Prechel, T. Richter, and J. Klinger (eds.) *Kulturgeschichten : altorientalistische Studien für Volkert Haas zum 65. Geburtstag*, 113–24. Saarbrücken, Saarbrücker Druckerei und Verlag.

Haas, V. (1970) *Der Kult von Nerik. Ein Beitrag zur hethitischem Kontext*. Rome, Päpstliches Bibelinstitut.

___ (1994) *Geschichte der hethitische Religion*. Leiden, Brill.

___ (2003) *Materia Magica et Medica Hethitica. Ein Beitrag zur Heilkunde im Altern Orient*. Berlin, De Gruyter.

___ (2006) *Die hethitische Literatur: Texte, Stilistik, Motive*. Berlin, De Gruyter.

Haas, V., and Jakob-Rost, L. (1984) Das Festritual des Gottes Telipinu in Hanhana und in Kasha. Ein Beitrag zum hethitischen Festkalendar. *Altorientalische Forschungen* 11, 10–91.
Habinek, T. (2005) *The World of Roman Song: From Ritualized Speech to Social Order.* Baltimore, The Johns Hopkins University.
Hazenbos, J. (2003) *The Organization of the Anatolian Local Cults During the Thirteenth Century BC: An Appraisal of the Hittite Cult Inventories.* Leiden, Brill.
Herington, C. J. (1985) *Poetry into Drama: Early Tragedy and the Greek Poetic Tradition.* Berkeley, University of California Press.
Hoffner, H. A., Jr. (1998) *Hittite Myths.* Second edition. Atlanta, Society of Biblical Literature.
Immerwahr, S. A. (1995) Death and the Tanagra Larnakes. In J. B. Carter and S. P. Morris (eds.), *The Ages of Homer: A Tribute to Emily Vermeule*, 109–21. Austin, University of Texas Press.
Jian, L. (1994) Hittite Women Singers. [munus]*zintuhi* and [munus]KI.SIKIL. *Journal of Ancient Civilizations* 9, 82–94.
Klinger, J. (1996) *Untersuchungen zur Rekonstruktion der hattischen Kultschicht.* StBoT 37. Wiesbaden, Harrassowitz.
Kontorli-Papadopoulou, L. (1996) *Aegean Frescoes of Religious Character, SIMA* 117. Göteborg, Äströms.
Laroche, E. (1947) Hattic Deities and their Epithets. *Journal of Cuneiform Studies* 1, 187–216
Matz, F. (1958) *Göttererscheinung und Kultbild in minoischen Kreta.* Wiesbaden, Akademie der Wissenschaften und der Literatur in Mainz.
McMahon, G. (1991) *The Hittite State Cult of the Tutelary Deities.* Chicago, Oriental Institute of the University of Chicago.
Melchert, H. C. (1998) Hittite *arku-* 'Chant, Intone' vs. *arkuwa(i)* 'Make a Plea.' *Journal of Cuneiform Studies* 50, 45–51.
Moritz, H. E. (1979) Refrain in Aechylus: Literary Adaptation of Traditional Form. *Classical Philology* 74, 187–213.
Morris, S. P. (2001) Potnia Aswiya: Anatolian Contributions to Greek Religion. In R. Laffineur and R. Hägg (eds.) *POTNIA. Deities and Religion in the Aegean Bronze Age*, 423–34. Aegaeum 22. Liège, Université de Liège, Histoire de l'art et archéologie de la Grèce antique.
Pecchioli Daddi, F. (1982) *Mestieri, professioni e dignità nell'Anatolia ittita.* Rome, Edizioni dell'Ateneo.
Popko, M. (1994) *Zippalanda: ein Kultzentrum im hethitischen Kleinasien. Texte der Hethiter* 21. Heidelberg, Universitätsverlag C. Winter.
Rutherford, I. C. (2001a) *Pindar's Paeans. A Reading of the Fragments with a Survey of the Genre.* Oxford, Oxford University Press.
___ (2001b) Prosodion. In *Der Neue Pauly* vol.10, 447–48. Stuttgart, J. B. Metzler.
___ (2004) Women Singers and the Religious Organisation of Hatti. On the Interpretation of CTH 235.1, CTH 235.2 and Other Texts. In M. Hutter and S. Hutter-Braunsar (eds.) *Offizielle Religion, lokale Kulte und individualle Religiosität. Akten des religionsgeschichtlichen Symposiums "Kleinasien und angrenzende Gebiete vom Beginn des 2. bis zur Mitte des 1. Jahrtausends v. Chr." (Bonn, 20–22. Februar 2003)*, 377–94. Münster, Ugarit-Verlag.
___ (2005) The Dance of the Wolf-Men of Ankuwa: Networks, Amphictionies and Pilgrimage in Hittite Religion. In *Acts of the 5th international Congress of Hittitology*, 623–40. Ankara.
___ (in press) Mycenaean Religion. In *The Cambridge History of Ancient Religions*, Vol. 1. Cambridge, Cambridge University.
Salvini, M., and Wegner, I. (1986) *Rituale des Azu Priesters.* CHS I.2. Rome, Multigrafica editrice.
Schachter, A. (1981–1994) *Cults of Boeotia.* 4 volumes. London, Institute of Classical Studies.
Schuol, M. (2004) *Hethitische Kultmusik: Eine Untersuchung der Instrumental- und Vokalmusik anhand hetitischer Ritualtexte und von archäoloischen Zeugnissen.* Orient-Archäologie Bd. 14. Rahden/Westfallen, Verlag Marie Leidorf.
Singer, I. (1983–1984) *The Hittite KI.LAM Festival. StBoT* 27–28. Wiesbaden, Harrassowitz.
Sokolowski, F. (1955) *Lois sacrées de l'Asie Mineur.* Paris, Boccard.
Soysal, O. (2004) *Hattischer Wortschatz in hethitischer Textüberlieferung.* Leiden, Brill.
Starke, F. (1985) *Die keilschriftliche-luwischen Texte in Umschrift.* StBoT 30. Wiesbaden, Harrassowitz.
Trümpy, C. (1986) *Vergleich des Mykenischen mit der Sprache der ChorlyrikL bewahrt die Chorlyrik eine von Homer unabhängige alte Sprachtradition.* Bern, Lang.
Watkins, C. (1970) Language of Gods and Language of Men: Remarks on Some Indo-European Meta-Lingusitic Traditions. In J. Puhvel (ed.) *Myth and Law among the Indo-Europeans*, 1–17. Berkeley, University of California.
___ (1986) The Language of the Trojans. In M. T. Mellink (ed.) *Troy and the Trojan War*, 45–62. Bryn Mawr, Bryn Mawr College.
___ (1995) *How to Kill a Dragon. Aspects of Indo-European Poetics.* Oxford, Oxford University.
Younger, J. G. (1998) *Music in the Aegean Bronze Age.* SIMA 144. Jonsered, Äströms.

8

HOMER AT THE INTERFACE

Trevor Bryce

I should at the outset make clear that my paper is based on the assumption that the *Iliad* is by and large the work of a specific individual called Homer, an Ionian Greek who lived on or near the western coast of Asia Minor in the second half of the eighth century BC.[1] Homer's composition is considered the account *par excellence* of the Trojan War. But in fact our knowledge of the Trojan War tradition owes much less to him than it does to other sources, like the poems of the so-called epic cycle. Of the entire ten-year operation, most of the *Iliad* is confined to just six days near its end. And the story stops short of the tradition's climactic event. The *Iliad* itself is not about the fall of Troy. Nor does it contain even a passing reference to what is commonly regarded as the archetypal symbol of the war – the Trojan horse. Homer's audiences were familiar with the large repertoire of tales that arose out of the tradition of a Trojan War, and Homer had no intention of going over well trodden ground.

Who were the audiences who first heard the *Iliad*?[2] What links did they have with their Bronze Age predecessors? In the *Odyssey*, Homer has Odysseus speak with pleasure of entertainments provided by bards in the banqueting halls of the nobility of his day (*Od.* 9.5–11). And it may well be that Homer's own audiences represented similarly elite elements from his own world, namely, the eighth-century Ionian region of Asia Minor. The Ionians' ancestors had migrated to their new homelands on the coast and offshore islands of Asia Minor in the aftermath of the upheavals at the end of the Bronze Age. Undoubtedly these upheavals, which affected many parts of the Greek and Near Eastern worlds, caused severe disruption to the existing social order, ethnic composition, and cultural environment of the regions most directly affected. But the so-called "Dark Age" was more of a bridge than a chasm between the Bronze and Early Iron civilizations. There was significant social and cultural continuity across the chronological divide. That is clear, for example, from the persistence of many Late Bronze Age elements in southern Anatolia and the Neo-Hittite kingdoms of northern Syria and eastern Anatolia during the early centuries of the first millennium.

In western Anatolia, the evidence for continuity between the Bronze Age cultures and ethnic groups, and the emerging Iron Age cultures and populations is less clear. During the Late Bronze Age, the Luwians were the most populous of the ethnic groups inhabiting western and southern Anatolia, and politically the most important. Many Luwians, including whole communities, may have shifted to new locations at the end of the Bronze Age, or to locations already occupied by kindred ethnic groups. But many others may have remained in their original homelands. We know, from both archaeological and written evidence, that Luwian population groups persisted in southern Anatolia during the first millennium, particularly in the coastal lands called Lycia (which formed part of the territory called the Lukka lands in Late Bronze Age texts) and Cilicia in Classical times.[3] And there may well have been a significant continuing Luwian presence amongst the descendants of the Late Bronze Age inhabitants of western Anatolia, particularly within and near the territories of the former Arzawan kingdoms. The populations of these kingdoms almost certainly contained a substantial Luwian component. Four of the kingdoms extended to the western Anatolian coast, from Milawata (Late Bronze Age Miletos) northwards to the Troad,[4] thus putting them at the closest points of contact between the Near Eastern and Aegean worlds. Archaeological and written evidence indicate intermingling of western Anatolian and Greek elements, of both a political and a commercial nature, for much of the Late Bronze Age. Undoubtedly there was cultural interaction as well.

To what extent did this interaction continue in the early first millennium? Unfortunately, evidence for an ongoing Luwian presence in western Anatolia in this period is meagre. As Professor Hutter notes in his discussion of Luwian religion, "it is possible (and even probable) that some Luwian traditions in the Arzawan lands continued to the Iron Age."[5] But as he also comments, we should not overestimate the Luwians' role in what he refers to as "a steady chain of contacts between Anatolia and the Aegean and Greek mainland since the fourteenth century ... (which) continued in the following centuries." Other Anatolian peoples may well have contributed to this process. It is possible, for example, that both the first millennium Carians and Lydians had ancestral roots amongst the Late Bronze Age peoples of western Anatolia, and played a role in the interaction of western Anatolians with the peoples of the Aegean and Mycenaean worlds.[6] To judge from later inscriptional evidence, the Carians and the Lydians were both of Indo-European origin. Whether or not they had close ethnic connections with the Indo-European-speaking Luwians remains a matter for speculation.

The influence, both political and commercial, that the Mycenaeans had exercized in western Anatolia from at least the early-fourteenth century seems to have terminated abruptly towards the end of the thirteenth century. Indirectly, this may be reflected in Hittite texts of the period.[7] But it is most unlikely that the Mycenaean presence entirely disappeared at this time. Indeed a residual Mycenaean population in the region may have provided one of the groups of the so-called Sea Peoples listed in the records of the late-thirteenth century pharaoh Merneptah.[8] When Ionian Greeks settled in Asia Minor towards the end of the second millennium, they were entering a region that already had a tradition of Greek-Anatolian interaction, and was almost certainly still occupied, even if now in small numbers, by descendants of the Bronze Age inhabitants of the region, of both Greek and indigenous origin. Homer's contemporary world was neither exclusively Greek nor Anatolian. Even if predominantly Greek, it was a mixture of the two.

Like his bardic predecessors, Homer probably enjoyed, and may indeed have depended upon, the patronage of a number of prominent families – in his case the families who constituted the local "aristocracies" of western Anatolia in the early centuries of the first millennium. Many were undoubtedly of Greek origin. It is possible that some of them could claim Anatolian connections extending back to the period of Mycenaean settlement in the region. But mostly, they were descended from the Greek immigrants who first settled on or near Anatolia's western coast in the twelfth and eleventh centuries. By Homer's time, several centuries had passed since these immigrants had departed their original homelands. Undoubtedly, the new settlers' descendants retained a strong sense of their Greek identity, as illustrated by their religion, social systems, folk traditions, and domestic architecture. But their families had by now spent many generations in an Anatolian environment, in close contact with local Anatolian peoples and cultures. Their loyalties and affinities lay at least as much with the homeland adopted for them by their forefathers as with the original homeland whence their forefathers had come.

The elite elements of western Anatolian society in Homer's day almost certainly included indigenous families. It is possible, for example, that Poseidon's prophecy about Aeneas in Book 20 of the *Iliad* was included by Homer at the prompting of an ambitious Troad family that sought to enhance its status by claiming Aeneas as its founder.[9] But while some families may have held firm to their original ethnic identity, no doubt there were many cases where ethnic distinctions were quickly blurred and eventually disappeared through generations of mixed marriages. To judge from later Greek tradition, the first mixed unions took place at the time of the first Ionian contact with western Anatolia. Herodotos (*Hist.* 1.146) talks of the marriages of aristocratic Ionian migrants on their arrival in Miletos with local Carian women, allegedly after murdering their prospective wives' fathers, husbands, and children.

We can perhaps compare the process of Ionian settlement in western Anatolia in the late-second millennium with that of Indo-European settlement in central Anatolia a millennium or more earlier, and the intermingling of Indo-European with native Hattian elements. This intermingling obviously influenced the ethnic profile of the Late Bronze Age Hittite civilization, whose ruling class nonetheless retained the language and many of the traditions of the original Indo-European settlers.

I have suggested that the audiences for whom Homer's epics were primarily composed consisted of prominent family groups of Greek, indigenous and mixed origins, located on or near Anatolia's Aegean coast. It was they who would most readily have identified with the elite class who constituted the Mycenaean and Trojan aristocracies in the *Iliad*, and most readily understood the code of honor that Homer's warrior-heroes embodied and shared. For the poet's story is of shared ideals, of shared suffering and tragedy.

Though the Trojan War is sometimes billed as the first great conflict between East and West, forerunner of the campaigns of Xerxes against Greece, Alexander against Persia, and Mehmet II against Constantinople, Homer does not present it as a contest between opposing cultures or races or belief systems. His is a tale told without bias towards or against one side or the other. Neither side outdoes the other in terms of the moral and physical qualities that its heroes display, or the weaknesses to which they are prone. And neither side consistently has the upper hand in the conflict. When Hector is killed, the Greeks' victory and Troy's fall are assured. But this is really quite incidental to the *Iliad's* tale. The Trojan hero's death provides no occasion for rejoicing. Throughout the last book of the *Iliad*, the mood is a markedly sombre one. The poem is no longer about a war approaching its climax. Homer stops short of this. Instead, as the poem draws to its end, his focus is solely upon a family mourning the loss of a beloved son and husband whose body they prepare for burial. In the *Iliad's* last lines, the conflict between Greeks and Trojans has faded from view.

That Homer should end his epic in this way probably tells us much about the audiences before whom his tale was first recited. Other poets, past and present, might well have taken a more partisan line, celebrating the Greek triumph, and highlighting Troy's final destruction. Homer approached the tale from a different perspective, aware that a non-partisan treatment of it would be more likely to strike a responsive chord with audiences whose sympathies lay equally with the heroes of both sides. He was sensitive to what pleased his audiences – as indeed he needed to be if they were made up of persons or families whose patronage he enjoyed. This had an important bearing on the shaping of the *Iliad*. The markedly contemplative character of the final book of the *Iliad*, with its reflections on human destiny and human mortality, was judged to be a fitting end to the epic by a poet well attuned to the tastes and expectations of his audiences.

Homer's social and cultural background may have been predominantly Greek in character. But longstanding Anatolian beliefs and traditions, preserved in one form or another to the poet's own day, must also have formed part of his cultural heritage. This is reflected in a number of episodes in the Homeric poems. For example, the chthonic rituals recorded in Late Bronze Age Hittite texts are closely paralleled by Homer's description of the procedures Odysseus follows in summoning up the spirits of the dead in Book 11 of the *Odyssey*. Patroklos' burial rites in Book 23 of the *Iliad* strikingly resemble in several respects the funerary rites prescribed in texts from Hattusa for Hittite kings and queens. Like Hittite royalty, Homer's dead heroes, Greek as well as Trojan, are generally consigned to the pyre. This practice appears to have no precedent in the kingdoms of Mycenaean Greece, but is well attested in the contemporary Anatolian world. It is remarkable that rites and procedures belonging to a non-Greek civilization that had ended centuries before Homer's time should not only resurface in his poems but also be set within a Greek context.

The story of Achilles' wrath has about it the feel of a morality tale, which would not have been out of place in a Mesopotamian context. In the *Greek* heroic code, personal honor is of paramount importance.

Achilles has suffered severe humiliation, and he reacts in a way that is understandable – even if taken to unacceptable extremes – in terms of the code by which he and his peers live. But from a *Mesopotamian* perspective, he might well be seen much less as a hero holding firm to an aristocratic code of conduct, than as a leader who has cast aside his responsibilities, consumed by his own arrogance and self-pity. By the story's end, however, he has come to a greater awareness of human mortality and all that it entails, particularly with his own death so close at hand. This awareness leads him to deeper understanding of and compassion for those with whom his mortality is shared, to "a moral vision about the universal suffering that unites all humankind."[10] Comparisons in matters of detail have often been made between the stories of Achilles and Gilgamesh. In overall concept too, the Gilgamesh tradition may not have been far from our poet's mind as he developed the *Iliad*'s primary theme.

Almost certainly Homer was acquainted with the Babylonian epic, or at least had heard tales from it. He lived at the interface of the Greek and Near Eastern worlds during the orientalizing period of Greek civilization. And westward-moving Near Eastern literary and folk traditions like those associated with Gilgamesh may well have been part of his cultural heritage. He in turn became an agent in the process of east-west cultural transmission – a process that had probably already begun in the Bronze Age, and that led eventually to the incorporation into Greek literature of traditions whose origins lay in Mesopotamia, Syria, and Anatolia.[11] But it is most unlikely that Homer was conscious of being an agent in this process. This would assign to his composition a dimension that was quite alien to his purpose. He composed with one main purpose in mind – to satisfy the expectations of a socially elite class of mixed, but predominantly Greek, origins who lived in the Ionian region of western Asia Minor.[12]

How, then, did the *Iliad* come to acquire its widespread popularity throughout the Greek world? Its association with the very beginnings of Greek literature, its artistic merit, its value as a repository of moral precepts, and its sheer monumentality have all been seen as contributing to its special status in Greek literature. But perhaps most important of all is the poem's panhellenic *inclusiveness*. In a political sense, panhellenism never took hold in the Greek world, for it was too fiercely countered by the forces of city-state parochialism. But sanctuaries like Delphi and festivals like the Olympic Games helped remind the Greeks of their fundamental kinship across city-state boundaries. It was a matter of individual city-state pride to be seen to be contributing to the maintenance of the Delphic sanctuary, and to be providing athletes for the panhellenic games. So too it was a matter of city-state pride to have a claim to participation in the expedition against Troy. To receive a mention in the *Iliad* was to acquire a sense of identification with it, and every state so mentioned, every state that could claim it had ancestors who fought in the war, helped contribute to the poem's popularity. Everyone wanted a piece of the action, if only in retrospect. A number of districts and communities listed amongst the Greek allies may well have owed their appearance in the epic to a latter-day poet (not necessarily Homer himself) willing to assign their ancestors a place in the great conflict as part of a *quid pro quo* arrangement – payment in kind for hospitality or other favors he had received from them.[13]

In the mid-sixth century, the Athenian tyrant Peisistratos incorporated performances of the Homeric epics into his city's newly reorganized Panathenaic festival. Under the Peisistratid regime, Athens became a major cultural as well as commercial center of the Greek world. The adoption of the Homeric epics was an explicit statement by Peisistratos of what he saw as Athens' role as the new focus of panhellenic culture. It was also the expression of an outlook that drew no distinction between those who fought on the Greek side and those who fought on the Trojan. Homeric tradition united them in a common culture, which included a similar set of beliefs and adherence to a common set of ideals and values.

That was to change with the rise of Persia, culminating in the invasions of Greece by Darius and Xerxes in the early-fifth century. After the repulse of these invasions, Athens attempted to give permanence to the fragile (and far from universal) Greek unity that had helped bring about the Greeks' ultimate triumph over Persia. The alliance of Greek states that now came into being, commonly called the Delian League, was from the outset effectively under Athenian leadership. It was an organization that had the ostensible aim of uniting the Greek world against any further threat from Persia. Athenian propaganda as expressed through art and literature now created a sharp division between Greek and non-Greek world by contrasting all the noble qualities that allegedly characterized the former and all the base qualities of extravagance, decadence and self-indulgence that were inherent in the latter. Troy was now represented as an integral part of the non-Greek world, with all the negative attributes that that implied.

Peisistratid Athens had clasped Homer to her bosom. Was there not scope now, in the post-Persian period, for using the *Iliad* to keep alive the panhellenic spirit, as a means of ensuring that the Greeks remained united against the enemy across the sea, inspired by the great triumph won by their ancestors in the heroic past? In fact, the *Iliad* was largely ignored by fifth-century Athenian writers and visual artists, for obvious reasons. It was a quite unsuitable instrument for fifth century Athenian propaganda. There is no glorious Greek triumph at the end of it, simply a statement of human grief and suffering that cuts across international boundaries. Greeks and Trojans share the same values and ideals, their characters are equally a mixture of good and bad. This could have no place in the propaganda that merged the image of the Trojan with that of the Persian. Both were now symbols of oriental decadence, far removed from the heroic image shared by Greek and Trojan in the Homeric poems.

Some 150 years later, the Homeric spirit gained a new lease on life from Homer's most avid fan who set foot on Trojan soil in 334 in preparation for his onslaught upon the Persian Empire: Alexander the Great. On the plains of Troy, Alexander conducted sacrificial rituals – faithfully imitating those performed by his heroic, Iliadic ancestors. He paid homage to Achilles, but also sought reconciliation with Priam. This was partly a personal family matter, for Priam had been slain by Neoptolemos, son of Achilles, and Alexander traced his descent on his mother's side from Achilles' family. But it was also in keeping with his vision of a world united across ethnic and cultural divides. Troy/Ilion was at the interface of this world. Alexander's pilgrimage there, Homer in hand, was a grand symbolic gesture. The Trojans' bad press was a thing of the past. Homer's heroes were reinstated.

In a material sense, Ilion did rather well out of the patronage of Alexander and his Hellenistic successors. It thrived on the juice of its legendary past. And never more so than under the patronage of Rome's first emperor Augustus. Which brings us to the Trojan prince Aeneas, member of a secondary branch of the Trojan royal family. The *Iliad* contains the prophecy that Aeneas will survive the fall of Troy and found a new dynasty that will rule over the Trojans. But *where* is not made clear. Though some argued that Aeneas re-established his kingdom in the Troad, it was a Greek tradition that took hold in the Roman world – that Aeneas sailed westwards and founded a new kingdom in Italy. In particular, Aeneas was linked through his son Ascanius also known by a spurious piece of nomenclature as Iulus, with Rome's Julian clan. The most illustrious members of this clan were Julius Caesar and his great-nephew Octavian, the later Augustus.

By a somewhat messy attempt to integrate Greek with native Italian tradition, Aeneas became the ancestor of Romulus, Rome's founder. Thus Julius Caesar via Iulus Ascanius could trace his family roots back to the very founder of the Roman nation, and Troy had been the ancestral home of this founder. But Caesar had little opportunity to benefit from his supposed family roots before his assassins cut him down. It was left to his great-nephew Octavian to exploit the full political potential of the link he had claimed with Aeneas and son. Literature provided one of the vehicles for doing this. Hence the commission bestowed upon the poet Virgil. In 31 BC, shortly before Virgil began work on the *Aeneid*, Octavian had triumphed over Antony and Cleopatra in the battle of Actium, and thus become the undisputed master of the Roman world.

It was a world that had been fragmented by a century of faction strife and civil war. The Republican institutions were no longer capable of restoring order and stability to this world. But what was the alternative? Julius Caesar's fate had but recently demonstrated the dangers faced by anyone suspected of harboring monarchical ambitions. In spite of the failure of the Republic, his countrymen still viewed the prospect of one-man rule with abhorrence. This was the challenge confronting Augustus, who in effect became the first emperor of Rome, with the deliberately bland title *princeps*, "first man," in the year 27 BC. He declared that he would hold the office of *princeps* only until the Republic could be restored. But doubtless there were many who had misgivings about his extraordinary status. To them in particular, he sought to present himself as the great peacemaker and reconciler, the restorer of old traditions and values, the legitimate and direct successor of his country's founder, and the one whose coming had been foretold back in the days of Aeneas himself.

These images of Rome's first emperor were to be incorporated in Virgil's great project – the composition of a national epic about the Roman nation's founding hero. And most importantly, an epic where Augustus appears, twice, as the one foretold by destiny, at the climax of Rome's progress through the ages:

> This is the man, this is the one whom you have so often heard promised to you,
> *Augustus Caesar, son of a god, the founder once more of a golden age*
> in Latium, throughout the lands where Saturn once ruled. (Virgil, *Aeneid* 6. 791–94)

It was a great piece of Augustan propaganda.

But there is something else as well. A critical turning point in the *Aeneid* occurs in Book 2 when Aeneas witnesses the brutal slaughter of Priam and his family. Immediately after, he catches sight of Helen – the cause of all Troy's sufferings – cowering by the threshold of the goddess Vesta. Consumed with a passion for revenge, he is on the point of leaping down and killing her, then rushing into the battle's midst and sacrificing his life in one last pointless act of heroism. But his mother Venus intervenes. She gently rebukes her son. It is fated that Troy should fall. It is the gods, not Helen, who should be blamed for this. She urges him to escape while there is yet time. He has a higher purpose to fulfill. This purpose becomes clear when the ghost of his wife Creusa appears to him, and lays before him the mission for which he is intended – to travel to Hesperia, the Land of the Evening Star, and establish there a new kingdom for his people.

By the end of Book II, the divine plan for Aeneas has been revealed. This book marks the transition from Homeric to Augustan hero. The former is characterized by the Latin word *furor* – a word with intensely negative associations, often including a single-minded obsession with revenge. It is an irrational emotion, a kind of madness, one of total self-absorption. It is epitomized in the *Iliad's* main theme – the wrath of Achilles. It is the emotion to which Aeneas almost succumbs. Indeed he shows many traits of the typical Homeric hero. But he overcomes this, with divine assistance, replacing it with the Roman quality of *pietas*. *Pietas* becomes Aeneas' defining quality. It is one that requires the subordination of all personal desires and emotions to one's duty to others – friends, family, gods and country. Adherence to a code in which the defence of personal honor and the pursuit of personal vendettas, as embodied in the conduct of a Homeric Achilles, are no longer appropriate in an age in which reconciliation and reconstruction are of paramount importance. Herein lies Virgil's most important message for the Roman of the Augustan era.

The epic of Gilgamesh and the *Aeneid* originated two thousand years and thousands of kilometers apart. The *Iliad* is a kind of midpoint between them – chronologically, geographically and thematically. There are themes common to them all. Above all, the harshness and immutability of one's mortal lot. Mesopotamian, Homeric and Virgilian heroes respond to this in different ways. Gilgamesh's futile quest for the secret of eternal life becomes a journey of self-discovery. The epic *begins* with his portrayal as a harsh, oppressive despot. It *ends* with his return to Uruk, a chastened and wiser man, ready to carry out the responsibilities of kingship.

The *Iliad* begins with an act of pitilessness: a king, Agamemnon, rejects the plea of an old man, Chryses, for the return of his daughter. This sets in motion the sequence of events that leads to the final contest between Achilles and Hector. The poem *ends* with an act of pity: the victor, Achilles, aware that he too must soon die, aware that his father like Hector's will be grief-stricken at his death, accedes to the plea of an old man, Priam, for the return of his son, in this case for burial.

Virgil's Aeneas reluctantly comes to terms with his destiny. The old heroic code of conduct must be set aside. All personal desires and emotions must be suppressed for the sake of the task that lies ahead – one that is concisely summed up in Aeneas's words to Dido: *Italiam non sponte sequor.* "Italy is my goal, but not of my choosing." Denial of self for the sake of a higher cause. It was a Roman heroic quality. And as far as such qualities go, this was for Virgil the noblest of them all.

NOTES

A number of the suggestions in this paper are further developed in my book *The Trojans and their Neighbours* (Bryce 2005b).

1 There has long been a view that "Homer" should be thought of as the personification of some sort of editorial process. This view is not in fashion at present, though there is still debate about what passages in the Homeric poems should be assigned to later interpolationists. Smyrna and the island of Chios are the most favored of a number of locations proposed in antiquity for Homer's birthplace.
2 A question discussed by Högemann (2000) and Latacz (2004, 274–47).
3 Houwink ten Cate (1965) still remains the most authoritative work on this topic.
4 Namely, Arzawa "Minor," Mira (which absorbed much if not all the territory of the former in the late-thirteenth century), Seha River Land, and Wilusa.
5 Hutter (2003, 270).
6 See Bryce (2006, 142–44)
7 See Bryce (2005, 309–10)
8 The group of people vocalized as Ekwesh or Akaiwasha in Merneptah's account of the Sea Peoples are commonly identified with the Ahhiyawans of the Hittite texts, who are in turn almost certainly to be identified with the Mycenaeans.
9 *Iliad* 20.320–328. Cf. Willcock (1976, 222–23).
10 Powell (2004, 1143).
11 The close parallels between episodes in the Hurrian Kumarbi cycle and Hesiod's *Theogony* provide the clearest example of this.
12 Of course the Homeric poems also had considerable popular appeal, and even in Homer's day may have been recited before gatherings who represented a much broader cross-section of the local populations.
13 This has been proposed, for example, in relation to some members of the list in the much debated Catalogue of Ships in Book 2 of the *Iliad*. For differing points of view, see the discussions of Anderson (1995, 188–89) and Latacz (2004, 219–49).

REFERENCES

Anderson, J. K. (1995) The Geometric Catalogue of Ships. In J. B. Carter and S. P. Morris (eds.) *The Ages of Homer: A Tribute to Emily Townsend Vermeule*, 181–91. Austin, University of Texas.

Bryce, T. R. (2005) *The Kingdom of the Hittites* (rev. ed.). Oxford, Oxford University.

___ (2005b), *The Trojans and their Neighbours*. London, Routledge.

Högemann, P. (2006) Zur Iliasdichter – Ein Anatolischer Standpunkt. *Studia Troica* X, 183–98.

Houwink ten Cate, Ph. H. J. (1965) *The Luwian Population Groups of Lycia and Cilica Aspera during the Hellenistic Period.* Leiden, Brill.

Hutter, M. (2003) Aspects of Luwian Religion. In H. C. Melchert (ed.) *The Luwians*, 211–80. Leiden, Brill.

Latacz, J. (2004) *Troy and Homer: Towards a Solution of an Old Mystery*. trans. K. Windle and R. Ireland. Oxford, Oxford University.

Powell, B. B. (2004) *Homer*. Oxford, Blackwell.

Willcock, M. W. (1976) *A Companion to the Iliad*. Chicago, University of Chicago.

9

THE POET'S POINT OF VIEW AND THE PREHISTORY OF THE *ILIAD*

Mary R. Bachvarova

In their landmark studies of the Mediterranean cultural *koiné*, Walter Burkert (1992) and M. L. West (1997) focused on proving that the Greeks had borrowed literary and religious motifs from the Near East. They were therefore interested in similarities between texts, not differences. Now that it has been accepted that borrowing did occur, we can turn our attention to the evolution of motifs, how the differing milieus shaped the texts over time, for the differences between stories that are part of the common eastern Mediterranean tradition are the key to understanding the development of this tradition.[1] A basis for this approach can be found in the scholarship on the multifarious *Ramayana* tradition in South Asia. A. K. Ramanujan (1991, 44–45, following Charles Sanders Peirce) categorized the interrelationships between the different texts within a single tradition as *iconic*: one structure is mapped onto the first structure, i.e., a faithful translation; *indexical*: the text considers itself to be telling the same story, but "the text is embedded in a locale, a context, refers to it, even signifies it, and would not make much sense without it;" and *symbolic*: "Text 2 uses the plot and characters and names of Text 1 minimally and uses them to say entirely new things, often in an effort to subvert the predecessor by producing a countertext." Particularly important to a proper understanding of the eastern Mediterranean epic tradition are Ramanujan's notions of indexical, that is, adapting a story to new milieus, genres and audiences; and symbolic, that is, responding to other known versions. With Ramanujan's scheme, I examine here Near Eastern and Greek versions of stories concerning the destruction of a city, seeing how the story evolved as it passed from the Sumerian Curse of Akkade to the Akkadian Cuthean Legend of Naram-Sin to the Hurro-Hittite Song of Release to Homer's *Iliad*. I will look particularly at the varying ways a ruler's role in the destruction of his city is explained in passages that seem to be responding to, and playing with, the earlier tradition.

Classical scholars have long mulled over the interaction between divine and human will/agency in the *Iliad* on the one hand while on the other they have used the text as evidence for political structures and means that were precursors to the great Athenian experiment of democracy (Hammer 2002, 49–58). While modern scholars have mostly looked at each aspect of the *Iliad* as separate and, to some extent, mutually contradictory issues, we would be missing something important if we did not understand that Homer himself sees action in the political sphere in response to events beyond the control of humans as a key element in the interaction between divine and human. Hammer has attempted to integrate the two fields of study by arguing that chance is culturally constructed: "Chance, thus, reveals both issues of community maintenance and the nature of human agency as individuals, through their deliberative and willful actions, seek to maintain a cultural equilibrium" (Hammer 2002, 58). As we will see, these same issues arise in the Near Eastern materials, and, like Homer, the poets and scribes who authored the various Near Eastern texts examined here were very interested in how humans used political means to decide on responses to divinely sent disasters that devastated the community:

> In the history of ancient Near East, a very marginal role is usually reserved to political debate, almost completely overwhelmed by the prejudice of a "despotical" relationship between ruler and governed people – where the former bears all the burden of decision, the latter just that of obeisance. Our texts may help us in perceiving a different situation, in which the decisional mechanism was built up of different and contrasting opinions. These opinions had sometimes to be substained [sic] by historical or mythical cases, by prototypes endowed with unquestionable authoritativeness. Besides the omens, which are the Mesopotamian form of expression for different options, also the historiographic literature had a role in this connection. (Liverani 1993b, 52)

Thus, by examining the continuous, yet flexible, eastern Mediterranean narrative tradition of stories concerning the destruction of cities, we can better understand the function of history and epic – both oral and written – and the relationship between politics and religion. Furthermore, the sympathetic portrayal of Hector in the *Iliad* as a leader who tries to do what is best for his city, but does not fully comprehend the will of the gods, has implications for the compositional history of the *Iliad*.

The story of the fall of Akkade (or not falling, as the case may be) is told from two different points of view, separated into different stories; the difference coincides in part with the use of different languages. The earliest copies of the Sumerian Curse of Akkade date to ca. 2000 BC (Cooper 1983, 11), and it is the earliest and most negative portrayal of Naram-Sin, who is blamed for the fall of the Sargonic dynasty, although we in fact know that the dynasty was still functioning for at least a generation after Naram-Sin, as was Akkade. The Curse of Akkade does not fit neatly into a single genre. On the one hand it makes use of phrases and themes that show up in (pseudo-)historical texts; on the other it draws on themes and phrases also found in the so-called "city laments," namely, Sumerian laments passed down in the scribal curriculum that described the destruction of a city (Cooper 1983, 20–28).[2]

The Curse of Akkade opens with a detailed description of a flourishing Akkade, which has replaced Uruk and Kish as the premier city of Mesopotamia, and its international fame:[3]

> After Enlil's frown
> Had slain Kish like the Bull of Heaven,
> Had slaughtered the house of the land of Uruk in the dust like a mighty bull,
> And then, to Sargon, king of Agade,
> Enlil, from south to north,
> Had given sovereignty and kingship –
> At that time, holy Inanna built
> The sanctuary Agade as her grand woman's domain,
> (1–8)
> ...
> [So t]hat foreigners would cruise about like unusual birds in the sky,
> That (even) Marḫaši would be reentered in the (tribute) rolls,
> (19–20)

Then, for some reason, the gods, especially Inanna, are offended and withdraw their favor:

> But the word from Ekur was as silence.
> Agade was reduced to trembling before her, and
> She grew anxious in Ulmaš.
> She withdrew her dwelling from the city.
> (57–60)

Naram-Sin has a dream that the future of Akkade is "altogether unfavorable" (84), but he fails to discuss the dream with anyone for seven years, withdrawing from society. "Because of Ekur he donned mourning garb." (88) Then, frustrated, he attempts to act, seeking the gods' opinion with regard to building a new temple. Extispicy denies him permission repeatedly. He then knocks down the Ekur temple in Nippur, a destructive act that is likened to sacking Nippur, Enlil's favorite city, and signals the descent of Akkade into *ate*:

> Large ships were docked at Enlil's temple, and
> The goods were removed from the city.
> As the goods were removed from the city,
> So was the political legitimacy[4] of Agade removed,
> The ships jarred the docks, and Agade's intelligence was displaced.
> (144–148)

It is unclear from the text whether the temple that Naram-Sin wished to build was one for Inanna in Akkade, in which case the demolition of Ekur was an act of revenge (so Jacobsen 1987, 359), or a new one in Nippur, in which case the destruction of the temple was in preparation for its rebuilding (so Cooper 1983, 239–41; 1993, 16–17).[5] The "word from Ekur" mentioned in l. 57 could refer to an attempt to obtain permission for the building or rebuilding of the temple.

Enlil responds by destroying all of Mesopotamia at the hands of the subhuman Gutians:

> Enlil, because his beloved Ekur was destroyed, what should he destroy (in revenge) for it?
> He looked toward the Gubin mountains;
> He *scoured* all of the broad mountain ranges –
> Not classed among people, not reckoned as part of the land,
> Gutium, a people who know no inhibitions,
> With human instincts, but canine intelligence, and monkeys' features –
> Enlil brought them out of the mountains.
> Like hordes of locusts they lie over the land,
> Their arms are stretched over the plain for him (Enlil) like a snare for animals,
> (151–19)

Notice the complete lack of sympathy for the invaders, who are compared to dogs or monkeys, as opposed to the earlier description of foreign visitors in Akkade as exotic birds.

Mesopotamia has been reduced to a shadow of its former self. In response to the lamentations of its inhabitants, "Enlil entered the holy bedchamber, and lay down fasting." The god's actions are in fact parallel with the actions of Naram-Sin. The other gods soothe him by cursing Akkade, and the text ends with "Akkade is destroyed – hail Inanna!"

I turn now to a later text describing the same event, but in Akkadian rather than Sumerian, and from Naram-Sin's point of view. This is the so-called Cuthean Legend of Naram-Sin. The version I quote here is the best preserved one (trans. Westenholz 1997, 301–31), in Standard Babylonian, dating to approximately 700 BC, but a longer, more fragmentary Old Babylonian version (1900–1500 BC) and a fragmentary Middle Babylonian version (1400–1300 BC) are extant (Westenholz 1997, 263).

Naram-Sin begins by casting the blame on another archetypal hero, Enmerkar, who failed to leave behind a stele advising his descendents of his own experiences, unlike Naram-Sin who has left behind this stele as an example to follow – that is, this tablet presents itself as a copy of a stele (ll. 1–3). The lack of example has prevented Naram-Sin from engaging in hero-worship or veneration of his ancestors. The Mesopotamian notion of history saw it as providing admonitory examples that legitimized actions in the present, and one key element of the instruction was to show the qualities necessary for kingship. The story of Enmerkar and the Lord of Aratta, part of the legend associated with Enmerkar alluded to by Naram-Sin, can be read in this way (Jacobsen 1987, 277). Clearly, Naram-Sin, when he criticizes the legendary epic hero Enmerkar, is making reference to traditional ideas concerning the purpose of commemorating great deeds of past heroes, on the one hand, to keep them happy, and on the other, to provide an education by example and experience. This matches both hero-worship in Greece and the Greek notion of Homer as a teacher, which Plato made such fun of in his *Ion*. The emphasis on the function of writing to preserve information across dynasties also spoke directly to the "real" audience of the text, the scribes who copied it as part of their training. As Michalowski points out, "the traditions fostered through the schools provided an ideological continuity for a bureaucratic class, independent, to a degree, from the vagaries of power at the top" (Michalowski 1987, 64; also see Tinney 1996, 57–58).[6]

Lacking the advice he needs, the king responds to the enemy invasion with the same sequence of actions found in the Curse of Akkade, attempting a series of divinatory inquiries into the wishes of the gods and then acting against the repeated responses, but the cause and effect are inverted. That is, his actions are precipitated by the enemy invasion, not the cause of it. The image of foreigners as birds that appeared in the first text is used to different effect here:

> A people with partridge bodies, a race with raven faces,
> the great gods created them.
> (31–32)
>
> ...
> At the beginning of their approach, they proceeded against Purushanda.
> Purushanda was completely scattered.
> (49–50)

Naram-Sin is unsure that the enemy is even human (63–71), and sends envoys to test if they can bleed. He then turns to divination to decide on a plan of action:

> I summoned the diviners and instructed (them). (72)
>
> ...
> The "latch-hook" of the great gods did not give me permission for my going and my demonical onrush.
> (78)

As in the previous narrative, the responses from divination prove to be unsatisfactory to Naram-Sin and he takes his own course:

> Thus I said to my heart (i.e., to myself), these were my words:
> "What lion (ever) performed extispicy?
> "What wolf (ever) consulted a dream-interpreter?
> "I will go like a brigand according to my own inclination.
> "And I will cast aside that (oracle) of the god(s); I will be in control of myself."
> (79–83)

Naram-Sin is portrayed as a good ruler, concerned with the prosperity of his people, yet his actions only lead to the destruction of his kingdom:

> I was bewildered, confused, sunk in gloom, desperate, and dejected.
> Thus I said to my heart, these were my words:
> "What have I left to the dynasty!?
> "I am a king who does not keep his country safe
> "and a shepherd who does not safeguard his people.
> "How shall I ever continue to act so that I can get myself out (of this)!?"[7]
> Terror of lions, death, plague, twitching of limbs,
> panic, chills, losses, famine,
> [wan]t, sleeplessness, (and) whatever (evil) existed descended [with] them.
> Above, in co[uncil,] the flood was decided.
> Below, on the [earth], the fl[ood] came into being.
> (88–98)

Two more rounds of omens are sought until, finally, a god decides to help him with some good advice:

Shining Venus from heaven approached me:
"To Naram-Sin son of Sargon,
"Desist! Destroy not the brood of destruction!
"In future days, Enlil will summon them for evil.
..."
(128–131)

...
I delivered them <to> the great gods for delivery(?).
I did not deliver them for my hand to kill.
You, whoever you are, be it governor or prince or anyone else,
whom the gods will call to perform kingship,
I made a tablet-box for you and inscribed a stela [sic] for you.
(147–151)

...
Read this stele!
Hearken unto the words of this stele!
Be not bewildered! Be not confused!
(154–156)

...
Strengthen your walls!
Fill your moats with water!
(160–161)

...
Let him roam through your land! Go not out to him! (166)

...
Let him murder, (and) let him return (unharmed)! (169)

...
Wise scribes,
let them declaim your inscription.
Your who have read my inscription
and thus gotten yourself out (of trouble),
you who have blessed me, may a future (ruler)
Bless you!
(175–180)

Here Ishtar is taking the opposite role her Sumerian correlate had in the Curse of Akkade. Staying true to its allegiance with Naram-Sin, the poem ends with an outcome opposite to that of the Sumerian version. Akkade is spared, and Naram-Sin as narrator makes sure that he supplies his descendants, the implied narratees, with the information he wished he had, fulfilling his role as hero and teacher. The "real" audience of the text, the scribes who copied it, were thus armed with an admonitory example should their ruler refuse their advice.

What are the reasons behind such differences in the narratives? This is a bone of contention among Mesopotamian scholars today. There was a time when the two texts were seen as taking sides in an ethnic conflict. But the analysis of ancient history on racial terms is currently frowned on.[8] Cooper (1993, 12, 14–15, 22) suggests that the earlier Curse of Akkade, whose earliest copies he dates to the Ur III period (1983, 11), presented an example of "the alienation of political power" not to be followed by the Ur III rulers, and provided a flattering contrast with the current prosperity of Mesopotamia. On the other hand, the more distant legendary kings of Uruk, such as Gilgamesh and Lugalbanda, provided a positive example, but with no anti-Akkadian bias (Cooper 2001, 131–42). Liverani (1993b) similarly sees these texts as admonitory history, but because he sees each text as responding to events contemporary to its composition, he dates the texts by finding an appropriate situation, and presuming it was contemporary events that dictated the attitude towards Naram-Sin, a point that seems accurate, but specifying which contemporary events they were is another matter.[9]

It is hard to deny however that the Sumerian Curse of Akkade takes the side of Nippur, a bastion of Sumerian scholarship, where it was a very popular part of the scribal curriculum (there are ninety-five copies extant). After Sumerian was reduced to a classical language, Akkadian began to make serious inroads into the literary use of Sumerian, which in the Ur III period were actively resisted, and Akkadian rulers replaced Sumerian ones in Mesopotamia.[10] And, despite the fact that the texts do not overlap in space and time, we can describe the relation between the two texts as symbolic – the later Akkadian one refutes the earlier Sumerian one, reusing and inverting the motifs found in the Curse of Akkade, especially ll. 131–146 in the Standard Babylonian version of the Cuthean Legend, a section specific to it describing the destruction of the land that would have occurred if Naram-Sin had not followed Ishtar's advice, rather than the devastation of the land that ends the Curse of Akkade. While we can infer that the Curse of Akkade was not known to the scribe who composed the Standard Babylonian version of the Cuthean Legend because the dates of the copies of the two texts do not overlap, we can assume that he was well aware of the standard images of the sacked city, which the Curse of Akkade shares in common with the Sumerian city laments dating to the Ur III and Old Babylonian period, and in the *balağ* laments that continued to be performed well into the first millennium BC. We are given then the barest glimpse of a thriving and multifarious oral tradition with interactions between the two great genres of "epic" and "lament," by its occasional appearance in the written record, which enables us to see how a composer could rework it to create his own version of a well-known tale.[11]

Let us now turn to Hattusa, the site where the Middle Babylonian version of the Cuthean Legend and the Hurro-Hittite Song of Release were found. The latter was written down in 1400 BC or so with the Hurrian original in one column and a translation into Hittite poetry in the other, but it may be based on a historical event that occurred centuries earlier (Neu 1996, 483; Wilhelm 2001, 82). It blames the destruction of the North Syrian city of Ebla not on the poor judgement of its king (here named Meki), but on the poor judgement of Zazalla, an opposing member of the assembly who carries the day, ignoring statements explaining why the Hurrian storm-god Teshub is angry.[12]

The implications of this text, found in 1983, for our understanding of the development of the eastern Mediterranean epic tradition have barely begun to be explored. In a recent article, I placed this text in the eastern Mediterranean epic tradition, showing that the assembly scene, which I will be examining here from a different angle, stands midway between the wider Near Eastern tradition and the Homeric tradition (Bachvarova 2005a). Like the Cuthean Legend, it responds to prior versions, inverting key motifs and, furthermore, it adds motifs that bring it closer to the *Iliad*.

We pick up the assembly scene with a description of Zazalla, the dominant speaker in assembly (*KBo* 32.16). Elsewhere I have compared Zazalla on the one hand to Agamemnon and on the other to Thersites (Bachvarova 2005a, 137–38). Like Thersites he is a powerful speaker, but the position of Thersites is inverted; he tells the truth, yet no one wants to hear it. The tablet breaks off here, but another tablet belonging to a different recension of the text (*KBo* 32.15), continues the scene with only a small gap. Most scholars agree that Zazalla seems to be speaking here. He seems to be replying to a claim that Teshub is in want, and that his suffering will be resolved if the people of Ikinkalis are released, as he has demanded (*KBo* 32.19). Meki, the king, has himself served as the go-between for Teshub, and has conveyed his threats to the Eblaite assembly (Wilhelm 1997, 292), apparently assuming the dissenting role given to the diviners in the Curse of Akkade and the Cuthean Legend. I translate the Hittite version, filling in the gaps from the Hurrian version of this passage:

> [If Tes]hub is injured by oppression
> and he [a]sks [for release], if Teshub
> [is o]ppressed, each will g[i]ve to the storm-god
> [one shekel of silver.]
> (ii 4′–6a′)
>
> We will rescue him, Teshub, the oppressed one.
> (But,) who harms him,
> we will not release.
> For you, Meki,
> does your heart rejoice inside?
> First of all, for you, Meki, your heart inside
> will not rejoice. ...
> (ii 18′–23′)
>
> In the case we let them go
> who will give us food? They are our cupbearers,
> and they give (emending the 1st pl. of the text) out (the food).
> They are our cooks,
> and they wash for us.
>
> And the thread which they spin is [thick]
> like the hair [of an ox.]
> But if for you releasing [is desirable,]
> re[lease] your male and female servants!
>
> Surrender your son! [Your] wife [...
> send! ...
> (ii 26′–iii 6)

The image of the suffering storm-god has presented an interpretive problem for some scholars who have argued that the situation of Teshub is a hypothetical example or a mythical tale (Neu 1993, 347–48; 1996, 482–83; de Martino 2000, 309, 314; Haas 1994, 552; Haas and Wegner 1991, 386; 1997, 439, 442–43; Wilhelm 1997, 281–82). I have argued that the description represents the real situation of the god, suffering from the neglect of his worshippers (Bachvarova 2005b).

Before the passage breaks off, Meki goes to beg for mercy from Teshub, casting the blame on his rival in the assembly:

> "Listen to me Teshub,
> great king of Kummi.
> I will [gi]ve it,
> (i.e.,) *pariššan*,
> but m[y c]ity will not give it.
> Nor will Zazalla, son of Pazz[anik]arri
> give release." Meki
> (tried to?) purify his ci[ty] from sin,
> the ci[ty of Eb]la. He (tried to?) waive the sins[13] for the sake of his city.
> (*KBo* 32.15 iii 13–20)

Meki's attempts at purification and compensation fail, and Ebla is destroyed – as far as we know. Even if the reason is not completely clear due to the current state of the text, there was some explanation given in this text for why Teshub was angry, unlike the texts concerning Naram-Sin.

One can compare the speech of Zazalla to Naram-Sin's refusal to accept the omens that give him an answer he does not want to hear. In particular, in the Curse of Akkade, Naram-Sin does understand that the gods are angry and does seek to find out how to propitiate them. Similarly, in the Song of Release there seems to be an understanding that Teshub is upset. It is unclear whether his demands are in response to a request for clarification, but Zazalla clearly repudiates the answer angrily, as Naram-Sin in the Cuthean Legend responded to his diviners with scorn. On the other hand, Zazalla's hostile reply can be compared to that of Agamemnon in the opening scenes of the *Iliad*, when he denies the claim that Apollo wants Chryseis to be returned, causing the plague that lays waste to his people. On a larger scale, the Trojan assembly has been persuaded by bribes from Paris to refuse to return Helen (11.122–142, see Sale 1994, 65–80), and this leads to the destruction of Troy. The Song of Release seems to follow this same trajectory – when Teshub's demand to release the captives is refused, he seems to cause the destruction of the city (*KBo* 32.11 i 8–9, iv 18′; 32.17, 18, 19).

The debate in the assembly is a new detail in the traditional Near Eastern plot. Although the addition of the humans debating before a human assembly is unique to this text before Homer, it is made up of typical motifs in the Near Eastern epic tradition, particularly the Sumerian epic Gilgamesh and Akka and the Akkadian narrative Atrahasis (Bachvarova 2005a). Moreover, this text has a symbolic relationship with the previous tradition in that it refutes the normal message of such stories, of which audience knowledge is presupposed.[14] Here the blame is placed squarely on Zazalla, not the king, who either conveys the information obtained from diviners, or – more likely because of his direct speech to Teshub in *KBo* 32.15 iii – directly relates the wishes of Teshub. The contrast with the Mesopotamian stories is striking, and implies that the Hurro-Hittite story is not intended for scribes training to be administrators or diviners but rather for the notables that made up the king's council, who were being admonished to obey his word.

Turning now to the *Iliad* and returning to its opening scene, the overriding issue in the debate between Agamemnon and Achilles is the hero's honor, a typically Greek theme not found in the earlier Near Eastern stories. Agamemnon refuses to give up Chryseis because he deserves to possess her as his prize. Furthermore, the leader who is blamed for the suffering he causes his people is called into question by being set against other types of leader. While Agamemnon is king by birth, Achilles deserves honor for his might, and skilled speakers such as Nestor and Thersites can contribute to the decision-making process. This clearly reflects Greek concerns about government, which first make an explicit appearance in Herodotus (*Hist.* 3.80–82), already fully blown, in the debate between the Persian conspirators concerning the best form of government, comparing tyranny or monarchy, aristocracy, oligarchy and democracy (Bachvarova 2005a, 145; see Hammer 1997 on Homer; Pelling 2002 on Herodotus). The *Iliad* continues the tradition, however, of exploring political responses to divine will that were found in the earlier Near Eastern texts, examining the decision-making processes among humans when faced with divinely sent disaster.

When it becomes clear that Agamemnon must return Chryseis to propitiate Apollo, Agamemnon then insults Achilles by taking his own concubine. After Achilles is publicly insulted by Agamemnon he turns to his mother, the goddess Thetis, and asks her to intervene. When Zeus is persuaded by Thetis to interfere and aid the Trojans so that the Achaeans might be brought to the brink of defeat and thereby Achilles receive the honor that is his due, this creates a situation in which the gods know more than they are telling the humans, and we, through the narrator, are privy to that knowledge, are reminded of it at every moment that the human characters within the story assert that they, relying on the messages the gods (especially Zeus) send to them, are sure that they will be victorious, even as we are sure that they will not. Just as the debate in the assembly motif is put to a very sophisticated use by Homer, the motif examined here, namely the role of the ruler as receiver of omens that presage his success or failure in actions that have consequences for his people, is manipulated in a very elaborate way by Homer to achieve maximum pathos and to fit with the concerns of his audience. This is true for the rulers in both sides of the conflict for, like Hector, Agamemnon is tricked by Zeus with a lying dream that convinces him to launch an attack on Troy, promising him victory (2.1–34). The manipulation of this convention is far more pathetic however in the case of

Hector, who we know will be maneuvered into the position in which he must be killed in defense of his city because of his ill-placed faith in the support of Zeus.

James Redfield, in *Nature and Culture in the Iliad: The Tragedy of Hector* (1994), argues in fact that the real hero of the *Iliad* is Hector, and traces the trajectory of his tragic error, beginning at the end of Book VIII, when Hector announces that the Trojans will win, and that he relies on Zeus for support. Hector is thinking of the moment when Zeus thundered thrice and drove Diomedes off (8.167–71), routing the Achaeans and leaving the Trojans in complete control of the plain before Ilios. Yet, Hector's confidence is expressed directly after we, the audience, have been allowed to witness a scene among the gods in which they discuss exactly how long he will be allowed to win, and why. And, the scene closes with the gods rejecting the sacrifices the Trojans make to them, since the city of Troy was hateful to them. Hector's confident decision to keep his men outside the walls of Troy for the night allows Diomedes and Odysseus to wreak all sorts of havoc on the camp. Hector apparently is not aware of the advice given to Naram-Sin, which he passed on to all his readers, to remain inside the city and let the enemy do their worst outside.[15]

Hector becomes more and more deluded during the course of the next few days, and a key turning point is the first time he rejects the cautious advice of the seer Poulydamas and refuses to retreat rather than attack:

> For a bird came to them (i.e., the Trojans), who were eager to go across, a high-flying eagle bounding the host on the right side, bearing a bloody snake in his talons, giant, living still, gasping, nor did it forget its lust for battle, for it struck him as he held it about the breast by the neck, bending around backwards; he hurled it away from himself onto the ground suffering from the pain, and threw it down into the middle of the throng; he himself, calling out (*klanxas*), flew on a gust of wind. The Trojans shivered when they saw the variegated snake lying in the center, an omen of shield-bearing Zeus. Then Poulydamas spoke standing before bold Hector, "Hector, always somehow you rebuke me in assemblies, although I am advising the right things, since it is not proper for (me) as a member of the *demos* to speak out of line, either in counsel or in war, but always to augment your power. Now however, I will speak out as seems best to me. Let us not go to fight the Danaans about the ships...." (12.200–216)
>
> Hector of variegated helm spoke to him, looking at him from under his brows, "Poulydamas, now those things you speak are not dear to me. You know how to think other advice (*mython*) better than this. If in earnest you tell that truthfully, then the gods themselves indeed have lost their minds, who would advise to forget the plans of loud-thundering Zeus, which he himself promised to me and agreed to. You yourself advise me to trust in slender-winged birds, which I don't care about at all, don't pay any attention to.... Let us trust in the plan of great Zeus, who rules all mortals and immortals...." (12.230–242)

The scribes who copied the Curse of Akkade and the Cuthean Legend as training to be administrators and diviners for the regime would have appreciated Poulydamas' comments on the difficulties of their role. Hector's reply meanwhile is reminiscent of Naram-Sin's in the Cuthean Legend:

> What lion (ever) performed extispicy?
> What wolf (ever) consulted a dream-interpreter?
> I will go like a brigand according to my own inclination.
> And I will cast aside the (oracle) of the god(s): I will be in control of myself.

Of course, the bird oracle that Hector repudiates is ambiguous: who is the snake and who the eagle?

This entire sequence of events is reprised in Book 18. Patroclus has been killed, Achilles has announced his intention to kill Hector, and the reply of Thetis, that this means his own death is imminent, presupposes that he will be successful. It has become clear to Achilles that the gods' intervention, the advice to avoid battle (the same advice that Hector ignores, causing his own destruction), which seemingly was to give him more honor, has been at the cost of his friend's life. He laments in words that many scholars have noticed bear remarkable resemblance to the words of Gilgamesh mourning the death of Enkidu (West 1997,

340–44). In this context, in which once again the intentions of the gods are made clear to the audience, Hector again disagrees with Poulydamas' cautious advice and insists that Zeus supports him.

> So Hector spoke, and the Trojans shouted assent, foolish ones, for Pallas Athena took from them their minds, for they agreed with Hector who advised badly, but no one did with Poulydamas, who advised a good plan. (18.310–313)

The delusion of the Trojans is reminiscent of the wrong decision made by the Eblaite council in the Song of Release, which ignores the advice of their king, the go-between for the Storm-god Teshub, and takes Zazalla's side.

Hector rejects cautious advice – now from his parents – most pitifully for the third and final time in Book 22:

> They did not persuade the heart of Hector, but rather he awaited giant Achilles as he came nearer. Like a snake in the mountains might wait for a man by his hole, having eaten evil poison; and an evil anger came over him, and he looked fiercely, circling his hole. (22.91–95)

Now it becomes clear which side was the snake in the earlier portent! Hector refuses to retreat, but:

> Anguished indeed, he spoke to his great-hearted soul, "Woe is me, if I take shelter in the tower and walls, Poulydamas would be the first to place shame on me, who advised me to lead the Trojans to the city at the fall of baneful night, when shining Achilles rose up. But I wasn't persuaded; indeed it would have been much better. But now, since I have destroyed the host with my recklessness, I am ashamed before the Trojan men and women with their trailing robes, lest some other person, who is less than me, might say, "Hector, trusting in his strength destroyed his people." (22.98–107)

Compare what Naram-Sin says to himself in the Cuthean Legend, when he realizes his grievous error:

> What have I left to the dynasty!?
> I am a king who does not keep his country safe
> and a shepherd who does not safeguard his people.
> How shall I ever continue to act so that I can get myself out (of this)!?

Hector goes on with a distinctively Greek answer, evoking the honor and duty of a Homeric warrior: "So they will say; but it would be much better for me, standing face to face in battle, to kill Achilles and return or to die myself with glory for the city..." (22.108–110). In fact he is unable to follow through on this brave thought, but "trembling seized him" (22.136), and he turned tail and ran. As Naram-Sin put it, "terror of lions, death, plague, twitching of limbs, panic, chills." The gods, interested spectators, realize this is the moment of truth and, atypically, hesitate (167–185).[16] Yet, as Naram-Sin says in the Cuthean Legend, "Above, in co[uncil,] the flood was decided."

To sum up, we can see in Homer a more sophisticated discussion of the responsibilities of the gods and the humans in the fall of a city, one that, unlike the stories of Naram-Sin, does not take sides and allows the audience insight into the thinking of the gods to which the intradiegetic characters are not privy. Amongst differences that can be explained by the concerns of the audience of the Homeric epics, we find striking similarities with the Near Eastern texts, from the intervention of Ishtar/Thetis ordering her favorite to keep out of a conflict, to the defiant response, to unwelcome omens, down to insignificant details such as the characterization of foreigners as birds, which is also found in the *Iliad* (2.459–68).

The relationship between a female goddess and the hero of the tale is a key element that is retained while undergoing adaptation. In the Sumerian stories, the king is legitimized by divine marriage between himself and Inanna. When Inanna abandons the king, his kingdom is doomed.[17] Ishtar's intervention, which saves Naram-Sin in the Cuthean Legend, presupposes such a relationship. Although we do not have enough of the Song of Release to see if the goddesses Allani and/or Ishara mentioned in the opening lines played such a role in the plot, in the Greek material the special relationship between man and goddess is maintained and reduplicated, with several heroes having a close bond with a goddess, from Diomedes and Athena to Paris and Aphrodite, to the two heroes who have divine mothers, Aeneas son of Aphrodite and Achilles son of Thetis. As Slatkin (1991, 53–84) discusses, the divine mother's intervention on behalf of her mortal son makes all the more poignant his destined death. This notion however was not new to the Greeks, but was already present in the story of Gilgamesh, a king born of a goddess and preoccupied with his own mortality.

We can also see that as the Near Eastern epic tradition gets closer to Greece, it becomes more like what we find in Homer. The Song of Release allows us to place the traditional motif of the destruction of a city in the Hurro-Hittite sphere along with other key themes that appear in Greek hexametric narrative poetry, such as the cosmogonic myth of Hesiod's *Theogony*, the fantastic wanderings of Odysseus, the mourning for a dead friend, and the assembly scene of the *Iliad*, for this text belongs to the same genre as Song of Kumarbi and the Hurro-Hittite version of Gilgamesh, as evinced by shared formulae (Bachvarova 2002, 120–26). The fact that themes from three different Hurro-Hittite songs match up with the themes from three different hexametric songs supports the possibility of transmission of a strain of the Near Eastern tradition closely related to the Hurro-Hittite tradition to the ancestors of Hesiod and Homer, either in the Mycenean period or later (Bachvarova 2005, 149–53).

One way in which the Near Eastern narrative tradition must have reached Greek-speaking poets is via continuity through the Dark Ages of an Anatolian tradition, whether as epic or as lament, or as both, about Troy, that Homer is responding to, and combining with, a Greek-centric version of the same story. I argue this based on William Merritt Sale's findings that Homeric formulae for Trojan heroes are scanty and rarely repeated, which I agree are good evidence that the sympathetic portrayal is late and replaced a more negative portrayal, deleting pejorative formulae for the Trojans. On the other hand, the calquing of Anatolian phrases and metaphors into the Homeric repertoire as discussed by Puhvel (1983; 1988; 1991; 1993) and Watkins (1998) needs to have occurred quite early in the tradition – perhaps at the very time Latacz (2004, 267–74) suggests the story of Troy was first immortalized in hexameters (some time between 1450–1050 bc).

Late transmission with continuity through the Dark Ages could also explain Homer's knowledge of, for example, the social structure of the Hittite nobility and the cities that made up the Middle Hittite Assuwan alliance, as evinced in the Trojan catalogue of allies, which matches the list of the lands of Assuwa, even following the same order (Watkins 1995, 150–51; 1998). Similarly the use of double names of some of the Trojans seems to match Anatolian customs in the second millennium (Bachvarova 2002, 47–48). The Hittite king Tudhaliya III also had a Hurrian name Tashmi-Sharri, for example, and de Jong (1987) has noted that Homer uses Greek names for Trojans such as Alexander when his narrative is focalized through Greek eyes, while he uses names with possible Anatolian origins such as Paris when telling his story through Trojan eyes. Therefore there were at least two times when transmission occurred, early (Late Bronze Age or Early Iron Age) and late. This is easier to believe, I think, if we agree with those, such as Geoffrey Horrocks (1997), who deny that there was an Aeolic phase in the Homeric dialect.

Finally, we can at least imagine how it is that Homer created a story that, unlike its predecessors, was sympathetic to both sides in the conflict – it would involve combining lays together, much as it has been postulated the story of Diomedes was inserted into the *Iliad*, or the story of Telemachus into the *Odyssey*. It has long since been suggested that the story of Achilles was added to a story of the Trojan War, and the final version of the *Iliad* was also a further blend of two narratives, one that was sympathetic to the Trojans and focused on Hector as a tragic hero, and another that took the side of the Greeks.

I turn now to some speculations as to how Homer could have become acquainted with a version of the fall of Troy that portrays Hector in such a sympathetic light. Lamentations performed by the losers for the fall of their city could have been an important source. Homer certainly acknowledges the power of lament when he describes Andromache and her handmaidens lamenting over Hector in the final book of the *Iliad*, and city-laments are found throughout the ancient Mediterranean, from Sumer, to the Old Testament, to ancient Greece, so we should not ignore the possibility of influence from this women's genre on epic.[18] Furthermore, we have seen that there is borrowing from motifs found in laments into Near Eastern texts we might define as epic.

The story line that I have traced from the third millennium to the first millennium BC, from Nippur to Anatolia, does not develop in a single direction and is not confined to a single genre. Furthermore, the relationship between the texts is not intertextual. Rather, the statement by Ramanujan (1991, 146) concerning the *Ramayana* fits well here:

> These various texts not only relate to prior texts directly, to borrow or refute, but they relate to each other through this common code or common pool. Every author, if one may hazard a metaphor, dips into it and brings out a unique crystallization, a new text with a unique texture and a fresh context.

NOTES

1 Haubold (2002) has been the first to discuss how one poet creatively adapted and responded to earlier versions of a well-known theme in the eastern Mediterranean poetic tradition. Using this approach, he deals effectively with the confusing variations in the theogonic traditions that appear in Hesiod and other Greek sources, and their relationship with the Sumerian, Akkadian and lost West Semitic versions.

2 It is slightly earlier than the four or five city laments, which start appearing near the end of the next great dynasty in Mesopotamia, the Ur III dynasty. On Mesopotamian city laments, see Tinney (1996, 19–25), Michalowski (1989, 4–8) and Hallo (1995, 1871–81).

3 I use the translation of Cooper (1983).

4 Following Cooper (1993, 17).

5 We do know that Naram-Sin did in fact refurbish Ekur, from inscriptions found there (Liverani 1993b, 57) and that it was traditional to sing *balağ* laments to propitiate the gods in the demolition phase of repairing a temple (Black 1991, 29).

6 Furthermore, as J. Westenholz (1993, 214–15) notes, one point of the criticism of Enmerkar is that he invented only writing on clay, not engraving words on stone for posterity.

7 The Old Babylonian version matches this passage up to this point (8–15, trans. Westenholz 1997, 273). Unfortunately, l. 93 can be translated in more than one way. An alternate translation is, "How shall I ever continue so that I can put myself out (in order to save the country)?" (Westenholz 1997, 269, 273).

8 See the review of scholarship by Cooper (1983, 39–40; 1993, 15; 2001, 131–42) and Liverani (1993a, 8–9; 1993b). Nissen (1993) discusses various differences that coincide with the switch from Sumerian rule to Akkadian rule.

9 Liverani (1993b, 56–59) pushes the date of composition of the "Curse of Akkade" forward into the Isin-Larsa period, about fifty years after the Ur III period, in order to date it to the rebuilding of the Ekur by Ishme-Dagan, arguing that the text expresses anti-Akkadian feelings appropriate to this period. While his revised dating is not widely accepted, Tinney (1996, 35–36) does note that the Nippur Lament, which alludes to the rebuilding of the Ekur by Ishme-Dagan, copies some themes and inverts others found in the Curse of Akkade. Similarly, the Sumerian city lament Lamentation over the Destruction of Sumer and Ur draws heavily on the traditional themes and phrases found in the Curse of Akkade, but does not blame the destruction of the land by the gods on its ruler Ibbi-Sin, the last king in the Ur III dynasty, rather attributing it to the workings of fate (Michalowski 1989, 8–9). The complex and interesting relationship between the Curse of Akkade and the Sumerian city laments cannot be gone into here. Liverani (1993b, 62–63) has less success finding a significant event that elucidates the point of the Cuthean Legend. The circularity of his approach has been commented on by other scholars (van de Mieroop 1999).

10 Michalowski (1987, 60–62) suggests that the reinstallation of Sumerian, by now a classical language, as an administrative language was part of a systematic bureaucratic reform.

11 On the relationship between the oral and written versions of the Naram-Sin stories, including others not discussed here, see J. Westenholz (1992), who describes the Old and Middle Babylonian texts as informal write-ups of a flexible oral tradition, as opposed to the fixed text of the Standard Babylonian version of the Cuthean Legend.

12 My translations are based on the edition of Neu (1996). Recent translations may also be found in Hoffner (1998, 65-80) and Wilhelm (2001), although they differ in crucial details from the ones I give here. I defend my interpretation in detail in Bachvarova (2005b).

13 The word I translate as "sin" (*waštul*) has been translated by Hoffner (1998, 73–75) as "debt" to fit with his theory

on why the people of Ikinkalis are being forced to work for the people of Ebla, namely, that they are debt slaves. Neu (1996, 9) has also followed this interpretation, but Otto (2001, 524–31) has shown that the people of Ikinkalis are prisoners of war. Also see Bachvarova (2005b) for a discussion of why Teshub demands their release.

14 We know that some educated Hittites were aware of the Cuthean Legend of "Naram-Sin" since two Middle Babylonian exemplars were found there, along with fragments of other stories about him in both Akkadian and Hittite (Westenholz 1997, 9, 102, 263).

15 West (1997, 374) cites a different set of Near Eastern parallels to the Doloneia.

16 This scene is a doublet of the scene among the gods when they decide that Sarpedon must die (*Il.* 16.431–461) and descends from the scene in Gilgamesh in which the gods debate whether he or Enkidu must die (West 1997, 179–80, 343–44).

17 This idea also appears in Enmerkar and the Lord of Aratta.

18 Another possibility is that there were different versions of the narrative recounting the fall of Troy, but both from the loser's side, for male and female losers may have different interpretations of the event. For the latter situation, we may turn to the biblical book of Lamentations, telling of the fall of Jerusalem. Nancy Lee (2002, 47–75) has argued that a male prophet is singing "in dialogue" with a female lamentation singer ("Jerusalem's poet"), and that they show different attitudes towards God.

REFERENCES

Bachvarova, M. R. (2002) From Hittite to Homer: The Role of Anatolians in the Transmission of Epic and Prayer Motifs from the Ancient Near East to the Ancient Greeks. Ph.D. diss. Chicago, University of Chicago.

___ (2005a) The Eastern Mediterranean Epic Tradition from *Bilgames and Akka* to the *Song of Release* to Homer's *Iliad. Greek, Roman and Byzantine Studies* 45, 131–54.

___ (2005b) Relations between God and Man in the Hurro-Hittite Song of Release. *Journal of the American Oriental Society*, 125, 45–58.

Black, J. (1991) Eme-sal Cult Songs and Prayers. In P. Michalowski et al. (eds.) *Velles Paraules: Ancient Near Eastern Studies in Honor of Miguel Civil on the Occasion of his Sixty-Fifth Birthday*, 23–36. Aula Orientalis 9. Barcelona, Editorial AUSA.

Burkert, W. (1992) *The Orientalizing Revolution: Near Eastern Influence on Greek Culture in the Early Archaic Age*, trans. M. E. Pinder and W. Burkert. Cambridge, MA, Harvard University.

Cooper, J. S. (1983) *The Curse of Agade*. Baltimore, Johns Hopkins University.

___ (1993) Paradigm and Propaganda: The Dynasty of Akkade in the 21st Century. In M. Liverani (ed.) *Akkad, the First World Empire: Structure, Ideology, Traditions*, 91–106. Padua, Sargon.

___ (2001) Literature and History: The Historical and Political Referents of Sumerian Literary Texts. In T. Abusch, P.-A. Beaulieu, J. Huehnergard, P. Machinist and P. Steinkeller (eds.) *Proceedings of the XLV Rencontre Assyriologique Internationale. Vol. 1: Historiography in the Cuneiform World*, 131–48. Bethesda, MD, CDL.

de Jong, I. J. F. (1987) Paris/Alexandros in the *Iliad*. *Mnemosyne* 40, 124–28.

Haas, V. (1994) *Geschichte der hethitischen Religion*. Handbuch der Orientalistik. Erste Abteilung. Der Nahe und Mittlere Osten 15. Leiden, Brill.

Haas, V. and Wegner, I. (1991) Review of *Keilschrifttexte aus Boghazköi 32: Die hurritische-hethitische Bilingue und weitere Texte aus der Oberstadt*, eds. Heinrich Otten and Christel Rüster. *Orientalistische Literaturzeitung* 86, 384–91.

___ (1997) Literarische und grammatikalische Betrachtungen zu einer hurritischen Dichtung. *Orientalistische Literaturzeitung* 92, 437–55.

Hallo, W. W. (1995) Lamentation and Prayers in Sumer and Akkade. In J. M. Sasson (ed.) *Civilizations of the Ancient Near East*, 1871–81. New York: Scribner's.

Hammer, D. (1997) "Who Shall Readily Obey?": Authority and Politics in the *Iliad*. *Phoenix* 51, 1–23.

___ (2002) *The Iliad as Politics: The Performance of Political Thought*. Norman, OK, University of Oklahoma.

Haubold, J. (2002) Greek Epic: A Near Eastern Genre? *Proceedings of the Cambridge Philological Society* 48, 1–19.

Hoffner, H. A. Jr. (1998) *Hittite Myths*. 2nd ed. Writings from the Ancient World 2. Atlanta, GA, Society of Biblical Literature.

Horrocks, G. (1997) Homer's Dialect. In I. Morris and B. Powell (ed.) *A New Companion to Homer*, 193–217 Leiden, Brill.

Jacobsen, T. (1987) *The Harps That Once ... Sumerian Poetry in Translation*. New Haven, Yale University.

Latacz, J. (2004) *Troy and Homer: Towards a Solution of an Old Mystery*, trans. K. Windle and R. Ireland. Oxford, Oxford University.

Lee, N. C. (2002) *The Singers of Lamentations: Cities under Seige, from Ur to Jerusalem to Sarajevo*. Leiden, Brill.
Liverani, M. (1993a) Akkad: An Introduction. In M. Liverani (ed.) *Akkad, the First World Empire: Structure, Ideology, Traditions*, 1–10. Padua, Sargon.
___ (1993b) Model and Actualization: The Kings of Akkad in the Historical Tradition. In M. Liverani (ed.) *Akkad, the First World Empire: Structure, Ideology, Traditions*, 41–67. Padua, Sargon.
Martino, S. de (2000) Il "Canto della liberazione": Composizione letteraria bilingue hurrico-ittita sulla distruzione de Ebla. *La Parola del Passato* 55, 296–320.
Michalowski, P. (1987) Charisma and Control: On Continuity and Change in Early Mesopotamian Bureaucratic Systems. In M. Gibson and R. D. Biggs (eds.) *The Organization of Power: Aspects of Bureaucracy in the Ancient Near East*, 55–68. SAOC 46. Chicago, The Oriental Institute of the University of Chicago.
___ (1989) *The Lamentation over the Destruction of Sumer and Ur*. Winona Lake, IN, Eisenbrauns.
Neu, E. (1993) Knechtschaft und Freiheit. Betrachtungen über ein hurritisch-hethitisches Textensemble aus Ḫattuša. In B. Janowski, K. Koch and G. Wilhelm (eds.) *Religionsgeschichtliche Beziehungen zwischen Kleinasien, Nordsyrien und dem Alten Testament. Internationales Symposium Hamburg 17.-21. März 1990*, 329–61. Orbis Biblicus et Orientalis 129. Freibourg/Göttingen, Universitätsverlag/Vandenhoeck & Ruprecht.
___ (1996) *Das hurritische Epos der Freilassung I. Untersuchungen zu einem hurritisch-hethitischen Textensemble aus Hattuša*. StBoT 32. Wiesbaden, Harrassowitz.
Nissen, H. J. (1993) Settlement Patterns and Material Culture of the Akkadian Period: Continuity and Discontinuity. In M. Liverani (ed.) *Akkad, the First World Empire: Structure, Ideology, Traditions*, 91–106. Padua, Sargon.
Otto, E. (2001) *Kirenzi* und *d^erôr* in der hurritisch-hethitischen Serie "Freilassung" (*parā tarnumar*). In G. Wilhelm (ed.) *Akten des IV. Internationalen Kongresses für Hethitologie. Würzburg, 4.-8. Oktober 1999*, 524–31. StBoT 45. Wiesbaden, Harrassowitz.
Pelling, C. (2002) Speech and Action: Herodotus' Debate on the Constitutions. *Proceedings of the Cambridge Philological Society* 48, 123–58.
Puhvel, J. (1983) Homeric Questions and Hittite Answers. *American Journal of Philology* 104, 217–27.
___ (1988) An Anatolian Turn of Phrase in the *Iliad*. *American Journal of Philology* 109, 591–93.
___ (1991) *Homer and Hittite*. Innsbrucker Beiträge zur Sprachwissenschaft, Vorträge und kleinere Schriften 47. Innsbruck, Institut für Sprachwissenschaft der Universität Innsbruck.
___ (1993) A Hittite Calque in the Iliad. *Historische Sprachforschung* 106, 36–38.
Ramanujan, A. K. (1991) Three Hundred Rāmāyaṇas. In P. Richman (ed.) *Many Rāmāyaṇas: The Diversity of a Narrative Tradition in South Asia*, 22–40. Berkeley, University of California.
Redfield, J. (1994) *Nature and Culture in the Iliad: The Tragedy of Hector*. 2nd expanded edition. Durham, Duke University.
Sale, W. M. (1994) The Government of Troy: Politics in the *Iliad*. *Greek, Roman and Byzantine Studies* 35, 1–100.
Slatkin, L. M. (1991) *The Power of Thetis: Allusion and Interpretation in the Iliad*. Berkeley, Los Angeles, University of California.
Tinney, S. (1996) *The Nippur Lament: Royal Rhetoric and Divine Legitimation in the Reign of Išme-Dagan of Isin (1953-1935 B.C.)*. Occasional Publications of the Samuel Noah Kramer Fund 16. Philadelphia, University Museum.
van de Mieroop, M. (1999) Literature and Political Discourse in Ancient Mesopotamia. In B. Böck, E. Cancik-Kirschbaum and T. Richter (eds.) *Munuscula Mesopotamica: Festschrift für Johannes Renger*, 327–39. AOAT 267. Münster, Ugarit-Verlag.
C. Watkins (1995) *How to Kill a Dragon: Aspects of Indo-European Poetics*. Oxford, Oxford University.
___ (1998) The Language of the Trojans. In L. Oliver (ed.) *Selected Writings*, 700–717. Innsbrucker Beiträge zur Sprachwissenschaft 80. Innsbruck, Institut für Sprachwissenschaft der Universität Innsbruck.
West, M. L. (1997) *The East Face of Helicon*. Oxford, Oxford University.
Westenholz, J. G. (1992) Oral Traditions and Written Texts in the Cycle of Akkade. In M. E. Vogelzang and H. L. J. Vanstiphout (eds.) *Mesopotamian Epic Literature: Oral or Aural?* Lewiston, Edwin Mellen.
___ (1993) Writing for Posterity: Naram-Sin and Enmerkar. In A. F. Rainey (ed.) *kinattûtu ša dârâti: Raphael Kutscher Memorial Volume*, 205–18. Tel Aviv, Tel Aviv University Institute of Archaeology.
___ (1997) *Legends of the Kings of Akkade: The Texts*. Mesopotamian Civilizations 7. Winona Lake, IN, Eisenbrauns.
Wilhelm, G. (1997) Die Könige von Ebla nach der hurritisch-hethitischen Serie "Freilassung." *Altorientalische Forschungen* 24, 277–93.
___ (2001) Das hurritische-hethitische »Lied der Freilassung«. In M. Dietrich et al. (eds.) *Ergänzungslieferung*, 82–91. Texte aus der Umwelt des Alten Testaments. Gütersloh, Gütersloher Verlagshaus.

10

HITTITE ETHNICITY?

CONSTRUCTIONS OF IDENTITY IN HITTITE LITERATURE

Amir Gilan

The nature of "identity" in general and ethnic identity in particular are currently being studied extensively in many fields of the humanities. Ethnicity in the ancient world has been a frequent topic of research in recent years. This work also provides a useful basis for a discussion of ethnic identity in second millennium Anatolia. Here I first consider the question of Hittite ethnicity within a larger framework of recent studies in sociology and social anthropology concerning the nature of ethnic identity. Second, I look at the role of literature in constructing Hittite identity. One such discursive strategy employed in the texts will be examined in detail.

1. Within Hittite studies, discussions of ethnicity are principally concerned with the formative period of Hittite history, that is, the emergence of the Hittite kingdom from the Old Assyrian period and onwards (eighteenth – sixteenth centuries BCE). The central issue at stake here is the role played by ethnic differences in the formation process of the Hittite kingdom in central Anatolia.

One model describes the emergence of the Hittite Kingdom as a result of a clash between two distinct ethno-political entities: The eventually triumphant Hittite (Nesite) speakers based around the city of Kanes (Hittite Nesa) south of the Kızıl Irmak River, and the Hattic inhabitants, mostly settled just to the north, in the basin of that same river. This interpretation is based on evidence suggesting what Singer terms, "a basic division of Anatolia into ethno-cultural zones, distinguishable by their onomasticon, pantheon and material culture, before Anitta's unification of the land" (2000, 638). These ethno-cultural divisions are considered roughly to correspond with the political map of Anatolia before Anitta's conquests. Thus, the rivalry between Kanes and the kingdoms of Hattusa or Zalpa, as reflected mainly in the Anitta text (for which see Hoffner 1997a), has been interpreted as an ethnic-flavored conflict between Hittites and Hattians.

In addition to the Hattic and Hittite speakers, several other linguistic groups were likewise settled in Anatolia. Palaic was spoken in the land of Palā, classical Paphlagonia, and Luwian was spoken in central and west Anatolia as well as in Kizzuwatna. The southern and southeastern parts of Anatolia were also inhabited by a Hurrian speaking population (Singer 1981, 124). In his recent treatment of Luwian prehistory, Melchert is, however, very careful not to invest his linguistic map with ethnic identities: "There can be little doubt," he writes, "that the societies of which Luwian speakers were a part were multi-ethnic, and this is almost certainly true of the Luwian-speaking population itself" (2003, 8). More generally, Melchert warns that language and culture do not always correspond to ethnicity or nationhood (2003, 2). In his history of the Hittite kingdom, Bryce argues that the notion of ethnic conflicts is "almost certainly meaningless" in the Middle Bronze Age (1998, 15). Furthermore, it has been questioned whether the sparse evidence available – relatively little is known about the true socio-linguistic or cultural situation in Anatolia in this period – allows any conclusions concerning ethnic identity in this, or in later, better-documented periods.

The picture that emerges from the century-long study of the archives in Hattusa indeed defies any simplistic cultural or ethnic definition. Hittite, the main administrative language of the kingdom, was named by its speakers as Nesite, that is, of the city of Nesa/Kanes. These Nesite speakers, however, identified themselves as the inhabitants of the Land of Hattusa, named after their originally "Hattic" capital city. Early Hittite religion and ideology of kingship are likewise a mixture of different components. The "Hittite" king and his queen both bear Luwian titles whereas the title of their son, the crown prince, is Hattic. The Storm-god of Hattusa is of Hattic origin, his name is however Indo-European (Melchert 2003, 18–21). In the light of this bricolage, the view that Old Hittite culture should be interpreted as the product of political supremacy of one distinct ethnic group of Indo-Europeans over the indigenous Hattic inhabitants within the Halys basin, is now generally being discarded in favor of a model of a long-term transculturation of a variety of cultural and linguistic elements (Klinger 2003: 95; Melchert 2003, 21; Oettinger 2002, 51). This process continued in later phases of Hittite history as well, in which Hurrian/north Syrian/Kizzuwatnean cultural elements were added to the mixture. For this bricolage of cultural and linguistic elements, Güterbock coined the term "Hittite civilization":

> We must strictly separate two spheres: linguistic and cultural. Since the name "Hittite" has, for forty years, been applied to the main language of the Boğazköy archives, we cannot easily abandon it (...). The speakers of this language took part in what may be called "Hittite civilization," but the latter is a mixed culture and cannot in its entirety be ascribed to a single ethnic group. Consequently, the name "Hittite" must mean one thing if applied to a language, another thing if applied to a civilization. (1957, 233–34)

Following Güterbock, the existence of "Hittite" ethnicity has been often rejected by modern scholarship. It has been claimed that the term "Hittite" itself as well as ethnic concepts such as *people*, *nation* or "*Volk*" are anachronistic for the period. Furthermore, there is nothing to suggest that ethnical, cultural or linguistic divisions corresponded to political borders, and the idea that they should do so, in other words, nationalism, is certainly anachronistic (Klinger 1996, 18). The Hittites' own term "Land of Hattusa" (*Ḫattušaš utnē*, KUR [URU]*ḪATTI*) designates merely a political entity named after its capital city (Starke 1998, 185–86). The term DUMU.MEŠ KUR [URU]*ḪATTI* denotes the inhabitants of that political entity, not exclusively the group of Hittite speakers (Klinger 1996, 85–87; Bryce 1998, 19). In his definition of the term "Hittite" cited above, Güterbock cannot, however, entirely dispense with the term ethnicity. "Hittite" Anatolia is often characterized in Hittitology as multi-ethnic, even by scholars who are otherwise reluctant to use the ethnic tag.

Yet, whereas "Hittite culture" certainly represents a bricolage of different elements, interwoven in a long-term process of transculturation, the political formation and later consolidation of the Hittite Kingdom throughout its history was actively carried out by a surprisingly constant, distinct group of actors. As the Egyptologist J. Baines notes, "the creation of a state and culture involves forging an ideology and an identity that will underpin its unity. Creating a collective 'self' that implies a collective 'other,' where the other is often axiomatically diverse and the self unitary" (1996, 361). Did such a collective identity emerge with the formation of the Hittite kingdom in Anatolia? Could it be described as ethnic identity?

Several methodological issues seem to me therefore fundamental for any discussion of ethnic identity in Hittite Anatolia. These include a definition of the term ethnicity, the possibility of its application to ancient Anatolia and its interpretative value to Hittitology. Another question concerns the relation between ethnic identity and culture. These matters will be addressed in the following sections.

2. In order to locate discussions of ethnicity in second millennium Anatolia within a larger framework, I begin with E. Gellner's pertinent remarks on social structure in pre-industrial, agro-literate political entities (Gellner 1983, 8–18). "In the characteristic agro-literate polity," Gellner writes, "the ruling class

forms a small minority of the population, rigidly separate from the great majority of direct agricultural producers, or peasants. Generally speaking, its ideology exaggerates rather than underplays the inequality of classes and the degree of separation of the ruling stratum" (Gellner 1983, 9–10).

According to Gellner's model, social stratification in agro-literate political entities is horizontal. Therefore, the ruling elite is inclined to stress and reinforce cultural difference in order for fortify its privileged position and has no interest whatsoever in promoting cultural homogeneity. As to the agricultural producers, peasant communities are economically and politically tied to their locality and seldom communicate with each other. Even if the nationalistic notion that cultural boundaries should define political entities had been invented in that period, according to Gellner it had no chance of success (Gellner 1983, 10–11). Gellner's argument that nationalism is anachronistic in the ancient world has also been extended to ethnicity (Hall 1997, 18 and n. 6). Yet ethnic identities are not exclusively modern and could also be found in antiquity (Malkin 1998, 55).

It is not difficult to identify Gellner's horizontal ruling stratum in Hittite Anatolia. It is well known that the extended royal family played an overwhelming role in Hittite politics throughout Hittite history (Beckman 1995, 539–60; Starke 1996). Starke even suggests equating the term LÚ.MEŠ [URU]*ḪA-AT-TI* (*ḫattušumeneš*) "Hittites" exclusively with members of this kinship group, which also constituted the *panku-*, the politically active "community (*Gemeinschaft*)" of the kingdom (Starke 1996, 153 and n. 54). As Watkins (2002, 167–69) shows, ideal Hittite social structure is defined in the first paragraph of the historical outline of the Telipinu Proclamation in terms of the individual's relation to the king. This relation is established either through family and kinship ties or through alliance, either by marriage or by political loyalty.

Patterns of participation in Old Hittite festivals reveal, however, a somewhat more complex situation than Gellner's model pertains. The participation of delegations from various cities in central Anatolia in the KI.LAM festival suggests, as Rutherford has recently argued (2002), the existence in this area of a "religious network," probably already pre-"Hittite." This pattern of religious participation expresses not only the horizontal allegiance to the king, but more importantly, a notion of common identity shared by the participating towns. Much of the same territory – north and central Anatolia – was later covered by elaborate trips by the king and other members of the royal family during the two great festivals, the AN.TAḪ.ŠUM festival in spring and the *nuntarriyašḫaš* festival in autumn (Nakamura 2002, 11–12, 438–39). An association with a specific territory and the notion of shared cult are important components of ethnic identity (Eriksen 1993, 34–35).

Ethnic studies are often characterized as a Ping-Pong match between two rivaling positions, usually termed the "primordial" and the "instrumentalist," "situationalist" or "circumstantial" (Siapkas 2004, 13; Sökefeld 1997, 30; Malkin 1998, 56; Fenton 2003, 83–84). Considered as primordial, ethnicity is a distinctive, privileged, deeply emotional attachment, determined at birth. In this sense it is often compared to kin relationship (Brown, cited by Sökefeld 1997, 29):

> The ethnic group is perceived by its members as a pseudo-kinship group, which promises to provide the all-embracing emotional security offered by the family to the child, which offers practical support, in the form of nepotism, such as the family gives to its members when they interact with others and which, precisely because it is based on the ubiquitous family and kinship ties, is widely and easily available for utilisation in politics.

Ethnicity, however, is a social construction rather than a biological phenomenon (Hall 1997, 32). Precisely for this reason instrumentalists view ethnicity as a context-bound social strategy, aimed to improve the group's socio-political situation (Eriksen 1993, 45–46; Siapkas, 2004, 13, 281). Ethnicity could thus be defined as the "associated phenomena and processes by which identities and affiliations are articulated" (Siapkas 2004, 15). According to this approach, ethnic identity is flexible and could be changed in relation to fluctuating historical circumstances (Malkin 1998, 56; Sökefeld 1997, 31; Hall 1997, 32). It is therefore not a universal phenomenon, but is restricted to certain historical situations. Instrumentalists are therefore mainly interested in the historical circumstances in which ethnicity is created in a specific historical context, in other words, in the process of ethnogenesis (Malkin 1998, 56–58). Ethnicity arises, according to Eriksen, "either from a process of social differentiation within a population, which eventually leads to the division of that population into two distinctive groups, or by an expansion of the system boundaries bringing hitherto discrete groups into contact with each other" (1993, 79).

The criteria that constitute ethnicity can vary (Eriksen 1993, 34). Cultural patterns as well as genetic, linguistic or religious traits do not necessarily correspond to ethnic boundaries (Hall 1997, 23–24; Fenton, 2003, 106–10). Especially pertinent to any discussion of ethnicity in Hittite Anatolia is, in my opinion, the notion that ethnic and cultural boundaries do not necessarily overlap (Jones 1997, 60). This point was made by F. Barth in his influential introduction to a volume of collected essays on ethnicity:

> We can assume no one-to-one relationship between ethnic units and cultural similarities and differences. The features that are taken into account are not the sum of "objective" differences but only those which the actors themselves regard as significant – some cultural features are used by actors as signals and emblems of difference, others are ignored. (Barth 1969, 14)

"Hittite" Anatolia provides, in my opinion, a perfect exemplification of this notion. Empire-period members of the royal family could bear Hurrian names and worship Hurrian-named deities in the rock sanctuary of Yazılıkaya and yet there is no reason to consider the empire-period king Hattusili any less "Hittite" than his namesake and forebear Hattusili I, who fought "Hurrian" troops on several occasions and whose religious world shows no signs of "Hurrian" cultural elements.

Common genetic, religious, cultural or linguistic features do not *objectively* define the ethnic group, but rather are social features *chosen* by a group, or by outsiders, to articulate its identity (Hall 1997, 32; Malkin 1998, 55–56). Yet most ethnic groups do tend to share a notion of common ancestry (Eriksen 1993, 35). Thus, the ethnic group could be defined as "a group in which members identify with each other, and against others, on the basis of a perceived notion of a common past" (Siapkas 2004, 15). To this definition Hall (1997, 32) adds another element: "The ethnic group is distinguished from other social and associative groups by virtue of association with a specific territory and a shared myth of descent." Furthermore, ethnic groups are often endogamous and may share a common religion (Eriksen 1993, 34–35). Yet ethnicity remains an elusive phenomenon and general definitions are often problematic (Sökefeld 1997, 34–35; Siapkas 2004, 15).

However, while claiming that ethnic identity is a historically determined, context-bound construction, one should not ignore the self-proclaimed primordial notions of a given group and underestimate the strength and "objectivity" of such notions of origin for that group (Malkin 1998, 56; Fenton 2003, 88; Siapkas 2004, 187). The Ping-Pong game between the two positions therefore also involves a shift of perspectives. The etic perspective – the observers/scholars attempt trying to establish the objective existence of an ethnic group – may sometimes contradict the emic (the group's own) notion of shared origins. Within this theoretical framework, scholars now investigate not only the historical circumstances that lead to ethnogenesis, but also the primordial notions of the group itself, thus combining the two approaches.

The above discussion has hopefully demonstrated the methodological difficulty of an *etic* definition of ethnicity in pre-Hittite and Hittite Anatolia. One may divide it into ethno-cultural or ethno-political divisions – or distinguish between "Hittite" and "Hattic" city-states – by interpreting the linguistic or cultural evidence in terms of ethnicity, but whether the use of this term really illuminates the social and cultural complexity of the period must remain questionable. It is perhaps preferable simply to speak of cultural, linguistic or religious groups rather than of ethno-cultural or ethno-linguistic, thus leaving the ethnic tag aside. Furthermore, the use of ethnicity for historical interpretation may reveal itself as tautological. Such an argument was offered, in my opinion, to explain, in ethnic categories, the difference between Anitta's ruthless destruction of Hattusa and the benevolent treatment of the inhabitants of Kanes/Nesa by his father

Pithana. Anitta's decisions may have been influenced by different factors, but once ethnic affiliation is a priori postulated, the outcome of the analysis has already been arrived at.

An "instrumentalist" approach, which investigates the contexts in which identities were constructed and articulated in "Hittite" Anatolia, may prove to be more promising than an a priori postulation or negation of ethnic identities. As we have seen, ethnicity emerges as a result of a process of social differentiation or in contact with other groups (Eriksen 1993, 79). Thus, the process of "Hittite" ethnogenesis could be studied in the context of territorial expansion, and the resulting contact with other "civilizations" or in relation to processes of social differentiation (such as the appearance of the Kaska in northern Anatolia?).

Secondly, the analysis should preferably focus on the emic perspective, on the notions of identity held by the "Hittites" themselves. Ethnic identity is, with J. Hall, "socially constructed and subjectively perceived." It is conceptual and should therefore be studied from the emic perspective, from the point of view of the group itself. Thus, the only notions of identity that could meaningfully be gleaned from the study of the textual evidence from the archives of Hattusa are "Hittite" notions of identity – that is, the ways in which the ruling stratum of the kingdom, which produced and consumed the texts, chose to assert and define its identity in different circumstances. The different strategies in which ethnic identities were constructed in Hittite Anatolia will be the subject of another study. In the next section, I will concentrate on one element of the ethnic definition, namely, the notion of a shared past. As Siapkas (2003, 14) argues, emic notions of ethnicity of "dead civilizations" are best studied where literary records are available. I will therefore consider ethnicity exactly where there is a good chance of finding it, in (Old Hittite) literature.

3. As the cruciform seal (Dincol et al. 1993) impressively demonstrates, the empire-period kings could look back and relate to a long ancestral tradition. The thirteenth-century king Tudhaliya IV gives the certainly inaccurate, but nevertheless impressive, *Distanzangabe* of four or five hundred years between himself and King Hantili (Beckman 2000, 22). Their selection of "throne-names," the offering-lists to deceased members of the royal family, and other cult practices within the great festivals likewise demonstrate the connection that the empire-period kings felt with the past.

From an Old Hittite perspective, however, the royal genealogy is rather short. The historical introduction to the Proclamation of Telipinu ascribes the beginnings of Hittite territorial expansion to Labarna I, whose independent existence is now confirmed by the cruciform seal (van den Hout 1997, 194, n. 2), that is, about six generations before Telipinu himself (Beckman 2000, 26). Based on further evidence, it is now possible to reconstruct several rulers before Labarna. The overall picture remains, however, basically the same. The Hittites of the Old Kingdom had – unless one chooses to interpret the legend at the beginning of the Zalpa text in terms of reflexes of ancient migration movements or foundation myths – a relatively short past (for the text, see Hoffner 1997).

Besides the association with the city of Kussara, which he shares with Hattusili I, there is nothing to suggests that the Hittites viewed Anitta, the destroyer of Hattusa, as their ancestor. Otherwise, it is hard to explain why no one bothered to erase his – from a Hittite point of view embarrassing – curse on the capital city from the different copies of the Anitta inscription. Both Anitta and his father Pithana are unknown to the offering-lists and are likewise missing in the section dedicated to the Old Hittite kings in the cruciform seal. The evidence seems to suggest that, at least in the Empire period, a certain Huzziya was considered as the founder of the ruling dynasty (Beal 2003, 31–32). A King Huzziya is indeed mentioned in the Anitta text, but interestingly as a king of Zalpa. Considering the evidence relating the institution of Hittite kingship to Zalpa (Klinger 1996, 125) and to the sea (Klinger 2000), this fact may give rise to some speculation.

In his study on collective memory, Assmann distinguishes between two kinds of memories, which he calls communicative and cultural memory respectively (2000, 48–59). Communicative memory is a living memory, experienced within a life time. Studies in oral history have shown that living memory does not span over eighty years, that is three or four generations (2000, 50–56). Cultural memory in contrast, registers myths, memories and symbols from time immemorial and is carried out in highly ritualized forms. Assmann's distinction may provide an explanation for the empty past of the Hittites. The observation that living memory does not extend longer than three or four generations fits perfectly with such phenomena as the historical narrative in the Zalpa text, which spans exactly three to four generations. In his Testament (CTH 6), Hattusili I can relate an anecdote about his grandfather, but the text contains nothing that goes earlier. It is perhaps not a coincidence that the little that was known about anything that preceded the beginning of the archives in Hattusa in more than a generation or two, comes from literary imports.

Yet, communities with almost no knowledge of their own past may integrate themselves into someone else's past (Malkin 1998, 58–59). Faced with a community with a "fuller" past, "empty handed" communities may find it easier to adopt themselves into other communities' pasts, rather than invent a wholly new one. Malkin gives the Roman adaptation of the Greek myth of the Trojan War as an ancient example for this phenomenon. The modern Palestinians' claim to be descended from the autochthonous Canaanite people, thus integrating themselves into the older, "fuller" Jewish biblical myth of origin, is given by him as a modern example. Hittite scribes may have used a similar strategy when they came into contact with literature that possessed a "fuller" past than their own, with the literature concerning the Akkadian kings Sargon and Naram-Sin.

4. *KBo* 3.13 is a Hittite version of a narrative concerning Naram-Sin's victory over a coalition of rebellious kings (Güterbock 1938, 66–80). The composition, the so-called Great Revolt against Naram-Sin is also available in several other versions. There are several Old Babylonian versions, which have been shown to be an adaption of an original Old Akkadian inscription (Michalowski 1980, 233–46). The most notable common feature of these different versions is that they contain a detailed catalog of enemy kings. Yet, as Frayne (1991, 381) concludes, "the various OB [Old Babylonian] versions of the 'Great Revolt' text do not appear to be a particularly reliable source for the names of the enemies of Naram-Sin as can be ascertained from the contemporary sources." Moreover, each version of the "Great Revolt" seems to represent a different geographical horizon (Jonker 1995, 125).

The Hittite text is unfortunately quite fragmentary, but its best-preserved part (obv. 8′–15′) contains a detailed list of seventeen kings who rose against Naram-Sin only to be defeated by him. A parallel catalog of kings is found in one of the Old Babylonian manuscripts, probably originating from Sippar (Westenholz 1997, 247). The names of the kings do vary, but the two lists share some place-names between them, sometimes even in a similar position within the list. The two texts manifest different geographical interests. The Hittite version lists more locations in the greater Anatolian region, the Old Babylonian list shows a wider geographical scope (Van de Mieroop 2000, 139).

Both catalogs of enemy kings are certainly a mixture of different textual layers, a product of scribal editing, adapting and compiling. One feature of the Hittite list is, however, especially striking. Whereas Kanes and Amurru are both listed in parallel sections of the two lists, Pamba, king of Hattusa, is featured exclusively in the Hittite version and is missing from the Old Babylonian parallel. Furthermore, the Hittite list has the beginning of the name ^{m}*Nu-u*[*r-* before the king of Amurru, which should very likely be restored, despite the small space, as Nūr-Dagan/Daggal, king of Purushanda (Singer 1981, 127). The story of this king's defeat by Sargon is told in the *šar tamhāri* (The King of Battle), yet another composition that, like the Naram-Sin text, was freely adapted into Hittite (Güterbock 1969; Gilan 2000; Rieken 2001). This fact suggests perhaps that both compositions had some kind of a life outside the scribal school. Another version of the composition, written in Akkadian, which was found in Tell el-Amarna in Egypt, was probably brought there from a Syro-Hittite source (Izre'el 1997, 71; Beckman 2001, 88). This cultural export suggests perhaps that the Hittites viewed the story as their own literary heritage (Singer 2000, 673 n. 4).

As already noted by Güterbock (1938, 78, 144), the Hittite scribe was clearly interested in placing the famous revolt story of Naram-Sin in an Anatolian setting and to involve further Anatolian kings in it. It is certainly not a coincidence that in both Hittite adaptations of narratives concerning the Akkadian kings both are facing, and defeating, Anatolian rulers.

Whether Sargon did in fact reach and conquer the Anatolian city of Purushanda cannot be definitely answered. There is no outside evidence to corroborate or to contradict this specific story-element (Klengel 1999, 20). A fictive letter written on an exercise tablet found in the southern Mesopotamian city of Ur implies that the story concerning Sargon's campaign to Purushanda was already known there in Old Babylonian times (Wilcke 1993, 67–68), at least a century before the Old Hittite period. The idea to plant the plot of the Sargon story in Anatolian Purushanda cannot, after all, be attributed to the Hittite adapter of the "King of Battle."

The listing of Pamba, an otherwise unattested king of Hattusa, in the catalog of enemy kings in the Naram-Sin text and his absence from the parallel catalog from Sippar are, however, more puzzling. One does not have to be a radical postmodern historian to acknowledge that it is very unlikely that Naram-Sin fought so many different coalitions of adversaries. But whereas the diversity of the Mesopotamian enemy catalogs could be explained as comprehensive attempts to define just what "all of the lands" or "the four corners of the world" might be or as variations on that theme, why would a Hittite scribe add a possibly fictional king of Hattusa to a catalog of a doomed coalition of the enemies? Why would a Hittite audience favor stories in which Anatolian rulers were defeated by invading Mesopotamian kings?

A far-reaching interpretation of this phenomenon, which concerns the ethnic identity of the Hittites, was recently advanced by van de Mieroop in his study of the different traditions concerning the Akkadian kings in Anatolia (2000, 158–59):

> The world the Sargonic kings inhabit in the Hittite traditions is that of the Hittites, namely greater Anatolia. That area is, however, portrayed as one to which the Sargonic rulers were alien: they fought against the local rulers of such places as Kaneš and Hattusa. The Hittites associated themselves with the non-Anatolian Akkadians, not with Anatolian rulers like Nūr-Daggan. There is certainly no indication at all of a primordial connection between the Hittite people and the land they inhabit.... If the Hittite rulers continued to maintain an association with the foreign Sargonic rulers throughout their history, this seems to indicate a persistent refusal to identify with their surroundings.

Yet, there is ample evidence to suggest that the Hittites associated themselves closely with their land, most notably through elaborate cult practices to the gods, the true proprietors of the land. The fervent dedication to land and deity is nowhere more impressively illustrated as in the royal prayers concerning the painful loss and the exultant liberation of the northern cult center Nerik.

Therefore, another interpretation of this phenomenon should be offered. Confronted with a "fuller" past than they themselves possessed – with the literature concerning the Akkadian kings – Hittite scribes were not able to top that rich tradition with legendary kings of their own, so they settled for the second best option, and "imported" the Akkadian kings into Anatolia. This, by the way, at a time when the Old Hittite kings themselves were conducting daring military campaigns in exactly the opposite direction, an enterprise that culminated in the destruction of Babylon by king Mursili I.

The adaption of the literature concerning the Akkadian kings not only enabled the Hittites to participate in the Babylonian textual community, it also provided their land with a past. By a conscious selection and adaptation of foreign cultural artifacts – in this case, the literature concerning the Akkadian kings, Hittite scribes found a way to express their own identity.

Since its very dawn, Hittitology tackled the task of distinguishing between the different cultural substratums that made up "Hittite civilization." The literary adaption of the Akkadian kings in Hattusa suggests, in my opinion, the need to consider the long-term transculturation process, which produced

"Hittite civilization" in relation to "Hittite" ethnogenesis – the processes by which identities and affiliations were created in Anatolia of the second millennium BC and the different circumstances in which they were articulated.

REFERENCES

Assmann, J. (2000) *Das kulturelle Gedächtnis: Schrift, Erinnerung, und politische Identität in frühen Hochkulturen*. Third edition. München, C. H. Beck.

Baines, J. (1996) Contextualizing Egyptian Representations of Society and Ethnicity. In J. S. Cooper and G. M. Schwartz (eds.) *The Study of the Ancient Near East in the Twenty-First Century. The William Foxwell Albright Centennial Conference*, 339–84. Winona Lake, IN, Eisenbrauns.

Barth, F. (1969) Introduction. In F. Barth (ed.) *Ethnic Groups and Boundaries. The Social Organization of Culture Difference*, 9–38. Oslo, Universitetsforlaget.

Beal, R. H. (2003) The Predecessors of Hattušili I. In G. Beckman, R. Beal and G. McMahon (eds.) *Hittite Studies in Honor of Harry A. Hoffner Jr. On the Occasion of His 65th Birthday, 13–35.* Winona Lake, IN, Eisenbrauns.

Beckman, G. M. (1995) Royal Ideology and State Administration in Hittite Anatolia. In J. M. Sasson (ed.), *Civilizations of the Ancient Near East* Vol. I, 529–43. New York, Scribner's.

___ (2000) Hittite Chronology, *Akkadica* 119–120, 19–32.

___ (2001) Sargon and Naram-Sin in Hatti: Reflections of Mesopotamian Antiquity among the Hittites. In D. Kuhn, H. Stahl (eds.) *Die Gegenwart des Altertums. Formen und Funktionen des Altertumsbezugs in den Hochkulturen der Alten Welt*, 85–91. Heidelberg, Edition Forum.

Bryce, T. (1998) *The Kingdom of the Hittites*. Oxford, Clarendon.

Cohen, Y. (2001) The Image of the "Other" and Hittite Historiography. In T. Abusch, P.-A. Beaulieu, J. Huehnergard, P. Machinist and P. Steinkeller (eds.) *Historiography in the Cuneiform World. Proceedings of the XLVe Recontre Assyriologique Internationale* Part I, 113–29. Bethesda, MD, CDL.

Dincol, A., B. Dincol, J. D. Hawkins, and G. Wilhelm (1993) The "Cruciform Seal" from Boğazköy-Hattusa, *Istanbuler Mitteilungen* 43, 87–106.

Eriksen T. H. (1993) *Ethnicity and Nationalism: Anthropological Perspectives*. London, Pluto Press.

Fenton, S. (2003) *Ethnicity*. Cambridge, Polity Press.

Frayne, D. R. (1991) Historical Texts in Haifa: Notes on R. Kutscher`s "Brockmon Tablets." *Bibliotheca Orientalis* 48/3–4, 378–409.

Gellner, E. (1983) *Nations and Nationalism*. Oxford, Blackwell.

Gilan, A. (2000) Sargon in Anatolia: The "King of Battle" in a Hittite Context. Unpublished M.A. Thesis. Berlin, Freie Universität.

___ (2004a) Sakrale Ordnung und politische Herrschaft im hethitischen Anatolien. In M. Hutter, S Hutter-Braunsar (eds.) *Offizielle Religion, lokale Kulte und individuelle Religiosität, Akten des religionsgeschichtlichen Symposiums "Kleinasien und angrenzende Gebiete vom Beginn des 2. bis zur Mitte des 1. Jahrtausends v. Chr."* Bonn, 20.-22. Februar 2003, 189–205. AOAT 318. Münster, Ugarit-Verlag.

___ (2004b) Überlegungen zu "Kultur" und "Außenwirkung." In M. Novák, F. Prayon, A.-M. Wittke (eds.) *Die Außenwirkung des späthethitischen Kulturraumes: Güteraustausch – Kulturkontakt – Kulturtransfer. Akten des zweiten Forschungstagung des Graduiertenkollegs "Anatolien und seine Nachbarn" der Eberhard-Karls-Universität Tübingen (20. Bis 22. November 2003)*, 9–27. AOAT 323. Münster, Ugarit-Verlag.

Güterbock, H. G. (1938) Die historische Tradition und ihre literarische Gestaltung bei Babyloniern und Hethitern bis 1200. Zweiter Teil: Hethiter. *Zeitschrift für Assyriologie und vorderasiatische Archäologie* 44, 45–149.

___ (1957) Towards a Definition of the Term "Hittite," *Oriens* 10, 233–39.

___ (1969) Ein Bruchstück der Sargon-Erzählung "König der Schlacht." *Mitteilungen der Detschen Orient-Gesellschaft zu Berlin* 101, 14--23.

Hall, J. M. (1997) *Ethnic Identity in Greek Antiquity*. Cambridge, Cambridge University.

Hoffner, H. A. Jr. (1997a) Proclamation of Anitta of Kussar. In W.W. Hallo (ed.) *The Context of Scripture*. Vol. 1: *Canonical Compositions from the Biblical World*, 182–84. Leiden, Brill.

___ (1997b) The Queen of Kanesh and the Tale of Zalpa. In W. W. Hallo (ed.) *The Context of Scripture*, Vol. 1: *Canonical Compositions from the Biblical World*, 181–82. Leiden, Brill.

Hout, T. van den (1997) The Proclamation of Telepinu. In W. W. Hallo (ed.) *The Context of Scripture*, Vol. 1: *Canonical Compositions from the Biblical World*, 194–98. Leiden, Brill.
Izre'el, S. (1997) *The Amarna Scholarly Tablets*. Cuneiform Monographs 9. Groningen, Styx.
Jones, S. (1997) *The Archaeology of Ethnicity: Constructing Identities in the Past and Present*. New York, Routledge.
Jonker, G. (1995) *The Topography of Remembrance*. Leiden, Brill.
Klinger, J. (1996) *Untersuchungen zur Rekonstruktion der hattischen Kultschicht*. StBoT 37. Wiesbaden, Harrassowitz.
___ (2000) "So weit und breit wie das Meer...": Das Meer in Texten hattischer Provenienz. In Y. L. Arbeitman (ed.) *The Asia Minor Connexion: Studies on the Pre-Greek Languages in Memory of Charles Carter*, 151–72. Orbis Supplementa 13. Leuven, Peeters.
___ (2003) Zum "Priestertum" im hethitischen Anatolien, *Hethitica* 15, 93–111.
Malkin, I. (1998) *The Returns of Odysseus: Colonization and Ethnicity*. Berkeley, University of California.
Melchert, H. C. (2003) Prehistory. In H. C. Melchert (ed.) *The Luwians*, 8–26. HbOr I/68. Leiden, Brill
Michalowski, P. (1980) New Sources Concerning the Reign of Naram-Sin. *Journal of Cuneifrom Studies* 32, 233–46.
Nakamura, M. (2002) *Das hethitische nuntarriyašḫa-Fest*. PIHANS 94. Leiden, NINO.
Oettinger, N. (2002) Indogermanische Sprachträger lebten schon im 3. Jahrtausend v. Chr. in Kleinasien. In *Die Hethiter und ihr Reich: das Volk der 1000 Götter*, 50–55. Bonn, Kunst- und Ausstellungshalle der Bundesrepublik Deutschland.
Rieken, E. (2001) Der hethitische *šar-tamḫāri*-Text: archaisch oder archaisierend? In G. Wilhelm (ed.) *Akten des IV Internationaler Kongress für Hethitologie, Würzburg 4.-8. Oktober 1999*, 576–85. StBoT 45. Wiesbaden, Harrassowitz.
Rutherford, I. (2002) The Dance of the Wolf-Men of Ankuwa: Networks, Amphictionies and Pilgrimage in Hittite Religion. Paper delivered at the 5th International Congress of Hittitology, Corum, 4 September 2002.
Siapkas, J. (2003) *Heterological Ethnicity. Conceptualizing Identities in Ancient Greece*. Acta Universitatis Uppsaliensis 27. Uppsala, Acta Universitatis Upsaliensis, Uppsala Universitet.
Singer, I. (1981) Hittites and Hattians in Anatolia at the Beginning of the Second Millennium B.C. *Journal of Indo-European Studies* 9, 119–34.
___ (2000) Review of Klengel, Geschichte des hethitischen Reiches, 1999. *Bibliotheca Orientalis* 57 5/6, 635–43.
Sökefeld, M. (1997) *Ein Labyrinth von Identitäten in Nordpakistan. Zwischen Landbesitz, Religion und Kaschmir-Konflikt*. Köln, Rüdiger Köppe.
Starke, F. (1996) Zur "Regierung" des hethitischen Staates, *Zeitschrift für Altorientalische und Biblische Rechtsgeschichte* 2, 140–82.
___ (1998) Hattusa. In H. Cancik and H. Schneider (eds.) *Der Neue Pauly*, Bd. 5, 186–98. Stuttgart, J. B. Metzler.
Van De Mieroop, M. (2000) Sargon of Agade and His Successors in Anatolia. *Studi miceni ed egeo-anatolici* 42/1, 133–59.
Watkins, C. (2002) Homer and Hittite Revisited II. In H. A. Hoffner Jr. and K. Yener (eds.) Recent Developments in *Hittite Archaeology and History: Papers in Memory of Hans G. Güterbock*, 167–76. Winona Lake, IN, Eisenbrauns.
Westenholz, J. G. (1997) *Legends of the Kings of Akkade: The Texts*. Mesopotamian Civilizations 6. Winona Lake, IN, Eisenbrauns.
___ (1998) Relations between Mesopotamia and Anatolia in the Age of the Sargonic Kings. In H. Erkanal, V. Donbaz, and A. Uguroglu (eds.) *XXXIVème Rencontre assyriologique internationale, 6.-10. VII 1987, 4-22*. TTKY 26. Ankara, Türk Tarih Kurumu Basımevi.
Wilcke, C. (1993) Politik im Spiegel der Literatur, Literatur als Mittel der Politik im älteren Babylonien. In K. Raaflaub (ed.) *Anfänge politischen Denkens in der Antike*, 29–75. Schriften des Historischen Kollegs 24. München, Oldenbourg.

11

WRITING SYSTEMS AND IDENTITY

Annick Payne

The Hittites used not one but two writing systems. On the one hand, thousands of clay tablets in cuneiform and, on the other, monumental inscriptions written in an apparently indigenous hieroglyphic script have survived. It is not at all clear where this script originated nor when, and moreover why the Hittites employed it. We easily note several disadvantages of the script: first, the shape of the hieroglyphic signs would be more difficult to write than cuneiform, especially on stone; second, the structure of the syllabary was even less suited to record the frequent consonant clusters of an Indo-European language; and last but not least, a return to a pictorial script seems to be a step backwards on the evolutionary ladder of writing systems.

EVOLUTION OF SCRIPTS

Before examining the textual evidence, let us first consider this last point. In his *Study of Writing*, Gelb prominently stated that "there is no reverse development," yet at the same time he conceeded that writing evolved "along a path of trial and error" and further, that "a circular line of development" could induce even alphabetic writing – presumably the final stage of the development – to incline towards the practices of earlier stages (Gelb 1963, 200–201). As a result, the development of writing seems to be wholly unpredictable – although knowledge of the context in which changes occur may help to understand the reasons behind them. Japan, for instance, predominantly used a syllabic script by the end of the ninth century AD, but the increasing use of foreign loanwords after 1868 effectively meant a return to mixed logographic-phonetic writing (Schmitt 1980, 232–40). Even modern, literate societies do not use purely alphabetic characters but also employ pictograms, logograms and even mixed logographic-phonetic writing. For instance, many traffic signs use pictures rather than words, conveying sense even beyond linguistic boundaries as anyone can "read" such a sign in his own language. Numbers, similarly, function as logograms. Even an established alphabetic character may be used in many different ways, not only with its phonetic value. Thus the letter *x* can be used to abbreviate the syllable "ex" (Xtra), or stand for the numeral 10 (X), and in rebus-like spellings may stand for the word "cross" as in "crossing" (Xing), and further, the cross may even symbolise Christ as in "Christmas" (Xmas). As this illustrates, writing, to this very day, clearly evolves in many directions, not always the most obviously "forward," and may also be used outside of standard writing practice.

HITTITE SCRIBAL PRACTICE

What do we know about the Hittite scribal tradition? Evidence for writing practices is, unfortunately, scarce and circumstantial. We may presume that only scribes and professionals who needed to consult written records, for instance doctors and priests, were literate. The large administrative centers of the empire, where archives of many thousand clay tablets have been uncovered, would have employed many scribes, who specialized in different areas such as redaction, copying or editing. The cuneiform texts differentiate two types of scribe, the ^{LÚ}DUB.SAR or "scribe" and the ^{LÚ}DUB.SAR.GIŠ or "wood scribe."[1] The numerous clay tablets that name their scribe tell us that the ^{LÚ}DUB.SAR wrote cuneiform on clay. Whatever the ^{LÚ}DUB.SAR.GIŠ wrote on wood, however, has perished. The cuneiform records provide scant information on this specialized profession. A fragmentary list of personnel from the Great Temple at Hattusa names nineteen ordinary and thirty-three wood scribes (*KBo* 19.28 obv. 5); but as it is the only such document we cannot know whether the numerical relationship between the two types of scribe is in any way representative.

Archaeological finds illuminate the practice of writing on wood a little. The Uluburun shipwreck, a merchant vessel that sank ca. 1306 BC near Kaş in southern Turkey, has, among other things, conserved a hinged, two-leaf wooden tablet. The inner surface of each leaf was recessed to retain the wax writing surface; this is now lost. The wooden frame, meanwhile, preserves three hieroglyphic symbols that cannot as yet be connected to a known script (cf. Neumann 1995, 413). Similar writing tablets are depicted on several Neo-Hittite reliefs from the Neo-Hittite state of Maraş, portraying young men with styli and writing tablets. The most elaborate representation, MARAŞ 9 – datable to the second half of the eighth century BC – shows a woman holding a boy; his name is given in hieroglyphs as "Tarhupiya" (cf. Hawkins 2000, 274–75 and pl. 125). In his right hand he holds a stylus, in his left a bird on a leash. Underneath the bird we see a closed, hinged writing board. A description of such a folded writing tablet is also found in the *Iliad*, where it is the only reference to writing and, further, it is connected to Anatolia: King Proitos of Tiryns, wrongly believing Bellerophon to have coveted his wife, writes a fatal letter ordering its carrier to be killed,[2] and sends Bellerophon to deliver it to his father-in-law, King Iobates of Lycia.

As early as 1939, Güterbock suggested that the Hittite wood scribes wrote hieroglyphs.[3] Theoretically, either cuneiform or hieroglyphs could be impressed on wax, and indeed, this might well have been the case. Yet the respective scripts would require styli of different shapes. The excavations at Boghazköy have unearthed over thirty writing tools, mainly made out of bronze but also bone. As the writing tips of most of the bone styli are damaged,[4] let us consider the bronze ones only in the following. They show a pointed tip used for writing at one end, at the other a flattened, chisel-like head for erasing or leveling the writing surface (Boehmer 1972, nos. 1207–1238, 2046–2050). Of course, one might question whether these objects were indeed styli used to write on wax-covered wood tablets. It seems likely, not just because of the depictions on the Maraş reliefs but also because the tips of some of the bone styli show signs of burns. Warming the tip in a fire would have softened the wax where it had made contact with the stylus and made it easier to write on, while not softening the remaining surface unnecessarily and smudging parts already written.

When regarding the shape of these writing tools, one cannot fail to notice that not one of the bronze styli has the triangular head needed to impress wedges; nor is it plausible that outlines of wedges would have been drawn when an impression would be a far quicker and more effective way to write. Therefore, if these styli were not used to write cuneiform, could they have been used to write hieroglyphs? The answer is decidedly affirmative. While we cannot illustrate this with material evidence from the Hittite Empire period, there is some handwritten confirmation from the Iron Age to support this hypothesis. The traces left by the writing tool used to incise hieroglyphs on lead strips found at Assur suggest that the writing implement used had a pointed head, like the styli discovered at Boghazköy.[5]

If correct, the assumption that the ^{LÚ}DUB.SAR.GIŠ, or wood scribe, wrote hieroglyphic texts in the employment of the Hittite state or temples has implications for the extent of hieroglyphic writing in Hattusa and thus of its role in Hittite society. Other factors, too, point towards a wide-spread usage of the script. We know of several stone blocks from Boghazköy that preserve scribal names (see Dinçol and Dinçol 2002). One of these, for instance, was found in a wall close to one of the northern gates at Hattusa, and names two scribes, Patasina (Bentesina) and Samituli.[6] Presumably, they were advertising their services as public scribes and may have had their stall underneath this sign. If the hieroglyphic script was confined to the surviving corpus of seals and royal inscriptions, Patasina and Samituli would hardly have found much business to advertize for. It is exceedingly more likely that a large part of the hieroglyphic text corpus is lost to us because it was written on perishable materials.[7] Only regular use of the script can explain two other facts: first, that the few surviving full-length empire inscriptions already show a fully functioning writing system, albeit not developed to the level encountered in the Iron Age; second, that during the empire period there is already evidence of cursive sign forms, notably on seals (see, e.g., *SBo II*, 130, 238). This move towards more abstract, simpler shapes is commonly interpreted as the result of frequent, handwritten usage.

ORIGINS OF THE SCRIPT

What do we know about where the script came from? Hittite records do not preserve any information on the invention and origin of the hieroglyphic script. Whether this is due to chance survival or lack of reflection on this matter, we cannot know. Material evidence provides little more than a rough time scale.

Hieroglyphic symbols were used in Anatolia as early as the eighteenth century BC, but as Mora has argued, these early hieroglyphs seem to record "complex messages" rather than "words" and cannot be connected either to a specific language or to the hieroglyphic script used during the Empire period (Mora 1991; 1994). Indeed, there is no evidence for the connection besides some analogous sign forms; yet it is conceivable that well-known symbols found their way into the new writing system because of whatever meaning they already held. As an organized writing system, hieroglyphs first appear on seals before making their appearance on stone inscriptions: New evidence in the form of the Ankara silver bowl may push the date for the latter as far back as ca. 1400 BC (Hawkins 2003, 145–46). Together these objects document how the medium of script from its early logographic phase slowly approached language: phonetic sign values were first introduced to write personal names, as at this stage logograms alone were no longer sufficient. Late Bronze Age inscriptions and also archaizing Iron Age ones seem to indicate that phonetic signs were used to record first the sound of words, and only secondarily the syntax, that is, case and verbal endings and sentence-introductory particle chains.

In light of the limited text corpus, many questions regarding the origin of the script must remain open until further discoveries hopefully provide new evidence. Nonetheless, to understand the rise and role of the script under the Hittite Empire, we should at least consider a few possible scenarios as to who invented the script, where and why. Güterbock's answer, "the Luwians, in Luwian countries, for the Luwian language" (Güterbock 1956, 518), is attractive because the language of the surviving inscriptions is almost exclusively Luwian. Yet there is no evidence placing the script distinctly in a context of Luwian people or countries outside of possible Luwian influences in the Hittite capital itself. Is there a possibility that it may have been Hittite scribes who organized the hieroglyphic symbols into a codified writing system, and if so, why did they employ a second script?

To narrow down the potential places where the script might have been invented, let us consider the question of influences from other writing systems, since a creation in complete isolation is at this time hardly conceivable. Knowledge of at least one of the contemporary writing systems – whether it be Egyptian hieroglyphic, cuneiform or one of the Aegean scripts – can be expected. It is generally ruled out that Egypt served as a model because the geographic distance makes a connection less likely, especially if one seeks a Luwian region as place of origin. Nonetheless, Egypt may yet have offered a stimulus for the execution of hieroglyphic monuments in Hatti; we shall return to this later. As regards a possible Luwian homeland of the script, one may consider the Arzawa lands in western Anatolia, or Kizzuwatna (Cilicia) to the south. The former region was presumably ignorant of cuneiform but in close proximity to the Aegean scripts, whereas the latter would certainly have been acquainted with cuneiform. Scholars have previously sought and found parallels with either Linear B or cuneiform.[8] In my opinion, the similarities with Linear B are few and insignificant.

Both on Crete and in Anatolia we find hieroglyphic symbols first appearing on seals, later as a codified writing system – yet at different periods in time. Although direction of writing and sign order of the two scripts differ, similar design of a number of signs has often been seen as proof of common roots. But while there are resemblances between some Linear and Hieroglyphic signs, the same can be claimed with regard to Sumerian! Further, both scripts show a similar range of and types of logograms – but their usage differs markedly. Linear B tends to separate logograms from the syllabic writing, whereas Hieroglyphic knows the following four stages: Logogram – logogram with phonetic complements (unknown in Linear B) – logogram acting as determinative plus full phonetic writing (Linear B does not use determinatives) – purely phonetic writing. Finally, like Linear B, Hieroglyphic shows a predominance of open syllable (CV) signs, only few signs have a different structure. The lack of closed syllable (CVC/VC) signs, however, may represent nothing other than an attempt to simplify the script and reduce the number of syllabic signs. Nor can we reconcile Linear B's full series of five vowels (a/e/i/o/u) with the tripartite hieroglyphic system (a/i/u). Since Hittite cuneiform already only partly differentiates i/e, this may be another attempt to simplify the script. Further, homophones, a feature that Hieroglyphic shares with cuneiform, are virtually non-existent in Linear B. The principles of phonetic writing differ also: Linear B omits all final consonants, Hieroglyphic only omits final dental stops. Linear B further omits preconsonantal *l*, *m*, *n*, *r*, *s*, whereas Hieroglyphic only omits preconsonatal *n*. Silent vowels of a cluster are indicated through repetition of the preceding vowel in Linear B, while Hieroglyphic, on the other hand, predominantly uses the *a*-series.

On balance, I would therefore hold it likely that the creators of Hieroglyphic were acquainted with cuneiform. One final argument may further strengthen the ties with the Hittite world. For a growing number of hieroglyphic signs, we can now prove that the syllabic value was derived acrophonically from the name of the object depicted, i.e. using the first syllable of the word, e.g., the sign "gazelle's head" has the value *sà* from the Hittite-Luwian *šaša-* "gazelle." This indicates that the script was the product of an educated scribal class; the same principle, incidentally, was employed by scribes in Hattusa to derive new phonetic values, e.g., the Sumerogram GEŠTIN "wine" got the phonetic value wi_5 because of Hittite *wiyan(a)-* "wine." On this basis, I would seek the origins of the script in an area acquainted with cuneiform, possibly Kizzuwatna if not Hattusa itself.

Can we decide at all whether the script was invented by Luwians purely for the Luwian language? While almost all surviving inscriptions use the script to write Luwian, exceptions, such as the Hurrian epigraphs of Yazılıkaya or Semitic names, for example, on seals from Emar, attest that other languages could be, and were, written with the script – to what extent, sadly, we shall never know. As mentioned, a good number of phonetic values were derived acrophonically. Unfortunately, we shall never prove that only Luwian words were used, because many symbols defy description, while even where we can identify what the sign shows, its Luwian name is often unkown to us. Nonetheless, could one also make a case for sign values being derived, using the same principle, from either Hittite or Hurrian words? This would build a reasonable case for an involvement of Hittite scribes in the creation of the script. Again, the same limitations apply, and additionally, there are only few instances where Hittite and Luwian would have realized the first syllable of a shared Proto-Anatolian word differently.[9] Also, there is no reason why a Proto-Anatolian root, which we so far know only from one of the two languages, may not have existed in the other. To sum up, while theoretically possible, there is no irrefutable example of an acrophonic value derived from a language other than Luwian. Whether or not the script was originally Luwian in the strictest sense, the ongoing debate on the Luwianization of Hattusa opens up yet further possibilities, namely that the Luwian homeland might even have lain in Hattusa itself. At any rate, the bigger question seems to be why the need or desire for a second script? Why did the Hittites write representative inscriptions in Hieroglyphic Luwian and not Cuneiform Hittite?

WHY DID THE HITTITES WRITE HIEROGLYPHS?

Two features seem to recommend the hieroglyphic script over and above cuneiform: first, it is used only within a Hittite context, and thus clearly represents an autochthenous script of some kind; second, it is highly visual. This may be why it is the only script used on Hittite monuments, and on seals one might view hieroglyphic symbols as a more personal and recognizable signature. As far as we can tell by the surviving material, hieroglyphs were used for monuments and documents aimed at a certain – one must assume largely illiterate – public. The advantages are obvious: a visual script can depict details, such as the shape of objects, that an abstract, "reading" script leaves out. Moreover, the pictorial character made it possible for people to recognize a number of important signs, thus achieving a basic understanding without actually learning to read and write. Testimony to such a recognition value are inscriptions set up marking boundaries and documenting territorial claims.[10]

Comparison of ancient and modern script inventions shows that writing arises chiefly out of an economic need and/or the desire to show off power. While the prior use of cuneiform under the Hittite Empire rules out an economic need for a new writing system, might demonstration of power have inspired the use of hieroglyphics? A not insubstantial part of the aesthetic appeal of a hieroglyphic script is that most people find it fascinating and impressive. Especially in light of the monumental character of the surviving inscriptions, it is hard not to view them as both an internal and an external display of power – a comparable case in point seems to be the invention of Persian cuneiform under Darius I. Within the Hittite Empire, such demonstrations could have been part of forging a collective identity that set them apart from their neighbors, while reminding the various vassal states of the power of their overlord. Without going into the question of Hittite identity (for which see Gilan in the present volume), suffice it to say that the "people of the land of Hatti," as they called themselves, clearly did not define themselves as a homogenous ethnic or linguistic group but as the inhabitants of a specific geographic area. A collective identity of some sort would have helped greatly to make such a geopolitical unit stable enough to last as long as the Hittite Empire did.

Externally, such monuments would serve to impress visiting foreigners, such as diplomats, merchants and craftsmen, displaying imperial might and splendor as well as claiming territories. Being credited, rightly or wrongly, with inventing your own script certainly carried prestige; in the case of the Hittites, it placed them on par with other great script inventors, namely the Mesopotamian fathers of cuneiform and, of course, the Egyptians. While comparative newcomers amongst the great powers, the Hittites had become Egypt's main rival, as various military campaigns, culminating in the battle of Qadesh and the ensuing peace treaty between Hattusili III and Ramses II attest. It may even be conceivable that the Hittites went as far as to invite comparison with Egypt by erecting monuments in a script that seemed to proclaim equal standing. While the two hieroglyphic scripts are clearly different, there are also some similar aspects. Both scripts held a similar role as indigenous writing systems used at home, particularly for monumental inscriptions. For outside contacts, a common medium, the internationally understood cuneiform script was utilized. I am not aware of any contemporary reaction to the Hittite hieroglyphs, but a well-known story from the Greek historian Herodotus illustrates that this script was at least once in antiquity thought to be Egyptian. In his *Histories* (2.102–111), he reports having visited two relief figures of the Egyptian pharaoh Sesostris on the road from Ephesos to Sardis. Authoritatively, he translates from "Egyptian": ἐγὼ τήνδε τὴν χώρην ὤμοισι τοῖσι εμõισι ἐκτησάμην, "I myself won this land with the might of my shoulders." Excessive fame, one might think, for Tarkasnawa, the king of Mira, one of the Arzawa lands, whose inscriptions of the Karabel pass have been identified as the reliefs of Herodotus's story, and simply state the king's name, title and ancestors (cf. Hawkins 1998).

To conclude, many open questions remain and it is not necessarily likely that explicit data will be forthcoming even through new discoveries. But even on the basis of the available material, it may still be worth investigating further the connection between the Hittites and this peculiar script.

NOTES

1 For the [LÚ]DUB.SAR.GIŠ see Pecchioli Daddi (1982, 166–68).
2 *Il.* 6.169: γράψας ἐν πίνακι πτυκτῷ θυμοφθόρα πολλά, "graving in a folded tablet many signs and deadly" (trans. A. T. Murray).
3 Güterbock (1939, 36). For a more recent and detailed study of Hittite writing on wood, see Marazzi (1994).
4 Boehmer (1972, nos. 2046–50). Note that nos. 2044–45 may show a triangular head such as would be needed to write cuneiform. Cuneiform writing on a wax tablet is preserved once at Nimrud (cf. Mallowan 1954; Wiseman 1955), and may conceivably also have been practiced at Hattusa.
5 See Payne, forthcoming.
6 BOĞAZKÖY 8, published by Bittel (1957); for the reading see Poetto (1987).
7 Dinçol and Dinçol (2002, 210) come to the same conclusion: "Diese Anzeigen oder Schilder legen nahe, daß es einen großen Bedarf für die öffentlichen Schreiber in der Haupstadt gab und daß das unoffzielle Schrifttum der hethitischen Gesellschaft viel reicher war, als wir von dem materiellen Befund entnehmen können."
8 See, e.g., Hawkins (2003, 168), Neumann (1992, 26–27 and n. 5).
9 Namely Proto-Anatolian **ḱe, *ḱœ, *gwe, *gwœ, *ǵe/ge, *ǵœ/gœ.*
10 One might view the YALBURT, KÖYLÜTOLU YAYLA and EMİRGAZİ inscriptions of Tudhaliya IV in central Anatolia in this manner; also the LATMOS and KARABEL pass inscriptions in the west.

REFERENCES

Bittel, K. (1957) Vorläufiger Bericht über die Ausgrabungen in Boğazköy im Jahre 1956. Untersuchungen in der Altstadt. *Mitteilungen der deutschen Orientgesellschaft* 89, 6–25.

Boehmer, R. M. (1972) *Die Kleinfunde aus Boğazköy*. WVDOG 87. Berlin, Gebr. Mann.

Dinçol, A., and Dinçol, B. (2002) Die "Anzeigen" der öffentlichen Schreiber in Hattuscha. In S. de Martino and F. Pecchioli Daddi (eds.) *Anatolia Antica. Studi in memoria di Fiorella Imparati*, 207–16. Eothen 11/1–2. Firenze, LoGisma.

Gelb, I. J. (1963) *A Study of Writing*. Chicago, University of Chicago.

Güterbock, H. G. (1939) Das Siegeln bei den Hethitern. In J. Friedrich, J. G. Lautner and J. Miles (eds.) *Symbolae Paulo Koschaker Didicatae*, 26–36. Studia et Documenta II. Leiden, Brill.

___ (1956) Review of: M. Riemschneider, *Die Welt der Hethiter*, Stuttgart 1954. *Orientalistische Literaturzeitung*, 513–22.

Hawkins, J. D. (1998) Tarkasnawa King of Mira. *Anatolian Studies* 48, 1–31.

___ (2000) *Corpus of Hieroglyphic Luwian Inscriptions. Vol. I. Inscriptions of the Iron Age*, Berlin, de Gruyter.

___ (2003) Script and Texts. In H. C. Melchert (ed.) *The Luwians*, 128–69. Handbuch der Orientalistik 68. Leiden, Brill.

Mallowan, M. E. L. (1954) The Excavations at Nimrud (Kalḫu), 1953. *Iraq* 16, 59–163.

Marazzi, M. (1994) Ma gli Hittiti scriveveano veramente su "legno"? In P. Cipriano, P. Di Giovine and M. Mancini (eds.) *Miscellanea di studi linguistici in onore di Walter Belardi*, 131–60. Rome, Il Calamo.

Mora, C. (1991) Sull'origine della scrittura geroglifica anatolica. *Kadmos* 30/1, 1–28.

___ (1994) L'etude de la glyptique anatolienne: Bilan et nouvelles orientations de la recherche. *Syria* 71, 205–15.

Neumann, G. (1992) *System und Ausbau der hethitischen Hieroglyphenschrift.* Nachrichten der Akademie der Wissenschaften zu Göttingen, I. Philologisch-historische Klasse, Nr. 4. Göttingen, Vandenhoeck & Ruprecht.

___ (1995) Annäherungen an Linear A. In S. Deger-Jalkotzy, S. Hiller and O. Panagl (eds.) *Floreant Studia Mycenaea. Akten des X. Internationalen Mykenologischen Colloquiums in Salzburg vom 1.-5. Mai 1995*, 407–17. Vienna, Österreichische Akademie der Wissenschaften.

Payne, Annick (forthcoming) *Überlegungen zur Hieroglyphenschrift der Assur-Briefe.*

Pecchioli Daddi F. (1982) *Mestieri, professioni e dignità nell'Anatolia ittita.* Incunabula Graeca 79. Rome, dell'Ateneo.

Poetto, M. (1987) L'iscrizione luvio-geroglifica HATTUSA VIII. *Oriens Antiquus* 26, 187–89.

Schmitt, A. (1980) *Entstehung und Entwicklung von Schriften.* Cologne-Vienna, Böhlau.

Wiseman, D. J. (1955) Assyrian Writing Boards. *Iraq* 17, 3–13.

12

LUWIAN MIGRATIONS IN LIGHT OF LINGUISTIC CONTACTS

Ilya Yakubovich

The study of ethnic movements in prehistoric Anatolia represents a field in which few issues are firmly settled.[1] Scholars such as V. Ivanov and C. Renfrew, advocating Anatolia as the homeland of the Indo-Hittite (Early Indo-European) language family, are opposed by those who treat the Indo-Hittite Anatolian languages as newcomers to Asia Minor. Within the second group, there are two major currents, one believing that Anatolians migrated to the Anatolian peninsula from the northeast, via the Caucasus (most recently, Stefanini 2002), and another tracing their way from northwest, via the Bosphorus (most recently, Darden 2001). It is probably fair to say that the last opinion has a larger number of adherents in Western European and American scholarship than either of the other two, but no consensus has been reached yet.

These attempts at remote ethnolinguistic reconstructions need not overshadow the importance of another aspect of Anatolian prehistorical research. Particular languages spoken over a vast territory within Anatolia in the second millennium BC must have had a starting point to their expansion. The principle of sequential reconstruction, in fact, dictates that one needs to decide where Hittites or Luwians "came from" before asking the same question about Proto-Anatolians or Proto-Indo-Hittites. In addition, we are better equipped to investigate the immediate prehistory of Anatolian peoples. Talking about Hittite or Luwian migrations, we can use early historical and literary texts, reflecting the national memory of the respective peoples, as well as the data coming from the analysis of linguistic contacts between Anatolian peoples and their known immediate neighbors. Neither of these two sources is available to us when we are discussing early Indo-European or Anatolian ethnic movements.

Many aspects of Hittite prehistory appear to be uncontroversial. The self-designation of the Hittite language, *nišili, nāšili, nešumnili* "Nesite" is derived from the ancient toponym Nesa, which has been identified with the site of Kültepe near Kayseri in central Anatolia. This city, also known in Hittite and Akkadian sources under the name Kanes, functioned as an important trade center in the twentieth to eighteenth centuries BC, hosting a large colony (*kārum*) of Assyrian merchants.[2] Most Anatolian names preserved in the excavated records of Assyrian merchants appear to be Hittite (Garelli 1963, 133–52). The status of Hittite increased during the reign of the Great King Anitta, an eighteenth century ruler of Kanes/Nesa who succeeded in defeating a coalition of hostile kings and established his dominion over much of central Anatolia. The Hattian town of Hattusa, destroyed by Anitta, was later refounded and repopulated by the Hittites as their new administrative and cult center. Hittite (Nesite) was the state language of the Hittite kingdom, whose political history between the mid-seventeenth and the early-twelfth century BC is well known from written sources. There is no evidence, however, that the Hittite dominion triggered linguistic assimilation among the subjects of the kingdom; on the contrary, the ever growing number of Luwian glosses in Late Hittite texts indicates a widespread Hittite-Luwian bilingualism in Hattusa, which cannot be observed in earlier periods (van den Hout 2006).

A scholar trying to investigate the early migrations of the Luwians faces more challenges. The speakers of Luwian inhabited a vast area stretching from the eastern shore of the Aegean Sea to the Euphrates valley. In the mid-second millennium BC, Luwian was apparently the language of ruling elites in the kingdoms of Arzawa in western Anatolia and Kizzuwatna in southeastern Anatolia, before they were absorbed by the Hittite Empire. On the other hand, the early Luwian texts composed in Istanuwa, located on or near the river Sahiriya (modern Sakarya) in northwest Anatolia, and in Kummanni, the capital of Kizzuwatna, display a degree of grammatical homogeneity that renders the very existence of an "Istanuwian dialect" a matter of dispute (Melchert 2003b, 174–75). After the collapse of the Hittite state in the early-twelfth century BC and the disappearance of the Hittite language from written records, Luwian principalities reemerged in central and southeastern Anatolia, as well as in northern Syria. The language of the Iron Age Hieroglyphic Luwian inscriptions reveals certain grammatical peculiarities of a dialectal nature, but no lexical change of any significance (Melchert 2003b, 171–72). A relatively uniform language used throughout Anatolia invites questions about the starting place and the direction of its proliferation. Unfortunately, the available historical sources do not give us a direct answer to these questions.

Bryce's (2003) first comprehensive attempt at reconstructing Luwian history offered a scenario of Luwian eastward expansion. Bryce hypothesized that by the seventeenth century BC "Luwian-speaking groups had occupied extensive areas in the western half of Anatolia" (p. 28). His conclusions appear to be based mainly on the identification of the countries of Luwiya and Arzawa, which seemingly alternate in the two versions of §19 of the Hittite Laws.[3] Bryce goes on to state that "by the middle of the millennium, Luwian-speaking groups had spread southwards and eastwards, occupying much of southern Anatolia, from the region of (Classical) Lycia in the west through (classical) Pamphylia, Pisidia, Isauria and Lycaonia to Cilicia in the East" (2003, 31). He concludes by reiterating the hypothesis that the basic migratory pattern of Luwians within Anatolia was a movement southeastwards (2003, 35), cautiously extrapolating this trajectory to the earlier period when Luwians had allegedly penetrated Anatolia via the northwest (2003, 40).[4] No systematic defense of this scenario has, however, been suggested, perhaps due to the fact that Bryce's paper represents a historical overview rather than a polemical article.[5]

In this paper, I am going to advocate a different theory, according to which the local *Urheimat* of the Luwians is to be sought in central Anatolia in the Lower Land (**katteran udne*) of the Hittite sources, which roughly corresponds to the area known today as the Konya Plain. My argumentation will be based primarily on linguistic data. In section 1, I am going to discuss the early linguistic contacts between Luwians and Hittites, while section 2 will be devoted to linguistic contacts between Luwian and Greek. I am going to argue that these contacts were much closer in the first instance, which speaks in favor of territorial adjacency between Hittite and Luwian homelands. In section 3, I will attempt to demonstrate the inconclusive nature of arguments advanced in favor of Luwian eastward migrations, and present some historical considerations that are compatible with my linguistic analysis.[6]

1. LUWIAN AND HITTITE

It was widely believed for many years that Luwian influence on Hittite was limited to the "Empire period" after 1400 BC. The refinement of Anatolian historical phonology and morphology has enabled scholars to detect a large number of Luwian lexical borrowings already in Old Hittite. The presentation by Craig Melchert at the Eleventh Conference of the *Indogermanische Gesellschaft* (Melchert 2005) was based on the list of some seventy-five certain or likely Luwian loanwords in Old Hittite, eleven of them occurring in the Old Script texts. Even if we make an unlikely assumption that up to one half of Old Hittite/Middle Script and Old Hittite/New Script loanwords were introduced by the copyists of Old Hittite texts, and then make an additional allowance of twenty-five percent for uncertain cases, we will wind up with more than thirty lexemes that were borrowed into Old Hittite from or through Luwian. This number is roughly similar to that of assured Hattic loanwords in Hittite (cf. Melchert 2003a, 17). A sampler of Old Hittite nouns derived from attested Luwian verbs is given below:

CLuw. *tabar-* "to rule"	Hitt. *tabarna-/labarna-* "a royal title" (OH/OS)[7]
CLuw. *uba-* "to establish"	Hitt. *ubati-* "demesne (vel sim.)" (OH/OS)[8]
CLuw. *tiššai-* "to cause, fashion(?)"	Hitt. *teššummi-/tiššummi-* "fired-clay vessel" (OH/OS)[9]
CLuw. *tūmmantī-* "to hear"	Hitt. *tūmantiya-* (c.) "obedience" (OH)[10]
CLuw. *šarlai-* "to exalt"	Hitt. *šarluma-* "exaltation" (OH)[11]

It is remarkable that many Luwian borrowings in Old Hittite belong to the administrative or ideological sphere. It is even more remarkable that six Hittite kings of the Old Kingdom period, namely Labarna, Hantili I/II, Zidanta I/II and the recently identified Muwatalli I (see Bryce 1998, 122–24) had names of Luwian origin.[12] One cannot agree more with Melchert (2003a, 21), who rejects the notion of Luwian substrate in Old Hittite on the basis of such data, preferring to talk about a Luwian adstrate. Thus, a significant number of Luwians lived side by side with Hittite speakers already in the seventeenth through fifteenth centuries BC. Furthermore, the prestige potential of the Luwian language must have been high enough to justify its usage in the regal onomastics.

The lexical evidence cited above can be supported by textual data. A Hittite ritual for the evocation of a disappearing deity (*CTH* 752) contains incantations in Palaic, Luwian and probably Hattic. The fragment 671/b = *KUB* 35.93+ belonging to this ritual, which contains a Luwian passage next to a Palaic one, has been written in the Old Script. The addressee of the ritual cannot be identified with certainty, but the usage of Palaic tips the scales in favor of the hypothesis that this is the god Ziparwa, who is in fact explicitly mentioned in a Palaic passage of the text. In any event, the myth of a disappearing deity belongs to the archaic Hattic stratum of Hittite religious tradition, and one could only wonder what would be the usage of Luwian incantations embedded in our text, if at the time of its composition, Luwian was an obscure language of the western Anatolian periphery. One has no choice but to admit that Luwian had its place in the Hittite state cult already in the Old Kingdom period, and furthermore its usage as a liturgical language was not restricted to the veneration of certain provincial deities. This conclusion can be supported further by adducing a Middle Script fragment 1109/v = *KBo* 19.155 and a New Script fragment Bo 5582 = *KUB* 35.5, which probably do not belong to *CTH* 752, but nonetheless display alternation between Hittite, Luwian and Palaic lines.

In fact, one can go even further backwards. Luwian personal names occur on the Assyrian tablets from Kanes, even though their number is predictably rather small. One must realize that it is frequently difficult to discriminate between Luwian onomastic material and archaic Hittite names. Thus, Kültepe personal names containing the Luwian theonym Sanda (Laroche 1966, # 1097-8) are likely to be of Luwian origin; yet one cannot exclude the theory that Sanda, also attested in Lydia, was a common Anatolian deity that later fell out of favor among Hittite worshippers. The same holds, *mutatis mutandis*, for the well-known onomastic element (-)*muwa*(-), which does seem to occur very frequently in the names of Luwian origin. One would be on safer ground assigning Luwian provenance only to those Kültepe names that display phonetic or morphological innovations peculiar to the Luwic subgroup. The following list is not meant to be exhaustive, but it is based on the rigorous application of this principle; for a list of other possible Luwian names see Garelli (1963, 139–41).

Laroche (1966, # 128)	*a-lá-ú-a-ni*	Contains Luw. *-wani-* (Laroche 1966, 259–60)
Laroche (1966, # 411)	*ḫu-da-ar-lá*	CLuw. *ḫūdarla-* "slave," Luw. *-la-*
Carruba (1992, 251)	*ḫu-tar-lá-ni*	See above
Laroche (1966, # 835)	*mu-a-na-ni*	**Muwa-nani*; Luw. *nana/i-* vs. Hitt. *negna-* "brother"
Laroche (1966, # 858)	*na-na-pí*	**Nana-piya-*, cf. above

Laroche (1966, # 1513)	*wa-šu-na-ni*	**Wašu-nani*, cf. above
Carruba (1992, 253)	*wa-li-a-ša-zu*	Contains Luw. *aša-z(a)-* "to say"
Laroche (1966, # 1520)	*wa-wa-li*	HLuw. *wa/i-wa/i-* vs. Hitt. **kuwau-* "cow"[13]
Laroche (1966, # 1521)	*wa-wa-la*	See above
Laroche (1966, # 1581)	*zu-a-ni-a*	HLuw. *sù-wa/i-ni-* "dog" vs. Hitt. *kuwan-* "dog"[14]

The addition of merely suggestive onomastic material, selected on the basis of the lexical evidence, would increase this list by three or four times. Special prosopographic research is needed in order to see whether the majority of these people are the inhabitants of the Kanes area, or come from other regions covered by the network of Assyrian trade in Asia Minor. In any event, they are not likely to represent the indigenous population of western Anatolia since the *kārum* trade does not appear to have been extended this far westwards. Therefore the presence of Luwians in central Anatolia must be reckoned with already in the twentieth through eighteenth centuries BC. In fact, the ethnonym "Luwian" may explicitly be attested in the Assyrian Colony period as *nuwa'um* (Carruba 1992).

The linguistic contacts between Luwian and Hittite were not necessarily limited to the lexicon. Both languages belonged to the Anatolian Linguistic Area that can be established on the basis of common structural innovations (Watkins 2001). Below, I am going to mention only two of them that demonstrably occurred after the genetic separation of Hittite and Luwian.

The clearest instance of the areal phonological development is the devoicing of word-initial stops in Hittite and Luwian (Melchert 1994, 16–21). The same process, at least in the case of dentals, can be observed in the history of late Anatolian languages, Lycian and Lydian, recorded in alphabetic writing. It also occurred in the genetically unrelated Hurrian language, but not in its close relative, Urartean, which vindicates the areal nature of this phenomenon. The fact that it occurred after the genetic separation of Hittite and Luwian is borne out by numerous irregular cases where the word-initial dental stop failed to devoice in one of the two languages, and is graphically rendered as *l-* (phonetically, possibly, [ð]); cf. Hitt. *tabarna-/labarna-* "a royal title," Hitt. (borrowed) *allappaḫḫ-* "to spit" vs. CLuw. *tappa-* "to spit," CLuw. *la-* vs. HLuw. *da-* "to take," and Melchert 2003b: 181, fn. 13.

In the morphosyntactic domain, one should compare the Hittite possessive construction with case attraction (*ammedaz* ŠU-*az* "with my hand") and the Luwian phrases with possessive adjectives (*zaššin* DUMU-*annaššin annin* "the mother (acc.) of this child"). Both constructions represent linguistic innovations from the Indo-Hittite point of view, and case attraction is more widespread in Late Hittite than in Old Hittite (cf. Luraghi 1993, 148). Both constructions can be viewed as a counterpart to the Hurro-Urartean construction with "double case" / *Suffixaufnahme*, described in Wilhelm (1995; Hurr. *ḫibapte=ne=da Šauška=we=ne=da* "to the *ḫibapte* of (the goddess) Shaushka"). All three constructions represent instances of case agreement between the possessum and the possessor, but the fusional Indo-Hittite morphosyntax happened to be not well compatible with the clusters of case endings, and so the agreement marker replaced the genitive case ending in Hittite. A typologically parallel development is provided by the instance of Old Georgian *Suffixaufnahme*, which was likely one of the factors triggering case attraction in Old Armenian (cf. Luraghi 1993, 164). The Luwian construction with the possessive adjective is structurally more similar to its Hurrian counterpart, in that both the case agreement and the syntactic subordination between the possessum and the possessor are overtly expressed in morphology.[15]

We do not have enough information at this point to conclude whether Early Luwian was in direct contact with Hurrian and/or Hittite, or its structural innovations were mediated by another language belonging to the same linguistic area.[16] In either case, however, the central Anatolian homeland of the Luwians appears to be compatible with such contacts, whereas pushing it westward would render their explanation more problematic. It is true that both the word-initial neutralization of stops and the possessive adjectives also existed in Lydian, a language that was spoken in western Anatolia in the first millennium BC. In my account, however, the spread of these areal innovations to western Anatolia can be connected directly with Luwian westward migrations.

2. LUWIAN AND GREEK

In order to test the hypothesis according to which the majority of western Anatolian population in the Bronze Age was Luwian-speaking, it is instructive to consider the Luwian borrowings into Greek. It is usually assumed that Proto-Greeks migrated to the south of the Balkan peninsula at some point in the early second millennium BC, while the earliest linear B tablets found in Crete date back to the fifteenth century BC. The Bronze Age Greek principalities (or perhaps one of them) were known to the Hittites as the (Great) Kingdom of Ahhiyawa, and we know from the Hittite records of the Empire period that Ahhiyawan kings frequently meddled in the political affairs of western Asia Minor, and on occasions exercised direct control over some parts of it, such as Millawanda/Miletos.[17] The abductions of the inhabitants of western Anatolia into Greece are confirmed by both Hittite and Mycenaean texts.[18] The frequent contacts between the Aegean islands and the Anatolian coastland allow Bronze Age archeologists to define the west Aegean–east Anatolian interface characterized by peculiar pottery styles (Mountjoy 1998).

If Luwians constituted the bulk of the Bronze Age population of the western coast of Asia Minor, one can expect many Luwian words to have been borrowed into Mycenean Greek around this time. This is emphatically not the case. The only likely borrowing from Luwian into Mycenean identified so far is Myc. *di-pa-* "a kind of vessel." This word, attested later as Gk. δέπας "cup" was compared with CLuw. *tappaš-* and HLuw. (CAELUM)*ti-pa-s°* "sky" (Melchert 2003b, 184 with references). The peculiar semantic shift "sky" > "cup," reflecting the naive image of the sky as a cup covering the flat Earth, is supported by the Luwian sign CAELUM that graphically represents a bowl (Hawkins 2000, I, 26), as well as by the Hittite cognate *nēbiš-*, which, besides "sky," can indicate a ritual object made of metal or of flour (Neu 1999, 621–22). As one can see from the above comparison, the Luwian word for "sky" displays a specifically Luwic assimilatory denasalization. Thus we can be sure that the Mycenean word could not be borrowed from Hittite, but only from Luwian or a closely related tongue. Yet, since Luw. *tappaš-/ ti-pa-s°* is not directly attested with the meaning "bowl," the Anatolian origin of Myc. *di-pa-* remains hypothetical.

This isolated and uncertain borrowing can be contrasted with five words borrowed by Mycenean from Semitic, according to the conservative count of Bartoněk (2002, 492). Our limited knowledge of Mycenean vocabulary, of course, leaves hope that more Luwian and Semitic loanwords will be identified in the future, yet even now one can get some sense of a proportion. If the Semitic borrowings into Early Greek can be explained, as they usually are, by intensive trade contacts, there is even more reason to suggest the same explanation for the borrowing of the Luwian word for "sky, *cup." These trade-driven loanwords can be contrasted with likely Mycenean borrowings from the Aegean substrate or adstrate, the selective presentation of which by Bartoněk (2002, 490–91) contains eighteen items.

Three to four more loanwords can be gained by extending the search for Luwian borrowings into Greek into the Iron Age period. Πήγασος "Pegasos," the horse carrying the lightning and thunderbolt for Zeus, is a Greek avatar of the Luwian Storm-god of Lightning (*piḫaššašša/i-*), chosen by the Hittite king Muwatalli I as his personal divine patron (Hutter 2003, 269 with references). HLuw. *tarwana/i-* "justice, judge," borrowed into Greek as τύραννος "tyrant," also made its way to the Levant, where it is reflected as Ugar. /zuranu/ "prince" and Hebr. *srn* "a title among the Philistines" (Yakubovich 2002, 11–12 with references).[19] HLuw. *tuwarsa/i-* "vineyard" has been compared with Gk. θύρσος "*thyrsus*, wand wreathed in ivy," but the irregular correspondence of word-initial stops suggests that this may be a common borrowing from a third source.[20] Phonetic irregularities likewise complicate the direct identification between Luw. (PANIS) *turpa/i-* "(a kind of) bread" and Gk. (dial.) δόλπαι / δόλβαι "small cakes."

These loanwords are clearly no match for several hundred Greek words of (likely) substrate origin collected, for example, in Furnée (1972). They can rather be compared with the small stock of likely lexical borrowings from or via Hittite into Greek, such as Hitt. *ešḫar* "blood" vs. Gk. ἰχώρ "the blood of gods"; Hitt. *ḫuḫubal* "a percussion instrument" vs. Gk. κύμβαλον "cymbal"; Hitt. *kuwanna(n)*- "copper ore" vs. Gk. κύανος "dark-blue enamel, lapis lazuli etc."; Hitt. *kubaḫi*- "a head gear" (< Hurrian) vs. Gk. κύμβαχος "crown of a helmet"; Hitt. *kurša*- "hunting bag" vs. Gk. βύρσα "leather, hide."[21] There are no reasons to think that the speakers of Greek and Hittite occupied directly adjacent areas in the second millennium BC, but these borrowings must rather be considered in the context of trade-driven cultural contacts in the eastern Mediterranean, similar to the contacts between the Greeks and the Phoenicians, but on a lesser scale.

As has already been said, distant maritime trade could likewise account for the only Luwian borrowing into Mycenaean attested so far. We know from archaeological data, such as the motley cargo of the sunken ship found near Uluburun, that international trade thrived along the coast of southern Anatolia in the Bronze Age. The linguistic evidence, however, seems to indicate that contacts between the two peoples continued throughout the Dark Ages, following the collapse of the Mycenaean city-states. The similarities between Cypriot and Pamphylian dialects of Greek on the one hand, and Mycenaean and Arcadian dialects of Greek on the other hand, suggest that the Greek colonization of the eastern Mediterranean was initiated by population groups displaced by the Doric migrations. With the mediation of Greek colonists, who no doubt kept some commercial ties with the Aegean area, new Luwian loanwords could penetrate the dialects of mainland Greece. Thus, Greeks did not borrow the common Luwian word for "king," **ḫantawati*-, albeit attested in Greek transmission as the name of a semi-legendary Lydian king Κανδαύλης (Gusmani 1964, 274). They, however, appropriated the Luwian word for "ruler, judge," a concept that gained prominence in the eastern Mediterranean during the Early Iron Age (Pintore 1979).

It cannot, of course, be excluded that individual Luwian words could enter Greek via land routes, or could even be borrowed from the pockets of Luwian populations living in western Asia Minor. But the overall comparison between the Luwian borrowings in Old Hittite and Greek suggests much closer lexical contacts in the first case. This conclusion is hardly compatible with the assumption that Luwian speakers inhabited western Anatolia in the early-second millennium BC.

It is true that the Greek dialects and the Indo-Hittite Anatolian languages share a number of structural similarities that are not likely to be coincidental (see most lately Högemann 2003, 6–9 with references). None of them, however, seems to be restricted to Greek and Luwian. These isoglosses can be divided into two small groups, those shared by Greek and most other Anatolian languages and those restricted to Greek and Lydian.

To begin with the first group, Proto-Greek and Common Anatolian share the constraint of the word-initial occurrence of *r*-, although *r*- secondarily emerges in Greek dialects and Hieroglyphic Luwian after the simplification of certain consonant clusters. This constraint may well have been caused by a common linguistic substrate. The Ionic iteratives marked by a suffix *-ske-* can be compared with Hittite *-ške-* and Luwian *-za-* marking the imperfective aspect. There is every reason to reconstruct *-sk'e-* as a common Anatolian imperfective marker, and the fact that its reflex is not identified in Lydian as yet may have to do solely with our poor knowledge of this language. In any event, it is easier to assume that East Ionic modified the function of the *-sk'e-* suffix by contact with an Anatolian language that did not assibilate Indo-Hittite palatals since Greek *-ske-* and Luwian *-za-* would hardly be identified as cognates by anyone but a historical linguist.

On the other hand, East Ionian psilosis (the loss of word-initial *h*-) can be ascribed to Lydian influence, as per Oettinger (2005), but a similar phenomenon is not known in Luwian. The Lesbian adjectival patronymics in *-ios*, perhaps secondarily diffused into the other Aeolic dialects, can be compared directly with Lydian patronymics in *-lis*, while in Hieroglyphic Luwian and Lycian the use the patronymic genitive is at least as common. The specific isoglosses between Lydian and the Greek dialects of the eastern Aegean are not surprising in view of their geographic proximity. The absence of specific isoglosses between Luwian and the same dialects represents yet another argument against the western Anatolian homeland of the Luwians.

3. FINAL CONSIDERATIONS

Now one has to address arguments that have been advanced in defense of the Luwian homeland in western Asia Minor. The claim that merits least consideration is the alleged continuity between Luwian and Indo-European eastward migrations, which clearly occurred in different time periods. The virtual absence of lexical distinctions between Cuneiform and Hieroglyphic Luwian contrasts with a large number of genetically unrelated words in the basic lexicon of Luwian and Hittite. The following list of thirteen items, partly based on Ivanov (2001), features only lexical items from Swadesh's one-hundred-word list.

Hitt. *ḫumant-* vs. Luw. *puna(da/i)-*, *tanima-* "all"
Hitt. *šalli-* vs. Luw. *ura-* "big"
Hitt. *warnu-* vs. Luw. *kinu-* "burn"
Hitt. *ak(k)-* vs. Luw. *wal-* "die"
Hitt. *ḫarsar/n-* vs. Luw. *ḫarmaha/i-* "head"
Hitt. *šakk-* vs. Luw. *un(a)i-* "know"
Hitt. *dalugi-* vs. *ārray(a)-* "long"
Hitt. *pešna-* vs. Luw. *zida/i-* "man"
Hitt. *palša-* vs. Luw. *ḫarwa-* "road"
Hitt. *mema-* vs. Luw. *aššaza-* "say"
Hitt. *au(š)-* vs. Luw. *manā-* "see"
Hitt. *ar-* (med.) vs. Luw. *ta-* "stand"
Hitt. *watar-* vs. Luw. *wār-* "water"

If we add to this that only about one half of Luwian lexical items belonging to the one-hundred-word list could be identified so far, and extrapolate that the total number of lexical divergences in the list could be around twenty-five, we wind up with a cognacy rate that is lower than that of Slavic languages (no more than twenty lexical divergences between any two given languages). The split of Proto-Slavic into distinct dialects is usually dated to the mid-first millennium AD on historical grounds. If we assume that the rate of lexical replacement was the same in the case of Anatolian, one has to hypothesize that the split of Hittite and Luwian occurred some 1500 years before the historical attestation of both languages, that is to say around 3000 BC.[22] While many linguists have doubts that the rate of lexical replacement must be constant within each and every language family, the statement of Bryce (1998, 14) that the existing difference between Anatolian languages "appear to be consistent with the theory that the main dispersion of Indo-European Speakers occurred ... perhaps no more than a few centuries before languages made their appearance in written records" is counterintuitive. The differences between Hittite and Luwian seem to be rather close to those observable in the case of Polish and Russian or Italian and Spanish.

The conclusions of Bryce appear much more legitimate when applied to the Luwian dialects. It would be impossible to explain their close similarities if we assume that the dispersal of Luwians throughout Anatolia occurred already in the third millennium BC. In the absence of a centralized state that could enforce the uniformity of language, the dialects of, say, Istanuwa and Kizzuwatna would have become mutually unintelligible over a period of a thousand years. One has no choice but to admit that extensive Luwian migrations must be synchronized with the period of Old Assyrian trade in Anatolia, if not with the Hittite Old Kingdom (cf. Bryce 2003, 31). If so, it is futile to look for the continuity between the migrations of Proto-Anatolians to Asia Minor, and the subsequent Luwian expansion, just as the German *Drang nach Osten* in the early-second millennium AD in no sense continues the westward migrations of Germanic tribes a millennium earlier. Neither is there any need for the basic direction of Luwian migrations to continue any old pattern, as the Germanic parallel clearly illustrates.

The identification between the lands of Luwiya and Arzawa would certainly represent a major piece of evidence in favor of Bryce's homeland theory. Yet, the scrutiny of the relevant context in the Hittite Laws prompts me to disagree with this identification. *KBo* 6.2 i 36–67 was reconstructed as [*ták-ku* LÚ.U$_{19}$].LỤ-*ạn* LÚ-*na-ku* MU[NUS-*na-ku* ^{URU}*Ḫa-at-tu-ša-az ku-iš-ki* LÚ ^{URU}*Lu-i-iš ta-a*]-*ị-ez-zi na-an A-NA* KỤR *Lụ-ụ́-ị-*[*ia p*]*é-ẹ-ḫụ-tẹ-ẹz-zị*, "If a Luwian abducts a free person, man or woman, from the land of Hatti, and leads him away to the land of Luwiya…." In the parallel passage of the later copy *KBo* 6.3 we read *tạ́k-kụ* LỤ́.Ụ$_{19}$.LỤ-*ạn* LỤ́-*ạn-nạ-kụ* MUNUS-*na-ku* ^{URU}*Ḫa-at-tu-ša-az ku-iš-*[*ki*] LÚ ^{URU}*Lu-ú-i-a-az tạ-ạ-ị-ẹz-zị nạ-ạn* A-*NA* KUR ^{URU}*Ar-za-u-wa pé-e-ḫu-te-e-zi* "If a man abducts a free person, man or woman, from the land of Hatti (or) from the land of Luwiya, and leads him away to the land of Arzawa." The syntax of the second version is admittedly quite awkward, and one should probably agree with Friedrich's suggestion, endorsed by Hoffner (1997, 30), and take *Lu-ú-i-a-az* (abl.) as a scribal error for **Lu-ú-i-a-aš* (nom.), matching **Lu-i-iš* (nom.) in the first version. Yet, once the error had been made, the sentence acquired a new possible interpretation, and a new scribe, confounded by the fact that the slave is lead to the same land of Luwiya from which he has been abducted, replaced Luwiya with Arzawa. This implies that Luwiya and Arzawa were *distinct* lands, at least in the opinion of the copyist of the Laws.

The traditional interpretation cannot explain why the original term Luwiya is preserved throughout *KBo* 6.3, and replaced with Arzawa only in the problematic context discussed above, and only in one of its two occurrences in this context. In addition, it creates an impression that Arzawa was under Hittite domination at the time of the drafting of the Laws. A different image can be inferred from the annals of Hattusili I (*CTH* 4); we learn that on one occasion he marched against Arzawa (not Luwiya!) and took from it cattle and sheep (de Martino 2003, 36). While there is tangential evidence that some parts of Arzawa may have been Hittite tributaries during the Old Kingdom period (cf. Bryce 2003, 47–48), one needs a vivid imagination in order to assume that they were abiding by Hittite legal regulations.[23]

The copiously attested Luwoid names of the Arzawan ruling elite leave little doubt that this independent kingdom was ruled by a Luwian dynasty by the fifteenth century BC. In view of the limited linguistic contacts between Luwian and Greek, I am inclined to view the Luwian presence there as a result of relatively short-lived military conquests.[24] One can further support this conclusion by considering the ethnolinguistic map of western Anatolia in the Iron Age. Lydians, a non-Luwic Anatolian population group that held sway in this region in the seventh–sixth centuries BC, are frequently regarded as invaders from the northeast, dislodging the Luwian population from the same area (e.g., Beekes 2002, 2003).[25] Yet, the Luwian lexical borrowings into Lydian texts are more compatible with the theory of a Luwian superstrate rather than substrate in this language. They are largely limited to Lydian personal names of Luwian origin appearing in Lydian and Greek texts, such as Lyd. PN Καδοας vs. HLuw. PN *ka-tú-wa/i-*; Luw. Lyd. PN Ουρπαλος vs. HLuw. PN *wa/i+ra/i-pa-la-wa/i*; Lyd. PN *Tiwdaś* vs. CLuw. *Tiwad-* "Sungod"; Lyd. PN *Walweś* vs. CLuw. *walwa-* "*lion"; Lyd. PN(?) Κανδαυλης vs. Luw. **ḫantawati-*, Lyc. *xñtawata-* "king" (cf. Carruba 1959, 401–3). The scenario according to which Lydian invaders borrowed personal names from their new Luwian subjects is typologically rather improbable. It is easier to assume that Luwian elites in Arzawa were wiped out by the turbulent events of the late-second millennium BC, or gradually assimilated by the autochthonous Lydians, but their prestigious names lived on in the tradition.[26]

Assuming that the local homeland of the Luwians was in central Anatolia places it in a reasonable proximity to the territory occupied by the speakers of the closely related Lycian, Milyan and Carian languages in the south, and the somewhat more distantly related Palaic in the north.[27] It also raises the likelihood that the Middle Bronze Age kingdom of Purushanda, located on the central Anatolian plateau, could be, wholly or in part, Luwian-speaking.[28] The king of Purushanda was the only Anatolian sovereign who was referred to by the title LUGAL.GAL "Great King" in the Old Assyrian tablets of the Karum II period. The situation apparently changed with the Hittite conquests of Anitta, which culminated in the surrender of the king of Purushanda. Anitta received from him as a gift an iron throne, probably to be interpreted as a regional symbol of supreme authority, and took him back to Nesa as a privileged vassal. Can it be that the Hittites inherited some bureaucratic infrastructures from this previous regional power (perhaps to be identified with Luwiya)? This would explain the early borrowings of administrative terms, such as *tabarna-* and *ubati-*, from Luwian into Hittite.[29]

The last remaining, and the least welcome task would be to comment on the factors that could prompt the Luwian sweep through the Anatolian peninsula. While the nature of the question precludes a definite answer, one can hypothesize that the importation of tin by Assyrian merchants dramatically increased the bronze production in certain parts of Anatolia, and those communities that benefited the most from international trade found themselves in a position of military superiority and could impose ruling elites upon less fortunate ethnic groups. Widespread local conflicts that mark the end of the *kārum* period seem to support the hypothesis that Assyrian trade in Anatolia led to a drastic shift in the balance of power. Can it be that the Luwians, alongside the Hittites, benefited from this situation? If we assume that the starting point of Luwian migrations was the Konya Plain, the historical Lower Land, this implies that the *kārum* of Purushanda (Burushatta) was probably on their territory, which would vindicate the suggested scenario.

NOTES

1 Subject to the usual disclaimers, I am grateful to Trevor Bryce, Theo van den Hout, and Itamar Singer, for their comments on the drafts of this paper, as well as to Thomas Wier, who assisted me in improving its style.

2 The most recent discussion of absolute dates in Middle Bronze Age Anatolia can be found in Veenhof (2003). The historical datings related to the Hittite Kingdom are taken from Bryce (1998) throughout the article.

3 More precisely, he writes, "Its [= Arzawa's] appearance is linked with the disappearance of the name Luwiya. Although the term *luwili* continued to be used as a linguistic term, the ethno-geographical designation Luwiya apparently dropped out of use, being replaced in later versions of the Hittite Laws by the name Arzawa" (Bryce 2003, 32).

4 Professor Bryce informs me in a personal communication that he prefers to leave quite open the question of where the Luwians came from before their arrival to Anatolia, allowing for the possibility that the main dispersion of Indo-European speakers occurred within Anatolia.

5 Nevertheless, the historical scenario advocated by Bryce has been perceived by some as a proven theory. Cf. a bold statement of Beekes (2003, 48): "It is generally accepted that the country of the (classical) Lydians was originally Luwian-speaking." Beekes makes two references to Bryce (2003, 32, 40), erroneously attributing one of them to Melchert.

6 In this paper, I am going to abstain from participating in the discussion about "the language of the Trojans" that gained momentum after the publication of Watkins (1986). However instrumental this process may be for raising public awareness about Anatolian studies, I believe that we simply do not have enough data to discuss this question in a scholarly fashion. Isolated Luwoid names of Trojan heroes occurring in the *Iliad*, the mention of Wilusa in a Luwian song embedded in a ritual, or the discovery of a single Hieroglyphic Luwian seal in Troy, may tell us something about the cultural contacts of Trojan elites, but are not particularly helpful for elucidating the sociolinguistic situation in the area. One might put together an equally convincing argument for Trojans being Greeks by adducing the Wilusan king Alaksandu, compared to Alexander, the Wilusan god *Appaliunas, reminiscent of Apollo, and the fact that Achaeans and Trojans speak without interpreters in the *Iliad*, whereas Carians are described there as "speaking a foreign tongue" (2.867).

7 The Luwoid character of Hitt. *labarna-/tabarna-*, borrowed in the two subsequent stages, is assured by the alternation *t-/l-*, as per Melchert (2003a, 19). The proponents of the Hattic origin of this royal title default by not being able to explain *labarna-* as a graphic alternant of *tabarna-* and/or disconnecting *tabarna-* from the obviously related Luw. *tabar-* "to rule." The ultimate origin of Luw. *tabar-* is a matter of dispute. I tried to explain this Luwian verb as a substrate term also lurking in Gk. λαβύρινθος (Myc. *da-pú-ri-to-*) "royal palace in Knossos, labyrinth" (Yakubovich 2002), whereas Melchert (2003a, 19) insists on the Indo-European origin of Luw. **tabar-* "powerful" (vel sim.) connecting it with MHG. *tapfer* "massive, firm, brave," and reconstructing the protoform *$dh_e b$-ro-*. I remain skeptical of this binary comparison between Anatolian and Germanic, which in addition implies a protoform containing the rare Indo-European phoneme **b*.

8 The direct cognate of Hitt. *ubati-* is attested in Luw. *ubatit-* "demesne (vel sim.)," while the occasional usage of the rare BA sign in the Hittite noun further supports its borrowed origin. Melchert (1993, 242) gives a somewhat different translation of Luw. *uba-*, namely "furnish, grant." For the justification of my semantic reconstruction, see Yakubovich (2005), while Melchert's ideas on this subject will soon be expounded in another Festschrift article.

9 Even though the adjectival suffix *-mna-* is Common Anatolian, the "*i*-mutation" in Hitt. *teššummi-* indicates the Luwian origin of this word.

10 Hitt. *tūm(m)antiya-* "obedience" is frequently accompanied by the gloss wedge. Luw. **tūmmant-* "ear" is a regular phonetic correlate of Hitt. *ištaman(a)-* "id."

11 Luw. *šarlai-* "exalt" is derived from Luw **šarla/i-* "supreme," attested as HLuw. SUPER-*la-* "id.," and cognate with Lyd. *serli-/selli-* "id." (Melchert 1993, 191). Hittite uses in the same meaning a more archaic adjective *šarezzi-*, which is endowed with an unproductive suffix.

12 On Labarna, see note 7 above. Hantili means "first" in Luwian, whereas Hittite employs a more archaic adjective *ḫantezzi-* in the same meaning. Zidanta cannot be separated from Luw. *zida/i-* "man." The name Muwatalli contains the suffix *-alli-* of Luwian origin (Melchert 2003a, 16).

13 Note that Pal. ...]*kuwawalla-* attested in a broken context may represent a precise match to Luw. *wawala/i-* "related to a cow (vel sim.)."

14 This etymology implies that the name *Zuwaniya-* is unrelated to a large family of names containing the element *zuwa/i-*. Alternatively, one can follow Garelli (1963, 141) and connect this name with Luw. *zuwa-* "bread, food."

15 These constructions should be distinguished from the Greek σχῆμα καθ' ὅλον καὶ μέρος, which is nearly restricted to the cases of the double accusative. Lühr (2002, 29–34) puts forth a theory regarding the historical origin of this construction that has nothing to do with linguistic contacts.

16 Some structural innovations of Luwian not shared by Hittite may also have been caused by areal diffusion. Here one can mention the elimination of the word-initial *st-* cluster, as well as the rise of agglutinative inflection of plural nouns, especially in Cuneiform Luwian. Both innovations can (although do not necessarily need to) be explained by early contacts between Luwian and Hurrian. On the likely preservation of **st-* in Hittite, see Kassian and Yakubovich (2001).

17 For the latest state of debate about the location of Ahhiyawa see Hawkins in Easton et al. (2002, 101). In spite of the lingering skepticism of individual scholars, the identification between Ahhiyawa and Mycenean Greece, or a part thereof, can be fairly referred to as *consensus majorum*.

18 On the Hittite side, see especially the letter concerning Piyamaradu (*CTH* 181). On the Greek side, the implicit evidence is provided by the lists of female workers employed in the palatial economy of Pylos, whose names link them to the eastern Aegean (PY A series; see the contribution by Stavroula Nikoloudis to this volume).

19 The Indo-Hittite origin of *tarwana/i-* is not assured, but Luwian emerges as the most likely immediate source of borrowing into the other languages for semantic reasons. In all probability, "justice" is the original meaning of this word, while "judge" represents a type of metonymy known from English "justices."

20 A similar correspondence between the Greek aspirate and the Luwian non-aspriated dental stop is attested in Gk. λαβύρινθος "royal palace in Crete, labyrinth" (Myc. *da-pú-ri-to-*), compared with the Carian toponym Λαβρυανδα. In general, it seems likely, although hardly provable, that the Greek suffix -ινθος, frequent in toponyms (e.g., Κόρινθος), has the same non-Indo-European substrate origin as the Anatolian toponymic suffix *–anda* (e.g., in Purushanda).

21 Hitt. *ešḫar* "blood" corresponds to Luw. *ašḫar*, which is a phonetically unlikely borrowing source for source for Gk. ἰχώρ. Hitt. *kuwanna(n)-* "copper ore" is presumably distantly related to Lith. *švìnas* "lead," which would indicate that its Luwian putative cognate would contain an initial afftricate *z-*. In the other cases, the assumption that the words listed above were borrowed from Luwian rather than Hittite is possible, but gratuitous, since none of them is actually attested in the Luwian corpus.

22 For a rich set of data regarding the rate of lexical replacement in the languages of Eurasia, see Starostin (2001). The special cases of quick lexical change caused by a periodical tabooing of lexical items do not need to concern us here since the available sources do not bear out the existence of lexical taboos in ancient Anatolia.

23 Note that, even if one accepts the equation Luwiya = Arzawa in *KBo* 6.3, this does not need to reflect any more than the opinion of the copyist of the Laws. The toponym Luwiya apparently fell out of use already in the Old Hittite period, whereas *KBo* 6.3 is at earliest a Middle Script copy, and probably belongs to an even later period (see Hoffner 1997, 230 for the discussion). But, even if the copyist knew exactly what Luwiya was, he may have been guided by the political realities of his own time. Itamar Singer reminds me that the Lower Land was under the Arzawan control in the early-fourteenth century BC when the Arzawan enemy "made Tuwanuwa (classical Tyana) and Uda (Hyde) his frontier" (*KUB* 6.28 obv. 8–9 as quoted in Bryce 2003, 56).

24 Gindin and Cimburskij argue that a very prominent role assigned in the *Iliad* to Lycians as the allies of the Trojans may reflect lingering memories about the Luwian military presence in western Anatolia (1996, 226–40). The cognate of the term *Luwiya*, *luwili*, is not attested in the Greek sources, and so one can speculate that the ethnikon

"Lycians" was at some point extended by the Greeks to their close linguistic relatives, the Luwians.

25 The derivation of the ethnonym Λυδός "Lydian" from the toponym *Luwiya*, attempted in Beekes (2003), runs into a number of formal problems, such as the uncertain absolute chronology of the sound change *-y-* > *-d-* in Lydian (cf. the contribution of Craig Melchert to this volume). Yet, even if we assume that this is a correct etymology, it by no means implies that Luwians were autochtonous to Lydia. Country names are frequently based on the ethnonyms of foreign invaders that subsequently undergo linguistic assimilation, as the names of France, Russia, Normandy, Burgundy, Lombardy, Andalusia, Seistan, and Tokharestan would suffice to illustrate.

26 The following argument in favor of Luwian migrations to Arzawa is intriguing, but not quite conclusive. The syntactic heads of *Anza-pa-ḫaddu*, lit. "protect our health" (?), the name of an Arzawan prince in the fourteenth century BC, or *Mana-pa-Tarhunta*, lit. "Tarhunt, protect the *mana*" (?), the vassal king of the Seha River Land, are likely to contain imperatives of the Luwian verb *pa-* "*to protect" (reconstructed in Melchert 1993, 162). The personal names containing imperative verbal forms are alien to the Indo-European tradition, but were quite common in Akkadian. Furthermore, the Akkadian imperative *uṣur* "protect!," the functional equivalent of Luw. **pa*, occurs specifically in Old Assyrian names from Kültepe (Kanes), e.g., *Uṣur-Anum* "Anu, protect (me)," *Uṣur-ša-Aššur* "protect (one) of Aššur," *Uṣur-ša-Ištar* "protect (one) of Ishtar" (Michel and Garelli 1997, 1, 327). Yet if we assume that the Luwian names in *-pa-* were calqued from Assyrian names in *Uṣur-* in the *kārum* period, and then carried over to western Anatolia, it remains unclear why the Hittites, who had to be in equally close contact with Assyrian tradesmen, do not appear to have similar calques in their onomastikon.

27 I generally accept the genealogical tree of the Anatolian languages suggested in Oettinger (1978). Note that the maps of Anatolian linguistic filiation printed on p. 91 of the same article implicitly assume the central Anatolian homeland of the Luwians.

28 This possibility has been raised already by Singer (1981, 130), who did not mean, however, to imply that this was the only Luwian kingdom of the time. As I argued above, the area occupied by the Luwians could not be as large in the early-second millennium BC as it was around 1300 BC. The fact that the mid-third millennium king of Purushanda, the legendary adversary of Sargon I, is provided with the Hurroid name Nurdah(h)i "the man of Nawar" in the Hittite recension of the *šar tamhāri* epic obviously should not be used as a basis for historical conclusions, as Archi (2000) correctly implies.

29 Stefanini (2002, 791–92) suggests on etymological grounds that the title *labarna-/tabarna-* could originally mean "governor/steward," and interprets it as the original title of the governors of Kussar, reflecting their subordinate position to the rulers of Nesa. The retention of the old vassal titles by independent rulers is a relatively common phenomenon that can be illustrated by the SUKKAL.MAḪ dynasty of Elam or the Ottoman sultans, not to mention the stewards of Minas-Tirith. Nothing, however, precludes the hypothesis that this title could be bestowed upon the rulers of Hattusa and/or Nesa by the Great Kings of Purushanda. This assumption would correlate better with the Luwian origin of the noun *labarna-/tabarna-*.

REFERENCES

Archi, A. (2000) Nawar-taḫe, king of Purushanda. *N.A.B.U.* 2000(4), 67.

Bartoněk, A. (2002) *Handbuch des mykenischen Griechisch.* Heidelberg, Carl Winter.

Beekes, R. (2002) The Prehistory of the Lydians, the Origin of the Etruscans, Troy and Aeneas. *Bibliotheca Orientalis* 59, 205–41.

___ (2003) Luwians and Lydians. *Kadmos* 42, 47–49.

Bryce, T. (1998) *The Kingdom of the Hittites.* Oxford, Clarendon.

___ (2003) History. In H. C. Melchert (ed.) *The Luwians*, 27–127. Leiden, Brill.

Carruba, O. (1959) Lydisch und Lyder. *Quaderni dell'Istituto di Glottologia, Università di Bologna* IV, 383–408.

___ (1992) Luwier in Kappadokien. In D. Charpin and F. Joannès (ed.) *La circulation des biens, des personnes et des idées dans le Proche-Orient ancien* (Actes de XXXVIIIe RAI), 251–57. Paris, Éditions Recherche sur les civilisations.

Darden, B. J. (2001) On the Question of the Anatolian Origin of Indo-Hittite. In R. Drews (ed.) *Greater Anatolia and the Indo-Hittite Language Family*, 184–228. Washington, Institute for the Study of Man.

Easton, D. F, Hawkins, J. D., Sheratt, A. G., and Sheratt, E. S. (2002) Troy in Recent Perspective. *Anatolian Studies* 52, 75–110.

Furnée, E. J. (1972) *Die Wichtigsten Konsonantischen Erscheinungen der Vorgriechischen.* Paris, Mouton.

Garelli, P. (1963) *Les Assyriens en Cappadoce.* Paris, Adrien-Maisonneuve.

Gindin, L. A. and Cimburskij, V. L. (1996) *Gomer i istorija vostochnogo sredizemnomorja*. Moscow, Vostochnaja literatura.

Gusmani, R. (1964) *Lydisches Wörterbuch mit grammatischer Skizze und Inschriften-sammlung*. Heidelberg , Carl Winter.

Hawkins, J. D. (1995) *The Hieroglyphic Inscription of the Sacred Pool Complex at Hattusa (Südburg)*. Wiesbaden, Harrassowitz.

___ (2000) *Corpus of Hieroglyphic Luwian Inscriptions. Vol. I. Part I, II: Texts*. Berlin, de Gruyter.

Hoffner, H. A., Jr. (1997) *The Laws of the Hittites: A Critical Edition*. Leiden, Brill.

Högemann, P. (2003) Die Ionische Griechentum und seine altanatolische Umwelt im Spiegel Homers. Pp. 1–24 in *Die Griechen und der Vordere Orient*, ed. M. Witte and S. Alkier. Göttingen: Vandenhoeck & Ruprecht.

Hout, T. van den (2006) Institutions, Vernaculars, Publics: The Case of Second Millennium Anatolia. In S. Sanders (ed.) *Margins of Writing, Origins of Culture. New Approaches to Writing and Reading in the Ancient Near East*, 217–56. Chicago, The Oriental Institute of the University of Chicago.

Hutter, M. (2003) Aspects of Luwian Religion. In H. C. Melchert (ed.) *The Luwians*, 211–80. Leiden, Brill.

Ivanov, V. V. (2001) Southern Anatolian and Northern Anatolian. In R. Drews (ed.) *Greater Anatolia and the Indo-Hittite Language Family*, 131–83. Washington, DC, Institute for the Study of Man.

Kassian, A. S. and Yakubovich, I. S. (2001) The Reflexes of IE Initial Clusters in Hittite. In V. Shevoroshkin and P. Sidwell (eds.) *Anatolian Languages*, AHL Studies in the Science & History of Language 6, 10–48. Canberra, Association for the History of Language.

Lühr, R. (2002) Badal- und Genitivkonstruktionen. *Historische Sprachforschung* 115, 23–36.

Laroche, E. (1966) *Les noms des Hittites*. Paris: Klincksieck.

Luraghi, S. (1993) La modificazione nominale nelle lingue anatoliche. *Archivio Glottologico Italiano* 68, 145–66.

Martino, S. de (2003) *Annali e Res Gestae Antico Ittiti*. Pavia, Italian University Press.

Melchert, H. C. (1993) *Cuneiform Luvian Lexicon*. Chapel Hill : self-published.

___ (1994) *Anatolian Historical Phonology*. Amsterdam, Rodopi.

___ (2003a) Prehistory. In H. C. Melchert (ed.) *The Luwians*, 8–26. Leiden, Brill.

___ (2003b) Language. In H. C. Melchert (ed.) *The Luwians*, 170–210. Leiden, Brill.

___ (2005) The Problem of Luvian Influence on Hittite. In G. Meiser and O. Hachstein (eds.) *Sprachkontakt und Sprachwandel. Akten des XI Fachtagung der Indogermanischen Gesellschaft*, 445–59. Wiesbaden, Reichert.

Michel, C. and Garrelli, P. (1997) *Tablettes Paleo-Assyriennes de Kültepe*. Paris, de Boccard.

Mountjoy, P. A. (1998) The East Aegean–West Anatolian Interface in the Late Bronze Age: Myceneans and the Kingdom of Ahhiyawa. *Anatolian Studies* 48, 33–67.

Neu, E. (1999) Altanatolien und das mykenische Pylos: Einige Überlegungen zum Nestorbecher der Ilias. *Archív orientální* 67, 619–27.

Oettinger, N. (1978) Die gliederung des anatolischen Sprachgebietes. *Historische Sprachforschung* 92, 74–92.

___ (2005) *Die griechische Psilose als Kontaktphänomen*. Münchener Studien zur Sprachwissenschaft 62, 95–101.

Pintore, F. (1979) Tarwanis. In O. Carruba (ed.) *Studia Mediterranea Pietro Meriggi dicata,* 473–94. Pavia, Aurora.

Singer, I. (1981) Hittites and Hattians in Anatolia at the Beginning of the Second Millenium BC. *Journal of Indo-European Studies* 9, 119–33.

Starostin, S. A. (2001) Comparative Historical Linguistics and Lexicostatistics. In A. Y. Aikhenvald, and R. M. W. Dixon (eds.) *Areal Diffusion and Genetic Inheritance: Problems in Comparative Linguistics*, 223–59. Oxford, Oxford University.

Stefanini, R. (2002) Toward a Diachronic Reconstruction of the Linguistic Map of Ancient Anatolia. In *Anatolia Antica. Studi in memoria di Fiorella Imparati*, 783–806. Florence, LoGisma.

Veenhof, K. R. (2003) *The Old Assyrian List of Year Eponyms from Karum Kanish and Its Chronological Implications*. Ankara, Turkish Historical Society.

Watkins, C. (1986) The Language of the Trojans. In M. J. Mellink (ed.) *Troy and the Trojan War: A Symposium Held at Bryn Mawr College, October 1984*, 45–62. Bryn Mawr, PA, Bryn Mawr College.

___ (2001) An Indo-European Linguistic Area and Its Characteristics: Ancient Anatolia. Areal Diffusion as a Challenge to the Comparative Method?. In A. Y. Aikhenvald and R. M. W. Dixon (eds.) *Areal Diffusion and Genetic Inheritance*, 44–63. Oxford, Oxford University.

Wilhelm, G. (1995) *Suffixaufnahme* in Hurrian and Urartian. In F. Plank (ed.) *Double Case. Agreement by Suffixaufnahme*, 113–35. Oxford, Oxford University.

Yakubovich, I. (2002) Labyrinth for Tyrants. In A. S. Kassian and A.V. Sidel'tsev (eds.) *Studia Linguarum 3 (Memoriae A. A. Korolëv dicata)*, 93–116. Moscow, Languages of Slavonic Culture.

___ (2005) Carian Monument. In N. Kazanskij (ed.) *Hẓda manasa. Sbornik statej k semidesiatiletiju s dnia rozhdenija Leonarda Georgijevicha Gercenberga (Studies Presented to Leonard G. Hertzenberg on the Occasion of His 70th Birthday)*, 240–51. St. Petersburg, Nauka.

13

"HERMIT CRABS," OR NEW WINE IN OLD BOTTLES: ANATOLIAN AND HELLENIC CONNECTIONS FROM HOMER AND BEFORE TO ANTIOCHUS I OF COMMAGENE AND AFTER

Calvert Watkins

THE LETTER *KUB* 26.91[1]

Early in August 2003, two press conferences were held at Manfred Korfmann's ongoing excavation in Troy, featuring presentations by the Hittitologist Frank Starke of a new interpretation of the Hittite letter *KUB* 26.91, as sent from the king of Ahhiyawa to the Hittite king rather than the other way around, and sundry other claims. After seeing the press releases of 7 and 9 August 2003 thanks to Peter Kuniholm, I discussed the matter at length over e-mail with Craig Melchert, and I am convinced that in his conclusion of the author and direction of the letter Starke was quite right, but that many of his further suggestions are highly unlikely, in particular, Starke's view that the writer of the letter spoke Greek rather than Hittite as his native language, and his forcible reading of a name Kagamunas as *Katamun=as, then identifying the latter with the Greek name Kadmos, and concluding that the letter must have originated in Thebes, and that Thebes was perhaps the "capital" of Ahhiyawa. Starke's conclusions, both the good and the shaky, are now unfortunately presented as "hard facts" by the distinguished Homerist Joachim Latacz, first in the second press release above and now in his newly revised book *Troy and Homer* (2004). The work has the merit of making these issues public; we await Starke's own publication.

As Sarah Morris reminded me, the late Oliver Gurney, in a posthumously published article, was in fact the first to state categorically and in print (2002, 135) that the letter *KUB* 26.91 "must have been written by the King of Ahhiyawa to the Hittite King rather than the reverse." Gurney (2002, 135 n. 13) also quoted a private communication received in 1981 from Sommer's student the late Prof. Annelies Kammenhuber proposing a restoration of the opening formula of the letter (i 1) as

> [*A-NA* ^{D}UTU-*ŠI QI-BI-MA UM-MA* LUGA]L KUR *Aḫ-ḫi-ya-w*[*a-a*]
> [To my Sun say: thus the Kin]g of Ahhiyawā

It would appear to fit the space perfectly. Kammenhuber rightly preferred LUGA]L to Sommer's E]N, as the same is argued for by her student A. Hagenbuchner (1989, 320). The letter continues, after a fragmentary three-line paragraph probably beginning the customary historical preamble, and containing reference to an outbreak of hostilities (*kurur ištarna ... kišat*), with another paragraph beginning:

I 5 *pa-*]*ra-an-ni* MU.KAM-*ti-mu* ŠEŠ-*YA ḫa-at-r*[*a-a-i*]*š*[
6 *t*]*u-e-el-wa :gur-ša-wa-ra ku-e* [
7 ^{D}U ÌR-*an-ni am-mu-uk pa-iš* LUGAL ^{KUR}*A-a*[*š-šu-wa*

> The year before (?) my brother had written [...]
> "Your islands which [...]
> the Storm God gave to me in vassalage. The King of Aššuwa [...

We owe to Starke in a study of a quarter-century ago (1981) the interpretation of Luwian *guršawara*, unknown in Sommer's time, as "islands" (see now Starke 1990, 535–36; Melchert, 1999, 113). What islands these were naturally invites further speculation. Lemnos, Imbros and Samothrace have been suggested. But more importantly, as Gurney states (2002, 135–36), "The reference to the Storm God surely proves that the quoted words [particle *-wa*, line 6 C.W.] were written by the Hittite King." Therefore the text through line 5 was written by the king of Ahhiyawa, and the letter is, with Gurney, "his protest at the claim by the Hittite King to the islands which had hitherto belonged to him."

Whether or not "this could be the origin of all the Hittite troubles in the West" (so Gurney), the letter as we have it attests and makes reference to correspondence, alliances and diplomatic marriages (*peran ḫamakta*, with Starke), and hostilities involving three sovereign(state)s:

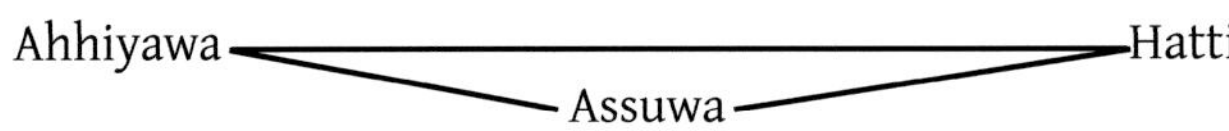

The Mycenaean Greek tablets make oblique reference to Assuwa [Aswa] in the personal and divine names *A-si-wi-jo* (KN, PY, MY) and *Po-ti-ni-ja A-si-wi-ja* (PY), Homeric PN Aswios, probably brought with refugees from the defeat of the As(su)wa coalition by Tuthaliya in the fifteenth century. Probably the same Tuthaliya is mentioned in our letter from the Ahhiyawan king (i 8) to the Hittite king, a cuneiform tablet that might argue for the presence of an Anatolian scribal school as part of the royal palace bureaucracy of Ahhiyawa itself. Mycenologists, archaeologists and philologists alike must take account of these testimonia of contemporary international contact and their implications; at the very least they should try to locate the LUGAL KUR *Aḫ-ḫi-ya-wa-a*. The "King of the land of Ahhiyawa" is real, and if Thebes for example cannot so far be proved to be his royal seat, it cannot so far be disproved either. Recall only the extraordinary collection of lapis lazuli cylinder seals found at Thebes; Porada (1981/1982) suggested the Kassite Babylonian examples might have been a gift of the Assyrian king Tukulti-ninurta I (contemporary and foe of Tudhaliya IV) to the king of Ahhiyawa. The collection includes also a number of Cypriot seals and one Hittite, inscribed with a Luwian name in hieroglyphs, as read by Güterbock.

A SYRO-HITTITE CONCEPT AND ITS CONTINUATION: LYCIAN FUNERARY ARCHITECTURE AND HOMERIC FORMULA

"The *sikkānu*-Stele in Late Bronze Age Syria" was the subject of a paper presented by Matthew Rutz (University of Pennsylvania) to the American Oriental Society in San Diego in March 2004. Syrian *sikkānu* may be a derivative of *sakānu*, Canaanite variant of Akkadian *šakānu* "to set up, set in place" though the etymology is contested. In Ugarit Rutz compares the *skn* offered to Dagan by Tharriyeli (*RŠ* 6.02) and examples are known from thirteenth-century Emar and Ekalte as well. For Hittite compare the ^{NA_4}*ḫuwaši*-stone, with its pseudo-sumerogram ^{NA_4}ZI.KIN from the Semitic (Haas 1994, 507–9). In contrast to scholars who view these "*baityloi*" as either "sacred" or "secular," Rutz offers a unitary function as *public visual representations of institutional authority*, from which can be derived the varying functions of the stelae as funerary monument, boundary marker curse and the like. This important cultural feature common to the southern Anatolian and West Semitic areal might well, with the Finnish archeologist Sanno Aro, have influenced Archaic Greek funerary art and architecture, specifically the stelae and (inscribed) statues.

Yet, the most notable and striking development of this cultural feature in the first millennium BC is found in Lycia: the funerary pillars treated by Deltour-Levie (1982). These tombs atop pillars, often on platforms, appear to be a purely Lycian creation (Deltour-Levie 1982, 200). Our preserved stone monuments date from the sixth to fourth centuries, and include the famous Xanthos stele (430–410); but architecturally the practice of stone mortise and tenon joints presupposes earlier wooden structures, later replaced by stone for durability (*ibid.* 201, following Mellink 1976).

It is noteworthy that these characteristically Lycian structures are themselves continued apparently to this day in Turkish folk architecture of the same region (Elmalı): stone and timber pillars with platforms for beehives to protect them from varmints (see Zahle [1975] and especially Mellink [1976]). These are thus the last *Nachwuchs* of our Syro-Hittite cultural feature three and a half millennia earlier.

Now, the funerary pillars must have been a salient and highly visible feature of Lycian culture already in the Archaic period, earlier than our attested monuments themselves, for they were apparently familiar enough to Ionian aoidoi to allow the generation of a Homeric formula "with tomb and pillar," τύμβωι τε στήληι τε, restricted to Lycian context: the death of Sarpedon (Myl. *Zrppedu*[*n-?*] TL 44d, 6 [Xanthos stele]), in *Il.* 16.456–7 = 673–75.

> ἔνθα ἑ ταρχύσουσι κασίγνητοί τε ἔται τε
> τύμβωι τε στήληι τε· τὸ γὰρ γέρας ἐστὶ θανόντων.
> There his brothers and his kinsmen will give him burial
> With tomb and pillar; for such is the privilege of the dead.

I have preferred "tomb" for τύμβωι to the more common "tumulus," since Lycian tombs are typically atop the pillars, which are not typically erected on tumuli.

Everything in this passage is Anatolian. In ταρχύω we have to deal "not only with a Lycian custom but with a Lycian word," as stated by Blümel (1925). Kretschmer (1939, 104) made more precise the meaning, "wie einen Gott bestatten" (Hittite *Tarḫu-*, Lycian *Trqq-*, base of the designation of the Storm-God), comparing such Homeric phrases as θεὸν ὣς τιμήσουσι, and the Hittite phrase DINGIR^{LIM} *kiš-* "become a god" = "die" of the king. The etymology, accepted by Chantraine, can stand, *pace* R. Janko, *Il. Comm. ad* Π 456.

Homeric στήλη in our formula is derived from the verb στέλλω "set out, make ready, fit out." Its formation recalls that of the Syrian *sikkānu*-stele, from the verb "to set up, set in place," and as such the word itself might be further evidence that the Greek institution of the στήλη might be a borrowing from Syro-Hittite tradition.

Lycian *sttala* by its phonological form must be a relatively late borrowing. But the real word for "stele, pillar, upright monument" in Lycian and other Anatolian languages is a different one.

HIEROGLYPHIC LUWIAN *TASA(N)-ZA*, LYDIAN *TAŚẼN*, LYCIAN *KUMEZIJẼ ΘΘẼ*

The South and West Anatolian word for "upright pillar, stele, altar, funerary monument, memorial, boundary marker" – essentially the same semantic range as that of Semitic *sikkānu* – is found most clearly in Hieroglyphic Luwian *tasa(n)-za*, Lydian *taśẽv*, Lycian *kumezijẽ θθẽ*, with their documentation. With the exception of the Palaic they were all seen by Eichner (1983).

Hieroglyphic Luwian *tasa*(*n*)*-za.* Hawkins (2000) discusses the word and gives its four attestations: ("256") *tà-sá-za* [acc.sg.neut.] KULULU 2 § 6 (mid-eighth century "for him may the black gods of Santas [(DEUS *sà-ta-si-i-zi* (DEUS)*pa*?*+ra/i-wa/i-i-zi-i*] attack [*a(n)ta* "CRUS"-*tu*] the memorial"; KARKAMIS A 6 § 28 (late-ninth to early-eighth century) *ta-sà* [acc.sg.neut.]=*pa=wa ta-si* [dat. sg.] NEG$_3$+*i* CUM-*ni ARHA tà-ia* "or whether he shall take away a stele for a stele," CEKKE § 15 (mid-eighth century) *a=wa* FINES-*ha+ra/i-ia ta-sa*[acc.pl.neut.] *ha-zi-mi-na* "we engrave(d?) frontier stelae." The formation is clearly that of a thematic neuter *tas-a(n),* with determiner *tasa(n)-za*, plural *tas-a*.

Lydian may attest a noun *taśẽv* in a poorly preserved bilingual Lydian-Greek inscription (no. 40) on a column drum from the temple of Athena at Pergamon (now in Berlin). For the reading I remain *pace* Gusmani

(1986) with Buckler's 1924 reading *taśẽv*, regarded as possible if not certain and accepted by Neumann (1967), the more so since the stress on the second syllable (Eichner 1985) is confirmed by Lycian. See however now Schürr (1999). If correct, this paragraph is moot.

Palaic may attest a derivative in the word *taš-ūra* (loc. sg.) "on the sacrificial table/stand," as suggested by Melchert (1994, 191). But the semantics of the formation are unclear, and Pal. *taš-* (if to the root "stand"?) might be wholly unrelated to the nouns *tasa(n)-za, taśẽv* (?), *θθẽ*. I remain sceptical.

Lycian attests the noun (nom.-acc. sg. neut.) *θθẽ* twice in the trilingual from the Letoon, N 320 lines 7, 16 (mid-fourth century). Eichner (1983, 59) first explained the history of the form: Common Anatolian **tasóm* > Pre-Lycian **tasẽ* > **tesẽ* by umlaut, whence **tehẽ*, syncopated to **t'hẽ*, whence *θθẽ* by rule. Compare CLuw. *tāta/i-* "father," HLuw. *tata/i-*, Lyc. *tede/i-*, genitive-adjective *teθθi* < **ted'hi* < **tedehi* = Milyan *tedesi*. For the forms and the rules see Melchert (1994, *passim*; 2004).

The two attestations on the trilingual stele are the following: (7) *m̃eitẽ : kumezijẽ : θθẽ* : "(the Xanthians and περίοικοι) built a sacred *kumezijẽ* (ἱερός) *monument* (for the divinities X. and A.)." The Greek version has ἱδρύσασθαι βωμόν "raise an altar" and the Aramaic just *krp' l-mᶜ bd* "o make a cult," with *krp'* an apparent Iranian loanword **karpa-* cognate with Vedic *kálpa-* "rite." (16–17) *sẽ-ñteñte-km̃mẽ : seyẽti : θθẽ : sttati-teli :* "and however much (is) inside (the temenos), and (the place) whereon the monument stands (are the property of X. and A.)." The Greek and Aramaic diverge somewhat: (15) καὶ ὅσον πρὸς τωῖ ἀγρῶι καὶ τὰ οἰκήματα "whatever appertains to the land, and the buildings." The Aramaic simply says (10) *w' yty by*[*t*] "and there is a property ('house')."

The *s* > *h* sound change is a feature of "normal" Lycian A, while it is not found in Milyan, Lycian B, nor in the Anatolian "Luvoid" languages of the Southeast in the first millennium. In Cilicia, the personal name Τεδι-νηνις corresponds to Τεδε-νη[νις] found in Lycia, and presupposes a southeastern Anatolian ("Luvoid") *tede/i-* "father" and *nẽne/i-* "brother," as in Lycian. By the same token, we may assume in this language a thematic stem **tese/i-* minus the *s* > *h* rule, and minus the syncope of the unstressed vowel. This word indeed exists; but in the Greek of Commagene in southeastern Anatolia. The word is ἱεροθέσιον, to which we now turn.

GREEK ΙΕΡΟΘΕΣΙΟΝ (ΣΩΜΑΤΟΣ ΕΜΟΥ) AND (ΣΩΜΑΤΟΣ ΕΝΘΑ ΘΕΣΙΝ)

Greek ἱεροθέσιον is the self-designation of the colossal sculptural and architectural complex and funerary monument of Antiochus I of Commagene (reigned ca. 69–ca. 36 BC) atop Nemrud Dağı in the Anti-Taurus range. It is "the outstanding landmark of the upper Euphrates River valley," (Sanders 1996, 91, to which I make global reference).

Antiochus's description of his monumental complex appears in lines 21–23 of the Nomos inscriptions: τόνδε χῶρον ἱερὸν ἁπάντων κοινὸν ἀναδεῖξαι θεῶν ἐνθρόνισμα προειλάμην "I chose to make this holy place a common consecrated seat of all the gods." It offers a fine example of the rhetoric of Antiochus's text. The hapax ἐνθρόνισμα presumably makes reference to the colossal seated deities on the East and West terraces.

The land of Commagene appears as Kummuh in first-millennium Assyrian sources. The kings of Kummuh bore or affected Hittite royal names in the Iron Age: Suppiluliuma and his son Hattusili are attested both in Hieroglyphic Luwian and Assyrian sources, the latter garbled to Ushpilulume, as is the last king Muttallu (= Muwattalli), deposed in 708 BC when the Assyrians conquered the country and deported the population to Babylonia (Hawkins 2000, 330–33). The land was probably the Kummaha of second-millennium Hittite sources as early as ca. 1500 (*IBoT* 1.36 iii 36).

The funerary complexes of Nemrud Dağı and others are all of Commagenian dynasts: Antiochus I, his father Mithradates I Callinicus and his grandfather Samos II. These complexes, where the word ἱεροθέσιον is uniquely attested and is clearly what they were called, have been aptly described by Joseph A. Greene, of Harvard's Semitic Museum as "Hellenistic architectural confections that combine aspects of mausoleums, royal sculpture gardens, dynastic monuments and political advertisements." He speculated that *hierothesion* could contain to some earlier, prehellenistic cultural feature "which only accidentally became fixed in an archeologically recognizable form owing to the outsized ego of the short-lived Commagenian dynasty, which built these monuments?" The foregoing discussion in this paper has clearly confirmed the correctness of his insight: *hiero-thes-ion* contains the word for "stele, memorial," which appears as HLuw. *tasa*(*n*)*-za*, Lyd. *taśẽv*, Lyc. *θθẽ* preceded by the adjective, which translates Lyc. (etc.) *kumezije-* "sacred, holy."

The word ἱεροθέσιον is found four times at Nemrud Dağı: note Nomos insc. 125 ἱεροθεσίωι σώματος ἐμοῦ "at the sacred tomb of my body." It is clear that for Antiochus ἱεροθέσιον designated both the totality of the mountaintop monument, colossal statues and all, and his own last resting place, the manmade tumulus proper.

While the other inscriptions attesting the word are texts of Antiochus I, internal evidence indicates that this word was the designation of the similar sanctuary complexes and tombs of his father and grandfather. Thus ἱεροθέσιον must have been current in the Greek of Commagene for such royal burial places by at least the second century BC (cf. Ramsey 2003).

Now the term "hermit crab" was coined by J. Heath (1998) for a process of linguistic change involving "formal renewal of morphology by phonologically mediated affix substitution." The process is not confined to morphology but extends to semantics, lexicon and syntax, as in our case of composition. The semantics of the Commagenean Anatolian noun phrase equivalent of Lycian *kumezijẽ θθẽ* "sacred **tese-*" "colonized" the phonetically similar Greek word θέσι-ς and brought about the creation of the compound ἱεροθέσιον. In just the same way the semantics of the imperfective Hittite *-ške-*, Luwian *-za-*, and its place in the Anatolian tense/aspect system, "colonized" the phonetically similar Greek morpheme -σκε- and brought about the creation of the augmentless imperfects and aorists in -εσκε- of East Ionic (see Puhvel 1991; Watkins 2001).

As Martin West reminds me, according to Buck-Petersen (1945) there are a dozen other words in late Greek in -θέσιον. All are transparent purely Greek creations, via several channels, but the presence of even just a few of them in the language at the time would surely have eased the creation and naturalization of ἱεροθέσιον.

It would appear that the "colonized" compound came first, qua SACRED + θεσι- = **tese-*. Only some centuries afterward could the Anatolian Greek simplex θέσις be extracted from the compound and come to be used simply for "burial place, grave." The pentameter line 2 of SEG 30.1479 reads ζῶν ἵ]ν' ἔχω φανερ[ὴν] σώματος ἔνθα θέσιν "so that living I may have a visible burial place for my body," which eerily echoes Antiochus's ἱεροθεσίωι σώματος ἐμοῦ and the other examples of the collocation noted above.

SOME PRECISIONS ON THE ETYMOLOGY OF GREEK ΘΕΟΣ

The Anatolian words Hieroglyphic Luwian *tasa*(*n*) *za*, Lydian *taśẽv*, Lycian *θθẽ* were etymologically related to Greek θεός "god" by Craig Melchert in lectures at Harvard University in the middle 1990s. My only contribution is to add ἱεροθέσιον to the dossier, and to insist that Greek θεός "god" < θεσό- (with Armenian *dik'*) and Anatolian **tas-ó-* make an essentially exact equation. The point of departure is an Indo-European apophonic root noun **d*^{h}*eh*$_1$*s-*/**d*^{h}*h*$_1$*s-* designating the sacred, Latin *fās*. (Whether this is an enlargement of the root **d*^{h}*eh*$_3$- is probable but uncertain.) With the secondary suffix **-nó-* we find both full grade of the base in Oscan *fíísnú* and zero-grade in Latin *fānum* < **fas-no-*, as well as full grade before **-tó-* in Latin *fēstus*. And with possessive secondary suffix **-ó-* (Schindler) and zero grade of the base we have a possessive adjective *d^hh_1s-ó-* "having the sacred." So Melchert (1994, 191; *qua* *d^hh_es-ó-*). Hajnal (1995) prefers full grade *d^heh_1s-ó-*, which eliminates the equation with θεός. This adjective was substantivized in the neuter in Anatolian as "sacred thing," whence "sacred structure," like Greek ἱερόν. In Greek or Greco-Armenian it was substantivized in the masculine to designate the "god" as "sacred being."

For the association between "sacred structure" and "god" recall my etymology (Watkins 1974, 102 n.) of "god" in Germanic: neuter *guđa^m < **Gu-tó-m* via "heaped-up earth, barrow, *kurgan*," Homeric χυτὴ γαῖα and the numinous presence therein.

The editor of *Nemrud Dağı*, Donald Sanders, cited a number of instances in excavator Theresa Goell's notes of "lingering Hittite traditions" in Commagene. In most of these, "Hittite" is to be understood as "Neo-Hittite" or just Hieroglyphic Luwian. I submit that the Greek word *hierothesion* itself is in this sense yet another "lingering Hittite tradition," and a not insignificant one.

NOTES

It is a pleasant duty to thank for their input all those with whom I have discussed aspects of this paper, not only Peter Kuniholm, but also Gary Beckman, Walter Burkert, Corinne Crawford, Ana Galjanić, Joseph A. Greene, John Huehnergard, Stephanie Jamison, Joshua Katz, Charles de Lamberterie, Craig Melchert, Sarah Morris, Norbert Oettinger, Hayden Pelliccia, Elise Ramsey, Matthew Rutz and Martin West.

1 Bo 1485 in F. Sommer (1932, ch. IX).

REFERENCES

Blümel, W. (1925) Homerisch ταρχύω. *Glotta* 15, 78–84.

Buck, C. D. and Petersen, W. (1945) *Precise Index of Greek Nouns and Adjectives*. Chicago, University of Chicago Press.

Deltour-Levie, C. (1982) *Les piliers funéraires de Lycie*. Publications d'Histoire de l'Art de l'Université Catholique de Louvain 31. Louvain-la-Neuve, Institut Supérieur d'Archéologie et d'Histoire d'Art.

Dörner, K. F. and Goell, T. B. (1963) *Arsameia am Nymphaios: Die Ausgrabungen im Hierothesion von Mithradates Kallinikos von 1953-1956*. Istanbuler Forschungen 23. Berlin, Gebr. Mann.

Eichner, H. (1983) Etymologische Beiträge zum Lykischen der Trilingue vom Letoon bei Xanthos. *Orientalia* 52, 48–66.

___ (1985) Malwa, eine hieroglyphenluwisch-sidetische Wortgleichung. *Münchener Studien zur Sprachwissenschaft* 45, 5–21.

Gurney, O. (2002) The Authorship of the Tawagalawas Letter. In P. Taracha (ed.) *Silva Anatolica: Anatolian Studies Presented to Maciej Popko on the Occasion of His 65th Birthday*, 133–41. Warsaw, Agade.

Gusmani, (1986) *Lydisches Wörterbuch*. Ergänzungsband Lf. 3. Heidelberg, Winter.

Haas, V. (1994) *Geschichte der hethitischen Religion*. Handbuch der Orientalistik. Leiden, Brill.

Hagenbuchner, A. (1989) *Die Korrespondenz der Hethiter, 2. Teil*. Texte der Hethiter 16. Heidelberg, Winter.

Hajnal, I. (1995) *Der lykische Vokalismus*. Arbeiten aus der Abteilung "Vergleichende Sprachwissenschaft" Graz, 10. Graz, Leykam.

Hawkins, J. D. (2000) *Corpus of Hieroglyphic Luwian Inscriptions*. Berlin: de Gruyter.

Heath, J. (1998) Hermit Crabs: Formal Renewal of Morphology by Phonologically Mediated Affix Substitution. *Language* 74, 728–59.

Laroche, E. (1979) L'inscription lycienne. In *Fouilles de Xanthos* 6, 49–127. Paris, Klincksieck.

Latacz, J. (2004) *Troy and Homer*. Trans. K. Windle and R. Ireland. Oxford, Oxford University.

Kretschmer P. (1939) Die Stellung der lykischen Sprache, *Glotta* 28, 101–16.

Melchert, H. C. (1993) *Cuneiform Luvian Lexicon*. Chapel Hill, NC, self-published.

___ (1994) *Anatolian Historical Phonology*. Amsterdam, Rodopi.

___ (2004) *A Dictionary of the Lycian Language*. Ann Arbor, Beech Stave.

Mellink, M. (1976) Local Phrygian and Greek Traits in Northern Lycia. *Revue Archéologique*, 23–25.

Neumann, G. (1967) Der lykische Name der Athena. *Kadmos* 6, 80–87.

Porada, E. (1981/1982) The Cylinder Seals Found at Thebes in Boeotia. *Archiv für Orientforschung* 28, 1–70.

Puhvel, J. (1991) *Homer and Hittite*. Innsbrucker Beiträge zur Sprachwissenschaft. Vorträge und kleinere Schriften 44. Innsbruck.

Sanders, D. H. (ed.) (1996) *Nemrud Dağı: The Hierothesion of Antiochus I of Commagene*. Winona Lake, IN, Eisenbrauns.

Schürr, D. (1999) Lydisches I. Zur Doppelinschrift von Pergamon. *Kadmos* 38, 163–74.

Sommer, F. (1932) *Aḫḫiyawā-Urkunden*. ABAW 6. Munich.

Starke, F. (1981. Die keilschrift-luwische Wörter für "Insel" und "Lampe." *Historische Sprachforschung* 95, 142–57.

___ (1990) *Untersuchung zur Stammbildung des keilschrift-luwischen Nomens*. Studien zu den Boğazköy-Texten 31. Wiesbaden, Harrassowitz.

Watkins, C. (1974) "god." In M. Mayrhofer et al. (eds.) *Antiquitates Indogermanicae. Gedenkschrift Hermann Güntert*, 101–10. IBS 12. Innsbruck, IBS.

___ (2001) An Indo-European Linguistic Area and Its Characteristics: Ancient Anatolia. In A. Y. Aikhenvald and R. M. W. Dixon (eds.) *Areal Diffusion and Genetic Inheritance*, 42–63. Oxford, Oxford University.

Zahle, J. (1975) Lykische Gräber. *Archäologischer Anzeiger* 1975, 344.

14

POSSESSIVE CONSTRUCTIONS IN ANATOLIAN, HURRIAN, URARTIAN AND ARMENIAN AS EVIDENCE FOR LANGUAGE CONTACT

Silvia Luraghi

As is well known, adnominal possession displays some peculiar features in Anatolian.[1] Noun phrases that contain a head noun and a nominal modifier (dependent noun) often display patterns that are different from the usual construction involving an adnominal genitive, which occurs in the other Indo-European languages. In the Anatolian languages of the Luwian group, the genitive case was replaced to varying extents by so-called genitival adjectives (Hajnal 2000). In Cuneiform Luwian, where substitution is complete, it already occurs in the most ancient written sources, and must date back to pre-literary times. Hittite, which retains the use of the adnominal genitive, displays case attraction (also called partitive apposition), especially in cases of inalienable possession (see below). Stefanini (1969) suggested that substitution of adnominal genitives by adjectives in Luwian is due to the influence of a Hurrian construction, suffix copying, described in §1. In Luraghi (1993a), I argued that influence from Hurrian can also explain the introduction of case attraction in Hittite (see further Luraghi 1993b). The only other ancient Indo-European language that displays case attraction to an extent similar to Hittite is Classical Armenian. According to Vogt (1932), case attraction in Classical Armenian was brought about by contact with Old Georgian, a language that also has suffix copying.

In the present paper, I would like to explore further the hypothesis of language contact and morphological borrowing in the light of our knowledge about contacts among Indo-European and non-Indo-European populations in Anatolia. I will start by surveying once more the data (§1). In §2, I will summarize our knowledge about movements and contacts of Indo-European and non-Indo-European populations in Anatolia. I will argue that early appearance of genitival adjectives in Luwian can be explained by early bilingualism in the area of Kizzuwatna, while later appearance of case attraction in Hittite may show that contacts with the Hurrians during the Old Kingdom mostly remained limited to military conquest, while later they increasingly extended to the cultural and linguistic levels. In §3, I will further suggest that the introduction of case attraction in Armenian may be dated back to contacts with the Urartians. Section 4 contains my conclusions.

1. THE DATA

1.1 Case Copying (Suffixaufnahme) in Hurrian, Urartian and Old Georgian

Case copying, also known by its German name, *Suffixaufnahme*, is known from several, genetically unrelated languages. Where is exists, it seems to be an areal phenomenon. This is best seen in Australia, where several languages belonging to different families have suffix copying (Plank 1995). In spite of the variety of languages that display this phenomenon, there appears to be a limitation to its occurrence: suffix copying is typical of agglutinative, rather than fusional languages. It can be described as follows: in an agglutinative language, the case suffix of a head noun is copied after the genitive suffix of a nominal modifier: X+case$_1$ Y+gen+case$_1$ = "Y's X," "the X of Y."

Some examples are given below:

(1) *eni(i)=n(a)=až(v)e=ne=da šarri=ne=da*
god-art.pl-gen-art.sg-dir king-art.sg-dir
"to the king of the gods" (from Wilhelm 1995, 118)

(2) *haldi=i=ne=ni alsuiši=ni*
Haldi-gen-art.sg-instr greatness-instr
"through the greatness of Haldi" (from Wilhelm 1995, 131)

(3) *šecevn-ita cmid-isa sameb-isa-jta*
help-instr holy-gen trinity-gen-instr
"with the help of the Holy Trinity" (from Boeder 1995, 159)

(4) *col-isa gan m-is mepc-isa-jsa*
wife-gen by art-gen king-gen-gen
"from the wife of the king" (from Vogt 1932)

In example (1) from Hurrian, the head noun is *šarri*, which takes the suffixes of definite article and directive case; both affixes are copied on the dependent noun *eni*, after the suffixes of the plural article and of the genitive. In (2) from Urartian, it is the suffix of the instrumental that is copied from the head noun *alsuiši* to its dependent *haldi*. In a similar way, the Georgian examples (3) and (4) contain genitival constructions in which the dependent in the genitive also bears the suffixes of the head noun. These three languages are agglutinative.

Suffix copying has the effect of creating agreement between a head noun and a dependent noun, in much the same way as agreement does when the dependent is an adjective. As remarked in Marr and Brière (1931, 231), "this formation typical of Georgian is called the 'double relation,' because it consists, on the one hand, in the genitive of the *nomen rectum* and, on the other, in the repetition of the case ending of the *nomen regens*, which already constitutes a 'relation.'"[2]

Through suffix copying the noun phrase acquires extra marking, and its boundaries are better indicated. The reason why suffix copying requires agglutinative morphology lies in the nature of the affixes, which in agglutinative languages have bigger autonomy that in fusional languages, and are always easily individuated and segmented. In fusional languages, on the contrary, inflectional affixes are often hardly segmented from the stem; furthermore, they often also convey information regarding inflectional class: this means that the endings are not easily identified as exponents of a certain case.[3] Because the Indo-European languages are fusional, suffix copying is unlikely to be borrowed without some changes that adapt it to fusional morphology.

1.2 Genitival Adjectives in Cuneiform Luwian and in Lycian

As remarked above, adjectival modifiers are found in all languages of the Luwian group but, while most languages also have a genitive case, in Cuneiform Luwian they are the only possible way to express adnominal relations. This situation held already at the time of the first written sources:

(5) *zassin* DUMU-*assassin annin*
this:ADJ.ACC child:ADJ.ACC mother:ACC
"this child's mother" (*KUB* 35.103 ii 13)

(6) *xntawaza xugasi enesi*
rulership:NOM grandfather:ADJ.NOM mother:ADJ.NOM
"the rulership of the mother's grandfather" (from Neumann 1982, 151)

(7) DINGIR.MEŠ-*assanzati wassarahitati*
gods-ADJ.PL.INSTR favor:INSTR
"by the favor of the gods" (from Melchert 2003, 188)

Examples (5) and (7) are from Cuneiform Luwian. In (5) the head noun *annin* is in the accusative; the dependent *zassin* DUMU-*assassin* contains a demonstrative and a noun, both take the adjectival suffix *-assa/i-* and agree in case with the head noun. Example (7) shows that a dependent noun can also be in the plural (see Melchert 2003, 188), while example (6) from Lycian shows that adjectival genitives can be recursive: the noun *xtawaza* is the head of the whole noun phrase, *enesi* is the modifier of *xtawaza* and *xugasi* is the modifier of *enesi*; they both take the adjectival suffix *-s-*.

Adjectival modifiers used in the place of genitives are known from many other Indo-European languages, but in none of them do they replace the genitive case completely (see the discussion in Luraghi 1993a). Some examples are given below from Latin (8) and Upper Sorbian (9 and 10):

(8) *ex Anniana Milonis domo*
"from Annius Milo's home" (Cic. *ad Att.* IV 3,3)

(9) *Janowa kniha*
Jan:ADJ-NOM.SG.F book:NOM.SG.F
"Jan's book"

(10) *mojeho muzowa sostra*
POSS.1SG.GEN husband:ADJ.NOM.SG.F sister:NOM.SG.F
"my husband's sister"

Possessive adjectives are most extended in the Slavonic languages, but even in Upper Sorbian, where they are most often used, they display some restrictions: they require definite referents and cannot be formed of all nouns; besides, they are not recursive (as shown in [18]), and plurality of the possessor cannot be expressed (Corbett 1987).

The adjectival suffix *-assa/i-* is also known from Hittite and Palaic, as shown by Hajnal (2000, 165–67), who also remarks that the usage of the genitive in Hittite (and presumably in Anatolian) had some limitations with respect to the other Indo-European languages.[4] If we accept Stefanini's (1969) hypothesis, according to which replacement of the genitive by the possessive adjective was brought about by contact with Hurrian, this phenomenon can be explained as a way to reproduce the same type of construction (agreement of a nominal dependent with its head noun) with Indo-European means that already existed in Anatolian. Stefanini writes, "such correspondences [i.e., with suffix copying] in Luwian could be received and understood only through an adjectival interpretation, in an Indo-European sense" (1969, 299).[5]

This interpretation is in keeping with our knowledge about morphological borrowing. Most often, morphological borrowing consists of the reinterpretation of an affix that already exists in the target language and takes over a function of an affix of the source language, as argued by Weinreich:

> If the bilingual identifies a morpheme or grammatical category of language A with one in language B, he may apply the B form in grammatical functions which he derives from the system of language A. What leads the bilingual to establish the interlingual equivalent of the morphemes or categories is either their FORMAL SIMILARITY or A SIMILARITY IN PRE-EXISTING FUNCTIONS. (Weinreich 1963, 39; emphasis mine)

In this perspective, the derivational suffix *-assa/i-* that derives an adjective from a noun corresponds to the suffix of the genitive in Hurrian, indeed their function is the same, because both mark a noun as a dependent of another noun. In this connection, it is interesting to note that descriptive grammars of Australian languages that also display suffix copying, similar to Hurrian, sometimes disagree in classifying the so-called genitive suffix. While some scholars consider it an inflectional suffix, others think that it should better be taken as derivational: "genitive could, strictly, be classified as a derivational affix rather than as an inflection ... genitive takes a case inflection agreeing with the head "possessed" noun and functions rather as a derived adjective" (Dixon 1980, 321).

1.3 Case Attraction in Hittite and Classical Armenian

Case attraction, which started occurring in Middle Hittite, and replaced an older construction involving possessive clitics (see Luraghi 1990 and below, § 1.4), consists of a dependent noun that takes the same case as the head noun (i.e., it is treated as an adjective), rather than be inflected in the genitive. It occurs with all cases, as shown in the examples below:

(11) *n= at= mu= kan* UKU-*az* KAxU-*az šara uizzi= pat*
CONN 3SG.N/A 1SG.OBL PTC man:ABL mouth:ABL out go:PRS.3SG PTC
"and it (sc. these words) comes out of my mouth of man" (*KUB* 6.45 i 30–31)

(12) *nu= kan* GAL-*in arunan* ᵈ*Ku(ma)rbiyaza* É-*irza* ...
CONN PTC big:ACC sea:ACC *K.*:ABL house:ABL
uwater n= an INA É- *ŠU arḫa peḫuter*
bring:PRT.3PL CONN 3SG.ACC into house his back bring:PRT.3PL
"they brought the big sea out of Kumarbi's house, and carried him to his (own) house" (StBoT 14 11.16–19);

(13) *tuedaš ššiyantaš pedaš*
2SG.DAT.PL beloved:DAT.PL sites:DAT.PL
"in your favorite sites" (*KUB* 36.90 16).

Examples (14) through (16) show how case attraction works in Classical Armenian. Example (16) is of special interest, because it is the translation of Georgian (4), which contains suffix copying:

(14) *yeresaç erkrē*
face:ABL earth:ABL
"from the face of the earth"

(15) *varowk' lawowt'eamb*
life:INSTR virtue:INSTR
"through a virtuous way of life"

(16) *i knoǰē t'agaworēn*
from wife:ABL.SG king:ABL.SG-ART
"from the wife of the king" (Armenian examples from Vogt 1932).

The above examples all contain occurrences where a dependent noun is inflected in the same case as the head noun. Examples (11) and (12) from Hittite involve the ablative; example (13) involves the use of the dative/locative and is especially interesting because it shows that pronouns could also undergo case attraction. Examples from Classical Armenian involve the ablative and the instrumental case.

Double case constructions are also known from other Indo-European languages, albeit sporadically. The closest parallel is the Homeric double accusative, as in:

(17) *Dēΐokhon dè Páris bále ... ômon ópisthe*
D.:ACC PTC *P.*:NOM hit:AOR.3SG back:ACC behind
"Deïochus hit Paris in the back from behind" (*Il.* 15.341)

In Homer, double case is limited to inalienable possession (mostly body parts), and it is productive only for the accusative. The limited small number of occurrences with the dative, as:

(18) *en dé te hoi kradiēi*
in PTC PTC 3SG.DAT heart:DAT
"in his heart" (*Il.* 20.169)

can be explained as involving a possessive construction (dative of possession, see also Jacquinod 1989).

In Homer, double case is limited to inalienable possession (mostly body parts), and it is productive only for the accusative (see Jacquinod 1989). In Hittite, case attraction is attested for all cases; it is limited to referents that can be seen as inalienably possessed, but their range is wider than in Homeric Greek. In Classical Armenian case attraction has no limitations.

Case attraction too can be seen as the over-extension of a construction that was possible in the Indo-European languages in order to reproduce a non-Indo-European construction. As with suffix copying, with case attraction, too, the dependent noun agrees with the head noun.

1.4 Diachrony of Case Attraction in Hittite

As I remarked above, case attraction did not occur in Old Hittite. As shown in Luraghi (1990), Old Hittite had a special possessive construction that was used for inalienable possession;[6] it involved a dependent in the genitive and a possessive clitic hosted by the head noun:

(19) *takku* LÚ.ULÙ^{LU}*-aš ELLAM-aš* KAxKAK=*šet* *kuiški* *waki*
if man-GEN free-GEN nose 3SG-POSS-N/A someone-NOM-SG bite-3SG-PRES
"if someone bites the nose of a free man" (*Laws* § 13 = A i 24, Old Hittite).

The occurrence of the clitic has the effect of cross-referencing the possessor with the possessee, in other words, it constitutes a sort of agreement between the dependent and the head noun. That this construction was functionally equivalent to case attraction is shown by the fact that in later manuscripts of the *Laws* it was substituted by case attraction:

(20) *takku* LÚ.ULÙ^{LU}*-an ELLAM* KAxKAK=*šet* *kuiški* *waki*
if man-ACC free nose 3SG-POSS-A someone-N-SG bite-3SG-PRES
"if someone bites a free man on his nose" (*Laws* § 13 = B i 33, Middle Hittite)

The occurrence of *-šet* in (19) must be explained as the result of a partial innovation: the copyist changed the genitive LÚ.ULÙ^{LU}*-aš* into an accusative LÚ.ULÙ^{LU}*-an* but did not leave out the possessive. This type of partial innovations is frequent in copies of Old Hittite texts.

1.5 Suffix Copying and Case Attraction

In the present section I will test the plausibility of the hypothesis that case attraction derives from borrowing of suffix copying. I will start by citing Vogt's (1932) explanation of suffix copying in Armenian as owing to influence from Georgian:

> In Georgian the case ending of the head noun ... is repeated after all modifiers, either adjectives, pronouns, genitives, prepositional phrases or noun phrases which already contain the expression of a case relation.... The difference between the two expressions [i.e. suffix copying in Georgian and case attraction in Armenian] is that Georgian allows cumulation of case endings whereas in Armenian the ending that marks the constituent forces away the ending that expresses the relation between head and modifier. Since the two languages have different [morphological] means, facts are not the same in detail. However, the general tendency of the two languages displays a striking similarity, making case endings also function as markers of noun phrases. (1932, 75)[7]

Indeed the similarity is striking, and the same holds for Hittite as compared to Hurrian: the only difference lies in the limitation of case attraction in Hittite to inalienable possession, while neither case attraction in Classical Armenian nor suffix copying in any of the languages cited here displays such limitation. In my opinion, the limitation is due to the fact that case attraction had been borrowed into Hittite as a replacement of the earlier construction with clitics, described in § 1.4, which already had the effect of making the head noun agree with the dependent.

Better dating of the Hittite tablets achieved in the 1970s helped work out a chronology of case attraction as described in §1.4, and clear the way for the idea that case attraction represented an older way of expressing possession in Proto-Indo-European, even older than the adnominal genitive (see Luraghi 1990 and 1993a for discussion).

Recently, Lühr (2001) offered another explanation of the development of case attraction in Hittite also connected with language contact and morphological borrowing (see also Lühr 2003). According to Lühr, Hittite case attraction was created due to influence of the Akkadian construct state. Lühr assumes that occurrences as (20) where case attraction is accompanied by the possessive clitic are indeed representative of an existing Hittite construction, rather that they are partial innovations, where the scribe has changed the genitive into the accusative, but then has not left out the possessive. Note however that such constructions only occur in the *Laws*, i.e., in a text that has been copied from an Old Hittite original, and not in Middle Hittite or New Hittite original manuscripts. Lühr then draws a parallel between (20) and occurrences such as (21):

(21) *rubu* *qas=* *su*
prince:NOM hand:CONSTR POSS
"the hand of the prince" (from Lühr 2001, 438),

and writes that "possessor and possessee or *rectum* and *regens* are placed in the same case next to each other."[8] However this is not the case, since the possessee (i.e., the word *qas*) is not inflected in the same case as the possessor: Here (as elsewhere in this construction) the possessor *rubu* is in the nominative case, while the possessee *qas* is in the construct state.[9] Furthermore, as I remarked above, the occurrence of the possessive clitic within case attraction in Hittite is only due to partial updating of the language. In original manuscripts written when case attraction started to be productively used, clitics did not occur.[10]

2. CONTACTS BETWEEN INDO-EUROPEAN AND NON-INDO-EUROPEAN POPULATIONS IN ANATOLIA

Stefanini (2002) explained the non-occurrence of adjectival genitives in Hittite as opposed to their occurrence in Luwian as owing to the influence of different substrates: while Luwian had Hurrian as its substrate at an early time, Hittite had Hattic, a language that does not have suffix copying.

Let us now turn to the distribution of genitival adjectives in the languages of the Luwian group. As I remarked above, the substitution of the genitive case is complete only in Cuneiform Luwian. Hieroglyphic Luwian and Lycian retained the genitive to different extents; Lycian also displays a tendency toward extending the genitive case at the expense of the adjectival construction (see Hajnal 2000).

The Hurrians were located in northern Syria, to the east of ancient Anatolia, so contact between them and the Indo-European populations must have taken place in an eastern area. In historical times, the Luwians were located in southern and western Anatolia, but, as Melchert puts it "that the Luwians *subsequently* moved from a western base south and east does not logically require that prior movement followed the same trajectory" (2003, 25). Indeed, the early Luwians, forefathers of those who later wrote the Cuneiform Luwian tablets, must have been located more to the east: "it seems certain that Luwian was present in Kizzuwatna by the Old Hittite period, and it was likely already there several centuries earlier" (Melchert 2003, 12). Furthermore, "in a few cases where a determination can be made, the Luwian rituals found in Hattusa are imported from the southern region of Kizzuwatna.... Our present evidence thus permits ... the view that the language of Cuneiform Luwian ritual texts represents an archaic (sixteenth–fifteenth century) dialect of Kizzuwatna" (Bryce 2003, 89).

I would like to suggest that at an early time, before the beginning of written sources, a group of Luwians lived in close contact with the Hurrians in the area of Kizzuwatna, experiencing a situation of bilingualism, which was the source for linguistic borrowing, attested by the extension of genitival adjectives. This group of Luwians constituted the speakers of second-millennium Luwian, that is, Cuneiform Luwian. The innovation then spread from east to west and touched the other Luwian varieties, which adopted the use of genitival adjectives without dropping the genitive case completely. The first-millennium languages of the Luwian group are descendents of the western varieties: first-millennium Hieroglyphic Luwian documents mostly come from the area of Arzawa (Melchert 2003, 142), while the Lycians had moved to Lycia from the west.

As for Hittite, Stefanini's explanation gives a reason for the fact that this language did not share the Luwian innovation. Indeed, the Hittites had contacts with the Hurrians at an early time, but such contacts were mostly limited to warfare, and were not likely to lead to a situation where bilingualism could develop to the high extent required for morphological borrowing.

Later, during the Middle Hittite kingdom, the impact of the Hurrians on the Hittite society grew dramatically. At this stage, members of the Hittite royal family bore Hurrian names, and contact between speakers of the two languages must have been increasingly high. This new situation may have led again to morphological borrowing; the Old Hittite possessive construction, which was endangered by the disappearance of possessive clitics, was replaced by the new case attraction construction, created under the influence of Hurrian suffix copying.

3. ARMENIAN

As we have seen, Vogt (1932) attributed the creation of case attraction in Classical Armenian to influence from Old Georgian. In the light of the evidence in §1, however, case attraction could also have been brought about by influence from Urartian. This would imply that Armenian speakers were already in the area of Lake Van at least at the beginning of the first millennium bc.

Vogt's hypothesis rests on solid ground: the influence of Georgian on Armenian has been pervasive, especially in the morphology. As is well known, during its attested history, Armenian has moved from the fusional type of Indo-European to the agglutinative type of the Caucasian languages: morphological borrowing went so far as to import a different morphological type into Armenian. However, the rise of case attraction attests to a different way of borrowing morphology. Rather than changing morphological type, Armenian reproduced the construction with Indo-European means. Case attraction developed before Armenian started to move toward the agglutinative type, so the difference in the two types of borrowing ultimately goes back to different temporal stages. Why did morphological borrowing start in a certain way, then stop, and then start again in a different way? A possible answer is that it does not only go back to different ages, but also to different source languages. This could be possible if case attraction owed to borrowing from Urartian. An early dating for case attraction in Armenian would also be in keeping with the hypothesis that agreement of a nominal modifier with the head noun was an areal phenomenon, as I will suggest in §4.

The precise age of the settlement of the Armenians in the area where they were at the time of the first written sources has been a debated matter. If case attraction indicates contact with Urartian, it could constitute an argument for early settlement of the Armenians in the Lake Van area, in keeping with current theories on the multiethnic and multicultural nature of the kingdom of Urartu (see Zimansky 2001).

4. CONCLUSIONS

Based on the evidence reviewed in the course of the paper, I would like to suggest that agreement of the head noun with a nominal modifier was an areal feature of a number of Indo-European and non-Indo-European languages spoken in the area of eastern Anatolia and western Caucasus in the second and first millennia bc. This type of agreement first manifested itself as suffix copying in the agglutinative non-Indo-European languages, then spread to the Indo-European languages, and was adapted to fusional morphology. Linguistic borrowing was the result of widespread bilingualism in this area.

NOTES

1 Research for this paper was partially supported by the Italian Ministry of Education, through an FIRB grant for the project "Europa e Mediterraneo dal punto di vista linguistico: storia e prospettive."

2 "Cette formation propre au géorgien est appellé la 'double relation,' puisqu'elle consiste, d'une part, dans le génitif du *nomen rectum* et, d'autre part, dans la répétition de la terminaison casuelle du *nomen regens*, laquelle répetition constitue déja la "relation.""

3 In other words, the same case in a fusional language has different endings depending on the inflectional class (for example, genitive singular in Latin has different endings depending on whether a noun belongs to the first, second, etc. declension); furthermore, in fusional languages, the same ending is often used for different purposes in different inflectional classes or even within the same inflectional class.

4 Hajnal points out that the adverbal use of the genitive in Hittite is restricted and almost nonexistent, when compared to the other Indo-European languages. For a similar remark see further Luraghi (1986).

5 "Corrispondenze come queste in luvio potevano essere ricevute ed intese solo attraverso un'interpretazione aggettivale, in senso indoeuropeo."

6 Inalienable possession involves entities that cannot be separated from the possessor. The notion of inalienability cannot be defined in the same way for all languages: while body parts are apparently inalienably possessed in all languages that distinguish between two types of possession, other entities, like various types of personal objects, can be the object of inalienable possession too, but the range of inalienable possession is language specific. For example, in Tungusian, domestic animals are inalienably possessed, while wild animals are not (see Beisenherz 2001). Thus, it is hard to see Lühr's argument (2001, 425) when she states that in Old Hittite, when possessive genitives co-occur with clitics "wie die Daten zeigen, kann der Besitz alienabel oder inalienabel sein." She apparently takes as an occurrence of "alienabel" the noun *assu* "good," but does not discuss the extent of alienable and inalienable possession in Hittite.

7 "En géorgien la désinence casuelle du nom déterminé ... se répète après tout déterminant, que ce soit un adjectif, un pronom, un génitif, une expression prépositionelle, ou encore un groupe pronominal comportant déjà l'expression de la relation casuelle.... La différence entre les deux expressions consiste en ceci, que le géorgien permet l'accumulation des désinences casuelles tandis qu'en arménien, la désinence marquant le group chasse la désinence marquant le rapport entre le déterminé et le déterminant. Comme les moyens dont disposent les deux langues sont différentes, le détail des faits n'est pas le même. Les tendances générales des deux langues n'en montrent pas moin une concordance frappante, en laissant les désinences casuelles servir aussi d'indicateurs des groupes nominaux."

8 "Possessor und Possessum oder Rektum und Regens stehen im gleichen Kasus nebeneinander."

9 I had already discussed this difference in Luraghi (1990, 313).

10 Note that case attraction did not occur in Old Hittite, and that Lühr's Old Hittite examples often are from later copies of Old Hittite texts. Indeed it is clear that case attraction could not exist in Old Hittite, if one does not analyze a single occurrence in isolation but rather the construction as a whole. As we have seen in the examples, case attraction typically occurred when the possessor was human, and often involved the ablative. But as Starke (1977) has shown, nouns with human referents did not take the ablative case in Old Hittite, so case attraction must be an innovation. Lühr (2001, 439) further mentions in a footnote that the so-called free genitive in Hittite could also owe to Akkadian influence. The free genitive consists in the occurrence of a noun in the genitive without a head noun, as *tayazilas* "of the theft" = "thief." This use of the genitive also exists in Akkadian: *ša abullim* "of the gate" = "guardian." Such free genitives also occur in Hurrian (and in other languages with suffix copying); they may be evidence for wider language contact.

REFERENCES

Beisenharz, A. (2001) Zum unveräuslichen Besitz im Tungusischen. In W. Boeder and G. Hentschel (eds.) *Variierende Markierung von Nominalgruppen in Sprachen unterschiedlichen Typs*, 31–47. Oldenburg: BIS

Boeder, W. (1995) Suffixaufnahme in Kartvelian. In F. Plank (ed.) *Double Case*, 151–215. Oxford, Oxford University.

Bryce, T. (2003) "History." In H. C. Melchert (ed.) *The Luwians*, 27–127. Leiden, Brill.

Corbett, G. (1987) The Morphology/Syntax Interface: Evidence from Possessive Adjectives in Slavonic. *Language* 63, 299–345.

Dixon, R. M. W. (1980) *The Languages of Australia*. Cambridge, Cambridge University.

Hajnal, I. (2000) Der adjektivische Genitivausdruck der luwischen Sprachen. In Ch. Zinko and M. Offisch (eds.) *125 Jahre Indogermanistik in Graz*, 159–84. Graz, Leykam.

Jacquinod, B. (1989) *Le double accusatif en grec, d'Homère à la fin du Ve siècle avant J. C.* BCILL 50. Louvain, Peeters.

Lühr, R. (2001) Der Ausdruck der Possessivität innerhalb der Determinans-Phrase in den ältesten indogermanischen Sprachen. In U. Junghaus, L. Szucsich (eds.) *Syntactic Structure and Morphological Information*, 415–46. Berlin, de Gruyter.

___ (2003) Badal- und Genitivkonstruktionen, *Historische Sprachforschung* 115/1, 23–56.

Luraghi, S. (1986) Der semantische und funktionelle Bau des althethitischen Kasussystems. *Zeitschrift fur vergleichende Sprachforschung* 99, 23–42.

___ (1990) The Structure and Development of Possessive Noun Phrases in Hittite. In H. Andersen and K. Koerner (eds.) *Historical Linguistics 1987*, 309–25. Amsterdam, Benjamins.

___ (1993a) La modificazione nominale nelle lingue anatoliche. *Archivio Glottologico Italiano* 78/2, 144–66.

___ (1993b) Suffix Copying and Related Phenomena: A Prototype Approach. *Linguistics* 32, 1095–1108.

Marr, N. and Brière, M. (1931) *La langue géorgienne*. Paris, Firmin-Didot.

Melchert, H. C. (2003) Language. In H. C. Melchert (ed.) *The Luwians*, 170–210. Leiden, Brill.

Neumann, G. (1982) Die Konstruktionen mit Adjectiva genetivalia in den luwischen Sprachen. In E. Neu (ed.) *Investigationes philologicae et comparativae*, 149–61. Wiesbaden, Harrassowitz.

Plank, F. ed. (1995) *Double Case*. Oxford, Oxford University.

Starke, F. (1977) *Die Funktionen der dimensionalen Kasus und Adverbien im Althethitischen*. Wiesbaden, Harrassowitz.

Stefanini, R. (1969) Il genitivo aggettivale nelle lingue anatoliche. *Athenaeum* 47, 290–302.

___ (2002) Toward a Diachronic Reconstruction of the Linguistic Map of Ancient Anatolia. In S. De Martino and F. Pecchioli Daddi (eds.) *Anatolia antica*, 783–806. Firenze, Logisma.

Vogt, H. (1932) Les groupes nominaux en arménien et géorgien anciens. *Norsk Tidsskrift for Spragvidenskap* 5, 57–81.

Weinreich, U. (1963) *Languages in Contact*. The Hague, Mouton.

Wilhelm, G. (1995) Suffixaufnahme in Hurrian and Urartian. In F. Plank (ed.) *Double Case*, 113–35. Oxford, Oxford University.

Zimansky, P. (2001) Archaeological Inquiries into Ethnolinguitic Diversity in Urartu. In R. Drews (ed.) *Greater Anatolia and the Indo-Hittite Language Family*, 15–27. JIES Monograph 38. Washington, DC, Institute for the Study of Man.

15

GREEK *MÓLYBDOS* AS A LOANWORD FROM LYDIAN

H. Craig Melchert

Beekes (1999, 7–8) has established that the oldest form of the Greek word for "lead" is Mycenaean *mo-ri-wo-do* (for attestations of the word see Aura Jorro 1985, 1, 457–58). Beekes reads the Mycenaean as /moliwdos/, but one must also consider /molivdos/, as suggested by Chantraine (1968, 710 and 1972, 205–6).[1] As per Beekes (1999, 10), all later variants of the word in Greek can be derived from the shape attested in Mycenaean.

The earliest Greek form /moliw/vdos/ precludes any connections of the word with Latin *plumbum* or Basque *berun* "lead" (thus with Beekes 1999, 10–11). Beekes, who argues for Asia Minor as the source of the Greek word, cites in passing Lydian *mariwda-* after Furnée, but merely as an example of the sequence *-wd-* in a language of Asia Minor. He can do nothing further with the Lydian word attested as a divine name.

Recent research, however, has removed the Lydian word from its isolation and provided it with a meaning and morphological analysis. The word occurs just once in Lydian in Text 4a in a curse formula against a potential tomb violator (text per Gusmani 1986, 148): *fak=mλ ś̃ãntaś kufaw=k mariwda=k ẽnsλibb[i]d* "Sanda and Kubaba and (the) *m.* shall *do harm* to him."

The association of *mariwda* with Sanda points to a connection with the Luwian divine name /marway(a)-/, as attested in Hieroglyphic Luwian in KULULU 2, §9 (text per Hawkins 2000, 488): *wa/i-ru-ta* | (DEUS)*sà-ta-si-i-zi* | (DEUS)*ma$_x$+ra/i-wa/i-i-zi-i* | ("*256")*tà-sá-za* | *a-ta* | "CRUS"-*tu* "Let the dark deities of Sanda step on his memorial." For the association of the *marwainzi*-deities (the form is animate nominative plural) with the god Sanda see Popko (1995, 93). For the reading as /marwainzi/ and interpretation "dark" see Melchert and Starke apud Oettinger (1989/1990, 97) and now Hawkins (2000, 489–90). As per Starke (1986, 162–63), the Cuneiform Luwian cognate is also attested in Hittite context as ^{d}*Mar-wa-ya-an-za* (dative plural), for which the Hittite equivalent is ^{d}*Mar-ku-wa-ya-aš*. The PIE root is **merg^w-* "dark" as in English "murk(y)" etc. (Neumann 1973, 298). Hittite *mark(u)waya-* and Luwian *marwaya-* form a direct equation reflecting an adjective **morg^{w}o-iyo-*. For this formation with the suffix **-iyo-* see Melchert (1990, 201–2).

It cannot be a coincidence that the single occurrence of Lydian *mariwda* accompanies one of only two instances of Sanda in our entire Lydian corpus.[2] Context argues that Lydian *mariwdaś* (with regular loss of *-ś* before *-k* "and") is also animate nominative plural "the dark ones" and refers to the deities who accompany Sanda. The Lydian word may reflect **morg^w-iyo-* (for the formation see again Melchert 1990, 201), with regular development to **marwida-* (Melchert 1994, 184–85). I now follow a suggestion of Norbert Oettinger (pers. comm.) in assuming that **marwida-* became **marwda-* with regular syncope (see Melchert 1997, 185) and then *mariwda-* with anaptyxis of *-i-* in the difficult cluster **-rwd-* (contra Melchert 2002, 242, n. 9, with the unlikely assumption of a direct metathesis **-rwi-* > *-riw-*).

We thus have good evidence for a Lydian adjective *mariwda-* "dark." Its phonetic shape is approximately [marivða-]. For Lydian *w* as a voiced labial fricative [v] or [β] compare *lewś/lefś* as the Lydian rendering of "Zeus," where *w* alternates with the voiceless labial fricative *f*. For Lydian *d* as something other than a stop

[d] see Melchert (1997, 45 with references). A voiced "flap" as in American English "ladder" is also quite possible instead of a fricative [ð] as in "lather."

Names for metals are commonly derived from color adjectives: compare Latin *argentum* "silver" < PIE *$h_2$erĝ- "bright white" or English "gold" < PIE *ĝhel- "yellow." For "lead" specifically as a "dark/black" metal we may compare Latin *plumbum nigrum* "black lead" (vs. *plumbum album/candidum* "white lead" = "tin").[3] Use of Lydian *mariwda-* "(the) dark (metal)" for "lead" would be a case of a "transferred epithet."

Greek substitution of /l/ for /r/ in the borrowing process is unsurprising. For variation between *l* and *r* within Lydian itself we may cite *mẽtlid/mẽtrid* "harm." The Greek word for a kind of "scraper" *stlengís/strengís/stelgís/stergís* (and further variants) probably represents a loanword from Anatolian to the root of Hittite *ištalk-* "make smooth, flatten" with original *l* (Neumann 1961, 94–95). The fact that /r/ and /l/ are contrastive sounds in both the source language Lydian and the borrowing language Greek does not in any way preclude the substitution. Speakers do not always make the expected identification of a sound of another language with the corresponding one in their own.[4] Since we do not know just when prehistoric *o became Lydian *a*, it is possible that the *o* of /moliwdos/ reflects a Lydian *o. Lydian *mariwda-* "dark, black" is thus a suitable source for Greek /moliwdos/ "lead" in terms of both form and meaning. The further plausibility of Greek /moliwdos/ as a loanword from Lydian depends on factors of chronology, geography and the material evidence for sources of lead in Mycenaean Greece.

I will first address the problem of chronology. The appearance of the word in Mycenaean requires borrowing by no later than the fifteenth century BC, but it may have happened earlier (thus also Beekes 1999, 12). Van den Hout (2003, 304–7) has argued that the Lydian change *y > *d* is already reflected in the place-name *Maddun(n)aš(š)a* and the personal names *Mad(d)unāni* and *Madduwatta* attested in Hittite cuneiform sources. He derives Lydian *madun- from *may-un- from *mǎi-won- with the "ethnicon" suffix seen in Luwian *-wann(i)-* (e.g., URU*Ninuwawann(i)-* "of Niniveh").[5] The same word, without the characteristic Lydian sound change, he sees attested in Greek *Me:ion/Maion-* "Maeonian." The name Madduwatta (compare for the formation with van den Hout [2003, 305] the Lydian names Alyattes and Sadyattes) is attested already from the late-fifteenth century.

The evidence just cited gives only a terminus ante quem. The borrowing could be considerably older. Differentiation of the Anatolian Indo-European languages must date minimally from ca. 2300 BC, but it probably begins far earlier: see among others Carruba (1995, 30–31), Starke (1997, 457) and Oettinger (2002, 52). Since we unfortunately cannot independently determine the relative chronology of pre-Lydian sound changes, that of *y > *d* could have happened any time during the period from roughly 2500–1500.

Beekes (2003) has now suggested that the Greek name for the Lydians *lūdó-* reflects the Lydian form of the name Luwiya.[6] He plausibly assumes that when the Lydians moved from northwestern Asia Minor into classical Lydia, which was Luwian territory in the second millennium, they adopted the name of their new dwelling place. He dates this event to some time after 1200 and suggests that this is also the likely date of the change *y > *d*. However, as he concedes, nothing at all precludes that the Lydians had had contact with the Luwians at a much earlier date and learned *luwiya-* as the name for the Luwians. It could then have undergone the change to Lydian *luw(i)da- at *any time*, long before the Lydians moved southward and adopted the name for their own new country. I therefore stand by the claim that the Lydian change *y > *d* and hence the borrowing of *mariwda-* into Greek could potentially have happened any time in the long period of approximately 2500–1500 BC.[7]

I turn next to the matter of geography. There is a growing consensus that the Lydians in the earlier-second millennium were located in the northwest of Asia Minor (later Mysia or Bithynia). See most extensively and emphatically Beekes (2002, 206–17), but compare also more tentatively Starke (1997, 457), Neumann (2001, 46), Högemann (2001, 59–60), Oettinger (2002: 52) and Melchert (2003, 22). If the Greek word for "lead" is a loanword from Lydian before 1500, then the Lydians must have found and exploited lead in northwestern

Asia Minor, not in classical Lydia. Buchholz (1972, 49) cites areas in northwestern, northeastern and south-central Asia Minor as possible sources for lead in Mycenaean Greece. Of those areas given for the northwest, one lies in Mysia and one in Bithynia. Either of these would be compatible with a Lydian source for the Greek word for "lead."

I come finally to the question of what we know about the source of lead objects found in Mycenaean contexts.[8] Buchholz opted very cautiously for northwest Asia Minor: "Die Galena-Vorkommen des kleinasiatischen Westens ... werden es gewesen sein, aus denen Troja und Teile der Ägäis beliefert wurden" (1972, 48). However, subsequent investigation, particularly lead isotope analysis, points to local sources of lead for objects found in Mycenaean contexts: the Cycladic island of Siphnos and the Laurion field in Attica (the former predominant in the Early and Middle Bronze Age, the latter in the Late Bronze Age; see Gale, Stos-Gale and Davis [1984, 390] and Mossman [2000, 87, 103–4]). There is no positive evidence for importation of lead from the western Mediterranean (Iberia, Sardinia) or from Asia Minor: see in detail Gale (1979). For negative evidence for at least some northwestern sites in Asia Minor see plots for 12, 14, 15 on his fig. 4 (for sites see fig. 1). Gale and Stos-Gale (1981, 217) arrive at similar conclusions.

Current evidence for the provenance of Mycenaean lead objects thus seems equally unfavorable to the two most popular hypotheses for the source of the Greek word for "lead": a loanword from the western Mediterranean or from Asia Minor. However, one fact about Mycenaean lead objects may still allow us to entertain northwest Asia Minor as the *earliest* source of lead for Mycenaean Greece. The distribution of lead objects appears to shift from the Early to Late Bronze Age. EBA objects cluster in Troy, Lesbos, the Cyclades, East and Central Crete, with very few on the Greek mainland. Those of the Late Bronze Age are concentrated in the Peloponnese, Argolid, Attica and Euboea (see Buchholz 1972, 23). Branigan (1974) reaches similar results indicating a possible east to west shift. Despite their results cited above pointing to Mycenaean exploitation of local sources of lead, allowance for a possible earlier source in Asia Minor is made by Gale (1979, 33) and Stos-Gale and Gale (1982, 472): "One interpretation of these facts (but an interpretation that awaits proof) is that sources of lead/silver for the Aegean may originally have been in the East."

In sum, the borrowing of Greek /moliwdos/ "lead" from Lydian *mariwda-* "dark, black" is linguistically viable. Lydians living in northwestern Asia Minor in the late-third and early-second millennium BC could easily have known and exploited local sources of lead. However, the evidence that Mycenaean Greeks were already chiefly exploiting local sources of lead for their use does seem to require that the putative first encounter of the Greeks with lead through the Lydians somewhere in northwestern Asia Minor – and hence the borrowing of the word for the metal – must have taken place at a relatively early date. Early in the second millennium or even late in the third would seem likely. Such a scenario is fully compatible with the Anatolian evidence (though it does require that the pre-Lydian sound change **y > d* be relatively early). One is then left to ask: Would the Indo-European-speaking Greeks have arrived in time for such an interaction? I can only raise this question here and must leave the further debate over the much-vexed question of the "arrival of the Greeks" to others better informed on the topic.

NOTES

1 Beekes admits (1999: 7, n. 1) that the Mycenaean spelling is unexpected for /moliwdos/ (one would not expect a syllable-final glide /w/ to be written), but he then rejects Chantraine's alternative with the odd assertion that "there is no reason to suppose it" (1999, 9). I cannot accept Beekes' claim that a fricative [v] or [β] "makes the assumed developments more difficult if not impossible." Such a sound would lead to Greek *b* just as easily as a [w], and rounding of the preceding vowel by a labial fricative is far from impossible. The unusual Mycenaean spelling may therefore be an attempt to write an unassimilated foreign sound. The issue is in any case of no

consequence for our purposes, since Greek would necessarily have adapted to a *b* either a labial fricative or a glide in the unusual position before stop.

2 The other is in Text 79, a fragment from Aphrodisias in Caria (see Gusmani 1986, 154).

3 German *Blei* "lead" and other Germanic cognates may also be derived from a color term seen in Lithuanian *blývas* "violet-colored."

4 For example, American English and Mandarin Chinese each have both a retroflex /r/ and an /l/, but the English /r/ is nevertheless treated as an /l/ in Mandarin, as in: Marilyn Monroe > Malilian Menglu. Loanword adaptation often involves folk etymological connections with words in the borrowing language, so we should also consider the possibility that the *l* in *mólybdos* is due to the influence of Greek *mélas* "black" or *moluū́no* "to soil, stain, pollute" (pers. comm. of Michael Weiss).

5 In view of other ethnic self-designations based simply on the word "people" or "human beings," Michael Weiss (pers. comm.) suggests the possibility that **mǎi-won-* is based on the same root as Hittite *maya(nt)-* "adult (male)" and Cuneiform Luwian *mayašša/i-* "of the community." This root would also be suitable semantically as the base of the name Madduwatta, a virtual **mǎi-wo-* *"vigorous, manly."

6 A derivation also made independently by Raphaël Gérard (2003; 2004, 125–32) and by Paul Widmer (2004). Gérard assumes that the source word is to be read *Lūya-*, which would lead directly to the Lydian by the change **y > d*, while Widmer argues alternatively that the standard reading *luwiya-* would also have led to **luwida-* and then syncopated **luwda-*, which could well have then contracted to **lūda-* with a long vowel preserved in the Greek form.

7 Such an early date for the change of **y > d* in Lydian does raise the question of how the Greeks received the version *me:ion-/maion-* with preserved **y*. However, it is by no means rare that a people become known not by their own name for themselves, but by the name that their neighbors call them. Thus the Greek may reflect a **māiwones* preserved in another adjacent Anatolian Indo-European dialect (cf. van den Hout 2003, 307–8).

8 I am most grateful to Eric Cline, James Muhly, and Susan Mossman for invaluable references and patient answers to my many questions on this complex issue. The standard disclaimer applies, and I am solely responsible for all views expressed here.

REFERENCES

Aura Jorro, F. (1985) *Diccionario Micénico*. Madrid, C.S.I.C.

Beekes, R. S. P. (1999) The Greek Word for "lead". *Münchener Studien zur Sprachwissenschaft* 59, 7–14.

___ (2002) The Prehistory of the Lydians, the Origin of the Etruscans, Troy and Aeneas. *Bibliotheca Orientalis* 59, 205–41.

___ (2003) Luwians and Lydians. *Kadmos* 42, 47–49.

Branigan, K. (1974) *Aegean Metalwork of the Early and Middle Bronze Age*. Oxford, Clarendon.

Buchholz, H.-G. (1972) Das Blei in der mykenischen Kultur und in der bronzezeitlichen Metallurgie Zyperns. *Jahrbuch des deutschen archäologischen Instituts* 87, 1–59.

Carruba, O. (1995) L'arrivo dei greci, le migrazioni indoeuropee e il «ritorno» dei eraclidi. *Athenaeum* NS 83, 5–44.

Chantrain, P. (1968) *Dictionnaire étymologique de la langue grecque*. Paris, Klincksieck.

___ (1972) Le témoignage du mycénien pour l'étymologie grecque: δαΐ, Κοπρεύς, Κυκλεύς, μολοβρός, μόλυβδος. In M. Ruipérez (ed.) *Acta Mycenaea*, 2, 197–206. Salamanca, Universidad de Salamanca.

Gale, N. H. (1979) Some Aspects of Lead and Silver Mining in the Aegean. *Miscellanea Graeca* 2, 9–60.

Gale, N. H. and Z. A. Stos-Gale (1981) Cycladic Lead and Silver Metallurgy. *Annual of the British School at Athens* 76, 169 –224.

Gale, N. H., Stos-Gale, Z. A., and Davis, J. L. (1984) The Provenance of Lead Used at Ayia Irini, Keos. *Hesperia* 53, 389–406.

Gérard, R. (2003) Le nom des Lydiens à la lumière des sources anatoliennes. *Le Muséon* 116, 4–7.

___ (2004) Quelques remarques autour de **y >* lydien *d*. *Res Antiquae* 1, 125–32.

Gusmani, R. (1986) *Lydisches Wörterbuch. Ergänzungsband, Lfg. 3*. Heidelberg, Carl Winter.

Hawkins, J. D. (2000) *Corpus of Hieroglyphic Luwian Inscriptions. Volume I. Inscriptions of the Iron Age*. Berlin, de Gruyter.

Högemann, P. (2001) Troias Untergang – was dann? Alte Dynastien, neue Reiche und die "Ionische Kolonisation" (12.-6. Jh. v. Chr.). In B. Theune-Großkopf et al. (eds.) *Troia: Traum und Wirklichkeit*, 58–63 Stuttgart, Konrad Theiss.

Hout, T. van den (2003) Maeonien und Maddunnašša: zur Frühgeschichte des Lydischen. In M. Giorgieri et al. (eds.) *Licia e lidia prima dell'ellenizzazione*, 301–10. Rome, CNR.

Melchert, H. C. (1990) Adjectives in **-iyo-* in Anatolian. *Historische Sprachforschung* 103, 198–207.

___ (1994) PIE **y* > Lydian *d*. In P. Vavroušek (ed.) *Iranian and Indo-European Studies. Memorial Volume of Otakar Klíma*, 181–87. Prague, Enigma.

___ (1997) PIE Dental Stops in Lydian. In D. Q. Adams (ed.) *Festschrift for Eric P. Hamp*, 2:32–47. Washington, DC, Institute for the Study of Man.

___ (2002) The God Sanda in Lycia? In P. Taracha (ed.) *Silva Anatolica. Anatolian Studies Presented to Maciej Popko on the Occasion of His 65th Birthday*, 241–51. Warsaw, Agade.

___ (2003) Prehistory. In H. C. Melchert (ed.) *The Luwians*, 8–26. Leiden, Brill.

Mossman, S. (2000) Mycenaean Age Lead: a Fresh Look at an Old Material. Pp. 85–119 in *Trade and Production in Premonetary Greece: Acquisition and Distribution of Raw Materials and Finished Products. Proceedings of the 6th International Workshop, Athens 1996*, eds. Carole Gillis et al. Jonsered, Åströms.

Neumann, G. (1961) *Untersuchungen zum Weiterleben hethitischen und luwischen Sprachgutes in hellenistischer und römischer Zeit.* Wiesbaden, Harrassowitz.

___ (1973) Review of Liane Jakob-Rost, *Das Ritual der Malli aus Arzawa gegen Behexung* (Texte der Hethiter 2). *Zeitschrift für Vergleichende Sprachforschung* 87, 295–99.

___ (2001) Der Große Nachbar in Anatolien. Die Hethither. In B. Theune-Großkopf et al. (eds.) *Troia: Traum und Wirklichkeit*, 46–50. Stuttgart, Konrad Theiss.

Oettinger, N. (1989/90) Die "dunkle Erde" im Hethitischen und Griechischen. *Welt des Orients* 20/21, 83–98.

___ (2002) Indogermanische Sprachträger lebten schon im 3. Jahrtausend v. Chr. in Kleinasien. In H. Willinghöfer and U. Hasekamp (eds.) *Die Hethiter und ihr Reich. Das Volk der 1000 Götter*, 5–55. Stuttgart, Konrad Theiss.

Popko, M. (1995) *Religions of Asia Minor.* Warsaw, Academic Publications Dialog.

Starke, F. (1986) Review of Hans G. Güterbock and Harry A. Hoffner, Jr., *The Hittite Dictionary of the Oriental Institute of the University of Chicago*, Vol. 3/2. *Bibliotheca Orientalis* 43, 157–65.

___ (1997) Troia im Kontext des historisch-politischen und sprachlichen Umfeldes Kleinasiens im 2. Jahrtausend. *Studia Troica* 7, 446–87.

Stos-Gale, Z. A. and Gale, N. H. (1982) The Sources of Mycenaean Silver and Lead. *Journal of Field Archaeology* 9, 467–85.

Widmer, P. (2004) Λυδία: Ein Toponym zwischen Orient und Okzident. *Historische Sprachforschung* 117, 197–203.

16

Kybele as Kubaba in a Lydo-Phrygian Context

Mark Munn

The Syro-Anatolian goddess Kubaba is among the most enduring cultural features of the ancient Near East and Mediterranean world. Contemporary documents attest her name as far apart in time and space as the Middle Bronze Age Assyrian merchant colony at Kanes in central Anatolia and Rome in the Age of Augustus. Across this span, Kubaba is named in cuneiform Akkadian and Hittite texts, in hieroglyphic Luwian, and in alphabetic Aramaic, Lydian, Phrygian, Greek and Latin texts. The very scope of this material, spanning such a linguistic, cultural and historical range, constitutes a major challenge to scholars interested in evaluating the cultural contexts that sustained the worship of Kubaba across the centuries. One of the problems that emerges from this long history is how to account for the forms of the name of this goddess in the various languages in which it was spoken. The present paper is devoted to a troublesome aspect of this problem, namely, the relationship between Kubaba and the Greco-Roman Kybele. Aware that others have argued to the contrary, I will argue that Kybele is indeed part of the legacy of Syro-Anatolian Kubaba, and that the transformation of her name finds explanation in the languages of Anatolia, particularly among the Lydians and Phrygians, where Greco-Roman sources place the home of her cult.

The Anatolian linguist Emmanuel Laroche most clearly outlined the evidence for the diachronic study of the cult of Kubaba in a seminal article from 1960, entitled "Koubaba, déesse anatolienne, et le problème des origines de Cybèle." Laroche argued that "Cybèle," or Kybele (Greek Κυβέλη) was the descendent of the older Syro-Anatolian Kubaba, whose especial home was at Carchemish in North Syria (see Hawkins 1981). In making this argument, Laroche assumed the identity of Kybele with Kybebe (Κυβήβη), a name that clearly derives from Kubaba. The name of Kybebe is most famously attested by Herodotus, who identifies her as the object of an indigenous cult at Sardis (Herodotus, *Hist.* 5.102.1). Charon of Lampsacus also mentions the cult of Kybebe among the Lydians and Phrygians, and the testimony of these fifth-century authors has been confirmed by Lydian inscriptions from Sardis, which give her name in the phonologically related form, *Kuvav-*.[1] Kybele is also identified with Lydia and Phrygia in fifth-century sources (most notably in Euripides' *Bacchae*), but the equation between Kybebe and Kybele is not explicitly attested until the late Hellenistic and Roman imperial eras. Strabo, Virgil and Catullus speak of the worship of Kybebe (or *Cybebe* in Latin) and the sacred places of Kybele (Latin *Cybele*) in the landscape of Lydia and Phrygia, suggesting that the names of Kybebe and Kybele were interchangeable.[2] Later lexicographers explained these names as references to the same divinity.[3] Many historians of religion have accepted this equation, and have followed Laroche in identifying both Kybele and Kybebe alike as the descendants of Kubaba.[4]

Since Laroche wrote, the antecedents to Greek Κυβέλη in Old Phrygian inscriptions have become better known through the work of Claude Brixhe. Brixhe has shown that the goddess is most often named in Old Phrygian inscriptions simply as *Matar*, "Mother," occasionally as *Matar Kubeleya*.[5] This evidence is consistent with the testimony of classical sources to the Phrygian origin of Kybele, and to her identification with the goddess also called "the Mother," or most often "the Mother of the Gods" (ἡ Μήτηρ τῶν Θεῶν). But the

Phrygian evidence has seemingly failed to reveal the connection to Kubaba that Laroche expected. Brixhe could find no way to derive the Phrygian name, *Kubeleya,* from Kubaba.

In the absence of a phonological explanation of the transformation of the name Κυβήβη into Κυβέλη, the connection between Kubaba of the Bronze and Iron Ages and classical Kybele has been called into question. As Brixhe has observed, Phrygian *Kubeleya* is an attributive adjective modifying *Matar.*[6] Unlike Kubaba, which is a proper name, *Kubeleya* in Phrygian is an epithet. As to the origin of Phrygian *Kubeleya,* Brixhe has pointed to Greek sources that derive the name of Κυβέλη from a place, most often identified as a mountain or mountains in Phrygia, called Κύβελον or Κυβέλα. Brixhe has postulated that Κύβελον or Κυβέλα derives from a Phrygian word for "mountain," and that *Matar Kubeleya* is therefore the Phrygian equivalent to the Greek Μήτηρ ὀρεία, "Mountain Mother," which is a well attested appellation of the Mother of the Gods.[7]

The most significant conclusion that Brixhe deduces from this line of analysis is that the name of Κυβέλη in Greek comes from Phrygian, and has nothing to do with the name of Kubaba and its descendant, Κυβήβη at Sardis.[8] Fritz Graf and Mary Rein have also argued that Phrygian Κυβέλη should be distinguished from Lydian Κυβήβη, largely on the basis of the common identification of Κυβέλη with settings in nature, contrasting with the shrine of Κυβήβη in an urban setting at Sardis.[9] Most recently, Lynn Roller has drawn attention to details in the iconography as well as the settings of the monuments of the Phrygian Mother and of Kubaba in North Syria that mark distinctions between them (Roller 1994, 66–68 and 1999, 121–41). The fact that the Greeks appear to have regarded Κυβήβη and Κυβέλη, the Phrygian Mother, as one and the same is taken as a sign of insensitivity to distinct, native origins. According to Roller: "The words Κυβήβη (Kybebe) and Κυβέλη (Kybele), while distinctive in their Anatolian languages, are only slightly different in Greek, and the Greeks may well have conflated them" (Roller 1999, 124).

The differences and distinctions seen by these scholars are real, but they are subtle features, and their significance is a matter of interpretation. The single strongest argument for a fundamental difference between the Phrygian deity, *Matar Kubeleya,* and her older, Anatolian counterpart, Kubaba, is the absence of any account of the relationship between their names. If, however, the epithet *Kubeleya* can plausibly be derived from the older name of Kubaba, then the connection between Κυβήβη and Κυβέλη observed in late-classical sources cannot be dismissed, and variations in iconography and cultic topography between Kubaba and Κυβήβη, on the one hand, and the Phrygian goddess on the other, must be explained as developmental variations, not fundamental distinctions. In fact, the present understanding of Anatolian languages allows Κυβέλη to be explained as a development, via Phrygian *Kubeleya,* from the older name of Kubaba. This explanation respects Brixhe's demonstration that *Kubeleya* is an epithet, and his argument that it refers to topographical features (although not to mountains alone). This explanation also takes into account the fact that the Phrygian language was a relative newcomer to Anatolia, and that the name of an Anatolian deity in Phrygian should reflect inflectional patterns attested among Anatolian languages, such as Lydian and Lycian, and should only secondarily show features imposed on it by speakers of Phrygian. Cultural as well as linguistic connections strongly support the derivation of a divinity known to the Greeks as Kybele from her more ancient forerunner, Kubaba.

The name of Kubaba at Sardis is attested as Κυβήβη by Herodotus, as has been noted above, and occurs in two Lydian inscriptions preserving the root form of her name: *Kuvav-.*[10] These two attested vocalizations indicate that where Lydians pronounced the fricative, *v,* in the name of Kubaba, others pronounced the labial stop, *b.*[11] Greek ears, and Phrygian as well, consistently heard a *b* in her name. Inflexions in Lydian and related Anatolian languages will have altered the ending of this name, according to its grammatical use. The genitive in Lydian is formed by an adjectival/genitive suffix, *-li-*, and a similar suffix, *-(ê)li*, is found in other Anatolian languages.[12] The adjectival or genitive form of the name of Kubaba in Lydian would thus, hypothetically, be **Kuvavli-*, pronounced by some as **Kubabli-*. Both Lydian and Lycian show examples of this suffix attached to the name of divinities to create theophoric names. So from the name of Artemis (which is *Artimuś* in Lydian, and *Ertemi* in Lycian) *Artimalis* is attested as a personal name in Lydian, and *Erttimeli* in Lycian, meaning "The One of Artemis."[13] Likewise, *Bakillis* is attested as the name of a Lydian month, formed from the name of the Lydian god, *Baki-*.[14] The formation of **Kuvavli-*, or **Kubabli-*, would therefore conform to a well-attested pattern for designating a person, place, or thing "of" or "pertaining to Kubaba."

Among speakers of Phrygian, the consonant cluster at the end of **Kubabli-* was probably simplified to **Kuballi-*, and through an attested shift in vowels, **Kuballi-* became **Kubelli-*.[15] This derivation is hypothetical, but it is based on attested forms, and does not require the hypothesis of an unattested lexical item, a Phrygian word for "mountain" (on which, see now Yakubovich 2007, 143). **Kubelli-* is probably the source of the Greek form Κύβελις, said to be an epithet or a name for Rhea, the mother of Zeus, used by Hipponax of Ephesos at the end of the sixth century. Ioannes Tzetzes, who preserves this information, goes on to say that the name comes from the worship of this goddess in a Phrygian town (πόλις) called Κυβέλλα.[16] According to the derivation described here, this town called Κυβέλλα can be understood as "a place of Kubaba."

Phrygian *Kubeleya* is a further formation from the same derivation. Like the Lydian suffix *-li-*, the Phrygian suffix *-eya* is used to form attributive adjectives.[17] The Phrygian *Kubeleya*, as an epithet modifying *Matar*, "Mother," can therefore be recognized as a Phrygian adjectival formation on **Kubelli-*, itself an adjectival formation from the name of Kubaba. *Matar Kubeleya* in the Phrygian inscriptions therefore designates "the Mother of the place of Kubaba," or "the Mother who is identified with the place of Kubaba." The name of Kubaba can thus be seen to have entered Phrygian as an attributive adjective in a form used in Lydian and in other Anatolian languages. The name *Kubeleya* was used to designate places that were especially associated with Kubaba or, as she was known in Greek, Κυβήβη.

Kybele in Greek might derive from the hypothetical form, **Kubelli-*, in Phrygian. At any rate, this is the probable origin of the attested place name, Κυβέλλα, as noted above. More probably, as Brixhe has argued, Kybele in Greek derives from the attested Phrygian epithet, *Kubeleya*. For this last is identical to Greek Κυβέλεια, attested as a place name (πόλις) in Ionia recorded by Hecataeus of Miletos at the end of the sixth century.[18] This may be the same Κυβέλεια identified by Strabo as a place near Mount Mimas in the territory of Erythrae, a "tall, well-wooded mountain, filled with wild game" (Strabo, *Geog.* 14.1.33), exactly the sort of place associated with the Mother of the Gods, and with Κυβέλη, by Greek sources.

Phrygian *Kubeleya* and Greek Κυβέλεια alike were the names of places, and they were also divine epithets that characterized those places as dear to Kubaba. Greek Κυβέλη can be recognized as the nominalization of an attributive name, Κυβέλεια, just as the deity Βασίλη, attested at Athens and associated with the Ionian heroes, Kodros and Neleus, can be understood as a personification of Βασιλεία, or "sovereignty."[19] Thus we can recognize Greek Kybele, known also as Μήτηρ Κυβέλη, and Phrygian *Matar Kubeleya* both as descendents of Kubaba.

Brixhe, Graf, Roller and others, are justified in seeing the Phrygian *Matar Kubeleya* as a distinctive expression of divinity, linked as she is with sacred places in the landscape, and especially mountains. But there is no justification for dissociating her ancestry from Kubaba, or in separating her from Kybebe at Sardis. Greek and Latin authors link Kybele and Kybebe, and the present argument demonstrates that this connection has a plausible linguistic basis. Moreoever, it is noteworthy that Greek and Latin authors frequently refer to the Mother of the Gods, to Kybele, and even to Kybebe, as both Lydian and Phrygian, as if one ethnic identity were equivalent to the other. The reason for this, I believe, is that the chief monuments of the Phrygian Mother are products of the era of the Lydian Empire in western Anatolia. While Kybebe was honored at her urban shrine at Sardis, the seat of Lydian sovereignty, she was also honored at the *Kubeleya*, the "place(s) of Kubaba," which were distributed over the land that the Lydians ruled. In both cases, the goddess signifies sovereignty.

This is clearly the case with the most famous of the Phrygian monuments associated with the Phrygian Mother, the rock-cut facade in the Phrygian highlands known as the "Midas Monument." As is the case with other such facades, the "Midas Monument" honored the Phrygian Mother, whose name, *Matar*, appears in inscriptions within the central niche, where a statue of the goddess once stood. This monument to the Mother was also a monument to kingship, for the Phrygian inscription over the top of the facade records a dedication by Ates to Midas, who is given the titles *Wanax* and *Lawag<e>tas* (to render these titles in Hellenized forms). Although some scholars have maintained that the Midas Monument was contemporary to the historical Midas, at the turn of the eighth to the seventh century, the preponderance of scholarly opinion now regards it to be a century or more later in date. The thorough study of this and related monuments in the Phrygian highlands by Susanne Berndt-Ersöz (2006a, see especially 126–34) confirms that the Midas Monument is a product of the mid-sixth century, in the time of Croesus. It was therefore most likely a posthumous monument to a heroized Midas, regarded as a paradigm of kingship by the Mermnad Lydians. The dedicator, Ates, bears a dynastic Lydian name, and most probably was none other than the Atys, son of Croesus, known from Herodotus.[20] The Phrygian Mother, whose statue stood within this monument, appeared to her worshipers as the agent of sovereignty, offering the kingship once held by Midas to a later generation of rulers. From this context we may recognize how the Greeks became familiar with Kybebe, a goddess of the Phrygians and the Lydians, and how they understood her to be the same as the goddess known from her many sacred places, called *Kubeleya*. To the Lydians and the Phrygians in the era of Mermnad tyranny, Kybebe was the ultimate source of all of the good things that came from perfect kingship. To the later Greeks, after the fall of Croesus and the manifest failure of the Lydian paradigm of kingship, she was abstracted from tyranny and became known, from the landmarks associated with her, as Kybele, the "Great Mother of Gods and Men."[21]

NOTES

1 Charon of Lampsacus, *FGrHist* 262 F 5 = Photius s.v. Κύβηβος. For the Lydian inscriptions, see Gusmani (1969).

2 Strabo, *Geog.* 10.3.12, 15. Virgil, *Aen.* 3.111 refers to *Mater Cybeli*, using *Cybelus* as a place name (cf. 11.768); at 10.220–33, Virgil names the goddess *Cybebe ... Genetrix.* Catullus 63 alternates between *Cybebe* (63.9, 20, 35, 84, and 91: *Dea magna, dea Cybebe, dea domina Dindymi*) and *Cybele* (63.12, 68, 76).

3 Hesychius s.vv. Κυβήβη, Κύβηβος; Photius, *Lexicon* s.v. Κύβηβος j; *Etymologicum Gudianum* s.v. Κυβήβη. These testimonia are usefully collected by Santoro (1973, 154–57).

4 So Fauth (1969, col. 383); Vermaseren (1977, 21–24); Diakonoff (1977); Burkert (1979, 102–5; 1985, 177–78).

5 Brixhe (1979), who notes the alternate spellings, *Kubileya* and *Kubeleya*.

6 Brixhe (1979). See also Brixhe and Lejeune (1984, 1, 45–47 no. W-04, and 62–68 no. B-01).

7 Brixhe (1979, 43–45), followed by Zgusta (1982), Gusmani (1980–1986, 68–69), Innocente (1995, 216), and Roller (1999, 66–69, 125, and 171). For the Phrygian antecedent to the Greek "Mountain Mother," see now Yakubovich (2007, 143), who identifies Phrygian *areyasti-*, attested as another epithet of *Matar*, as a derivation from Luwian **areyatti-*, "mountain." (I thank Ilya Yakubovich for bringing this identification to my attention.)

8 Brixhe (1979, 45), concludes that his deductions "excluent que *Kubaba* et Κυβέλη dérivent d'un même thème ou que le second soit issu d'une altération du premier."

9 Graf (1984, 119; from a paper delivered in 1979); Rein (1993, 10–18; 1996).

10 One text, Gusmani (1964, 252, no. 4a line 4), names Kybebe as one of three deities protecting a tomb from desecration (for corrected readings see Gusmani 1975, 266–67); the second text, Gusmani (1980–1986, no. 72; see Gusmani 1969) is a graffito on a potsherd partially preserving her name. For the most likely readings of these texts, see Gusmani 1969, and 1980–1986, 68 (revising an earlier reading in Gusmani 1964, 156).

11 Melchert (1994, 128–29; 2003, 175–77), summarizes phonological characteristics of first-millennium Anatolian languages. Gusmani (1964, 31–32) demonstrates the not infrequent alternation of labials, *b*, *v*, and *f*, in Lydian.

12 On Lydian *-li-*, See Gusmani (1964, 36; 1980–1986, 71); Heubeck (1969, 416–17); Georgiev (1981, 209; 1984, 9–10, and 34

n. 13). The possessive suffix *-(ê)li* is common to Carian, Lycian, Luwian, Lydian, and Etruscan; see Georgiev (1981, 211; 1984, 8–9) and Melchert (2003, 195).

13 Lydian *Artimalis*: Gusmani (1964, 63). Lycian *Erttimeli* and Αρτεμηλις: Laroche, in Metzger (1979, 58 and 114). Cf. Heubeck (1959, 21–23); Georgiev (1984, 9–10).

14 Gusmani (1964, 74). Cf. Greek Βάχχιος as a personal name, and Βακχιών as an Ionian month; see Trümpy (1997, 57, 60, 64–65).

15 The consonant cluster *-vl-* or *-bl-* is not attested in surviving Old Phrygian texts, and may have been avoided in Phrygian. Brixhe (1994, 175–76), notices the tendency for Phrygian to adopt personal names from the Hittite/Luwian languages that Phrygian speakers came into contact with, yielding irregular nominal morphologies. Gusmani (1976, 79), discusses the vocalic phonology in the shift *â* > η. The Lydian vocalic phonology is preserved in the earliest Greek text to name Kybele, a graffito on a sherd from Epizephyrian Locri, in southern Italy, probably dating to the early-sixth century. It reads: [τᾶ]ς Κυβάλας (."... of Kubala," using koppa instead of kappa). See Guarducci (1970); the sherd is illustrated in a line drawing in Vermaseren (1977, 23, fig. 12).

16 Hipponax fr. 156 (West = 121 Bergk), cited in Santoro (1973, 155).

17 On the Phrygian adjectival or attributive suffix *-eyo/a* used in name formations, see Brixhe 1979, 43 n. 32; Neumann (1988, 7–8, 21).

18 Hecataeus, *FGrHist* 1 F 230 (from Stephanus of Byzantium, s.v. Κυβέλεια).

19 On Basile and the shrine she shared with Kodros and Neleus, see *IG* I^3 84, and Plato, *Charmides* 153A.

20 As argued by Berndt-Ersöz (2006a, 130, and 2006b).

21 The interpretation outlined here of the Phrygian Mother as a symbol of sovereignty is presented in greater detail in chapters 2 through 4 of Munn (2006). I would like to thank H. Craig Melchert for his advice on many of the linguistic points covered in this paper, without, however, implying that he is responsible for how I have used his advice.

REFERENCES

Berndt-Ersöz, S. 2006a. *Phyrgian Rock-Cut Shrines: Structure, Function, and Cult Practice*. Culture and History of the Ancient Near East 25. Leiden, Brill.

___ 2006b. The Anatolian Origin of Attis. In M. Hutter and S. Hutter-Braunsar (eds.) *Pluralismus und Wandel in den Religionen im vorhellenistischen Anatolien: Akten des religionsgeschichtlichen Symposiums in Bonn (19.-20 Mai 2005)*. Münster, Ugarit-Verlag.

Brixhe, C. (1979) Le nom de Cybèle. *Die Sprache* 25, 40–45.

___ (1994) Le phrygien. In F. Bader (ed.) *Langues Indo-Européennes*, 165–78. Paris, CNRS.

___ and M. Lejeune (1984). *Corpus des inscriptions paléo-phrygiennes*. 2 vols. Paris, Recherche sur les civilisations.

Burkert, W. 1979. *Structure and History in Greek Mythology and Ritual*. Sather Classical Lectures 47. Berkeley, University of California Press.

___ (1985) *Greek Religion*. Trans. J. Raffan, Cambridge, MA, Harvard University Press.

Diakonoff, I. M. (1977). On Cybele and Attis in Phrygia and Lydia. *Acta Antiqua Academiae Scientiarum Hungaricae* 25, 333–39.

Fauth, W. (1969) Kybele. *Der Kleine Pauly. Lexikon der Antike*. Vol. 3, cols. 383–89. Stuttgart, A. Druckenmüller.

Georgiev, V. I. (1981) *Introduction to the History of the Indo-European Languages*. Sofia, Bulgarian Academy of Sciences.

___ (1984) Lydiaka und lydisch-etruskische Gleichungen, *Linguistique balkanique* 27, 5–35.

Graf, F. (1984) The Arrival of Cybele in the Greek East. In J. Harmatta (ed.) *Proceedings of the VIIth Congress of the International Federation of the Societies of Classical Studies*, Vol. 1, 117–20. Budapest, Akadémiai Kiadó.

Guarducci, M. (1970) Cibele in un' epigrafe arcaica di Locri Epizefiri. *Klio* 52, 133–38.

Gusmani, R. (1964) *Lydisches Wörterbuch*. Heidelberg, Carl Winter.

___ (1969) Der lydische Name der Kybele. *Kadmos* 8:2, 158–61.

___ (1975) Lydiaka. *Oriens Antiquus* 14, 265–74.

___ (1976) Zum Alter des ionischen Wandele α > η, In A. Morpurgo Davies and W. Meid (eds.) *Studies in Greek, Italic, and Indo-European Linguistics Offered to Leonard R. Palmer on the Occasion of his Seventieth Birthday, June 5, 1976*, 77–82. Innsbruck, Institut für Sprachwissenschaft der Universität Innsbruck.

___ (1980–1986) *Lydisches Wörterbuch: Ergänzungsband*. 3 fascs. Heidelberg, Carl Winter.

Hawkins, J. D. (1981) Kubaba at Karkamiš and Elsewhere. *Anatolian Studies* 31, 147–76.

Heubeck, A. (1959) *Lydiaka. Untersuchungen zu Schrift, Sprache und Götternamen der Lyder*. Erlanger Forschungen A/9. Erlangen, Universitätsbund Erlangen.

___ (1969) Lydisch. In J. Friedrich (ed.) *Kleinasiatischen Sprachen*. HdO I/2.1–2, 397–427. Leiden, Brill.

Innocente, L. (1995) Stato degli studi frigi. In O. Carruba, M. Giorgieri, and C. Mora (eds.) *Atti del II Congresso Internazionale di Hittitologia*, 213–24. Pavia, Gianni Inculano.

Laroche, E. (1960) Koubaba, déesse anatolienne, et la problème des origines de Cybèle. In *Éléments orienteaux dans la religion grecque ancienne. Colloque de Strasbourg 22-24 mai 1958*, 113–28. Paris, Travaux du Centre d'Études supériores specialisé d'histoire des religions, Strasbourg, Presses universitaires de France.

Melchert, H. C. (1994) Anatolian. In F. Bader (ed.) *Langues Indo-Européennes*, 121–36. Paris, CNRS.

Metzger, H. ed. (1979) *Fouilles de Xanthos*, Vol. 6: *La stèle trilingue du Létôon*. Paris, Klinksieck.

___ ed. (2003) *The Luwians*. HbOr I/68. Leiden, Brill.

Munn, M. (2006) *The Mother of the Gods, Athens, and the Tyranny of Asia: A Study of Sovereignty in Ancient Religion*. Berkeley, University of California Press.

Neumann, G. (1988) *Phrygisch und Griechisch*. Österreichische Akademie der Wissenschaften, philosophisch-historische Klasse, Sitzungsberichte, vol. 499. Vienna, Verlag der Ôsterreichischen Akademie der Wissenschaften.

Rein, M. J. (1993) The Cult and Iconography of Lydian Kybele. Unpublished PhD diss. Harvard University.

___ (1996) Phrygian Matar: Emergence of an Iconographic Type. In E. Lane (ed.) *Cybele, Attis and Related Cults: Essays in Memory of M. J. Vermaseren*, 223–37. Leiden, Brill.

Roller, L. E. (1994) The Phrygian Character of Kybele: The Formation of an Iconography and Cult Ethos in the Iron Age. In A. Çilingiroðlu and D. French (eds.) *Anatolian Iron Ages 3: The Proceedings of The Third Anatolian Iron Ages Colloquium Held at Van, 6-12 August 1990*, 189–98. London, British Institute of Archaeology at Ankara.

___ (1999) *In Search of God the Mother: The Cult of Anatolian Cybele*, Berkeley and Los Angeles, University of California.

Santoro, M. (1973) *Epitheta Deorum in Asia Graeca cultorum ex auctoribus Graecis et Latinis*. Testi e documenti per lo studio dell' antichità 44. Milan, Istituto deitoliale cisalpino-Lo goliardica.

Trümpy, C. (1997) *Untersuchungen zu den altgriechischen Monatsnamen und Monatsfolgen*. Heidelberg, Carl Winter.

Vermaseren, M. J. (1977) *Cybele and Attis: The Myth and Cult*, London, Thames and Hudson.

Yakubovich, I. (2007) Review of H. C. Melchert (ed.) *The Luwians. Journal of Near Eastern Studies* 66.2, 140–44.

Zgusta, L. (1982) Weiteres zum Namen der Kybele. *Die Sprache* 28, 171–72.

17

KING MIDAS IN SOUTHEASTERN ANATOLIA

Maya Vassileva

King Midas of Phrygia entered modern consciousness by means of Greek mythology, which presented an image of a fabulously wealthy, greedy and rather stupid Oriental monarch. He is remembered primarily for his "golden touch," as well as the ass's ears with which Apollo punished him. However, since the discovery of the Assyrian documents of King Sargon II, the identification of King Mita of Mushki with the Midas in the Greek literary sources has been accepted (Winckler 1898). Thus, the identification of the Mushki with the Phrygians was established, although there are still scholars who do not accept it (e.g., Laminger-Pascher 1989, 24). The historical claim of King Midas became even stronger when his name was found in Old Phrygian inscriptions (Brixhe and Lejeune 1984, M–01a). Progress in the archaeological study of Phrygia in particular and of Anatolia in general have confirmed the political might of the Phrygian kingdom and its influence over both the East Greek world and its Anatolian neighbors. Exactly how the historical Midas took on legendary and mythological character in Greek literature and how much Phrygian reality is reflected in the Greek texts are questions that remain open.

Although the Mushki are mentioned earlier, the most informative group of Near Eastern texts on King Mita/Midas is the royal inscriptions and letters of Sargon II. This corpus sheds light on the political situation in southeastern Anatolia at the end of the eighth century BC and reveals that King Mita of Mushki was a mighty adversary of Assyria who endlessly organized anti-Assyrian coalitions with other rulers of the smaller kingdoms of Tabal, Tyana, Que and Carchemish, only finally to become an ally of Assyria.

The historical geography of southeastern Anatolia is very difficult to restore according to the Assyrian texts and the Luwian inscriptions discovered there. The exact location and the boundaries of the numerous small kingdoms, or city-states, are yet to be defined. Tabal was the name by which the Assyrians referred to the southeastern corner of the Anatolian plateau (Hawkins 2000b, 425). Sargon II's texts provide secure evidence for the intense political activity of Mita in the region for about a decade, from 718 to 709 BC.

The first possible reference to a conspiracy pitting Mita against Assyria appears in 718 BC. Sargon II had removed Kiakki of Sinuhtu (one of the Tabalian kingdoms) from the throne, because of his anti-Assyrian activity together with Mita (in the fragmentary Nimrud cylinders; Gadd 1954, 180; Lafranchi 1988, 61; Hawkins 2000b, 427). He gave his city to Kurtî of Atuna (Tunna?; Fuchs 1993, Ann. 70–71). In turn Kurtî, or Gurdî, after flirting with Mita and after being frightened by the fate of Ambaris, was forced to submit to Assyria.[1]

In 717 BC, Pisiris of Carchemish was also accused of disloyalty to the Assyrian king and of allying himself with Mita (Fuchs 1993, Ann. 72–76; Gadd 1954, 179; Hawkins 2000a, 76). In 715 BC Sargon claimed that he took over fortresses in Que that had previously been conquered by the king of the Mushki (Fuchs 1993, Ann. 199–20, 125–26; Hawkins 2000a, 42). Sometime before 718 BC, Sargon set Ambaris, "the Tabalian," on the throne and gave him his daughter and the land of Hilakku as a dowry (Fuchs 1993, Ann. 194–198; Prunk

29–30; Hawkins 2000b, 427). But, accused of conspiring with Mita, the Urartian king Rusa and the Tabalian kings, he was deprived of his throne in 713 BC (Fuchs 1993, Ann. 198–200; Hawkins 2000b, 428). Probably at that same time Sargon turned Bit-Burutas (Tabal) and Hilakku into an Assyrian province (Hawkins 2000b, 427). The same accusations were made against Tarhunazi of Melid in 711 BC and provoked the Assyrian intrusion into the country (Fuchs 1993, Ann. 204–210; Hawkins 1993–97a, 38; 2000a, 285).

Finally, the letter of Sargon to the governor of Que, discovered in Nimrud, informs us that Mita had intercepted an embassy that Urik of Que had sent to Urartu and handed it over to the Assyrians, declaring his friendship (Parpola 1987, no. 1). Sargon instructs his governor to return Phrygian subjects held by the Assyrians, probably from a previous political and military encounter between both countries. The very favorable answer of the Assyrian king, showing readiness to accept the Phrygian as a friendly ruler, shows the political and strategic importance of this alliance. The letter was initially dated to 738 BC, to the time of Tiglath–pilesar III, then to 710/709 BC (Saggs 1958, 202–5; Postgate 1973, 33; Mellink 1979, 250; 1991, 622; Hawkins 1993–1997b, 272). Recently, Lafranchi has dated it to 715 BC, placing Urik's envoys to Urartu, the Assyrian attack against Mita in Que, Mita's forwarding the envoys to Assyria, and the writing of the letter all at around the same time (Lafranchi 1988). However, most scholars agree that the date of this letter is 710/709 BC. Thus, for a decade, Mita's political partners ranged from Melid to Que.[2]

One of the possible implications of Sargon's good disposition towards Mita in 710/709 BC, as already noted by others, was his intention to control the kings of Tabal through the Phrygian ruler (Hawkins 2000a, 42). This demonstrates Mita's close relations with, and the influence he wielded over, Tabal and Tyana. The Phrygian presence in the east was probably earlier than the above-mentioned events, at least in the first half of the eighth century BC, as shown by the inscription of Yariris of Carchemish and the one from Til-Barsip, which speak of the Mushki (Hawkins 2000a, KARKAMIS A6, 126; Thureau-Dangin and Dunand 1936, 149).

The Near Eastern texts suggest that Mita had the closest political relations with the Tabalian rulers. Some scholars even propose a common Phrygian-Tabalian kingdom, which Sargon had to deal with, or a Phrygian protectorate in the border area between Tabal and Tuwana (Börker-Klähn 2003, 85).

More than twenty years ago, Diakonoff suggested that *Kurtî/Gurdî* can be identified with the legendary Phrygian ruler Gordias, known from the Greek texts as King Midas's father.[3] Scholars continue to debate the possible identification of *Kurtî/Gurdî* from the Assyrian texts with Kurtis from Hieroglyphic Luwian inscriptions and the relation/identification between the several individuals attested under the name of *Gurdî* (Aro-Valjus 1999, 431–32). *Kurtî* of Atuna/Tuna received the house of Sinuhtu after Kiakki's removal, only to become disloyal to Assyria himself. A certain Gurdî concluded a vassal treaty with Sargon II. *Gurdî*, "the Kulummean," is known from Sargon's Eponymous Chronicle in 705 BC and *Gurdî* of Til-Garimu in the time of Sennacherib (695 BC; Aro-Valjus 1999, 431). *Gurdî/Kurtî* was most probably the same person as Kurtis of Atuna, who left his name in the Hieroglyphic Luwian inscription from Bohça and on the Kululu lead strips (Fuchs 2000, 642). J. D. Hawkins considers this identification very probable but has some doubts about the locations of Atuna/Tuna (and Tyana; Hawkins 1979, 166; 2000b, 431–32; Hawkins and Morpurgo-Davies 1979, 390; accepted also by Fuchs 2000, 642, contra Aro 1998, 142–43; Aro-Valjus 1999, 431).

The inscriptions from Bohça give the name of Kurtis's father, Ashwis(is),[4] whom Diakonoff suggests is Askanios, one of the Phrygian chieftains in the *Iliad*.[5] Linguistically *Kurtî/Gurdî/Kurtis* is not impossible, but we simply do not have enough evidence to be certain. Could a Phrygian ally from Atuna be turned into a member of the dynasty by the Greek mythographers, while his father becomes another Phrygian epic hero? In the present state of the data one can only hypothesize that the Greeks were aware of the close political and cultural relations between the Phrygians and the kingdoms in southeastern Anatolia.

The above-mentioned written evidence has been referred to, but usually very briefly, in general entries about the Mushki/Phrygians, or in attempts to interpret certain archaeological finds. While considering the finds from the tumuli at Bayındır in Lycia, the political situation of the late-eighth century in southeastern Anatolia has often been brought up (most recently by Börker-Klähn 2003). However, Lycia is further west from the area in question and, more importantly, this spectacular discovery has not yet been published properly.

Phrygian political involvement in southeastern Anatolia has often been discussed in relation to Warpalawa, king of Atuna, the best-attested Tabalian king. He is estimated to have reigned at minimum between 738–710 BC (Hawkins 2000b, 432). He was not a Phrygian vassal or client state (as suggested by Berges 1998, 187), but was a Phrygian ally and a strong ruler in his own right, as his inscriptions demonstrate.[6] It has long been proposed that Warpalawa is wearing a Phrygian fibula and possibly a Phrygian garment on his rock-cut relief at Ivriz.[7] Indeed, there is an almost exact parallel of Warpalawa's fibula in a piece found in the so-called "Midas Mound" at Gordion.[8] Most scholars interpret it as a royal gift by Mita to his ally.[9] In view of the political and cultural context, one can also make the case for the adoption of a status symbol.

The archaeological record of Tyana and Tabal has also occasionally been quoted. Many scholars have noted the Phrygian affinities of the pottery discovered in Porsuk.[10] The numerous tumuli, unfortunately unexcavated and many of them looted, are also worth noting (Aro 1998, 243; Berges 1998, 186). A tomb near Kaynarca yielded a bronze belt and bronze vessels comparable to the inventory of the Gordion tombs (Akkaya 1991). They attest to a Phrygian tradition, regardless of whether they are interpreted as belonging to members of Tyana royal family, as some do (Akkaya 1991, 27; Berges 1998, 187), or to Phrygians.

There are also Old Phrygian inscriptions discovered in Tyana, the so-called Black Stones (basalt slabs), which might be among the earliest ones.[11] Although the texts are fragmentary, Midas's name is distinguished in one of them.[12] Most scholars agree that it is the great Midas who is mentioned. One of the suggestions about the nature of the monument is a historical text, commemorating the alliance with Warpalawa (Dupré 1983, 110). M. Mellink claims that these might be the Phrygian equivalent of Warpalawa's stele from Bor (1991, 626). A kenotaph or a "tomb-like" monument (Sams 1995, 1157) seems to me less probable, while a public text after the model of the Assyrian royal inscriptions (Brixhe 1991, 45–46; 2004, 103) is hardly possible in view with the current Phrygian epigraphic data.

A variant of a title, known from two rock-cut inscriptions from "Midas City" (*memevais* - *memeuis*; Brixhe and Lejeune 1984, M-01b and M-02), is mentioned in the same Tyana stone, where Midas's name is detected. Variants of the peculiar Phrygian sign ↑ are used next to the normal form both in the above-mentioned inscriptions from "Midas City" and on the Tyana stones. It might be worth noting that the name of the dedicator of the two texts from "Midas City," is accompanied by other titles, besides *memevais*. *K↑iyanaveyos/ k↑ianaveyos*, occurring in both texts, is considered either as a title, or as an ethnonym (Brixhe and Lejeune 1984, 10). It has been suggested this word be interpreted as "of Tyana."[13]

It is very unlikely that these are political or historical texts comparable to the Near Eastern and Neo-Hittite traditions, as most of the Old Phrygian inscriptions are dedicatory. So, if we assume that this is some kind of royal representation or claim of political domination by the Phrygian king, this would have rather been done through a dedication or religious type of message. On the other hand, inscribing a stele was not so often the Phrygian practice. Besides the rock-cut inscriptions and the numerous sherd graffiti, we have few texts carved on stone slabs.[14] The most plausible reconstruction of the monument(s) from Tyana[15] makes it very similar to the stelae known from Tabal. They have rounded tops and usually are inscribed on all sides, just like the Tyana "Black Stones." Recently, J. Börker-Klähn has been concerned with a relief from Gökbez. Two such steles, attached together, are represented on the background of the relief (Börker-Klähn 2004, Abb. 27). One cannot help but compare them with the Phrygian rock-carved "double idols" (Haspels 1971, fig. 36). Could these round-topped stelae from Tyana and Tabal have influenced Phrygian "idols"?

Mellink has drawn attention to the representation on a second, smaller relief from İvriz (Bier 1976, Abb. 5): A man in a long garment, followed by another person who carries a sacrificial animal, probably a servant, heads to a platform cut into the rock (Mellink 1979, 252; cf. Börker-Klähn 2000, 39, 62; 2004, 173–74). There are a few steps and a rectangular opening, interpreted as a libation basin. This setting conforms very well with the Phrygian megalithic rituality related to the Mother-Goddess worship.[16]

I will not enter here into the discussion of the relationship between Kubaba and Kybele (for which see Roller 1999, 44–53 and Munn in this volume). However, one cannot miss the fact that the rulers of the Neo-Hittite kingdoms were also closely associated with goddess worship. The kings of Carchemish were her dear servants; they were responsible for the restoration of her image(s), shrines, and temples (see "set" and "reseated Kubaba" in the Luwian Hieroglyphic inscriptions from Carchemish; Hawkins 1981).

Although of a later date, another "black stone" is worth mentioning. Not far from the area under discussion, in Cappadocia, a basalt slab was discovered, inscribed this time in Aramaic. It is dated to the fifth to fourth centuries BC and mentions "Kubaba from PWSD/R which is in Kastabalay." This is probably a city or place sacred to the goddess, whose name possibly relates to the Anatolian toponym *Piwassura*, derived from *Pirwa* and corresponding to Artemis's epithet *Peraisia* in a passage in Strabo (Strabo, *Geog.*, 12.2.7; Iamblichus, *De Myst.*, 3.5; Dupont-Sommer 1964, 13). Strabo speaks about the priestesses of Artemis *Peraisia* in Kastabala "who walk with naked feet over hot ambers without pain." The survivals of this ritual practice have been observed by ethnographers in modern Bulgarian and northern Greek villages and have long been discussed in the literature (Robert 1964, 50–64; A. Fol 1998, 58–59; V. Fol 2000, 187–92).

The combined data of the monuments demonstrate that the Phrygian involvement in southeastern Anatolia was not so short-lived or occasional as initially assumed. The closer examination of the written sources suggest that the Phrygians under King Midas played a paramount role in the area, probably for a couple of decades in the eighth century BC, while their presence might have been much longer. The first quarter of the seventh century BC saw the Mushki again in the area, probably allied with the Cimmerians (Starr 1990, no. 1; Aro 1998, 151–53; Börker-Klähn 2004). Neither the "Black Stones" from Tyana, nor the tombs at Bayındır, Lycia, look isolated anymore. We would not be able to estimate securely what kind of Phrygian population there was in southeastern Anatolia, but the evidence of the cultural interactions can not be assigned only to isolated contacts, garrisons or diplomats.[17] Here is the spot where most probably the Phrygians were in touch with the ancient Near Eastern cultural heritage and experienced the influence of the Neo-Hittite/North Syrian world. Here, another stele of Warpalawa from Ivriz is worth mentioning: it contains a bilingual Luwian-Phoenician text, the latter of which is still unpublished (Dinçol 1994, 117–28). Thus, one of king Mita's allies was setting up his stele written in Phoenician as well. Phoenician and Aramaic inscriptions of the ninth to seventh centuries were found in southeastern Anatolia, in a well-attested Luwian-speaking area. Perhaps some traditional views on the Phrygian adoption of the Semitic script should be reconsidered or modified, especially in light of the new dates for the Gordion destruction level (Brixhe 2002, 25–28; DeVries et al. 2003).

Thus, Phrygians played a significant role in the cultural interactions between the East and the West. These interactions occurred in a zone that exhibits distinguishable typological parallels in kingship, cult practice and rituality, which ran from the Balkans through the Phrygian Highlands and is echoed in southeastern Anatolia. At the same time, echoes from the Neo-Hittite world were heard in, and absorbed by, "western" Phrygia.

NOTES

1 In 713 BC or shortly after (ARAB II § 214; Hawkins 2000b, 428)

2 Even if Lafranchi's arguments are accepted for a shorter period of Phrygian domination in Que, Sargon's letter is quite eloquent about Mita's role in the political events in southeastern Anatolia. Besides, as noted above, Kiakki's conspiracy with Mita, dated before 718 BC, is evidence for an earlier Phrygian involvement in the area.

3 Diakonov (1981, 51), Diakonoff and Neroznak (1985, XIII). Röllig's suggestion for a Lycian name (1957–1971, 703) can hardly be accepted.

4 Hawkins (2000b, 431, 479), who is more inclined to compare the name with that of Ušhitti; according to C. Melchert (personal communication) the name should be read As(a)ku(a)sis.

5 *Il.* 2.862; Diakonov (1981, 57). He argues that Kurtis's elaborated title "the king heard of by the west and the east" is foreign to the local tradition.

6 See Aro's interpretation of Urballa's appearance in Sargon II's letter to his governer of Que (Aro 1998, 138).

7 Muscarella (1967a, 83–84; 1967b, 19–20; 1988, 422, note 5); Boehmer (1973, 151–52); Berges (1998, 185–86, n. 27); Börker-Klähn (2004, 168). It is debatable whether the entire garment and the belt represented on the relief matches the Phrygian finds as Boehmer and Berges assume.

8 Type XII.9 according to Blinckenberg's classification (Young 1981 MM187A, 160, pl. 76. F). Aro argues for a Tabalian origin of Warpalawa's fibula (1998, 221).

9 Boehmer (1973, 156); Dupré (1983, 110). Other explanation have been offered; for example, the fibula could have been imported, or the result of diplomatic marriage.

10 The first period of Porsuk level III was compared to Gordion pre-destruction and destruction levels (Dupré 1983, 111; Sams 1994, 53–54, 155), the latter being recently dated a century earlier, i.e., ca. 800 BC (see also Mellink 1979, 254; Börker-Klähn 2003, 75).

11 Brixhe and Lejeune (1984, T-01-03); Brixhe (1991; 2004, 94–103); Vassileva (1992).

12 Brixhe and Lejeune (1984, T-02b, 264–66):]*tumida* is yet unclear, but *mida*[in the fourth line could be Midas.

13 Orel (1997, 13) with the earlier bibliography. Although rejected by Brixhe and Lejeune (1984, 257), this hypothesis is worth further exploration.

14 There are several stone inscriptions from Gordion (G-01, G-02), some of them on small stone pieces (G-03-09); there is a Graeco-Persian stele from Bithynia (B-02). It seems that the number of inscribed bigger stone slabs or stelae is larger in the eastern areas of the spread of Phrygian script: C-01, P-02, -03, -04. The ones from Pteria (near Boğazköy) are fragments of parallelepid stone blocks.

15 Mellink (1979, fig. 1d). Although very similar, the three pieces of stone slabs from Tyana belonged most probably to three different monuments of the same type (Brixhe 1991, 41; 2004, 103).

16 Thus the interpretation of the opening as meant for the erection of a stele, suggested by Mellink, seems less probable.

17 Brixhe argues that there was no Phrygian-speaking population in Tyana (Brixhe 1991, 45).

REFERENCES

Akkaya, M. (1992) Objets phrygiens en bronze du tumulus de Kaynarca. In B. Le Guen-Pollet, O. Pelon, *La Cappadoce méridionale jusqu'à la fin de l'époque romaine: état des recherches. Actes du Colloque d'Istanbul 1987*, 25–27. Paris, Éditions Recherche sur les Civilisations.

Aro, S. (1998) Tabal. Zur Geschichte und materiellen Kultur des zentralanatolischen Hochplateaus von 1200 bis 600 v. Chr. Unpublished Ph.D. Diss., Helsinki, Helsinki University.

Aro-Valjus, S. (1999) Gurdî. In S. Parpola, *The Prosopography of the Neo-Assyrian Empire. 1.2*, 431–32. Helsinki, The Neo-Assyrian Text Corpus Project.

Berges, D. (1998) Neue Forschungen in Tyana. In R. Rolle and K. Schmidt (eds.) *Archäologische Studien in Kontaktzonen der antiken Welt*, 179–204. Göttingen, Vandenhoeck & Ruprecht.

Bier, L. (1976) A Second Hittite Relief at Ivriz. *Journal of Near Eastern Studies* 35, 115–26.

Boehmer R. M. (1973) Phrygische Prunkgewänder des 8. Jahrhunderts v. Chr. Herkunft und Export. *Archäologischer Anzeiger* 1973/2, 149–72.

Börker-Klähn, J. (2000) Nachlese an phrygischen Fundplätyen. *Rivista di archeologia* 24, 35–69.

—— (2003) Tumulus D von Bayındır bei Elmalı als historischer Spiegel. In M. Giorgieri, M. Salvini, M.-C. Trémouille, P.

Vannicelli (eds.) *Licia e Lidia Prima dell'ellenizzazione. Atti del Convegno internationale Roma, 11-12 ottobre 1999*, 69–105. Roma, Consiglio Nazionale delle Ricerche.

___ (2004) Die Leute vom Göllüdağ und im Königreich Tyana. In T. Korkut (ed.), *Anadolu'da Doğdu. Festschrift für Fahri Işık zum 60. Geburtstag*, 163–99. Istanbul, Ege Yayınları.

Brixhe, C. (1991) Les inscriptions paléo-phrygiennes de Tyane: leur intérêt linguistique et historique. In B. Le Guen-Pollet and O. Pelon (eds.) *La Cappadoce méridionale jusqu'à la fin de l'époque romaine: état des recherches. Actes du Colloque d'Istanbul 1987*, 37–46. Paris, Éditions Recherche sur les Civilisations.

___ (2002) Corpus des inscriptions paléo-phrygiennes. Supplément I. *Kadmos* 41, 1–102.

___ (2004) Corpus des inscriptions paléo-phrygiennes. Supplément II. *Kadmos* 43, 1–130.

Brixhe, C., and Lejeune, M. (1984) *Corpus des inscriptions paléo-phrygiennes*. T. I–II. Paris, Éditions Recherche sur les Civilisations.

DeVries, K., Kuniholm, P. I., Sams, G. K. , and Voigt, M. M. (2003) New Dates for Iron Age Gordion. *Antiquity* 77/296. Online: http://antiquity.ac.uk/ProjGall/devries/devries.html.

Diakonov, I. M. (1981) Malaya Azia i Armenia okolo 600 g. do n.e. i severnie pohodi vavilonskih tsarei. *Vestnik drevnei istorii* 2, 34–64.

Diakonoff, I. M. and Neroznak, V. P. (1985) *Phrygian*. Delmar, NY, Caravan Books.

Dinçol, B. (1994) New Archaeological and Epigraphical Finds from Ivriz: A Preliminary Report. *Tel Aviv* 21, 117–28.

Dupont-Sommer, A. (1964) Une inscription araméenne et la déesse Kubaba. *Bibliothèque archéologique et historique de l'Institut français d'archéologie d'Istanbul* 16, 7–15.

Dupré, S. (1983) *Porsuk I. La céramique de l'âge du bronze et de l'âge du fer.* Paris, Éditions Recherche sur les civilisations.

Fol, A. (1998) Sabas/Sabazios/Sabo. In N. Tuna, Z. Akture and M. Lynch (eds.) *Thracians and Phrygians: Problems of Parallelism. Proceedings of an International Symposium on the Archaeology, History and Ancient Languages of Thrace and Phrygia. Ankara 3-4 June, 1995*, 55–60. Ankara, METU.

Fol, V. (2000) The Rock and the Fire. In A. Fol (ed.) *Ancient Thrace*, 171–92. Sofia, Europa Antiqua, Institute of Thracology.

Fuchs, A. (1993) *Die Inschriften Sargons II. aus Khorsabad*. Göttingen, Cuvillier.

___ (2000) Kurti. In S. Parpola (ed.) *The Prosopography of the Neo-Assyrian Empire*. Vol. 2/1, 642. Helsinki, The Neo-Assyrian Text Corpus Project.

Gadd, C. J. (1954) Inscribed Prisms of Sargon II from Nimrud. *Iraq* 16, 173–201.

Haspels, C. E. H. (1971) *The Highlands of Phrygia. Sites and Monuments*. Vol. 1–2. Princeton, Princeton University.

Hawkins, J. D. (1979) Some Historical Problems of the Hieroglyphic Luwian Inscriptions. *Anatolian Studies* 29, 153–67.

___ (1981) Kubaba at Karkamis and Elsewhere. *Anatolian Studies* 31, 147–75.

___ (1993–97a) Melid. *Reallexikon der Assyriologie* 8, 35–42.

___ (1993–97b) Mita. *Reallexikon der Assyriologie* 8, 271–73.

___ (2000a) *Corpus of Hieroglyphic Luwian Inscriptions*. Vol. I: *Inscriptions of the Iron Age. Part 1: Text, Introduction, Karatepe, Karkamiš, Tell Ahmar, Maraş, Malatya, Commagene*. Berlin, de Gruyter.

___ (2000b) *Corpus of Hieroglyphic Luwian Inscriptions. Vol. I: Inscriptions of the Iron Age. Part 2: Text, Amuq, Aleppo, Hama, Tabal, Assur Letters, Miscellaneous, Seals, Indices*. Berlin, de Gruyter.

Hawkins, J. D., Morpurgo-Davies, A. (1979) The Hieroglyphic Inscription of Bohça. In O. Carruba (ed.) *Studia Mediterranea Piero Meriggi dicata*. II, 387–405. Pavia, Aurora.

Lafranchi, G. B. (1988) Sargon's Letter to Aššur-Šarru-Usur: An Interpretation. *State Archives of Assyria Bulletin* 2.1, 59–64.

Laminger-Pascher, G. (1989) *Lykaonien und die Phryger*. Österreichische Akademie der Wissenschaften. Philosophisch-Historische Klasse. Sitzungsberichte 532. Vienna, Österreichische Akademie der Wissenschaften.

Mellink, M. J. (1979) Midas in Tyana. Pp. 249–57 in *Florilegium Anatolicum. Mélanges offerts à Emmanuel Laroche*. Paris, Boccard.

___ (1991) The Native Kingdoms of Anatolia. In *CAH*[2] 3.2, 619–65. Cambridge, Cambridge University.

Muscarella, O. W. (1967a) Fibulae Represented on Sculpture. *Journal of Near Eastern Studies* 26, 82–86.

___ (1967b) *Phrygian Fibulae from Gordion*. London, Quaritch.

___ (1988) *Bronze and Iron: Ancient Near Eastern Artifacts in The Metropolitan Museum of Art*. New York, The Metropolitan Museum of Art.

Orel, V. (1997) *The Language of Phrygians. Description and Analysis*. Delmar, NY, Caravan Books.

Parpola, S. (1987) *The Correspondence of Sargon II. Part I. Letters from Assyria and the West*. Helsinki, Helsinki University.

Postgate, J. N. (1973) Assyrian Texts and Fragments. *Iraq* 35, 13–36.

Robert, L. (1964) La déesse de Hiérapolis-Castabala. *Bibliothèque archéologique et historique de l'Institut français d'archéologie d'Istanbul* 16, 50–64.

Roller, L. E. (1999) *In Search of God the Mother. The Cult of Anatolian Cybele.* Berkeley and Los Angeles, University of California.

Röllig, W. (1957–1971) Gurdi. *Reallexikon der Assyriologie* 3, 703.

Saggs, H. W. F. (1958) The Nimrud letters, 1952, Part IV. *Iraq* 20, 182–212.

Sams, G. K. (1994) *The Early Phrygian Pottery. The Gordion Excavations, 1950-1973: Final Reports.* Vol. IV. ed. E. L. Kohler, Philadelphia, University of Pennsylvania Museum.

___ (1995) Midas of Gordion and the Anatolian Kingdom of Phrygia. *CANE* 2, 1147–59.

Starr, I. (1990) *Queries to the Sungod. Divination and Politics in Sargonid Assyria.* State Archives of Assyria 4. Helsinki, Helsinki University.

Thureau-Dangin, F. and Dunand, M. (1936) *Til-Barsib.* Paris, Paul Geuthner.

Vassileva, M. (1992) Notes on the "Black Stones" from Tyana. *Epigraphica Anatolica* 19, 1–3.

Winckler, H. (1898) *Die Reiche von Kilikien und Phrygien im Lichte der altorientalischen Inschriften.* Altorientalische Forchungen II.2. Leipzig.

Young, R. S. (1981) *Three Great Early Tumuli: The Gordion Excavations Final Reports, Vol. 1.* Philadelphia, University of Pennsylvania.

18

THE GALA AND THE GALLOS

Patrick Taylor

"There is a class of Babylonian priests called *kalu*, Sumerian *gala*, concerned especially with the temple tympanon and bull sacrifice ... whom it is tempting to connect with the Meter cult, too...." With these words, Walter Burkert revived the search for the origins of the *gallos* of Rome and Hellenistic Greece among the Bronze Age cultures of the Near East (1979, 198 with previous literature).[1] Burkert himself prefers to relate the *galloi* to the beings called *gallu* who carry Ishtar's consort Dumuzi to the Underworld in Mesopotamian myth. Nevertheless, a possible relationship between the GALA of Mesopotamia and the Hellenistic *gallos* (Latin *gallus*) is suggested not only by the phonetic resemblance of their names, but also by the striking agreement of certain characteristics of the two cultic functionaries. The typological similarity between them has received detailed examination in recent cross-cultural studies of the role of transgendered individuals in religion and ritual (e.g., Roscoe 1996). The Hittite texts, however, offer evidence for the historical continuity of tradition between the GALA and the gallos beyond mere typological resemblance.

The galloi were self-castrated eunuch devotees of Cybele, the mother goddess of the Greek and Roman world, whose cult was overwhelmingly associated with Phrygia in antiquity.[2] They are noted for their wailing and lamentation of Attis, Cybele's mythological companion who died after castrating himself. The processions of the galloi, accompanied by the clanging of cymbals, were characterized by ecstatic self-mutilation and bloodletting. The stereotypical *gallus* of Roman literature wore feminine dress and heavy makeup, had long yellow-tinted hair, and was willing to perform sex acts considered degrading by the Romans. Martial (3.81), for example, reproaches a *gallus* for cheating on his vows to Cybele by engaging in oral sex with women, rather than men.

The GALA priests, on the other hand, were professional cultic singers, attested in texts from the third millennium onwards. They were not eunuchs, as Renger demonstrated (1969). Their repertoire included songs in various genres, including the BALAG (performed to the BALAG-drum and usually translated "lamentation") and the ÉR.ŠEM$_5$.MA ("wail of the šem drum").[3] The cultic songs of the GALA are composed in emesal (EME.SAL), a variety of Sumerian whose exact nature has been a subject of much dispute. Emesal may simply be the "refined" dialect of Sumerian, considered softer or more beautiful, or it may at one time have been an actual female *genderlect*, the existence of which is paralleled in other languages (Schretter 1990, 105–23). Whittaker provides a summary upon we may base a discussion: "Emesal occurs only as a literary dialect: that is, as the vehicle of specific literary and cultic genres and as a literary device employed, among other things, to identify female speakers generically" (2002, 641).

Although the exact nature of the GALA and the evolution of his role in Mesopotamian cult over the millennia remain topics of controversy, some evidence suggests that Mesopotamian society considered the GALA to have transgendered characteristics. Steinkeller provides evidence for the original transgendered status of the GALA in his analysis of the origin of the Sumerian sign GALA (UŠ.TUŠ; 1992, 37). He notes that the Sumerian word for "son-in-law," usually written $mussa_x$(SAL.UŠ)[sá], "contains the logogram SAL.UŠ (more correctly: GAL_4.GÌŠ 'vagina + penis'), which is used in third-millennium sources (mostly ED [Early Dynastic – *P.T.*]) to write various words connected with the idea of heterosexual intercourse.... In this connection, we may also mention the logogram UŠ.TUŠ (more correctly, GÌŠ.DÚR 'penis + anus'), standing for GALA, which is clearly the 'homosexual' equivalent of SAL.UŠ."

In the Sumerian myth of the Descent of Inanna, the god Enki creates two cultic personnel from the dirt underneath his fingernails and sends them to revive Inanna, who lies dead in the Underworld. He forms a GALA.TUR (perhaps "lowly gala, low-ranking gala,") with another cultic functionary called a KUR.GAR.RA. The KUR.GAR.RA is also suspected of engaging in homosexual sex and behaviors that we may consider transgendered within the context of Mesopotamian society (Bottéro and Petschow 1972, 463; Henshaw 1993, 289). In the Akkadian versions of the myth, the Descent of Ishtar, the GALA.TUR and KUR.GAR.RA are replaced by a single figure, an *assinnu* or *kulu'u*, also males who engage in prostitution or transgendered behavior. The Sumerian Proverb Collections depict the GALA as ridiculous in general, and Alster interprets the following proverb as a crude joke (Sumerian Proverb Collection 2, 100, ed. Alster 1997, 1, 65): gala-e bìd-da-ni ḫa-ba-an-da-zé-er / èm ga-ša-an-an-na ga-ša-an-mu / ba-ra-zi-zi-dè-en-e-še "A lamentation priest wiped his anus and said, 'I must not stir up that which belongs to the Queen of Heaven, my lady'." The quoted speech contains the emesal forms ÈM for NIĜ, "thing," and GAŠAN for NIN, "lady," and the low humor of this proverb recalls the origin of the sign GALA.

Some of the first attestations of the word γάλλος in Greek indicate the preservation of Mesopotamian tradition. Five epigrams in the Greek Anthology, 6.217–21 and 6.237, tell slightly differing versions of story about a devotee of Cybele who encounters a lion. As a typical example of these poems, we may quote *AP* 6.217 (attributed to Simonides, ed. Gow and Page 1965, 1: 180, translation mine):

Χειμερίην νιφετοῖο κατήλυσιν ἡνίκ' ἀλύξας
  Γάλλος ἐρημαίην ἤλυθ' ὑπὸ σπιλάδα,
ὑετὸν ἄρτι κόμης ἀπομόρξατο, τοῦ δὲ κατ' ἴχνος
  βουφάγος εἰς κοίλην ἀτραπὸν ἵκτο λέων·
αὐτὰρ ὁ πεπταμένῃ μέγα τύμπανον, ὃ σκέθε, χειρὶ
  ἤραξεν, καναχῇ δ' ἴαχεν ἄντρον ἅπαν·
οὐδ' ἔτλη Κυβέλης ἱερὸν βρόμον ὑλονόμος θὴρ
  μεῖναι, ἀν' ὑλῆεν δ' ὠκὺς ἔθυνεν ὄρος,
δείσας ἡμιγύναικα θεῆς λάτριν, ὃς τάδε Ῥείᾳ
  ἐνδυτὰ καὶ ξανθοὺς ἐκρέμασε πλοκάμους.

A gallos, taking shelter from the wintry falling of snow, entered a desolate cave. He had just wiped the sleet from his hair, when in his footsteps came a cattle-devouring lion down the hollow path. But the gallos with outspread hand beat the big tympanon that he held and the whole cave echoed with the sound. The forest-dwelling beast could not bear the holy noise of Cybele, but rushed swiftly up the tree-covered hill, in fear of the half-woman servant of the goddess, who dedicated to Rhea these robes and yellow locks.

The poems from the Greek Anthology curiously echo a Sumerian proverb from the Old Babylonian period (Sumerian Proverb Collection 2, 101 ed. and trans. Alster 1997, 1: 101–2): gala-e ur-maḫ-e edin-na ù-mu-ni-in-te / ḫe-en-du èrim(?)[ki] ká [d]inana-še / ur-šika-da-ra / šeš-zu edin-na ta-àm mu-un-na-ak-e-še "A lamentation priest, after he had met a lion in the desert, said, 'Let him come! In the town ... at Inanna's gate, oh dog, chased away with potsherds, what is your brother doing in the desert?'" The agreement in motifs between the Greek poems and the Sumerian proverb suggests the possible transmission of elements of the institution of the GALA from Mesopotamia to the Hellenistic world.

The typological similarity between the institutions also invites an etymological equation of the words GALA and γάλλος. The Sumerian word, first borrowed into Akkadian, would have entered – perhaps through the mediation of Hurrian – the local languages of Anatolia, eventually to be passed to Phrygian and Hellenistic Greek. However, the preservation of the initial *g* is somewhat surprising in light of constraint against initial voiced stops characteristic of the Anatolian linguistic area in the Bronze Age. Moreover, the word GALA appears in Akkadian as *kalû* with a *k*, the usual realization of Sumerian *g* in early borrowings into Akkadian. However, the consonant *k* seems peculiarly susceptible to voicing in the process of borrowing, as exemplified for example by Italian *gamba*, French *jambe* from Greek καμπή "bend (in a limb)," or Latin *guberna* "rudder" beside Greek κυβερνάω "steer," and the same voicing may have occurred during the transmission of the term to Greece. As for the geminate *l*, we may again reckon with the vagaries of borrowing or influence from other word.[4] A variety of other etymologies of Greek γάλλος have been proposed, however. Lane (1996) has advocated the derivation of γάλλος from the name of the Gaulish tribes who occupied parts of Phrygia in the third century BC, while Puhvel (*HED* 2, 414) has proposed that the word is native Phrygian and related to Greek κόλος, "docked," referring to the self-mutilation practiced by the galloi.

Evidence for a historical continuity of tradition between the institutions of the GALA and the gallos would strengthen the case for Burkert's association of the two, whether or not the Sumerian word is the ultimate source of the Greek word. The local cults of Anatolia provide an obvious means of transmission of the institution of the GALA from Mesopotamia of the third and second millennium to Phrygia of first millennium, and thence to Greece. Roller notes the paucity of evidence for eunuch priests resembling the galloi in Iron Age Phrygia, with the possible exception of a figurine from Bayandir (1996, 105). She also disputes a Phrygian origin for the drum that formed an essential part of the later Hellenistic and Roman conception of Cybele (1996, 148): "the tympanon was a Greek addition to the Meter iconography.... Thus the Greek iconography of Meter/Kybele presented a goddess who had departed quite far from her Anatolian origins.... And one key symbol, the tympanon, had acquired a prominence that it did not have in the Anatolian tradition."

Textual evidence, however, suggests a cultic continuity from the Hittites and Luwians of the Bronze Age to the Phrygians of the Iron Age and thence to the Hellenistic world. Several scholars have remarked on one cultic practice shared by Bronze Age Anatolia and the later cult of Cybele, namely, the distinctive ritual gesture of drinking from a musical instrument (Polvani 1988, 173; *HED* 3, 359). Clement of Alexandria preserves the *symbolon* of the mysteries of Cybele (*Protrep.* II): ἐκ τυμπάνου ἔφαγον· ἐκ κυμβάλου ἔπιον· ἐκερνοφόρησα· ὑπὸ τὸν παστὸν ὑπέδυν "I ate from the *tympanon*-drum, I drank from the cymbal, I carried the sacred dish, I went behind the curtain of the nuptial bed." Firmicus Maternus (*De err. prof. rel.* 18.1) transmits another version of the same formula as spoken by the initiates of Attis.

A strikingly similar ritual practice is described in the group of Hittite and Luwian texts edited by Starke (1985, 294–353) under the rubric of the "Kult des Pantheons von Ištanuwa" and partially translated by Güterbock (1995). Istanuwa is located in the Lower Land, in south-central Anatolia. The festivals associated with the city involve the participation of group of people called the Men of Lallupiya, and a musical instrument called the *ḫuḫupal*-instrument occupies a central place in this cult. The word *ḫuḫupal* has been adduced as a possible relative of Greek κύμβαλον "cymbal," an instrument that played a large role in the worship of Cybele (*HED* 3, 359). Güterbock (1995, 71), however, interprets the *ḫuḫupal* as a drum of some sort, rather than a metallic cymbal.

Before they begin to drink from the *ḫuḫupal*, the Men of Lallupiya first beat on the instrument. They then pour *marnuan*-beer into the *ḫuḫupal*, and the *marnuan* flows out into another *ḫuḫupal.* They begin the ritual drinking (*KUB* 25.37 i + *KUB* 51.9 obv., translation following Güterbock 1995, 66): [*m*]*aḫḫan=ma=kan* ^{GIŠ}*ḫuḫupal IŠTU* GEŠTIN *šunnanz*[i] *n=at=kan ḫantezzi palši* ^{LÚ}SAGI.A=*pat waršuli arḫa ekuzi* LÚ.MEŠ ^{URU}*Lallupiya=ma kiššan =*⸢*iš*⸣*ḫamiškiuan* ⸢*tian*⸣z[*i w*]*īntar wīntar taruwaliy*[*a*]*n wīntar* ⸢*nu kuitman ak*⸣ *kuškanzi kuitman a*[*kuan*]*na ḫūmanteš* ⸢*irḫānzi*⸣ *išḫamiškan=ma apā*[*t*] SÌR [*n*]=*at išhamiyauanzi* EGIR=⸢*pa*⸣ *w*[*aḫnu*]*škanzi* "When they fill the *ḫuḫupal* with wine, the first time, only the cupbearer drinks it up, sniffing. The Men of Lallupiya sing as follows, *wīntar, wīntar taruwiliyan wīntar*, while they drink, and while they finish drinking, that song is sung. They reply(??) singing." The cupbearer and the others then continue to drink from the *ḫuḫupal*. Surely this is the Anatolian rite antecedent to those carried out in honor of the Phrygian goddess Cybele later in the Roman world.

However, a curious incident immediately follows, another singular detail linking the cult of Istanuwa to that of Cybele a thousand years later. The cupbearer offers the *ḫuḫupal* to the head of the Men of Lallupiya, and he sings like a woman (KUB 25.37 i 41′ + KUB 35.131 i 1′ff. trans. after Güterbock 1995, 66): *[n]=ašta maḫḫan* ^{GIŠ}*ḫuḫupal* ^{LÚ}SAG[I.A ... *n]=at šunnai=pat šanḫazi=ma=at=k[an? UL Š]A* LÚ.MEŠ ^{URU}*Lallupiya kuiš* LÚ.GAL-*ŠU[NU nu]* ⸢*a*⸣*pēdani pāi nu=šši* GIM-*an* L[Ú ...] *šūw[a]n[n]a(?) menaḫḫanda ēpzi [nu=šši men]aḫ[ḫanda Q]A-TAM-MA* MUNUS-*nili i[šḫamāi]* "When the cupbearer ... the *ḫuḫupal*, he just fills it, but [does not] wipe it out.... He gives it to him who is the head of the men of Lallupiya. When a man of Lallupiya holds out to him [...] and a full one, he s[ings] opposite [him] like a woman in the same way." Güterbock's restoration of the verb *i[šḫamāi]* here is supported by a somewhat similar procedure found later in the festival (*KUB* 25.37 iii) that does not involve "singing like a woman." Occurring as part of a festival that otherwise resembles of the rites of Cybele, this incident of transgendered behavior (MUNUS-*nili išḫamāi*), suggests the existence of cultic functionaries who may have developed into the galloi of Hellenistic and Roman times.

A third detail suggests continuity between the cult of Istanuwa and the later cult of Cybele. The Sahiriya is the only river-deity to be mentioned in the festivals of Istanuwa (*KUB* 35.135 iv 14′–17′): "Then the king and queen, sitting, drink to the Storm-god of Istanuwa, Kinaliya, Gurnuwala, Maliya of the horn, the Hurrian Inar, and the River Sahiriya three times." Forlanini (1987, 115 note 23) has identified the Sahiriya with the Sangarios (modern Sakarya) in western Anatolia and proposed that Istanuwa may have been situated near Gordion. We may add that in the myths of Cybele, the Sangarios plays a significant role. The Sangarios is the father of Attis's mother according to the accounts of Pausanias (VII, 17) and Arnobius (*Adv. nat.* 5.6). According to Ovid (*Fasti*, 4.229), on the other hand, Attis is unfaithful to Cybele with a nymph named Sangaritis. Among the other deities toasted in this list of gods, a deity called *ḫurlaš* ^{d}*Inar*, "the Hurrian Inara," is otherwise unknown, as noted by Kammenhuber (1976, 73), and it remains unclear why a Hurrian version of the goddess Inara should appear in this Luwian context. However, we may note that both Cybele and the Hittite goddess Inara are known for their attachment to mortal lovers, Cybele to Attis and Inara to Hupasiya – attachments that have unfortunate consequences in Attis' case and probably also in Hupasiya's.

A further link between the cult of the Istanuwian Pantheon and the cult of Cybele is suggested by an incident of ritual bloodletting (*KUB* 53.15 i 13′ff + *KUB* 41.15 i(!) 3′ff, lines 13′–24′ translated by Beckman 1985, 143).

13′ [... *aku]wanna* 3-*ŠU irḫāizzi nu* ^{LÚ}A.ZU-*aš* 1 *ḫuḫupalli*
14′ [-*a]z dāi nu walḫannai* DINGIR.MEŠ-*ašš=a* SÌR.ḪI.A-*uš*
15′ [*išḫa]miškizzi* ^{URU}*Ištanumnili*

16′ [2 ^{URUDU}*š]epikušteš n=aš=šan šuppiyanti* NINDA.KAŠ
17′ [*dā]i nu* 1 LÚ *karapzi* ^{LÚ}A.ZU-[*aš*]*š=a šarā tizzi tā* GUNNI
18′ 4-*ŠU ḫūyanzi* ^{GIŠ}*ḫuḫupal walḫannai išḫamiškizzi=ya*

19′ *mān* 4-*ŠU ḫūyanzi nu=za* ^{LÚ}A.ZU-*aš* 2 ^{URUDU}*šepikuštuš dāi*
20′ *nu=za=kan ḫatta nu=za namma* ^{GIŠ}*ḫuḫupalli dāi nu* ^{GIŠ}BANŠUR-*aš piran*

21′ *tar-uk*$^{\text{!}}$*-zi mān* 3-*ŠU wē[ḫz]i n=uš=z=ašta arḫa* SUD-*ya nu* GEŠTIN(!) NAG-*zi*
22′ *piraššet kuiēš ašanzi nu-uk(!)-kán apušš=a ḫatta kuiš*
23′ *aniyaēzzi n=an=kan ḫatta kuiš=za MIMMA IDU*
24′ [*nu*] *ANA* DINGIR-*LIM tezzi*

> ... makes the rounds 3 times ... The "physician"... one *ḫuḫupal*-instrument. He beats on it and sings the songs of the gods – in the manner of the city of Istanuwa.
>
> [Two copper] pins – they are stuck into the holy bread (and) beer (portion[?]). He [pla]ces (them) on the table. One man lifts (it – the portion[?]), and the "physician" steps up. Then they run around the hearth four times striking the *ḫ*-instrument and singing continually.
>
> When they (have) run around four times, the "physician" takes the two copper pins and pierces himself. He takes the *ḫ*-instrument again and dances before the table. When he spins three times, then he pulls them (the pins) out and drinks (some) wine. Whoever are seated before him, them he pierces – whoever participates, him he pierces! Whoever knows something tells it to the deity...

We may compare this incident with the ecstatic dancing and bloodletting that formed a well-known part of the cultic performances of the galloi in Rome (Graillot 1912, 126, n. 4). Many Romans found this behavior disturbing and senseless, as exemplified by the following vivid lines of Propertius (2.22a, 5–16): *cur aliquis sacris laniat sua bracchia cultris / et Phrygis insanos caeditur ad numeros?* "Why does anyone lacerate his own arms with sacred knives. And why is he wounded to the mad measures of a Phrygian (musician)?"

Not only do the Istanuwian festivals hold evidence for the survival of Bronze Age Anatolian elements in the cult and myth of Cybele, but they also resemble the cultic performances of the Mesopotamian GALA. Hutter offers an analysis, worth quoting at length, of the Istanuwian festivals based on the names of the songs recorded on the tablets:

> In the shelf list KUB 30.42 i 1 we read...: "First tablet. Song(s) of conciliation of the men of Istanuwa." The same we read in Luwian language in broken context in KUB 32.13 i 6–11: "I will conciliate, I will conciliate [...] they shall conciliate him, the gods [...], the pure ones [...] they shall conciliate him [...] above the Sun-god [...]." It is neither clear who is the one to be conciliated nor why this has become necessary, but some general rite of conciliation or pacifying is possible within a festival.
>
> Another aspect of one of the purposes of the festival we see in KBo 4.11 when we read the colophon: "They sing the songs of thunder".... [I]f we combine "the songs of thunder" with the "songs of conciliation" we can understand a little bit more concretely the reason for the festival: it is celebrated (annually) as a reconciliation of the people of Istanuwa and Lallupiya with their gods, removing all the "misdeeds" which might have caused the Storm-god's anger and thus also his thunder. (2003, 241)

When we consider Hutter's analysis together with the cultic incident of singing like a woman (MUNUS-*nili išhamāi*), a possible ritual "missing link" between the GALA and the gallos emerges in the Men of Lallupiya. The GALA sings a genre of compositions that can aptly be characterized as "songs of thunder" and "songs of soothing": the BALAG, often translated "lamentation." The BALAGs are composed in emesal, suspected of being the female genderlect of Sumerian, which recalls the head of the Men of Lallupiya singing "like a woman." Black summarizes the typical contents of the BALAG as follows: "praise, or self-praise of the deity ... all-powerful, violent and irrational gods whose purpose cannot be divined, laments over the destruction, by an unknown enemy, of now deserted temples, haunted buildings, and ruin mounds ... the enemy, the sheepfold, the cowpen, the flood, the storm, abandonment, humiliation, lamentation, nostalgia...." (1991, 25–26).

The BALAG-compositions can be considered "songs of thunder" in several respects. The name of the Mesopotamian genre is taken from the BALAG-drum, and the sound of drums is likened to thunder in Sumerian literature (Curse of Akkad ll. 200–201, ed. Cooper 1983, translation partly following Renger 1969, 190): balağ imin-e an-úr gub-ba-gim ki mu-un-ši-ib-úš ùb me-zé li-li-iš [d]Iškur-gim šà-ba mu-na-an-tuk "(The people of Akkad) put in place seven BALAG drums, as if they stood at heaven's base and played ub, meze, and lilis-drums loudly like Iškur [the Storm-god] among them for him (Enlil)." A cultic drum plays a large role both in the performances of the GALA and in the Istanuwian festivals. Moreover, the storm, considered as the manifestation of the power of the gods, is a ubiquitous motif of BALAG-incantations, as illustrated by a litany from the BALAG *Immal Gudede* "The Lowing Cow" (translated by Cohen 1988, 2, 625): "Storm, destructive heart of Enlil! Furious storm killing people.... Storm which has no regard for a mother! Storm which has no regard for a father! Storm which has no regard for a spouse! Storm which has no regard for a child!"

The BALAG can also be identified as "songs of soothing," comparable to those identified by the Hittites as *li-la-u-wa-aš* SÌR. The compositions often contain a section in which forms of the Sumerian word *ḫun*, "soothe, pacify" are reiterated as part of an attempt to soothe the deity. The long lamentation *Elum Gusun* "Honored One, Wild Ox" offers a typical example (lines 164 and 167–169, ed. and trans. Cohen 1988, 1, 280, 295, boldface mine):

164 balag dìm-me-er mu-lu šùd-da ^{d}Mu-ul-[líl-šè mu]-
...
167 me-en-dè ki-e-šè a-ra-zu-a mu-un-re_7-en-dè-en ^{d}Mu-[ul-líl-še mu]-
168 ù-mu-un **šà-ab ḫun-e-da** in-gá-re_7-dè-en ^{d}Mu-[ul-líl-še mu]-
169 **šà-ab ḫun-gá bar ḫun-gá-da** in-gá-re_7-dè-en ^{d}Mu-[ul-líl-še mu]-

---

164 With lamentations god and man going in prayer going to Enlil.
...
167 We go to that place in prayer. We go to Enlil.
168 We go **to calm the heart** of the lord. We go to Enlil.
169 We go **to calm the heart**, **to calm the liver**. We go to Enlil.

Another BALAG relates a myth in which Enki fashions the GALA specifically to soothe Inanna (BM 29616, ed. Kramer 1981, 3–5, boldface mine):

21 **gala-mu-lu-ír-šà-ḫun-e** da(?)-ni(?)- ?- ? mu-na-an-dím
22 ír-šà-ne-$ša_4$-i-si-iš-ma-al-la-ni ? ? [si] bí-ni-sá
23 ^{kuš}ub-li-li-ès-mùš-àm-di-da-ni šu-ni-šè bí-in-mar
24 ^{d}am-an-ki-ke_4 kù-ga-ša-an-na-ra mu-lu da(?) MEŠ(?) mu-ši-in-gi_4
25 nin-da(?) **šà-zu ḫa-im-ḫun-e** ^{giš}gu-zu-za tùš-ù

---

21 He fashioned for her **the *gala*, him of the heart-soothing laments**...
22 He arranged his mournful laments of supplication...
23 He placed the *aḫulap*-uttering *ub* and *lilis* (drums) in his hand.
24 Enki sent him who... to holy Inanna:
25 "Oh queen, **may your heart be soothed**, seat yourself on your throne"

In the Ištanuwian festivals, we may compare the Luwian "song of soothing" that repeats forms of the verb *lila-* "soothe, pacify, conciliate" (*KUB* 32.13 i 6–11, translated by Hutter above): *[li-]⸢la⸣-i-lu li-la-i-lu* [... *l]i-la-an-du-an* DINGI[R^{MEŠ}...]⸢*ku*⸣*-um-ma-i-in-zi* ⸢*a*⸣[...] *wa-ti-in-az-ḫa* ⸢*a*⸣-×[...] *li-la-an-du-an* [...] *šar-ra* ^{d}UTU-*w*[*a* ...].

The Mesopotamian BALAG and ÉR.$ŠEM_5$.MA also invoke the theme of the destruction of the god's temple, and these genres show certain similarities with the Mesopotamian city laments. This in turn suggests another connection with the repertoire of Istanuwa and Lallupiya. Among the incipits of the Songs of Thunder collected on *KBo* 4.11, there is a sentence that Watkins (1986, 58–60) has interpreted as the beginning of a Luwian poem about the city later known as Troy, a "Wilusiad": EGIR-*ŠU* ^{d}*Šuwašunan ekuzi aḫḫ=ata=ta alati auienta wilušati* "Afterwards he drinks to Šuwašuna. [He says in Luwian:] 'When they came from steep Wilusa...'." Watkins compares the opening line and refrain of the Old Welsh poem *Y Gododdin,* which begins *Gwyr a aeth Gatraeth,* "Men who went to Catraeth." Just as the Welsh poem describes a disastrous military defeat and laments the loss of great warriors, we may suggest that the song for Suwasuna functions as a "Lament over Wilusa," an Anatolian echo of the city laments of Mesopotamia, which exalt the power of the gods. The Men of Lallupiya address Suwasuna with the song appropriate to him, just as the GALA addresses the deity with the appropriate BALAG-lamentation and ÉR.ŠEM$_5$.MA about the destruction of the city and the deity's temple.

Thus we observe several striking similarities between the GALA and certain cultic personnel among the Men of Lallupiya, and these suggest either the regional diffusion of a cultic institution of Mesopotamian origin or the inheritance of a transgendered institution developed in common within the Near Eastern region. The practices carried out by the Men of Lallupiya may have survived into the Iron Age to form a characteristic part of the developing cult of the Mother Goddess in western Anatolia. These cultic practices may then have become typical of the worship of Cybele among the galloi as her cult expanded to Greece and Rome, preserving a Bronze Age heritage into Hellenistic times and beyond.

NOTES

1 I would like to thank Paul-Alain Beaulieu, Yoram Cohen, Piotr Steinkeller, and Calvert Watkins for discussing with me various aspects of the ideas presented herein. All errors remain my own.

2 For full documentation of the cult of Cybele, the reader is referred to the magisterial works of Graillot (1912) and Roller (1999).

3 Black (1991, 28 n. 39) presents evidence for the interpretation of the Mesopotamian BALAG-instrument as a drum, rather than a harp.

4 We should also note that the Sumerogram GALA was used by the Hittites to write the their word *ḫalli(ya)ri-*, a word referring to a kind of cultic singer and of unknown etymology (Puhvel *HED* 3, 30). I will not speculate if the [LÚ]*ḫalliyari* had a role in the transmission of the institution of the GALA to Anatolia.

REFERENCES

Alster, B. (1997) *Proverbs of Ancient Sumer: The World's Earliest Proverb Collection.* 2 vols. Bethesda, CDL.

Beckman, G. (1985) Review of KUB LIII. *Bibliotheca Orientalis* 42, 142–44.

Black, J. A. (1991) Emesal Cult Songs and Prayers. *Aula Orientalis* 9, 23–36.

Bottéro, J. and Petschow, H. (1972) Homosexualität. *Reallexikon der Assyriologie* 4, 459–68.

Burkert, W. (1979) *Structure and History in Greek Mythology*. Berkeley and Los Angeles, University of California.

Cohen, M. E. (1988) *The Canonical Lamentations of Ancient Mesopotamia.* Potomac, MD, Capital Decisions.

Cooper, J. (1983) *The Curse of Agade.* Baltimore, MD, Johns Hopkins University.

Forlanini, M. (1987) Toponymie antique d'origine hattie? *Hethitica* 8, 105–22.

Gordon, E. I. (1959) *Sumerian Proverbs: Glimpses of Everyday Life in Ancient Mesopotamia.* Philadelphia, University Museum, University of Pennsylvania.

Gow, A. S. F. and Page, D. L. (1965) *The Greek Anthology: Hellenistic Epigrams.* Cambridge, Cambridge University.

Graillot, H. (1912) Le Culte de Cybèle, mère des dieux, à Rome et dans l'empire romaine. Paris, Fontemoing.

Güterbock, H. (1995) Reflections on the Musical Instruments *arkammi, galgalturi*, and *ḫuḫupal* in Hittite. In *Studio historiae ardens: Ancient Near Eastern Studies Presented to Philo H. J. Houwink ten Cate on the Occasion of his 65th Birthday*, 57–72. Leiden, Nederlands Historisch-Archaeologisch Instituut te Istanbul.

HED. Puhvel, J. (1984–) *Hittite Etymological Dictionary*. Trends in Linguistics. Documentation 1, 5, 14, 18, 22. Berlin, de Gruyter.

Henshaw, R. A. (1993) *Female and Male: The Cultic Personnel: The Bible and the Rest of the Ancient Near East.* Princeton Theological Monograph Series 31. Allison Park, PA, Pickwick Publications.

Hutter, M. (2003) Aspects of Luwian Religion. In H. Craig Melchert (ed.) *The Luwians*, 211–81. Leiden, Brill.

Kammerhuber, A. (1976) Die hethitische Göttin Inar. *Zeitschrift für Assyriologie* 66, 68–88.

Kramer, S. N. (1981) BM 29616: The Fashioning of the Gala. *Acta Sumerologica* 3, 1–11.

Lancellotti, M. G. (2002) *Attis Between Myth and History: King, Priest and God.* Religions in the Graeco-Roman World 149. Leiden, Brill.

Lane, E. N. (1996) The Name of Cybele's Priests the "Galloi." In E. N. Lane (ed.) *Cybele, Attis, and Related Cults: Essays in Memory of M. J. Vermaseren*, 117–34. Leiden, Brill.

Polvani, A. M. (1988) Appunti per una storia della musica cultuale ittita: lo strumento huhupal. *Hethitica* 9, 171–79.

Renger, J. (1969) Untersuchung zum Priestertum der altbabylonischen Zeit. 2. Teil. *Zeitschrift für Assyriologie* 39, 104–30.

Roller, L. E. (1999) *In Search of God the Mother: The Cult of Anatolian Cybele*. Berkeley and Los Angeles, University of California.

Roscoe, W. (1996) Priests of the Goddess: Gender Transgression in Ancient Religion. *History of Religions* 35, 195–230.

Schretter, M. K. (1990) *Emesal-Studien: Sprach- und Literaturgeschichtliche Untersuchungen zur sogenannten Frauensprache des Sumerischen*. Innsbrucker Beiträge zur Sprachwissenschaft Innsbruck 69. Innsbruck, Institut für Sprachwissenschaft der Universität Innsbruck.

Starke, F. (1985) *Die keilschrift-luwischen Texte in Umschrift*, StBoT 30. Wiesbaden, Harrassowitz.

Watkins, C. (1986) The Language of the Trojans. In M. Mellink (ed.) *Troy and the Trojan War*, 45–62. Bryn Mawr, Bryn Mawr University.

Whittaker, G. (2002) Linguistic Anthropology and the Study of Emesal as (a) Women's Language. In S. Parpola and R. M. Whiting (eds.) *Sex and Gender in the Ancient Near East*, 633–34. CRRAI 2001. Helsinki, Neo-Assyrian Text Corpus Project.

19

PATTERNS OF ELITE INTERACTION: ANIMAL-HEADED VESSELS IN ANATOLIA IN THE EIGHTH AND SEVENTH CENTURIES BC

Susanne Ebbinghaus

Written sources provide sparse but valuable information about Phrygian contacts with other peoples east and west. From Assyrian cuneiform documents of the last decades of the eighth century BC King Mita of Mushki, known to the Greeks as Midas, emerges as a troublemaker on the northwestern fringes of the Neo-Assyrian Empire, engaging in alliances with Urartu and the Neo-Hittite kingdoms. The defeat and subsequent integration into the Assyrian Empire of several independent principalities in southeast Anatolia and North Syria, and advances of the Assyrian governor of Cilicia into Phrygian territory seem to have persuaded Midas to make conciliatory moves and improve his diplomatic relations with the Neo-Assyrian Empire (Muscarella 1989, 149–50; Mellink 1991, 622–24; Hawkins 1994; Wittke 2004, 48–51, 106–30). Close connections between Phrygia and the kingdom of Tuwana, later Tyana, to the north of the Cilician Gates are attested by the finds of Phrygian alphabetic inscriptions in the area (Mellink 1991, 625–26). Looking west, contacts between Greeks and Phrygians in this time period are of a more legendary nature. Herodotos (*Hist.* 1.14.2–3) reports that King Midas sent his throne to Delphi, the first foreigner to make a dedication at a Greek sanctuary. Midas is also said to have married a woman from Aeolian Cyme (Heraclides Lembus 37 Dilts; Pollux 9.83).

Looking for manifestations of these contacts in the material record, archaeologists have identified Near Eastern imports and influences in Phrygia, and Phrygian as well as Phrygian-inspired objects in Greece (Sams 1993; Muscarella 1989). Somewhat puzzling is the apparent lack of Greek material at Phrygian sites; for example, only very little pottery of the Greek Geometric period has been excavated at Gordion (DeVries 2005, 37–43, figs. 4–3, 4–6; Kerschner 2005, 122–23, pl. 10, 1). Foremost indicators for Phrygian-Greek contacts are the bronze belts and fibulae of Phrygian type found in the Greek cities of Asia Minor. Recent excavations at Ephesos and Miletos have brought to light many belts and fibulae made by local Ionian workshops in imitation of Phrygian prototypes (Donder 2002; Klebinder 2002). Actual imports from Phrygia that may have reached the west before the end of the eighth century include an elaborate bronze fibula with a separately made lock plate from the sanctuary of Hera on Samos (Jantzen 1972, 48–49 B 1513, pl. 44; Ebbinghaus 2006, 208–9, fig. 6).[1] This object finds close parallels among the fibulae from the so-called Midas Mound Tumulus at Gordion (Young 1981, 156–162, pls. 76–77). A similar fibula is worn by Warpalawas, king of Tuwana, on the rock relief at İvriz, a further indication of this king's alliance with Phrygia (Caner 1983, 173–74, pls. C, 67).

The present paper focuses on animal-headed vessels in the form of beakers and buckets (or *situlae*) as one facet of the contacts between Anatolia and the Near East in the eighth and seventh centuries. It is argued that this class of material provides tangible evidence for the inclusion of the Phrygian elite and perhaps also some Greeks from Asia Minor into a network of diplomatic exchanges centered on the Neo-Assyrian Empire. In a paper delivered at the Assyriology Congress in Istanbul in 1987, Oscar Muscarella drew attention to some of the questions raised by the two animal-headed *situlae* from Gordion (Muscarella 1998). In the following, these issues are addressed in a broader context.

1. BUCKETS AND BEAKERS FROM GORDION AND SAMOS

Two bronze *situlae* with the heads of a lion and a ram, respectively, have come to light in the Midas Mound Tumulus at Gordion (figs. 1, 2; Young 1981, 121–23, pls. III–IV, 62–63; Öztürk 1992, 142–43, 214 nos. 121–22).[2] This royal tomb is now dated to ca. 740, which means that rather than for the historic Midas/Mita, it was built for one of his predecessors (DeVries et al. 2003). The animal-headed vessels are sizeable containers hammered of thin bronze sheet and equipped with an inner liner, as was common practice for such vessels in the Neo-Assyrian period. Their heads are carefully modeled and the eyes inlaid.

Very similar vessels are depicted on the reliefs of the palace that the Assyrian king Sargon II (721–705 BC) built for himself at his new capital city Dur-Sharrukin, modern Khorsabad, in the last decades of the eighth century. Here, lion-headed *situlae* occurred both in procession scenes and in the context of a banquet (Botta and Flandin 1849, pl. 162; Albenda 1986, pl. 144). The latter representation points to one, and perhaps the most basic, function of such buckets. They were used to draw liquid from a cauldron, and to distribute it among the participants of the banquet (fig. 3; Botta and Flandin 1849, pl. 76; Albenda 1986, pl. 123). The lion's head of the *situla* from Gordion appears to be a three-dimensional version of the lion's heads depicted on the reliefs; indeed, the stylization of the Gordion head fits well into the canon of Assyrian art. Because of the impact of Neo-Assyrian culture on neighboring regions, however, it cannot be excluded that the vessel was made outside of Mesopotamia, for example in northern Syria, the place of origin of two cauldrons with siren attachments deposited in the same tumulus (Young 1981, 104–10, pls. 51–57).[3] The ram-headed *situla* from Gordion has the ears placed behind the horns in a highly idiosyncratic fashion, but it is otherwise closely related to ram-headed vessels of terracotta found at Assyrian sites, including Ashur, Nineveh and Nimrud (ancient Kalhu; Curtis 2000, 195–99, figs. 1–20).

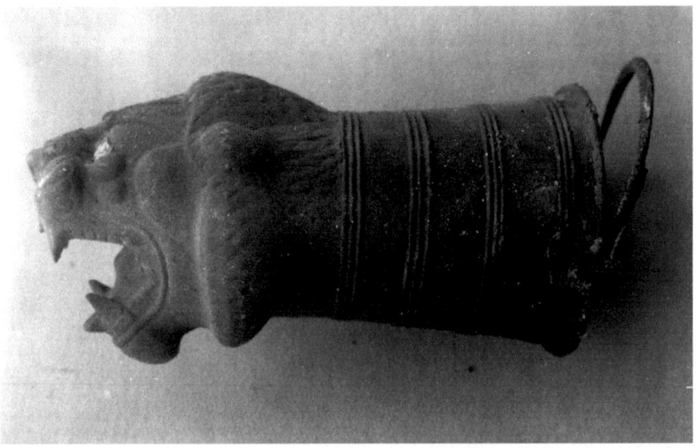

Fig. 1. Lion-headed *situla* from the Midas Mound Tumulus. Photo courtesy of Gordion Archives.

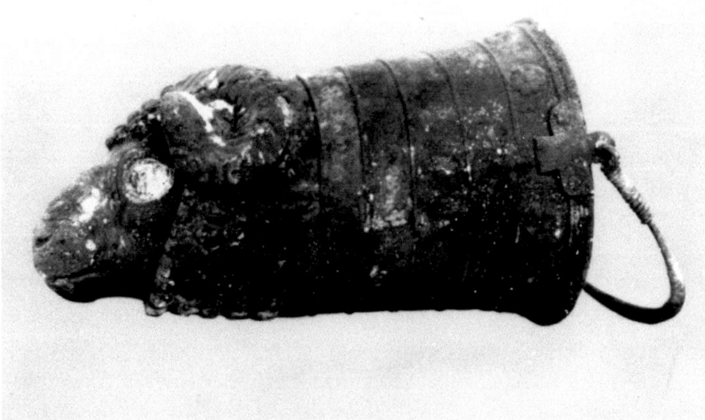

Fig. 2. Ram-headed *situla* from the Midas Mound Tumulus. Photo courtesy of Gordion Archives.

The circumstances of their deposition indicate that the function of the two *situlae* from the Midas Mound Tumulus was basically the same as that of the lion-headed buckets featured in the Assyrian court banquets. Analysis of organic residues from the interior of the *situlae* revealed that they had contained a mixed fermented beverage of grape wine, barley beer and honey mead – a potent potion likely prepared in the large cauldrons that were present in the burial chamber (McGovern 2003, 279–98). In addition, the impressive banqueting set included five pairs of small cauldrons with ring and bucket handles, several jugs, two ladles and more than one hundred drinking bowls, all of bronze (Young 1981, 110–47, pls. 58–73). The two *situlae* were recovered wrapped in textile behind one of two wooden serving stands; they were probably suspended in linen bags from nails in the wall above (Young 1981, 101, 121, fig. 66, pl. 44c). The stands, whose fronts were covered with intricate inlay, were thought to be screens by the excavator (Young 1981, 176–81, pl. 44a–b), but each had a top shelf with three openings for the insertion of vessels. The small cauldrons and ladles were found nearby. Elizabeth Simpson has suggested that "the situlas may also have been used with the screens, perhaps as dippers to fill the small cauldrons, from the three large cauldrons found alongside the tomb's south wall" (Simpson and Payton 1986, 45–46). On the eastern periphery of the Neo-Assyrian Empire, the seventh- or early sixth-century bronze bowl from the Neo-Elamite tomb at Arjan in western Iran depicts two ram-headed vessels set in a pot stand – albeit of a different type (Majidzadeh 1992, 136, fig. 1; Alvarez-Mon 2004, 209–211, fig. 3).

To the west of Phrygia, two animal-headed containers of bronze have been excavated in the sanctuary of Hera on the Greek island of Samos. The smaller, damaged vessel is a *situla* with the head of a calf, which used to be mistaken for a bull but may be recognized by its budding horns (fig. 4; Jantzen 1972, 71 B 275, pl. 73).[4] It is of lesser size and quality than the specimens from Gordion, and was probably manufactured somewhere on the periphery of the Assyrian Empire, not least because a calf is not yet attested for animal-headed vessels from Assyria (Curtis 2000, 201). The larger vessel from Samos preserves no traces of a handle,

Fig. 3. Khorsabad, Room II. Servants with lion-headed *situlae*. Botta and Flandin (1849, pl. 76).

and is best classified as a cup or beaker. Instead of terminating in a simple animal's head, it is janiform, with the upper part of a lion's head embossed on opposite sides (Kyrieleis 1986, 189, pl. IIc).[5] The facial features of the lions are coarsely rendered and bear some similarity to Neo-Hittite sculpture. Both vessels from Samos conform to standard Neo-Assyrian production techniques; they are hammered of sheet metal and equipped with an inner liner.

The beaker and *situla* recovered in the sanctuary of Hera were brought there as votive offerings, either by a Greek or by a foreigner. They provide no indication of any practical use they may have fulfilled within the sanctuary, or of the purpose they might have served in a Greek context prior to their dedication. The example of somewhat later, locally produced animal-headed vessels, however, allows us to draw some conclusions that may be relevant also for the earlier period. The most important piece of evidence is a bull- or cow-headed bronze beaker dated to ca. 600 BC, which follows a new bent type of Iranian origin (further discussed by Ebbinghaus 2006, 215–16, fig. 12). Both the style of the animal's head and the fact that the vessel is single-walled and cast suggest that it is a product of local Samian workshops. It is inscribed *chaire o hiereu* ("cheers, oh Priest!"), which implies that it served as a drinking cup on the occasion of ritual banquets, an integral part of the cult of Samian Hera. May we infer similar uses for the calf's head *situla* and the lion-faced beaker?

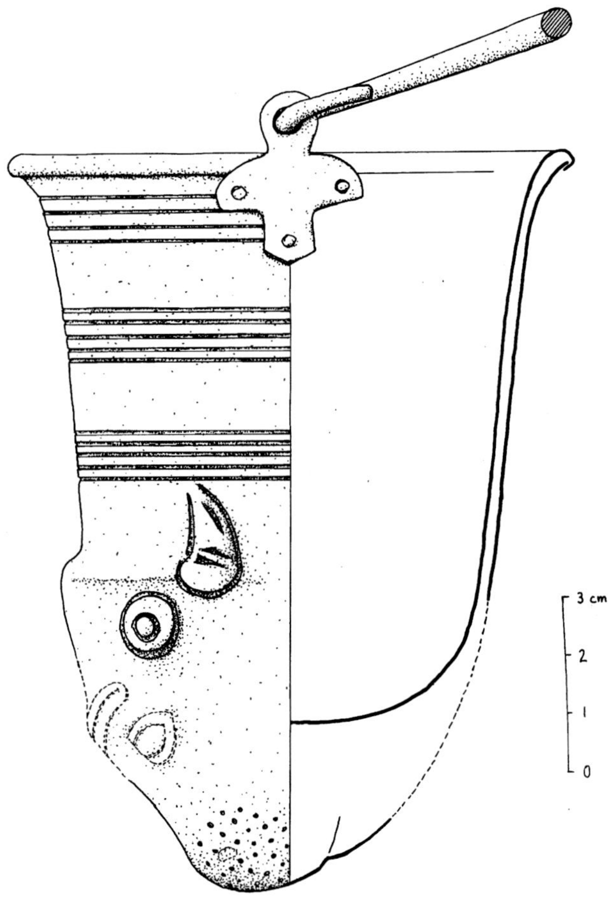

Fig. 4. Calf-headed *situla* from the sanctuary of Hera on Samos. Drawing by author.

Situlae and beakers with the heads of rams, gazelles and lions are also known from northern Syria, Urartu and western Iran (Tuchelt 1962, 57–64, pls. 7–9; Calmeyer 1979; Muscarella 1988, 24–26 no. 5; Curtis 2000). The finds from these regions include examples of terracotta. This indicates that their use reflected longer-standing traditions and was not restricted to elite contexts, unlike at Gordion, Samos and Veii in Etruria, where another lion-headed bronze vessel of eastern origin was found (Sciacca 2003). Which factors promoted the wide diffusion of animal-headed vessels during the Neo-Assyrian period, including their spread to more distant lands? The following sections aim to answer this question.

2. IN SARGON'S PALACE

The contexts in which animal-headed containers are depicted on the walls of Sargon's palace at Khorsabad are quite informative. The reliefs preserve two representations of banquets; in both, lion-headed cups and *situlae* constitute the main elements of the drinking set. The banquet in Room II is most probably a victory feast celebrating Sargon's campaign in the east, illustrated in the frieze in fig. 3 (Botta and Flandin 1849, pls. 52, 57–67, 76; Albenda 1986, 81–82, pls. 110, 113, 116–123; Stronach 1995, 180–85, fig. 12.3). The banquet in Room VII is shown above and may be understood as following upon the excursion of the king and his retinue in a royal park (Botta and Flandin 1848, 108–14; Albenda 1986, 80–81, 104–5, pls. 85–90). It seems that the relevant scenes represented feasts for court and military officials hosted by the king – who apparently did not participate – on two different occasions. Accordingly, each feast is likely to have highlighted a different aspect of Sargon's kingship, with lion-headed vessels felt to be appropriate for both. The pictorial record is complemented by written documents from the Assyrian court. These attest that lion-headed vessels could be employed as drinking cups at banquets for foreign tributaries as well as in religious rituals; they could even hold the drink provided by the king for a god (Deller 1985, 328–34, 344; Stronach 1995, 182).

A letter mentions a lion-headed silver vessel that was sent to the Assyrian king, probably Sargon II, together with other items of precious metal that may have constituted gift, tribute or booty (Deller 1985, 331). The reliefs at Khorsabad confirm the secondary function of animal-headed containers as items of exchange. On Facades L and N and in Room VI, lion-headed *situlae* are among the objects presented to the king by Assyrian attendants and foreign tributaries (Botta and Flandin 1849, pls. 10–11, 16, 30, 103; Albenda 1986, 63–66, 71–73, pls. 16, 43, 47, 55, 66, figs. 35, 63, 85). The attendants carry vessels, furniture and chariot equipment, which might represent the contributions of Assyrian provincial governors, in analogy to the tribute brought by the representatives of vassal states (Bär 1996, 229). In any case, the objects are highly appropriate as gifts to the king, since they consist of the essential furnishings of the royal court, and, on Facade N, more precisely the furnishings of the royal banquet. Besides lion-headed buckets, the vessels include a relatively large lion-headed beaker without handle, which was possibly destined for the use of the king himself (Deller 1985, pl. 30b). The lion's head as an emblematic finial recurs elsewhere on the reliefs, for example on jewelry, fly whisks and weapons, while furniture such as stools and tables incorporate lion's paws and, more rarely, heads (Botta and Flandin 1849, pls. 22–23, 159, 161; Albenda 1986, 93–95, pls. 50, 139, 143). This iconographic choice reflects the traditional notion of the lion as a prime symbol of royal power. Ashurnasirpal II (883–859 BC) and Ashurbanipal (668–627 BC) displayed royal prowess in the lion hunts carved on the walls of their palaces at Nimrud and Nineveh; the walls of Sargon's palace at Khorsabad were emblazoned with the figure of a hero grasping a lion (Magen 1986, 29–36, pls. 1–4; Albenda 1986, 52–53, 101–102, pls. 15, 17, figs. 7–8).

Two groups of foreign tributaries bring lion-headed *situlae* at Khorsabad. The tribute bearers on Sargon's reliefs are quite standardized in their dress and goods (Bär 1996, 243). Accordingly, their respective countries of origin are hard to identify – with one exception. At least one of the *situla*-carrying groups may be assumed to hail from Anatolia, most likely Phrygia, because of the large fibula of Phrygian type attached to the coat of one of its members (fig. 5; Botta and Flandin 1849, 106 *bis*; Albenda 1986, pl. 69; commented by Muscarella 1998, 150–52). If this identification is correct, it leaves us with the fairly puzzling scenario of members of the Phrygian elite bringing owls to Athens, as it were – that is animal-headed *situlae* to the Assyrian court, while they themselves used imported vessels of this type. In any case, the representation at Khorsabad does not imply a special connection between Phrygians and animal-headed buckets. Such *situlae* were also associated with tributaries from other lands, most prominently a Zagros people on the Assyrian-style bronze coffin allegedly from Ziwiye. The members of the relevant delegation carry city models, wine skins, animal horns and *situlae* with what appear to be the heads of a lion and a gazelle (Muscarella 1988, 342–49 no. 473).[6]

Proceeding under the assumption that Sargon's reliefs illustrated what actually happened – although as he cautions, that need not be the case – Oscar Muscarella (1998, 155–56) has wondered whether the Phrygians brought *situlae* to Sargon's court because "they gave the Assyrian king what he wanted and expected." Even if the reliefs do not depict real events, their iconography must have been plausible. Maybe no Phrygian ever presented a lion-headed *situla* to Sargon. From an Assyrian point of view, however, Phrygia seems to have belonged to the circle of states that acknowledged Assyria's superior power by sending a certain range

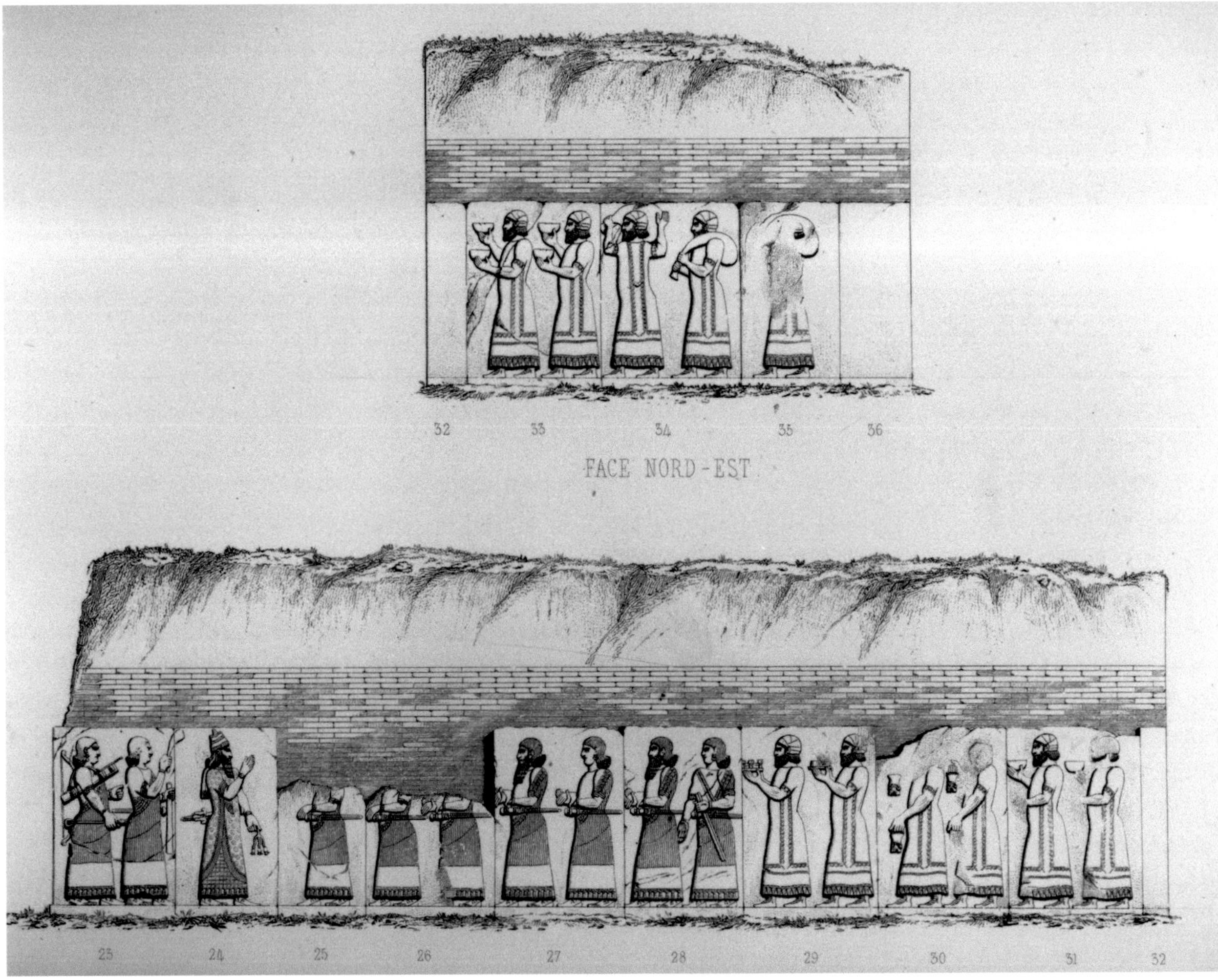

Fig. 5. Khorsabad, Room VI. Tributaries with lion-headed *situlae*. Botta and Flandin (1849, pl. 103).

of gifts to her king. Gifts and especially tribute often reflected local availability of raw materials and sought-after resources as well as local traditions of craftsmanship, but the overall impression conveyed by the offerings in the tribute scenes at Khorsabad, as later at Persepolis, is that of internationally acknowledged trappings of elite lifestyle. The wide diffusion among local elites of these items – witness the animal-headed *situlae* from Gordion – leaves no doubt that we are dealing with more than just artistic convention or lack of imagination on the part of the craftsmen responsible for the carving of the reliefs. In fact, animal-headed vessels were present not only at the court of Sargon II and one of Midas' predecessors, but at other royal courts, as well. The ram-headed vessels on the above-mentioned Neo-Elamite cup occur in the context of what appears to be a royal banquet (Alvarez-Mon 2004). A gazelle-headed vessel of bronze engraved with an Assyrian-style presentation scene, moreover, reinforces the conceptual link between animal-headed vessels and gift giving (Tuchelt 1962, 59 no. 12, pls. 8–9; Calmeyer 1979, 196 B4, fig. 3).

3. BRONZE AGE PRECEDENTS

There is good evidence from the Bronze Age for the use of animal-shaped vessels as standard gifts in diplomatic exchanges. As the information available for this period is comparatively rich, it is briefly reviewed in the following paragraphs, in order to render some depth to the scenario proposed for the Iron Age. Zoomorphic vessels were very much at home in Bronze Age Anatolia. Numerous terracotta vessels in the form of standing animals and animal's heads have come down to us from the Assyrian Colony period (Tuchelt 1962, 28–33, 46–49, pl. 3; Özgüç 2002). In the Old Hittite and Hittite Empire periods, the tradition of animal-shaped vessels standing on all fours continued with several pairs of large, bridled terracotta bulls from Boghazköy and elsewhere (Haas 1994, 534). Preserved metal vessels include the silver cups with the *protomai* of a stag and a bull formerly in the Norbert Schimmel collection (Muscarella 1974, nos. 123–24) and the bull-headed cups found with other metal vases near Kastamonu in the Black Sea area (Emre and Çınaroğlu 1993, 676–78, figs. 1–4, pls. 126–29).[7] In contrast to the animal-headed vessels of the Aegean, the Anatolian head and *protome* vessels did not have a second outlet. They were cups to be drunk over the rim rather than *rhyta* for the pouring of liquids.

The Minoan and Mycenaean *rhyta* in the form of an animal's head were basically zoomorphic funnels. This and in some cases also the findspots suggest that many served to pour libations in a sanctuary or funerary context (Tuchelt 1962, 36–45; Koehl 1981 and 2006; Petit 1984). The ritual function of their Anatolian counterparts emerges clearly from surviving texts. Hittite *BIBRI* are listed in inventories of cult equipment and were used by the royal couple to drink in honor of a deity, or perhaps literally to imbibe the deity associated with the particular animal (Tuchelt 1962, 49–55; Carruba 1967; Haas 1994, 520–23, 525–26, 530–38, figs. 100, 107–8, 110–11; Güterbock 1998). The bull-headed cups from the region of Kastamonu, for example, may have been used "to drink" the Storm God. An association with cult is also suggested by relevant finds from the Levant. In Ugarit, a lion-headed terracotta cup was dedicated to the god Reshef (Zevulun 1987, 96–98 no. 5c, fig. 9). At the same time, however, rulers from the same areas engaged in the exchange of animal-shaped vessels as diplomatic gifts.

The earliest evidence for such vessels circulating as diplomatic gifts between rulers in Syria, southern Anatolia, Mesopotamia and Iran comes from texts found at Old Babylonian Mari, which refer to gold and silver cups with the heads of bulls, calves, deer, gazelles, ibexes and lions (Dunham 1989). The Amarna Letters include a letter of the Hittite king Suppiluliuma I (ca. 1355–1320 BC) to the pharaoh, which records a stag and a ram *BIBRU* of silver among the greeting-gifts sent to Egypt (Moran 1992, EA 41, 39–43). Pictorial evidence for the exchange of zoomorphic vessels is provided by the wall-paintings in the tombs of officials of the 18th Dynasty at Egyptian Thebes. The tombs of Useramun, Mencheperresonb and Rechmire show Aegeans (*keftiu*) bringing bull-headed and bull-shaped vessels of various materials, as well as lion- and griffin-headed specimens of gold (Vercoutter 1956, 311–21, 357–39, pls. 37–41, 61; Wachsmann 1987, 55–61, pls. 26b, 27–29, 32, 34–37, 40–41, 55–58; Laboury 1990, 96–100 pl. 25; Dziobek 1994, 91–92, pls. 20–23, 92–93). Animal-headed vessels are also shown among tribute and booty from Syria (Wachsmann 1987, 57–59, pl. 53; Zevulun 1987, 98–99). An actual example of an Anatolian vessel presented to an Aegean ruler may be preserved in the stag-shaped silver vessel from Shaft Grave IV at Mycenae; the spout on the back betrays its Anatolian origin (Koehl 1995). A number of ram-headed cups from the Uluburun shipwreck attests the exchange of such vessels at a somewhat lower level (Bass et al. 1989, 7–8, fig. 12).

In essence, the zoomorphic vessels of the Bronze Age were banqueting utensils for kings and gods, their practical purpose being heavily overlaid or replaced by symbolic considerations. An ivory inlay from Canaanite Megiddo depicts animal-headed vessels within the sphere of the banquet, a gazelle's and a lion's head cup are placed atop a large jar that stands behind the throne of a ruler and is framed by two cupbearers (Zevulun 1987, 100–101, fig. 11).[8] Their shared basic function as drinking utensils meant that specimens received from abroad could be employed by their new owners, although local customs may have called for minor modifications. It has been suggested that the hole drilled in the proper right nostril of the Anatolian stag vessel from Mycenae might result from an attempt to transform the object into a *rhyton* appropriate for its new Aegean context (Koehl 1995).[9]

4. CONCLUSION

It was precisely their inherent function as banqueting utensils that made the animal-headed vessels highly suitable as prestige gifts. Gifts were often given in the context of a banquet, and communal consumption of food and drink was – then as now – a prime occasion for expressing wealth and social standing through the provision of foodstuffs and the display of sumptuous furnishings and banqueting equipment. The efficacy of the latter would be enhanced significantly if it included rare gifts from abroad (or at least imitations thereof), reflecting diplomatic contacts and recognition by foreign powers. In the case of zoomorphic vessels, their iconography could be exploited further to enhance intended statements, as for the lion-headed beakers and buckets at Sargon's court.

Although it cannot be determined with certainty where in the Near East the Iron Age fashion for animal-headed vessels began, it is quite clear that they became a standard gift in the Assyrian-dominated court culture of the eighth century. This, in turn, further promoted their spread in the Near East and, to a lesser degree, in the Mediterranean. The Phrygians encountered animal-headed *situlae* through their contacts with North Syria, Assyria or Urartu. Assyria is an unlikely source for the *situla* and beaker from Samos, which probably reflect Samian exchanges with North Syria, Cilicia or even Phrygia. The vessels from Gordion and Samos illustrate how these foreign objects could be employed to fulfill particular local purposes, at the funerary feast for a Phrygian king and in a ritual meal in honor of a Greek goddess. Some two centuries after Sargon II, lion-headed beakers in the Neo-Assyrian tradition made their last appearance at the Greek symposion. Equipped with a handle in the Greek fashion and decorated in the Attic red-figure technique, these vessels still betray their eastern pedigree in the overall form and the inner liner replicated in clay (Hoffmann 1962, 13–14, nos. 18–19, pl. 4).

NOTES

1 The fragment of an oversize fibula of Blinkenberg type XII 3 from Samos mentioned in Ebbinghaus (2006, 208) may also have come from Phrygia.

2 Ankara, Museum of Anatolian Civilizations 18505 (lion): height 22.5 cm, rim diameter 11.3 cm; 12508 (ram): height 20.5 cm, rim diameter 12.5 cm.

3 As noted by Sams (1974, 191), the raised cheeks of the lion occur similarly in Neo-Hittite sculpture.

4 Samos Heraion B 275; height as restored 12.7 cm, rim diameter 9.8 cm.

5 Samos Heraion B 2519; height 17.2 cm, rim diameter 12.5 cm. Compare beakers with triple ram's heads (Curtis 2000, 198 no. 11, fig. 16; Seipel 2001, 200, 204–5 no. 116).

6 At least one animal-headed *situla* has been recognized also among the vessels brought by unidentified tributaries on the reliefs of the Assyrian provincial palace at Arslan Tash in North Syria (Albenda 1988, 20–23, figs. 8, 29; Curtis 2000, 195).

7 For examples made of clay see Sevin (1993).

8 A new lion-headed vessel from Tell Hazor has been connected with royal feasting by S. Zuckerman (lecture at Harvard University, 3/15/2005).

9 Koehl (1995, 62–63) suggests that the pierced nostrils of the Anatolian animal-shaped vessels of terracotta constitute firing rather than pouring holes, and that the *BIBRI* "standing on all fours" were emptied with the help of drinking tubes.

REFERENCES

Albenda, P. (1986) *The Palace of Sargon, King of Assyria*. Paris, Editions Recherche sur les Civilisations.

___ (1988) The Gateway and Portal Stone Reliefs from Arslan Tash. *Bulletin of the American Schools of Oriental Research* 271, 5–30.

Alvarez-Mon, J. (2004) Imago Mundi: Cosmological and Ideological Aspects of the Arjan Bowl. *Iranica Antique* 39, 203–37.

Bär, J. (1996) *Der assyrische Tribut und seine Darstellung: Eine Untersuchung zur imperialen Ideologie im neuassyrischen Reich.* AOAT 243. Neukirchen-Vluyn, Neukirchener Verlag.

Bass, G. F. et al. (1989) The Bronze Age Shipwreck at Ulu Burun: 1986 Campaign. *American Journal of Archaeology* 93, 1–29.

Botta, P.E. and Flandin, E. (1849) *Monument de Ninive* I, II. Paris, Imprimerie Nationale.

Calmeyer, P. (1979) Zum Tongefäß in der Form eines Gazellenkopfes. Pp. 195–201 in *Bastam* I, ed. W. Kleiss. Berlin, Gebr. Mann.

Caner, E. (1983) *Fibeln in Anatolien.* PBF XIV, 8. Munich, C. H. Beck.

Carruba, O. (1967) Rhyta in den hethitischen Texten. *Kadmos* 6, 88–97.

Curtis, J. (2000) Animal-Headed Drinking Cups in the Late Assyrian Period. In R. Dittmann et al. (eds.) *Variatio Delectat: Iran und der Westen: Gedenkschrift für Peter Calmeyer*, 193–213. AOAT 272. Münster, Ugarit-Verlag.

Deller, K. (1985) SAG.DU UR.MAḪ, "Löwenkopfsitula, Löwenkopfbecher". *Baghdader Mitteilungen* 16, 327–46.

DeVries, K. (2005) Greek Pottery and Gordion Chronology. In L. Kealhofer (ed.) *The Archaeology of Midas and the Phrygians: Recent Work at Gordion*, 36–55. Philadelphia, University of Pennsylvania Museum of Archaeology and Anthropology.

DeVries, K. et al. (2003) New Dates for Iron Age Gordion. *Antiquity* 77/296. Online: http://antiquity.ac.uk/ProjGall/devries/devries.html.

Donder, H. (2002) Funde aus Milet XI. Die Metallfunde. *Archäologischer Anzeiger*, 1–8.

Dunham, S. (1989) Metal Animal Headed Cups at Mari. In O. M. C. Haex, H. H. Curvers, and P. M. M. G. Akkermans (eds.) *To the Euphrates and Beyond: Archaeological Studies in Honour of Maurits N. van Loon*, 213–20. Rotterdam, A. A. Balkema.

Dziobek, E. (1994) *Die Gräber des Wesirs User-Amum Theben Nr. 61 und 131.* Archäologische Veröffentlichungen 84. Mainz, von Zabern.

Ebbinghaus, S. (2006) Begegnungen mit Ägypten und Vorderasien im archaischen Heraheiligtum von Samos. In A. Naso (ed.) *Stranieri e non cittadini nei santuari greci. Atti del convegno internazionale*, 187–229. Florence, Le Monnier Università.

Emre, K. and Çınaroğlu, A. (1993) A Group of Metal Hittite Vessels from Kınık-Kastamonu. In M. J. Mellink, E. Porada, and T. Özgüç (eds.) *Aspects of Art and Iconography: Anatolia and its Neighbors. Studies in Honor of Nimet Özgüç*, 675–713. Ankara, Türk Tarih Kurumu Basımevi.

Güterbock, H. G. (1998) To Drink a God. In H. Erkanal, V. Donbaz, and A. Uğuroğlu (eds.) *XXXIVth International Assyriology Congress 6-10/VII/1987, Istanbul*, 121–29. Ankara, Türk Tarih Kurumu Basımevi.

Haas, V. (1994) *Geschichte der Hethitischen Religion.* HbOr 15. Leiden, Brill.

Hawkins, J. D. (1994) Mita. *Reallexikon der Assyriologie* 8.3–4, 271–73.

Hoffmann, H. (1962) *Attic Red-Figured Rhyta.* Mainz, von Zabern.

Jantzen, U. (1972) *Ägyptische und orientalische Bronzen aus dem Heraion von Samos.* Samos 8. Bonn, Habelt.

Kerschner, M. (2005) Die Ionier und ihr Verhältnis zu den Phrygern und Lydern: Beobachtungen zur archäologischen Evidenz. In *Neue Forschungen zu Ionien*, 113-46. Asia Minor Studien 54. Bonn, Habelt.

Klebinder, G (2002) Ephesos und Phrygien. Eine Untersuchung der Beziehungen anhand der Bronzen aus dem frühen Artemision von Ephesos. In B. Asamer et al. (eds.) *Temenos, Festgabe für Florens Felten und Stefan Hiller*, 75–82. Wien, Phoibos.

Koehl, R. B. (1981) The Functions of Aegean Bronze Age Rhyta. In R. Hägg and N. Marinatos (eds.) *Sanctuaries and Cults in the Aegean Bronze Age, Proceedings of the First International Symposium at the Swedish Institute in Athens, 12-13 May, 1980*, 179–88. Stockholm, Åströms.

___ (1995) The Silver Stag "Bibru" from Mycenae. In J. B. Carter and S. P. Morris (eds.) *The Ages of Homer: A Tribute to Emily Townsend Vermeule*, 61–66. Austin, University of Texas.

___ (2006) *Aegean Bronze Age Rhyta.* Philadelphia, INSTAP Academic Press.

Kyrieleis, H. (1986) Chios and Samos in the Archaic Period. In J. Boardman and C. E. Vaphopoulou-Richardson (eds.) *Chios: A Conference at the Homereion in Chios 1984*, 187–204. Oxford, Oxford University.

Laboury, D. (1990) Réflexions sur les vases métalliques des tributaires *keftiou*. *Aegaeum* 6, 93–119.

Magen, U. (1986) *Assyrische Königsdarstellungen - Aspekte der Herrschaft: Eine Typologie.* Baghdader Forschungen 9. Mainz, von Zabern.

Majidzadeh, Y. (1992) The Arjan Bowl. *Iran* 30, 131–44.

McGovern, P. (2003) *Ancient Wine.* Princeton, Princeton University.

Mellink, M. (1991) The Native Kingdoms of Anatolia. In *CAH* III^2.2, 619–65.

Moran, W. L. (1992) *The Amarna Letters.* Baltimore, Johns Hopkins University.
Muscarella, O.W. (1974) *Ancient Art: The Norbert Schimmel Collection.* Mainz, von Zabern.
___ (1988) *Bronze and Iron: Ancient Near Eastern Artifacts in the Metropolitan Museum of Art.* New York, The Metropolitan Museum of Art.
___ (1989) King Midas of Phrygia and the Greeks. In K. Emre et al. (eds.) *Anatolia and the Ancient Near East: Studies in Honor of Tahsin Özgüç*, 333–44. Ankara, Türk Tarih Kurumu Basımevi.
___ (1998) Relations between Phrygia and Assyria in the 8th Century B.C. In H. Erkanal, V. Donbaz, and A. Uğuroğlu (eds.) *XXXIVth International Assyriology Congress 6-10/VII/1987 - Istanbul*, 149–57. Ankara, Türk Tarih Kurumu Basımevi.
Özgüç, T. (2002) Opfer und Libation. In H. Willinghöfer and U. Hasekamp (eds.) *Die Hethiter und ihr Reich: Das Volk der 1000 Götter*, 122–27. Stuttgart, Theiss.
Öztürk, J. (ed.) (1992) *Museum of Anatolian Civilizations: Metal Vessels.* Ankara, T. C. Kültür Bakanlığı.
Petit, F. (1984) Les rhytons égéens en forme de tête animale. *Art & Fact* 3, 71–80.
Sams, G. K. (1974) Phrygian Painted Animals: Anatolian Orientalizing Art. *Anatolian Studies* 24, 169–96.
___ (1993) Gordion and the Near East in the Early Phrygian Period. In M. J. Mellink, E. Porada, T. Özgüç (eds.) *Aspects of Art and Iconography: Anatolia and its Neighbors. Studies in Honor of Nimet Özgüç*, 549–55. Ankara, Türk Tarih Kurumu Basımevi.
Sciacca, F. (2003) Nota sul *rhyton* a protome di leone da Veio: confronti e produzione. *Archeologia Classica* 54, 301–19.
Seipel, W. (ed.) (2000) *7000 Jahre persische Kunst: Meisterwerke aus dem Iranischen Nationalmuseum in Teheran.* Milan/Vienna, Skira.
Sevin, V. (1993) An Old Hittite Rhyton from İmikuşağı. *Istanbuler Mitteilungen* 43, 195–98.
Simpson, E. and Payton, R. (1986) Royal Wooden Furniture from Gordion. *Archaeology* 39/6, 40–47.
Stronach, D. (1995) The Imagery of the Wine Bowl: Wine in Assyria in the Early First Millennium B.C. In P. E. McGovern and S. J. Fleming (eds.) *The Origins and Ancient History of Wine*, 175–95. Philadelphia, Gordon and Breach Publishers.
Tuchelt, K. (1962) *Tiergefäße in Kopf- und Protomengestalt: Untersuchungen zur Formengeschichte tierförmiger Gießgefäße.* Istanbuler Forschungen 22. Berlin, Gebr. Mann.
Vercoutter, J. (1956) *L'Égypte et le monde égéen: Étude critique des sources égyptiennes.* Cairo, Imprimerie de l'Institut Français d'Archéologie Orientale.
Wachsmann, S. (1987) *Aegeans in the Theban Tombs.* Leuven, Peeters.
Wittke, A.-M. (2004) *Mušker und Phryger: Ein Beitrag zur Geschichte Anatoliens vom 12. bis zum 7. Jh. v. Chr.* Beihefte zum Tübinger Atlas des Vorderen Orients B 99. Wiesbaden, Reichert.
Young, R. S. et al. (1981) *Three Great Early Tumuli.* The Gordion Excavations Final Reports. Volume I. Philadelphia, The University Museum, University of Pennsylvania.
Zevulun, U. (1987) A Canaanite Ram-Headed Cup. *Israel Exploration Journal* 37, 88–104.

20

"A FEAST OF MUSIC": THE GRECO-LYDIAN MUSICAL MOVEMENT ON THE ASSYRIAN PERIPHERY

John Curtis Franklin

It was once believed that Lydia was a crucial intermediary for the Greek importation of Near Eastern cultural artifacts, that Sardis was "un vaste champ d'études, un merveilleux foyer d'inspiration" (Radet 1893, 304). But growing archaeological evidence has led many scholars to see in the wide-ranging Greco-Levantine maritime routes a more general and efficient explanation for the circulation of orientalia both in the Late Bronze Age and the later Orientalizing Epoch (ca. 750–650 BC; Dunbabin 1957, 24–43, 62, 65–71; Akurgal 1962; Boardman 1964; Morris 1992; West 1997a, 3–4). Lydia has thus come to be regarded by many as somewhat backward and provincial, learning more from the Greeks than the reverse; the two usual examples are the alphabet and the orientalizing style in pottery, which appear in Lydia somewhat later than in other parts of the Aegean (Hanfmann 1953; Dunbabin 1957, 62–71; Greenewalt 1970; Powell 1991, 11 n. 16). On the other hand, it is certain that Lydia was a principle inspiration for the Greek cultivation of *habrosunê*, the "luxurious living" that was a cardinal ideal of the Archaic elite (Bowra 1941; Mazzarino 1947, 192–246; Bowra 1957; Lombardo 1983; Nenci 1983; Kurke 1992; Miller 1997, 252). Here I will attempt to reconcile these two positions by arguing that, with the accession (coup?) of Gyges and his revamping of the royal court in the early-seventh century, we may detect a sudden spike of Mesopotamian influence on the culture of the Lydian elite, due to the Mermnads' emulation of Assyrian court life. Sardis was thus able to make a unique contribution to Archaic Greek orientalism through a continuous, focused infusion of classical Mesopotamian art and learning into the Greco-Lydian, and thence wider Greek, world. Interestingly, rather extensive evidence for this phenomenon emerges in the musical sphere, and this has important implications for the nature of Archaic Greek lyric. (Naturally, the Greco-Lydian musical movement must have involved a strong local Anatolian element; but this dimension I will consider in a separate publication.)

In the early Iron Age, Lydia's geographical position probably lay beyond the sphere of significant Mesopotamian contact. This began to change, however, with the Neo-Assyrian expansion. Already the Heraclid fortification of the acropolis at Sardis (ca. 700 BC) reveals Mesopotamian construction techniques, although this is balanced by traditional Anatolian elements (Hanfmann 1983, 75, 89). Legendary material recorded by later historians, and deriving in part from a Lydian king list, links the Heraclids to Mesopotamia through a mythological descent from Belus < Bel and Ninus < Ninurta or Nineveh (Herodotus, *Hist.* 1.7; Ctesias, *FGrH* 688 F 1). But this material was probably not contrived until the seventh century (see below), and Gyges (r. ca. 685–52 BC), the first Lydian king recorded in Mesopotamian annals, seems to have been the first to establish substantial links with Assyria. This at least is the impression one gets from the well-known tale recorded by the scribes of Nineveh. Early in the reign of Ashurbanipal (ca. 668–633 BC), Cimmerian incursions compelled Gyges, like Midas before him, to appeal for Assyrian military intervention. Approached with the proper form of ingratiating (and, for Gyges, face-saving) diplomacy – that the god Ashur himself had so instructed the Lydian king in a dream – the Assyrians recorded the fact, or claim, that no imperial interpreter could understand the envoys' language (Cogan and Tadmor 1977, 78 n. 25, with adjusted date of ca. 645 BC for the death of Gyges; cf. Hartman 1962; Spalinger 1978). It may be, of course, that this episode only reflects Ashurbanipal's condescending reaction to a parvenu. At any rate, Gyges now came under Assyrian protection, and Lydia was probably regarded as a subject state for the first time; Sardis may appear in a damaged Neo-Assyrian province list (Fales and Postgate 1995, 1), and such claims would explain why, centuries later, Ctesias included Lydia, with the rest of Anatolia, among the states conquered by "Ninus" (*FGrH* 688 F 1). In reality, Lydia must have belonged, like Cyprus (Reyes 1994, 49–68), to the tribute-paying periphery beyond the provinces proper. Although Gyges later conspired with the Egyptian pharaoh Psammetichus I, his death in the Cimmerian sack of Sardis forced Ardys (ca. 652–630 BC) to return to the fold (Herodotus, *Hist.* 1.15, 2.152). The Assyrians probably now required royal Lydian hostages. This was certainly the case under the Neo-Babylonian state in the sixth century, when a handful of Lydians – seemingly a Mermnad prince and attendants – is found residing at the palace of Nebuchadnezzar II (Weidner 1939, 934). Such guests would certainly have been well treated – hence the relatively generous allowances recorded in Assyrian archives – and quite possibly received a formal education, or at least prolonged exposure to classical Mesopotamian culture. Relations of this sort recall the figure of Meles, one of the semi-legendary Heraclid kings, who was said to have retired voluntarily, on the basis of an oracle, to Babylon for expiation of a murder (Nic. Dam., *FGrH* 90 F 16, 45). Whatever its historical value, the tale at least demonstrates Lydian reverence of Mesopotamian wisdom and science.

Under Alyattes (ca. 610–560 BC) came Hanfmann's "diffusion jump" of Assyrian influence in the remodeling of the ancient Heraclid palace, and the construction of a massive wall enclosing the traditional mudbrick, reed-roofed huts of lower Sardis. These improvements were paid for by a profitable gold harvest from the Pactolus, the same stream that had enriched the golden-touched Mita of Mushki. A Lydian "gold rush" made a vigorous overland trade with Assyria fully intelligible, and accords well both with the explosion of their commercial activities in the seventh century, and the fact that Babylonian weight and value standards underlie the Greco-Lydian coinage that arose in the seventh century under a royal monopoly (Hanfmann 1983, 71, 75–78, 80–85; cf. Burkert 1992, 14, 37–38). It has been held that Cimmerian incursions prevented significant trade between Lydia and points eastwards at this time (Dunbabin 1957, 68, cf. 62; Roebuck 1959, 53; Birmingham 1961, 195). Yet, what else would have motivated Assyria to intervene? They must have been protecting a profitable tributary to their own commercial system, with probably more than sporadic success. This was an old Hittite route, renovated previously during the Phrygian ascendancy, which would eventually form a western spur of the Persian "Royal Road," itself an adaptation of a comprehensive Assyrian network of communications and trade (Ramsay 1927, 145–170; Osten 1951; Birmingham 1961; Young 1963; Kessler 1997).

Lydian prosperity culminated at this time in the monumental aspirations of Alyattes, who campaigned much more vigorously against the Greek coastal cities than had his predecessors (Herodotus, *Hist.* 1.16–25). Alyattes employed typical Near Eastern strategies in his destruction of orchards and crops, and was inspired by specific Assyrian tactics in the siege mound and sapping, which led to the fall of Smyrna (ca. 600 BC), and the mass (if relatively local) deportation of its inhabitants (Herodotus, *Hist.* 1.17–19; Strabo, *Geog.* 14.1.37; cf. Cook 1958–1959, 24–25; Oded 1979; Cole 1997). He raised for himself an enormous burial tumulus at Bin Tepe which, according to Herodotus, rivaled anything in Babylon or Egypt (Herodotus, *Hist.* 1.93; Strabo, *Geog.* 13.4.7; cf. Xenophon, *Cyr.* 7.2.11). That of course was the intention. A similar bid for Near Eastern-style monarchy may be inferred from the construction of the Lydian king list, which lies somewhere behind the accounts of Herodotus and Xanthus, whence variously Nicolaus of Damascus and the Greek chronographers. While this document's use of varying lengths of rule for the pre-Mermnad kings suggests at first an authoritative and accurate record, like other such lists, this is undermined by its eventual resort to legendary and mythological figures (here spanning twenty-two generations). In fact, it is doubtful whether any such list existed in written form before the Mermnads. As Burkert has argued, the genealogy via Belus and Ninus was probably contrived under the Mermnad dynasty, perhaps in the reign of Gyges, to reflect the new diplomatic ties with Assyria and to provide the usurper with a credible pedigree. The alleged descent from Heracles, and hence genealogical involvement with Greeks, may have come even later, a Greco-Lydian poetic derivative of the sixth-century alliance with Sparta (Burkert 1995, 144–45; but cf. Mazzarino 1947, 172–73). At the same time, it is important that the sequence Ninus-Belus faithfully preserves a Mesopotamian mythological construct, one not found in the remains of Hesiod's genealogies (see Talamo 1979, 40–41, 53). Here is strong evidence for direct Greco-Lydian exposure to Mesopotamian poetics; it is tempting to suspect the involvement of Magnes, Gyges' ostentatious praise-singer.

In the vacuum and struggle following the destruction of Nineveh in 612 BC, Lydia came to blows with first the Medes and then the Persians. It has been much debated whether Thales, while employed by Alyattes as a military engineer, could have had recourse to Babylonian astronomical records when he is said to have predicted the eclipse of May 28, 585 which halted the battle between Lydians and Medes, or indeed whether Babylonian savants could have made an accurate prediction of this sort for Anatolia. Neugebauer has pronounced its impossibility (Neugebauer 1957, 141–44; 1963; cf. *inter alios* Panchenko 1994; Dalley et al. 1998, 103, 129–30). It is worth recalling, however, that the ensuing truce via diplomatic marriage was negotiated by the kings of Babylon and Cilicia. In the post-Assyrian conflicts, the Mermnads remained closely aligned with Babylon; Nebuchadnezzar II, like Ashurbanipal before him, claimed Lydia as the western limit of his empire (Lambert 1965, 2). Clearly Lydia had become a permanent presence in Mesopotamian power politics. And when the Persians captured Sardis in 546 BC, the Babylonians duly recorded the defeat of Croesus' defeat (Smith 1924, 101, 116, 120; Cargill 1977).

Given this orientation of the Mermnad court, it would not be surprising if Lydian musicians of the time cultivated a taste for the contemporary and/or classical Mesopotamian art. It is probable in fact that the Neo-Assyrian emperors promoted such a fashion among their client states for ideological purposes. Their archives and reliefs attest the frequent transfer of musicians, as prizes of conquest or diplomatic gifts, to Nineveh from various subject states. Records of wine rations from Nimrud, spanning perhaps half of the eighth century, show that as many as two hundred and forty musicians, both male and female, might be resident in the palace at any one time, including a large proportion of foreigners: Kassite, Chaldaean, (Neo-)Hittite, Aramaean, Tabalites, Arpadites, and Kommagenes are all specified, and we have only a small fraction of the original records (Kinnier Wilson 1972, nos. 6.40–42, 15.7–11, 16.27–31, 21.6 [discussion 76–78]; Dalley and Postgate 1984, no. 145.iii.19–23; cf. 22 for redating of texts; cf. Cheng 2001, 68, 118–20). Similarly, one bread list from the palace of Sargon (ca. 721–705 BC) contains a large enough distribution for perhaps two hundred musicians (Kinnier Wilson 1972, no. 35). A relief from the reign of Sennacherib (704–681 BC) shows three foreign lyre-players being driven into captivity; it is generally thought that these are the Judaean musicians mentioned in the emperor's annals, sent as tribute by Hezekiah after the campaign of 701.[1] (The famous lament of Ps 137:1–4, "how shall we sing the lord's song in a strange land?" relates rather to the great exile in the Neo-Babylonian period; but it is worth noting that Ezra itemizes 328 singers among those liberated by Cyrus half a century later [2:41, 65, 70], while Nehemiah makes it 245 [7:1, 67, 73, 12:27–47]). From Esarhaddon (680–669 BC) we have a list of sixty-one foreign musicians being housed for some special event, including perhaps Anatolian "Corybantes" alongside Tyrians, Kassites, Aramaeans, and (Neo-) Hittites (Fales and Postgate 1992, no. 24.20–27 [discussion XVII–XIX]; cf. nos. 26.8, 140, 142.5). A propaganda piece from Ashurbanipal's reign shows the so-called Elamite Orchestra – a large ensemble of vertical and horizontal harps, pipes, drum and possibly singers/dancers – celebrating the accession of Ummanigash, the emperor's appointee after the defeat of Teuman (BM 124802, Rashid 1984, 136–39, figs. 151–153). Another relief from the same period seems to show a performance of Arab musicians, echoing a cuneiform source that describes Arab prisoners toiling with song to the delight of their Assyrian captors, who clamored for more.[2] Other groups of unknown ethnicity are marked as non-Assyrian by differences of instrument, dress, and hairstyle, and some may even be shown in Assyrian garb (Cheng 2001, 68–69, 78–83, cf. 118–19).

A pavement inscription from Sargon's palace at Khorsabad seems to describe this musical cosmopolis in a sort of imperial proclamation:

> From the princes of the four regions (of the world), who had submitted to the yoke of my rule, whose lives I had spared, together with the governors of my land, the scribes and superintendents, the nobles, officials and elders, I received their rich gifts as tribute. I caused them to sit down at a banquet and instituted a feast of music [*nigûtu*].[3]

This material might suggest that political alignment with Assyria also entailed cultural opportunities, with music serving as a sort of common language in the banquet halls where recipients of the Assyrian peace mingled. And, where a spotlight was always on the central power at Nineveh – reflected. All this may be reflected in the famous relief of Ashurbanipal reclining in a one-man symposium among his women (BM 124920, Rashid 1984, 130 and fig. 147). This moment of fertile tranquility was originally the centerpiece of a large composition that included scenes of military triumph over Egypt, Elam and Babylonia, a novel counterpoint of traditional motifs intended to evoke appreciation for the ultimate rewards of the Assyrian imperial endeavor (Albenda 1976–1977). It has been observed that eight of the ten musical representations known from the palace were found among these fragments, and plausibly suggested that this complex was a banqueting hall that featured performances by the many musicians of the emperor's "harem" (Cheng 2001, 154–55). If so, we may assume a very international, if intimate, atmosphere. At the same time, it is striking that all of the musical representations – with the exception of the banquet scene itself – feature Assyrian male musicians in the overtly public and nationalistic contexts of triumph, hunt and religious ritual. If one may assume that the musical imagery is consistent with the ideology of the larger composition – and this would be entirely consistent with the conventions of other imperial relief-groups (see, e.g., Winter 1981) – there emerges a picture of Assyrian music, with its classical Mesopotamian basis, in a dominant position. The music of subject nations, represented in large part by captive female musicians, is gathered, mingled, fertilized by the emperor himself. The resulting fusion is presented "in Assyrian dress" (Cheng 2001, 117–25) as the same form of celebration that Sargon had used to symbolize the Assyrian peace. Access to these delights of the imperial *penetralia* was restricted to those who had submitted to the emperor and were absorbed into the Assyrian cosmos.

The musical representations, then, accord with the allegory of the larger composition. But there is no reason to doubt that the individual scenes have some basis in reality, granting the inevitable distortions introduced, consciously or unconsciously, by ideological and cultural bias. It is reasonable to assume, therefore, that from the late-eighth century, and perhaps earlier, the Assyrian emperors actively cultivated a cosmopolitan but Mesopotamianizing musical movement in their own palaces, and encouraged the "princes of the four regions" to do the same. Ashurbanipal especially is known to have been an enthusiastic patron of arts and letters; the musical program proposed here would accord well with his aim, in establishing his great library, to assemble in one place all of Mesopotamian learning (cf. Livingstone 1989, XVI–XXXI).

In the absence of Lydian records and the relative paucity of material evidence from Sardis, we must turn to the Greek poets and musicians to find support for the present hypothesis. The Greco-Lydian *koiné* of the seventh and sixth centuries, and the real or alleged involvement of Terpander, Magnes, Alcman, Aesop, Alcaeus, Hipponax, Sappho and Solon, need not be reviewed here.[4] The statement of Herodotus, that "the Greeks and Lydians make use of very similar customs" and that "all the *sophistai* of Greece came to Sardis at the height of its wealth" (Herodotus, *Hist.* 1.29, 1.94), will suffice.

The crucial indicator of Assyrian emulation is the prominence in Lydia of harps. These were almost certainly a novelty in seventh-century western Anatolia, where the musical inheritance from the Bronze

Age was a tradition rather of lyres (Schuol 2004, 57, 107–8). As I will argue elsewhere, these Lydian lyres probably underlie the enigmatic "Asiatic *kithara*" of Euripides, Aristophanes and the Greek lexicographers, and should be connected with the classical form of the Greek kithara, which begins to appear in the ceramic record only in the late-seventh century (Maas and Snyder 1989, 31–32, 41).

Various types of harp are directly attested in Archaic poetry from the late-seventh century.[5] Pindar (fr. 125), who elsewhere reveals a keen interest in and knowledge of musical history (Nagy 1990; Franklin forthcoming), offers a still earlier association when he attributes, to the symbolic founding-father of Greek citharody, the invention of the *barbitos*,

> Which once upon a time, it seems, the Lesbian Terpander
> First devised, when hearing at Lydian banquets
> The octave-answering strum of the lofty harp (*hupsêlâs ... paktidos*).[6]

The *barbitos*, or *barmos* as it appears in Alcaeus, Sappho and Anacreon, was the Greek baritone lyre (Maas and Snyder 1989, 39–40, 113–38). It was most at home when "taking part in the symposium," in the words of Alcaeus (fr. 70.3–4). In the Classical period, harps were generally familiar in Greece, being well attested in Athenian drama (West 1992, 72 n. 105 for sources). But the Archaic material relates principally to poets of the eastern Aegean, and especially Lesbos: Terpander, Sappho, Alcaeus and Anacreon (Maas and Snyder 1989, 40–41; West 1992, 71). Alcman, with Lydian associations ranging from circumstantial to essential, is readily included in this musical world. These instruments were apparently in vogue among the Archaic gentry here for use in the symposium, alongside the *barbitos*. By contrast, the ceramic record clearly demonstrates that the *kithara* was, by the end of the Archaic period, the instrument of professional musicians; a constant attribute of Apollo among the Olympians, one may conclude that its distribution had become pan-Hellenic by ca. 525 BC (Maas and Snyder 1989, 41, 53–78). From the late-fourth century onwards, however, Aristoxenus and other antiquarians display some confusion about the exact identity of the various harps mentioned by the early poets, and Aristotle refers to both harps and *barbitoi* as instruments of "the ancients," as though they had been out of fashion for some generations – and certainly Plato and Aristotle rejected the harp as being unsuitable for gentlemen's edification.[7] In Attic drama these instruments appear as an archaism in romanticized visions of Lydia and Phrygia, often with an erotic flavor; this relates to the continued use of harps by women, both *hetairai* and respectable wives, as seen in Attic vases from the second half of the fifth century (see below). The period of the "Greek" harp's respectability as a male instrument thus coincides quite closely with the rise and fall of Mermnad Lydia. This should be added to the abundant evidence for the vilification of Lydia following the Persian conquest and especially the Persian Wars (for which Miller 1997 *passim*).

To the best of my knowledge, no musical representation has yet been found from Archaic Sardis (cf. Hanfmann 1983, 89). But while the Greeks believed that their triangular harp (*trigônos*) was a Lydian invention, their own representations of the instrument clearly resemble Mesopotamian models (already Flach 1883, 105; Radet 1893, 265; West 1997a). Juba (*FGrH* 275 F 15) indeed asserts for the harp an origin among the "Syrians," which in Greek sources may often be taken for "Assyrians;" but the value of this testimony is limited, since other historians proposed other derivations, and by the Hellenistic period it seems that many varieties of harp were known from many places. In Assyrian reliefs, the upright triangular harp was not a military instrument but appears in garden and banquet scenes of the sort we may imagine in Pindar's portrait of Terpander at Lydian feasts (BM 124922, 124920, Rashid 1984, 126 and figs. 145, 130, 147). This instrument clearly included a deep register, and it should be this aspect of the *pêktis* that served as a model for the *barbitos*, if there is any historical value in Pindar's account; for the *barbitos*, at least in its classical form, differed from other Greek lyres by its register, and not its number of strings, which must have been seven usually.[8] That said, it is intriguing to note that Theocritus calls the *barbitos* of Simonides *poluchordos* (Theocritus 16.45), as though some vestige of its origin in harps had survived into the fifth century and via Alexandrian antiquarianism.

The Assyrian horizontal harps certainly *were* used in military contexts (BM 124696, 124948; cf. Rashid 1984, figs. 71–74, 134–138, 141, 146). Its players are always standing or walking, and appear in triumphal and ritual scenes where we may suppose them to be, or to have been, marching or parading. There is also the victory procession of singers, harps and percussion mentioned in the account of Sargon's eighth campaign (Thureau-Dangin 1912, line 159 with 27 n. 4; Luckenbill 1926–1927, 2, 83). And whatever the Assyrian practice, processions of *vertical* harps seem to have been normal elsewhere, as shown by the Elamite Orchestra. As objects of Assyrian representation and manipulation, these musicians have been somewhat displaced from their native context (Cheng 2001, 23, 91). But the same combination of horizontal and vertical harp, apparently in procession, appears independently in an Elamo-Persian context ca. 700 BC (the Malamir relief: Duchesne-Guillemin 1969, pl. V, fig. 13), and elsewhere upright harpers are shown standing as often as not. We may assume, therefore, that the Elamite Orchestra is at least shown in normal performance conditions, and that processions of upright harpers were a familiar part of the Neo-Assyrian musical *koiné*.

One can now detect an Assyrian flavor in Herodotus's description (*Hist.* 1.17) of Alyattes marching against Miletus "to the accompaniment of panpipes (*suringes*), harps (*pêktides*), and bass and treble pipes (*auloi*)." It may well be that Herodotus's source (using the term loosely) was able to specify this information because it had struck contemporary observers as a novelty, and so had stuck in cultural memory. One can only wonder whether the Lydians would have maintained the Assyrian custom of excluding upright harps from military use. (This question might be answered if one could be sure that Herodotus and Pindar intended the same instrument by *pêktis*, and if one understood the sense of the latter's *hupsêlâs*; as it is, the word might mean either "high-pitched" or "lofty/tall," one suitable for one kind of harp, one for the other.) Note also the distinction of two sizes of pipes in Herodotus' account, which might recall those in one Assyrian relief (BM 124922, Rashid 1984, 126 and fig. 145), since this is clearly not an attempt at perspective; and that "long pipes" may be distinguished in Akkadian texts (Cheng 2001, 35). Large military bands on the Near Eastern model may have become popular at this time, adapted to local instrumentation. According to Pausanias (3.17.5; cf. Thucydides 5.70; Athenaeus 517A, 627D), the Spartans had once marched to the *lura*, *kithara* and *aulos* (whereas in the Classical period the *aulos* seems to have been the sole instrument of the Spartan military). One of the so-called Cypro-Phoenician bowls from the early-seventh century shows a military procession of lyre, double-pipe, and frame-drum (New York 74.51.4556 = Markoe 1985, Cy7). To the best of my knowledge, however, there is no parallel for the Lydian use of military harps outside of Mesopotamia, or indeed Assyria. The Lydian inclusion of panpipes might then be seen as an eccentric, perhaps quaint local touch.

The predominantly sympotic role of the *barbitos* and the popularity of harps in the Archaic period, along with the association of both in the mind of Pindar with Lydian feasts, suggest that Sardis made an important contribution to the conventions, or at least outward style, of the early Greek symposium.

Central to the creation and maintenance of aristocratic social identity throughout the Archaic and Classical periods, the symposium's main socio-structural features and most of its practical manners were already in place before the end of the eighth century, being supposed behind several Homeric banquet descriptions, as well as the famous Cup of Nestor, whose find-context at Pithekoussai supplies a rough but secure *terminus* ca. 725 (Murray 1984; 1994a; Wecowski 2002a, 2002b). By contrast it is only at the end of the seventh century that the custom of reclining appears in the ceramic record. Corinth apparently leads, followed by Attica, Laconia, Boeotia and the east Greek cities (Dentzer 1982, 78–130), but it must be stressed that this chronology may well need adjustment as new finds come to light, since for some areas, especially in the east Aegean, the material record is quite unevenly represented. Alcman gives the first unambiguous testimony of reclining in Archaic poetry (fr. 19 *PMGF*), roughly contemporary with the ceramic evidence. But it is hard to doubt that, when Archilochus sang "and reclining on my spear I drink" (fr. 2 West, *IE*[2]), he was contrasting a mercenary's hardships with the pleasures of the symposium – where, after all, these verses were likely to have been heard (Murray 1984, 52–53). This would take us back to the middle of the seventh century or earlier, and bolster significantly the dossier of east Greek evidence (cf. Fehr 1971, 26). To this one may now add the banqueting hall at Hyria on Naxos, constructed around ca. 625 BC, seemingly built to accommodate *klinai*.[9]

The lack of earlier evidence notwithstanding, it is generally assumed that the custom of reclining was as old as the new aristocratic symposium itself, to be counted among other orientalizing imports from the Levant, where the *banquet couché* is attested for the eighth century by Amos (6:3–7; Murray 1994b, 48–49). Several Levantine representations of the reclining banquet have now been found on Crete and Euboea in contexts as early as the ninth century (Popham et al. 1988–1989; Popham 1995; Matthäus 1993; 1999–2000). But these few examples are not proof that the custom had been adopted widely or even at all in the Aegean at this time, any more than, for example, Mycenaean pottery at Avaris proves a colony at the Hyksos capital (cf. Wecowski 2002a, 626 n. 3). In general terms, Murray thinks of a gradual downwards proliferation of the symposium from an obsolescent warrior elite to the emergent hoplite class (1984, 264–65). By this plausible view, the relatively late representations of reclining symposia might be seen in terms of a devolution of status markers, appropriately reflected in a downmarket version of *paterai* in precious metals. That this process could be extended far enough backwards to account for the isolated ninth-century examples, however, must remain uncertain. It may well be, as Wecowski suggests, that the custom of reclining "does not belong to what we may call the very core of the symposion" (2002a, n. 3).

An important factor that has been overlooked in this debate is Greek emulation of Lydian *habrosunê*, known from many other indications. Wherever and whenever the origins of Greek reclining, it is striking that the ceramic evidence coincides not with the great age of Levantine expansion in the ninth and eighth centuries – even if this can account for the isolated examples from Crete and Euboea – but rather with the Lydian acme. I have argued that the prosperity of the Mermnad dynasty was itself due in no small part to a sort of client-patron relationship with Assyria, also at the height of its wealth. The reclining banquet was known in Nineveh at this time, even if the Assyrians themselves probably adopted the practice from abroad, perhaps a result of conquests in Syria and the Levant, in appropriating the luxuries of the vanquished (Dentzer 1982, 51–58; Rathje 1990, 284; Carter 1995; Reade 1995, 47–48). The relief of Ashurbanipal shows that reclining was, if not a royal prerogative (cf. Reade 1995, 45–47), one at least with the highest cachet. There is every reason to suppose that the Mermnad kings would have imitated this posture, invested with much more prestige by the Assyrian emperors than any Greek contemporaries or predecessors could have given it. And once reclining was practiced in "Sardis at the height of its wealth" and witnessed by "all the *sophistai* of Greece," its mainstreaming throughout Hellas would have been heavily accelerated, to be complete by the middle of the sixth century. Gyges and his successors were, if not the original *turannoi* – often supposed to be an Anatolian loanword, and first attested in Archilochus, who used it of Gyges (Archil., fr. 19; cf. Hippias, *FGrH* 6 F 6) – at least the most conspicuous and influential at this time. A close connection between Sardis and Corinth, the city that leads Dentzer's chronology, is seen from the alliance between Alyattes and Periander, that the Lydian dedications at Delphi were stored in the Corinthian treasury, and that Arion of Lesbos, resident at Periander's court, was a Greco-Lydian musician in the Terpandrian mold (Herodotus, *Hist.* 1.14, 1.23, 3.48–49; Nic. Dam., *FGrH* 90 F 59; Apollodorus, *FGrH* 244 F 332a; Plutarch, *Mor.* 859F; Diog. Laert. 1.95, 1.99). Alcaeus of course had Lydian support in his bid for power in Mytilene (e.g., Page 1955, 226–34).

But most interesting for this discussion is Polycrates of Samos who, according to Clearchus, vigorously pursued the Lydian lifestyle. While he comes relatively late (fl. ca. 540–522) – emerging in aftermath of

Croesus's defeat by the Persians – this very fact shines light on his establishment of a sort of red-light district or "lovers' lane" to rival that of Sardis, and that he "filled Hellas" with all sorts of decadent treats. We may infer that after the fall of Sardis the party had to move elsewhere, and that Samos became a hot new destination (Clearchus frr. 43a/b, 44 W = Ath. 540F–541a, cf. 516C–D, 540D–E). Polycrates also has special musical significance given his patronage of Anacreon, the "*barbitos*-loving," "Lydopathic" symposium poet who eventually became a symbol of symposium poetry and a stereotyped subject of poetic romance (Anacreon *PMG* 481; Herodotus, *Hist.* 3.121; Critias, DK 88 B 1.4; Athenaeus 673D).

A strong parallel for the reclining banquet as an adaptation of Lydo-Assyrian custom is the Greek use of parasols in the late Archaic and Classical periods (for which see Miller 1992; Miller 1997, 193–98). A prominent emblem of royalty in Neo-Assyrian reliefs, its adoption on the imperial periphery is attested for the Levant, Urartu, and among the Persians, who would incorporate it into their own royal iconography. Despite the lack of finds or representations from Lydia, these parallels make it virtually certain that the parasol was in use there prior to the Persian conquest. This derives strong support from fragments of parasols found at Gordion and Samos in seventh-century contexts (cf. Kurtz and Boardman 1986). To this one may add the further testimony of Clearchus, who describes the (putatively) pre-conquest Lydians as "thinking it more luxurious that the rays of the sun never fall on them" (fr. 43a). Here then is striking "material" confirmation of an Assyrianizing fashion in Lydia, once again with sympotic resonances.

It is now recognized that the symposium provided the primary stage for the composition and performance of Archaic monody (Reitzenstein 1893; West 1974, 11–17; Vetta 1983, xi–lx; Murray 1984, 264, 271–72; Bowie 1986; Gentili 1988, 89–104; Schmitt-Pantel 1990). It would be here that a novel aristocratic musical movement would be most energetically developed. Pindar, perhaps in the same poem in which he sang of Terpander's invention of the *barbitos* at Lydian feasts, asserted that the Lesbian singer also invented the genre of *skolia*, sympotic drinking songs (Pindar, fr. 126; cf. Dicaearchus, fr. 88 W; Plutarch, *Mor.* 615B–C; Athenaeus 693F–696A, incl. Artemon fr. 10 *FHG* 4.342; Hesychius, s.v. *skolia*). There is an important connection to be made here with the classical Mesopotamian tuning system, which is known to have been used for both love-songs and divine hymns (Franklin 2002, 698–99). Erotic lyrics are of course prominent in the corpus of Archaic Greek monody (Sappho, Ibycus, Anacreon, Theognis, et al.). The Lydians' practice of prostituting their daughters, and the common use of harps by *hetairai* in Athens, where the Lydian-style symposium lived on in the fifth century, is surely also relevant – and accords well with an Assyrianizing Feast of Music with its bevies of female musicians. As to divine hymns, Terpander came to symbolize the citharodic preludes (*prooimia*), songs to the gods that preceded epic recitation, and, perhaps originally a sort of *paian* to Apollo, began a symposium.[10] Menander Rhetor asserts the prevalence of cletic hymns in "Sappho, Anacreon, and the other melic poets" (3.333.8–20 Spengel; cf. Himerius, *Or.* 19), and indeed the various lyric appeals to Aphrodite or Eros may themselves be seen as a form of divine summoning. Thus we find a considerable coincidence of Greek and Mesopotamian genre and performance practice, with the evidence converging especially on "Sardis at the height of its wealth." That these various instruments and practices became associated with the symbolic Terpander is suggestive of the extent to which the Hellenic tradition as a whole was influenced by the Greco-Lydian musical movement and, by extension, elements of the Mesopotamian art.

NOTES

1 BM 124947, Rashid (1984, 122 and pl. 142). Textual sources: Luckenbill (1924, 70 [32]; 1926–1927, 2, 143, no. 312). Cf. 2 Kgs 18:13–37, Isa 36:1–2; Herodotus, *Hist.* 2.141.

2 Louvre AO 19908, Rashid (1984, 134–35, figs. 149–50). For the identification, Cheng (2001, 73–74). Text, Schrader (1889–1892, ii.234).

3 Pavement inscription 3.37–45, translation Luckenbill (1926–1927, 2, 50–51); cf. Fuchs (1994, 254–59, 358). *Nigûtu*, "revelry/jubilation," is common of music-making occasions, see Meissner (1920, 1, 331); Kilmer (1997, 468).

4 See generally Radet (1893, 82–83, 93, 260–66, 278–80); Mazzarino (1947, 192–99); Hanfmann (1983, 87–90).
5 [Homer] *Marg. POxy.* 3964; Sapph. 22.11, 156; Alcaeus, 36.5; Anacreon, *PMG* 373, 374, 386; cf. Menaechmus, *FGrH* 131 F 4; Euphorion (*ap. Ath.* 635A). For the *magadis* of Alcman, cf. West 1992, 73. Classical authors, Pindar, fr. 125; Sophacles, fr. 412; Arostophanes, *Thesm.* 1217; Diogenes, *TrGF* 45 F 1.9–11; for Telestes; cf. Phrynichus, *TrGF* 3 F 11.
6 The extensive scholarly discussion of this fragment cannot be addressed here. See most recently West (1997b), with further references.
7 Plato, *Resp.* 3.399C–E; Aristophanes, *Pol.* 1341a39–1341b1; Athenaeus 634F–636F; cf. Barker (1984–1989, 1, 265, n. 21); West (1992, 70–78).
8 The strong literary evidence for a seven-stringed standard in the Archaic period (see Franklin 2002, 686) must take precedence over the unreliable ceramic record (on which Maas and Snyder 1989, 124).
9 I owe this reference to a lecture at the Center for Hellenic Studies in March 2006 by M. Wecowski, who will examine the chronological problem of reclining in a forthcoming study.
10 *Theog.* 1–10; Xenophanes 1.11–14; Ion, fr. 27 *IEG*; Plutarch, *Mor.* 615B–C; Pseudo-Plutarch, *De mus.* 1133C. Cf. West (1971, 307); West (1981, 116, n. 24); Schmitt-Pantel (1990); West (1992, 18–19); Furley and Bremer (2001, 1, 161–62).

REFERENCES

Akurgal, E. (1962) Early Period and Golden Age of Ionia. *American Journal of Archaeology* 66, 369–79.

Albenda, P. (1976–1977) Landscape and bas-reliefs in the bit-hilani of Ashurbanipal. *Bulletin of the American Schools of Oriental Research* 224–225, 49–72; 29–48.

Barker, A. (1984–1989) *Greek Musical Writings*. Cambridge, Cambridge University Press.

Birmingham, J. M. (1961) The Overland Route across Anatolia in the Eighth and Seventh Centuries B.C. *Anatolian Studies* 11, 185–95.

Boardman, J. (1964) *The Greeks Overseas*. Harmondsworth, Penguin.

Bowie, E. L. (1986) Early Greek Elegy, Symposium and Public Festival. *Journal of Hellenic Studies* 106, 13–35.

Bowra, C. M. (1941) Xenophanes, fragment 3. *The Classical Quarterly* 40, 119–26.

__ (1957) Asius and the Old-Fashioned Samians. *Hermes* 85, 391–401.

Burkert, W. (1992) *The Orientalizing Revolution: Near Eastern Influence on Greek Culture in the Early Archaic Age*. Cambridge, MA, Harvard University.

__ (1995) Lydia between East and West or How to Date the Trojan War: A Study in Herodotus. In Carter and Morris 1995, 139–48.

Cargill, J. (1977) The Nabonidus Chronicle and the Fall of Lydia. Consensus with Feet of Clay. *American Journal of Ancient History* 2, 97–116.

Carter, J. B. (1995) Ancestor Cult and the Occasion of Homeric Performance. In Carter and Morris (1995), 285–312.

Carter, J. B. and Morris, S. P. (eds.) *The Ages of Homer. A Tribute to Emily Townsend Vermeule*. Austin, University of Texas.

Cheng, J. (2001) Assyrian Music as Represented and Representations of Assyrian Music. Unpublished Ph.D. dissertation, Harvard University.

Cogan, M. and Tadmor, H. (1977) Gyges and Ashurbanipal: A Study in Literary Transmission. *Orientalia* 46, 65–85.

Cole, S. (1997) The Destruction of Orchards in Assyrian Warfare. In Parpola and Whiting 1997, 29–40. Helsinki, Helsinki University.

Cook, J. M. (1958–1959) Old Smyrna, 1948–1951. *Annual of the British School at Athens* 53–54, 1–34 and plates 1–6.

Dalley, S. and J. N. Postgate (1984) *The Tablets from Fort Shalmaneser*. London, British School of Archaeology in Iraq.

Dalley, S., A. T. Reyes, D. Pingree, A. Salvesen, and H. McCall (1998) *The Legacy of Mesopotamia*. Oxford, Oxford University.

Dentzer, J.-M. (1982) *Le Motif du banquet couché dans le Proche-Orient et le monde grec du VIIe au IVe siècle*. Rome, Bretschneider.

Duchesne-Guillemin, M. (1969) La Harpe à plectre iranienne: son origine et sa diffusion. *Journal of Near Eastern Studies* 28, 109–15.

Dunbabin, T. J. (1957) *The Greeks and their Eastern Neighbours. Studies in the Relations between Greece and the Countries of the Near East in the Eighth and Seventh Centuries B.C.* London, Society for the Promotion of Hellenic Studies.

Fales, F. M. and Postgate, J. N. (1992) *Imperial Administrative Records, Part I: Palace and Temple Administration*. Helsinki, Helsinki University.

___ (1995) *Imperial Administrative Records, Part II: Provincial and Military Administration*. Helsinki, Helsinki University.

Fehr, B. (1971) *Orientalische und griechische Gelage*. Bonn, Bouvier.

Flach, H. (1883) *Geschichte der griechischen Lyrik nach den Quellen dargestellt, Vol. 1*. Tübingen, Fues.

Franklin, J. C. (2002) Diatonic Music in Greece: A Reassessment of its Antiquity. *Mnemosyne* 56.1, 669–702.

___ (in press) "Song-Benders of Circular Choruses": Dithyramb and the "Demise of Music." In P. Wilson and B. Kowalzig (eds.) *Song Culture and Social Change: The Contexts of Dithyramb*. Oxford, Oxford University.

Fuchs, A. (1994) Die Inschriften Sargons II aus Khorsabad. Göttingen, Cuvillier.

Furley, W. D. and Bremer, J. M. (2001) Greek Hymns: Selected Cult Songs from the Archaic to the Hellenistic Period. Tübingen, Mohr Siebeck.

Gentili, B. (1988) Poetry and Its Public in Ancient Greece: From Homer to the Fifth Century. Baltimore, MD, The Johns Hopkins University Press.

Greenewalt, C. H. (1970) Orientalizing Pottery from Sardis: The Wild Goat Style. *California Studies in Classical Antiquity* 3, 53–89.

Hanfmann, G. M. A. (1953) Ionia, Leader or Follower? *Harvard Studies in Classical Philology* 61, 1–37.

___ (1983) *Sardis from Prehistoric to Roman Times*. Cambridge, MA, Harvard University.

Hartman, L. F. (1962) The Date of the Cimmerian Threat against Ashurbanipal according to ABL 1391. *Journal of Near Eastern Studies* 21, 24–37.

Kessler, K. (1997) "Royal Roads" and other Questions of the Neo-Assyrian Communication System. In Parpola and Whiting 1997, 129–36.

Kilmer, A. D. (1997) Musik. A. I. In Mesopotamien. *Reallexikon der Assyriologie* 8, 463–82.

Kinnier Wilson, J. V. (1972) *The Nimrud Wine Lists*. London, British School of Archaeology in Iraq.

Kurke, L. (1992) The Politics of ἁβροσύνη in Archaic Greece. *Classical Antiquity* 11/1, 91–120.

Kurtz, D. C. and Boardman, J. (1986) Booners. In *Greek Vases in the J. Paul Getty Museum*, Vol. 3, 35–70. Malibu, J. Paul Getty Museum.

Lambert, W. G. (1965) Nebuchadnezzar King of Justice. *Iraq* 27, 1–11.

Livingstone, A. (1989) *Court Poetry and Literary Miscellanea*. Helsinki, Helsinki University.

Lombardo, M. (1983) Habrosyne e habra nel mondo greco arcaico. In *Forme di contatto e processi di trasformazione nella società antiche*, 1077–1103. Pisa/Rome, Scuola normale superiore/Ecole française de Rome.

Luckenbill, D. D. (1924) *The Annals of Sennacherib*. Chicago, University of Chicago.

___ (1926–1927) *Ancient Records of Assyria and Babylonia*. Chicago, University of Chicago.

Maas, M. and Snyder, J. (1989) *Stringed Instruments of Ancient Greece*. New Haven, Yale University.

Markoe, G. (1985) *Phoenician Bronze and Silver Bowls from Cyprus and the Mediterranean*. Berkeley and Los Angeles, University of California.

Matthäus, H. (1993) Zur Rezeption orientalischer Kunst-, Kultur- und Lebensformen in Griechenland. In K. Raaflaub (ed.) *Anfänge politischen Denkens in der Antike: die nahöstlichen Kulturen und die Griechen*, 165–86. Munich, R. Oldenbourg.

___ (1999–2000) Das griechische Symposion und der Orient. *Nürnberger Blätter zur Archäologie* 16, 41–64.

Mazzarino, S. (1947) *Fra Oriente e Occidente; ricerche di storia greca arcaica*. Florence, La Nuova Italia.

Meissner, B. (1920) *Babylonien und Assyrien*. Heidelberg, Winters Universitätsbuchhandlung.

Miller, M. C. (1992) The Parasol: An Oriental Status-Symbol in Late Archaic and Classical Athens. *Journal of Hellenic Studies* 112, 91–105.

___ (1997) *Athens and Persia in the Fifth Century B.C.: A Study in Cultural Receptivity*. Cambridge, Cambridge University.

Morris, S. P. (1992) *Daidalos and the Origins of Greek Art*. Princeton, Princeton University.

Murray, O. (1984) The Greek Symposion in History. In E. Gabba (ed.) *Tria corda: Scritti in onore di A. Momigliano*, 256–72. Como, Edizioni New Press.

___ (1994) Nestor's Cup and the Origins of the Symposium. *Annali di archeologia e storia antica* n.s. 1 (Apoikia: scritti in onore di Giorgio Buchner), 47–54.

Nagy, G. (1990) *Pindar's Homer: The Lyric Possession of an Epic Past*. Baltimore, MD, The Johns Hopkins University.

Nenci, G. (1983) Tryphe e colonizzazione. In *Modes de contacts et processus de transformation dans les sociétés anciennes*, 1019–31. Pisa/Rome, Scuola normale superiore/Ecole française de Rome.

Neugebauer, O. (1957) *The Exact Sciences in Antiquity*[2]. Providence, RI, Brown University.

___ (1963) The Survival of Babylonian Methods in the Exact Sciences of Antiquity and Middle Ages. *Proceedings of the American Philosophical Society* 107, 528–35.

Oded, B. (1979) *Mass Deportations and Deportees in the Neo-Assyrian Empire*. Wiesbaden, Reichert.

Osten, H. H. van den (1951) Anatolische Wege. *Eranos* 49, 65–83.

Page, D. L. (1955) *Sappho and Alcaeus*. Oxford, Oxford University.

Panchenko, D. (1994) Thales' Prediction of a Solar Eclipse. *Journal of the History of Astronomy* 25, 275–86.

Parpola, S. and R. M. Whiting (eds.) *Assyria 1995. Proceedings of the 10th Anniversary Symposium of the Neo-Assyrian Text Corpus Project, Helsinki, September 7-11, 1995*. Helsinki, Helsinki University.

Popham, M. (1995) An Engraved Near Eastern Bronze Bowl from Lefkandi. *Oxford Journal of Archaeology* 14.1, 103–7.

Popham, M. R., Calligas, P. G. and Sackett, L. H. (1988–1989) Further Excavation of the Toumba Cemetery at Lefkandi. *Archaeological Reports* 35, 117–29.

Powell, B. (1991) *Homer and the Origin of the Greek Alphabet*. Cambridge, Cambridge University.

Radet, G. (1893) *La Lydie et le monde grec au temps des Mermnades (687-546)*. Paris, Thorin.

Ramsay, W. M. (1927) *Asianic Elements in Greek Civilization*. London, Murray.

Rashid, S. A. (1984) *Mesopotamien*. Leipzig, Deutscher Verlag für Musik.

Rathje, A. (1990) The Homeric Banquet in Central Italy in the Orientalizing Period. In O. Murray (ed.) *Sympotica: A Symposium on the Symposium*, 279–88. Oxford, Oxford University.

Reade, J. E. (1995) The Symposion in Ancient Mesopotamia: Archaeological Evidence. In O. Murray and M. Tecuosean (ed.) *In Vino Veritas*, 35–56. London, British School at Rome.

Reitzenstein, R. (1893) *Epigramm und Skolion*. Giessen, Rickersche Buchhandlung.

Reyes, A. T. (1994) *Archaic Cyprus. A Study of the Textual and Archaeological Evidence*. Oxford, Oxford University.

Roebuck, C. (1959) *Ionian Trade and Colonization*. New York, Archaeological Institute of America.

Schmitt-Pantel, P. (1990) Sacrificial Meal and Symposion: Two Models of Civic Institutions in the Archaic City? In O. Murray (ed.) *Sympotica: A Symposium on the Symposium*, 14–33. Oxford, Oxford University.

Schrader, E. (1889–1892) *Keilinschriftliche Bibliothek: Sammlung von assyrischen und babylonischen Texten in Umschrift und Übersetzung*, 3 volumes. Berlin, Reuther.

Schuol, M. (2004) *Hethitische Kultmusik. Eine Untersuchung der Instrumental- und Vokalmusik anhand hethitischer Ritualtexte und von archäologischen Zeugnissen*. Rahden, Verlag Marie Leidorf.

Smith, S. (1924) *Babylonian Historical Texts Relating to the Capture and Downfall of Babylon*. London, Methuen.

Spalinger, A. (1978) The Date of the Death of Gyges and its Historical Implications. *Journal of the American Oriental Society* 98, 400–409.

Talamo, C. (1979) *La Lidia arcaica: tradizioni genealogiche ed evoluzione istituzionale*. Bologna, Pàtron Editore.

Thureau-Dangin, F. (1912) *Une relation de la huitième campagne de Sargon (714 av. J.-C.)*. Paris, Geuthner.

Vetta, M. (1983) *Poesia e simposio nella Grecia antica: Guida storica e critica*. Rome and Bari, Laterza.

Wecowski, M. (2002a) Homer and the Origins of the Symposion. In F. Montanari and P. Ascheri (ed.) *Omero tremila anni dopo*, 625–37. Rome, Edizioni di storia e letteratura.

___ (2002b) Towards a Definition of the Symposium. In T. Derda, J. Urbanik and M. Wecowski (ed.) *Euergesias Charin: Studies Presented to Benedetto Bravo and Ewa Wipszycka by Their Disciples*, Warsaw, Fundacja im. Rafala Taubenschlaga.

Weidner, E. F. (1939) Jojachin, König von Juda, in babylonischen Keilschrifttexten. In *Mélanges syriens offerts à Monsieur René Dussaud*, 923–35. Paris, Geuthner.

West, M. L. (1971) Stesichorus. *The Classical Quarterly* n.s. 21, 302–14.

___ (1974) *Studies in Greek Elegy and Iambus*. Berlin, de Gruyter.

___ (1981) The Singing of Homer. *Journal of Hellenic Studies* 101, 113–29.

___ (1992) *Ancient Greek Music*. Oxford, Oxford University.

___ (1997a) *The East Face of Helicon*. Oxford, Oxford University.

___ (1997b) When is a Harp a Panpipe? *The Classical Quarterly* 47, 48–55.

Winter, I. J. (1981) Royal Rhetoric and the Development of Historical Narrative in Neo-Assyrian Reliefs. *Studies in Visual Communication* 7, 2–38.

Young, R. S. (1963) Gordion on the Royal Road. *Proceedings of the American Philosophical Society* 107/4, 348–64.

INDEX

F

G

H

N

O

P

T